Applied production analysis

Applied production analysis
A dual approach

ROBERT G. CHAMBERS

University of Maryland

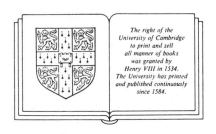

The right of the
University of Cambridge
to print and sell
all manner of books
was granted by
Henry VIII in 1534.
The University has printed
and published continuously
since 1584.

CAMBRIDGE UNIVERSITY PRESS

Cambridge
New York   Port Chester   Melbourne   Sydney

Published by the Press Syndicate of the University of Cambridge
The Pitt Building, Trumpington Street, Cambridge CB2 1RP
32 East 57th Street, New York, NY 10022, USA
10 Stamford Road, Oakleigh, Melbourne 3166, Australia

First published 1988
Reprinted 1989

Printed in the United States of America

Library of Congress Cataloging-in-Publication Data
Chambers, Robert G.
Applied production analysis / Robert G. Chambers.
p.   cm.
1. Production (Economic theory)   I. Title.
HB241.C452   1988   87–12511
338.5 – dc 19
ISBN 0 521 30699 X hard covers
ISBN 0 521 31427 5 paperback

British Cataloguing-in-Publication Data applied for.

For
MY PARENTS

Contents

Contents

Figures

Preface

This book's subject matter is the economics of production. What differentiates this book most markedly from other books on production economics is that it relies almost solely on the use of "dual" techniques. Since the late 1960s, developments in duality theory and in its application to microeconomic data have radically transformed applied production analysis. Where before, most analyses focused on estimation of production or transformation functions, the use of dual cost or profit functions now dominates applied production economics. To some extent, this dominance is based on the "newness" of the dual approach, which makes many people anxious to learn about it and use it. But it also is quite apparent that the dual approach is often simply much easier to use and to interpret. And although dual treatments now dominate the journal literature and many excellent monographs on duality exist, as this book is being completed, a unified treatment of the basic matter of production economics from a dual perspective that is readily accessible to graduate students and nonspecialists does not exist. This book attempts to close this gap.

The book mimics a semester-long course on production economics that I have been teaching at the University of Maryland since 1979. Of course, in that time, many topics that I once thought important and spent a good deal of class time on gradually became either less interesting to me or so transparently useless that they were dropped from the course. What remains represents, I hope, a reasonable survey of producer decision making under certainty and of some of the more important tools for applying these developments. The book does not address decision making under risk and uncertainty. These topics are missing, not because they are uninteresting or transparently useless, but because they are so important that they merit a separate treatment. Moreover, Anderson, Dillon, and Hardaker (1977) have already provided a good book-length treatment.

The introduction surveys in a relatively succinct manner the chronology of production economics as seen through the eyes of an agricultural economist whose main interest in these tools and the theory behind them has been in applying them to agricultural problems. Thus, the book relies quite heavily on examples and intuition cast in an agricultural context.

xiii

Chapter 1 examines the properties of the single-output production function. In writing the book, much thought was given to whether the discussion should dispense with the production function from the start and rely solely on multioutput representations of the technology. My decision to start with the production function is based primarily on two reasons: First and foremost, my experience as a graduate instructor has shown me that, for whatever reason, students grasp the notion of a production function more readily than they do the more general concept of a technology; second, starting from the production function allows the theory and results developed in the first two chapters to be extended in a straightforward manner to the consumer case simply by changing definitions and terminology. But multioutput technologies are not ignored completely: They form the subject matter of Chapter 7.

The second and third chapters deal with the cost-minimizing decision. This is really the core of the book since most of the analytical tools used in other sections are developed at length in these chapters. The decision to develop the tools and the analytical concepts in terms of the cost function is largely based on a prior pedagogical accident: That was the way that I learned them. It is not intended to cast the cost minimization paradigm as inherently more important than the profit maximization framework; indeed, it is obvious that the former is always a special case of the latter.

Chapter 4 moves on to profit functions and is considerably less detailed in terms of mathematical exposition than the second and third chapters. An attempt has been made in this chapter to use as many heuristic arguments as possible without deviating too much from the straight and narrow of mathematical formalism. Perhaps it is well to point out here that the book relies heavily on mathematical arguments. The reader will encounter relatively few pages where he or she is not obligated to read at least one equation. Although this book and the course it emerged from are not and were never intended to be courses in mathematical economics, the use of so much mathematics is inevitable in a book such as this. But the reader can rest assured that with some distinctly minor exceptions, the arguments in this book only require a sound understanding of the differential and integral calculus.

Chapter 5 is devoted to an analysis of functional forms and aggregation. The decision to include half a chapter on functional forms in a book on applied production economics is obvious and needs little explanation even to the uninitiated. But the emphasis on aggregation may seem a little less obvious. I included this treatment because experience has taught me that only rarely does one encounter data sets that do not require aggregation across firms or across industries. Thus, I felt that the reader should be well acquainted with the aggregation problem. Chapter 6 is devoted to different methods of measuring technical change. The chapter splits naturally into two parts: The first views technical change continuously and concentrates on the representation of technical change in both primal and dual functions; the second concentrates on the more discrete approach of using index numbers to measure technical change. As stated, Chapter 7 is devoted to multioutput representations of the technology.

During the years that I have been writing and rewriting this book, I have had many professional and personal experiences that have contributed greatly to the final product. I would like to take a few lines here at the reader's expense to thank some of the people involved. Strangely enough, the two people I want to thank first taught me virtually nothing about production economics. Although Richard Just and Andy Schmitz may have taught me nothing about production economics, they taught me much about economics, economic research, and being an economist. Without their help and advice in the formative stages of my professional career, this or any other professional endeavor would not have been possible. Over the years, a number of professional colleagues and former students have either read parts of the manuscript or helped me to understand many of the concepts used in the manuscript by engaging in joint research and just plain conversation: Ted McConnell, Ramon Lopez, Rulon Pope, John Antle, Rolf Färe, Mike Weiss, Ana Aizcorbe, Tom Lutton, Bruce Gardner, Darrell Hueth, Ivar Strand, Ian Hardie, Utpal Vasavada, Hyunok Lee, and Eldon Ball all fall in this category. I especially want to thank Arne Hallam, however, for reading the entire manuscript several times. Special thanks also go to Virgil Norton, who first convinced me to come to the University of Maryland and who, as chairman of my department, provided me with the ideal research support for a new assistant professor. Finally, I want to thank Virginia Smith, Ginger Kuykendall, Kathy Banvard, and Saroj Bhandari for typing and retyping bits and pieces of the manuscript.

Notation

$V(y)$	input requirement set
x	input vector
y	output vector
w	input price vector
p	output price vector
$\nabla(y)$	lower boundary of $V(y)$
$c(w, y)$	cost function
$\Pi(p, w)$	profit function
$R(p, w)$	revenue function
σ	elasticity of substitution
σ_{ij}	Allen elasticity
σ_{ij}^{M}	Morishima elasticity
σ_{ij}^{s}	shadow elasticity
ϵ_{ij}	demand elasticity, cost minimizing
$\epsilon_{ij}(p, w)$	demand elasticity, profit maximizing
T	production possibilities set
$Y(x)$	producible output set
$R(y)$	factor price frontier
$V^{*}(y)$	implicit input requirement set
$c^{*}(w, y)$	implicit input cost function
$\Pi(q, \theta)$	restricted profit function
$\mathbf{I}$	set of input indexes
$\hat{\mathbf{I}}$	partition of $\mathbf{I}$

Introduction

This book considers the theory of producer behavior and its implications for applied production analysis. Although the theoretical results are relatively standard, the presentation makes almost exclusive use of "dual" techniques and concepts. The main reason for the heavy reliance on dual results is that, in many important instances, the dual approach considerably simplifies and clarifies derivations and results that are otherwise quite difficult. Moreover, since it deals with observable market phenomena such as demands, prices, costs, and profits, the dual approach has natural and obvious advantages for applied production analysis.

With these points in mind, however, one should remember that duality is not so much a panacea as it is an alternative way of looking at the economic world. And since the questions one investigates often depend on this view, it is beneficial to have more than one way of looking at things. The book has two major parts: The first consists of Chapters 1–4 and 7 and deals mainly with theoretical results for the production, cost, and profit functions. The second part of the book, Chapters 5 and 6, addresses the more empirically oriented issues of functional form, aggregation, and technical change measurement. A brief mathematical appendix is included for readers who may find some of the mathematical arguments either arcane or exotic.

In writing a book like this, it is inevitable that a heavy dose of mathematics ultimately creeps in. This is peculiarly true for a long-established area like producer theory, where relatively few "new" results are being established and the emphasis has shifted toward making well-known results more rigorous while relying on the weakest possible assumptions. Thus, I do not shy away from mathematical arguments in what follows. But with the sole exception of Chapter 7, which is intended for more advanced readers, I have tried to keep the mathematical prerequisites to a minimum and illustrate as much as possible with examples and graphical analysis. Any student possessing the usual amounts of linear algebra and calculus should find the vast majority of the material accessible. A necessary by-product of any attempt to make the book more accessible mathematically is that the argument becomes somewhat loose at many points. This is not a book for mathematical purists (or probably even semipurists). After teaching this material for a number of years, I am convinced that sacrificing some rigor for more economic intuition is usually a more than fair trade. I hope the reader agrees. Sections set off with an asterisk (*), however, contain more advanced material.

Since this book focuses somewhat narrowly on dual approaches, it is worthwhile to put the book in somewhat of a historical perspective by casually surveying applied production economics more broadly defined. The best place to initiate such a discussion is with Von Thuenen, who in addition to being with Cournot, the major innovator in early nineteenth-century economics, was probably the first truly applied production economist and agricultural economist. For a 10-year period (1820–30), Von Thuenen meticulously collected and recorded data from his farming operation in northern Germany. These data were used as a basis for his theoretical speculations on economics. By keeping a clear idea of the relation between "theory" and "reality" while using observed data to suggest the direction of his theorizing, he was able to formulate early versions of the marginal productivity theory of distribution, the principle of substitution, and a locational theory of rent that deduced the optimal location of various types of agrarian activities.

Although there were many intervening theoretical contributions of great importance, the next major development in applied production analysis awaited the second decade of the twentieth century and H. L. Moore (1929). Born in Charles County, Maryland, after receiving his Ph.D. at Johns Hopkins, Moore embarked on the then largely uncharted course of using statistical techniques to examine economic phenomena. His first major effort was an attempt to test marginal productivity theory as formulated by the neoclassical economists of the late-nineteenth century. Although his work was nearly always flawed in some respects, he probably did more than any other economist to foster the use of statistical tools in economic analysis. Like Von Thuenen, Moore worked frequently with agricultural commodities and eventually attempted to estimate both demand and supply curves for a number of agricultural products. One of Moore's major contributions to pure economics was the realization that in considering the laws of demand and supply, one had to go beyond the ceteris paribus notions that dominated the discussion of his day. Working with data apparently convinced him of the need to address cross-commodity effects in applied and theoretical analysis.

In 1924, a trio of agricultural economists working under the auspices of the Bureau of Agricultural Economics at the U.S. Department of Agriculture used statistical techniques to construct an empirical framework to help agricultural producers in their entrepreneurial decisions. Although the tools they used are primitive by today's standards (mainly correlation techniques), the work of Tolley, Black, and Ezekiel (1924) appears to be one of the first attempts by economists to isolate the technology in a manner that would allow constructive application of the marginal productivity principle by decision makers. Black himself was an important innovator in the use of empirically based cross-classification tables in production analysis. Although rarely seen nowadays, cross-classification tables were heavily used in the 1920s and 1930s. Perhaps the best evidence of this is Cassels's (1936) use of them in his path-breaking formulation of the laws of variable proportions.

One might conclude that agricultural economists were at the forefront of innovations in applied production economics. In fact, in reviewing the impact of Moore's work, Stigler (1965) notes that of Moore's contemporaries only agricultural economists truly appreciated the depth of Moore's contribution and tried to build on it immediately. Since I am an agricultural economist, this may seem somewhat self-serving. But there are good reasons why this should have occurred. Above all else, being an applied discipline, it is natural that agricultural economics should be interested in applied production problems. Second, the period following World War I, when the statistical tools necessary to the analysis were becoming readily available, was a period when agriculture was sorely depressed. Some of Moore's own work addressed the proposals of certain farm groups for the restriction of cotton acreage as an income-enhancement mechanism. And third, many economists of that time apparently felt that the principle of substitution and the laws of variable proportions were most closely approximated by agricultural production techniques. It was no accident that Von Thuenen formulated this principle on the basis of his agricultural observations.

Although a number of agricultural scientists had formulated and estimated yield and production relationships [in fact, this was an impetus for many innovations in classical statistics], it was not until the appearance of Cobb and Douglas's (1928) paper, "A Theory of Production," that the estimation of production functions became commonplace in economics. Besides contributing perhaps the most ubiquitous function in all of economics, this study touched off a spate of empirical studies that has not yet truly abated. The Cobb–Douglas study is interesting because for a long time it diverted attention away from the study of supply-and-input-demand relationships and increasingly focused attention on the examination of technical relationships and, after the work of Marschak and Andrews (1944), on estimating the first-order conditions for a given production function.

After the estimation of production functions became relatively commonplace, the next major development for applied production economics was the discovery of the simplex method and other algorithms for solving complicated mathematical programming problems. For the first time, economists had available a method for numerically prescribing what optimal behavior should be given a technology and a set of resource constraints. Although Stigler (1945) had effectively solved the diet problem in the early 1940s, the 1950s witnessed a veritable explosion of empirical studies using these programming methods. From a purely practical perspective, this was probably one of the two or three greatest contributions (along with the evolution of modern computers) to applied production analysis. Closely related to this work was the study of engineering cost and production functions and the efficiency frontier techniques pioneered by Farrell (1957). Unfortunately, this book cannot hope to address any of this literature or the closely related literature on nonparametric applied production analysis. Good starting points for an analysis of these areas are any of the many excellent texts on operations research methodology and the Hanoch and Rothschild (1972) paper on nonparametric approaches. This latter work [and the related work by Afriat (1972), Varian (1983), and Färe, Grosskopf, and Lovell (1985)] is particularly important because it offers sound methods for examining whether existing data sets conform to the usual neoclassical postulates that play such an important role in modern producer theory.

At the same time that programming developments were consuming applied production economics, a major breakthrough for applied economics had already occurred and been overlooked. In 1953, Shephard published a relatively short monograph entitled *Cost and Production Functions* giving the first rigorous treatment of duality relationships [others, including Hotelling (1932) and Samuelson (1948), had already alluded to them] that simultaneously anticipated almost all of the major developments in production economics that occurred in the late 1960s and 1970s. Although a basically theoretical treatment, Shephard clearly had a strong grasp of the problems to be encountered in applied production analysis. This short book also introduced the concept of homotheticity into economics, solved versions of the input aggregation problem, and set the stage for the use of his techniques on applied problems. It was not until the work of Uzawa (1962) and Nerlove (1963), however, that the importance of Shephard's work began to be realized. Full fruition came with the work of McFadden and his associates at Berkeley. They greatly extended and developed tools that made possible application of Shephard's results in a relatively straightforward fashion. The present book is basically an examination of their work and later contributions that have built upon it.

The 1950s and early 1960s also witnessed significant attempts to expand applied production analysis in two important directions. The first was a concerted effort by Heady and a host of associates at Iowa State (e.g., Heady et al., 1964) to use carefully controlled experimental agricultural data to estimate technical production relationships for a number of agricultural products. Heady's work is one of the earlier instances where economists relied on experimental data closely conforming to usual statistical assumptions rather than on market-based data. Although largely forgotten, with the immense popularity of the dual approach, this remains an extremely important effort. Someday somebody will return to those studies and data sets with a more modern array of tools than Heady possessed. The second major contribution was Mundlak's (1963) work on the empirical modeling of multioutput production relationships. It is only in the last few years that this path-breaking effort has been followed up to any reasonable degree with the appearance of multioutput cost and profit function studies.

Since this survey is so brief, a number of important developments have been omitted. I apologize to all concerned. To compensate, I offer a relatively complete bibliography of the literature on applied production economics at the end of the book. [Interested readers should also consult the excellent monograph edited by Fuss and McFadden (1978) which contains an even more voluminous bibliography.] In closing, my only regret is that I have said nothing (nor will say anything) about risk and uncertainty. This is an important area that has warranted and received a vast amount of attention. But most unfortunately, many applied economists have the mistaken notion that dual approaches cannot be extended to cover such problems. Although there are obvious problems that have to be surmounted in this regard, this notion is wrong. Epstein's (1983) work on generalized duality appears to offer an excellent starting point for such developments.

CHAPTER 1

The production function

The logical place to initiate a discussion of applied production analysis seems to be with the technology. Although recent developments in production theory have distracted economists' attention somewhat, the technology and attempts to adumbrate characteristics of the technology are still the bedrock of applied production analysis. Thus, this first chapter is devoted to a consideration of a particular representation of technology that has assumed a dominant place in the minds of many economists, the scalar-valued production function. As we shall see, this concept is limited in many respects and is rapidly being replaced with alternative representations that permit the existence of intermediate inputs and outputs, joint products, and a host of other generalizations. However, starting with the production function is very convenient since most applied economists are familiar with its general properties. Thus, discussions based on it build continuously on a preexisting basis and do not require a discrete jump in the learning process. Additionally, it is relatively easy to illustrate the most important concepts of applied production analysis for the single-output case. Once these are clearly understood, proceeding to the more general representations, which promise to provide the general tools of production analysis for years to come, is a simple matter.

Because the production function is so ubiquitous, it is easy to forget sometimes that it represents a set of very extreme assumptions and that there was ever a time when its properties or even its existence was seriously debated. However, as is now commonly defined, the concept of a production function did not come into popular usage until at least the first decade of this century. An excellent indicator of its late entrance on the stage of economic analysis is that in 1920 Marshall (1961) never explicitly employed the production function in his *Principles,* despite the fact that this same book is sprinkled with depictions (verbal as well as graphic) of a declining marginal productivity contour. Well into the 1930s, significant contributions were being made to the general understanding of the production function.

Any attempt to isolate a sole originator of the production function is likely doomed.[1] One can say, however, that the classical economists, although likely grasping the rudiments of such a formulation, did not clearly define the production function. But the concept was firmly rooted in the professional jargon of economists by the 1930s. Therefore, it is perhaps best to attribute origination of the concept to the entire school of early marginalists and neoclassical economists. After all, the marginal revolution in economics clearly encouraged the development and refinement of analytical concepts like the production function that facilitate exact reasoning in economic analysis.

Before proceeding with a discussion of the exact properties of the production function, it is important to pause and reemphasize a point that all economists have drilled into them from their first course in economics. The production function (and indeed all representations of technology) is a purely technical relationship that is void of economic content. Since economists are usually interested in studying economic phenomena, the technical aspects of production are interesting to economists only insofar as they impinge upon the behavior of economic agents. In instances where the technical aspects of production impose no restrictions on economic behavior, the production function is likely to be of only ancillary interest to an economist. Because the economist has no inherent interest in the production function, if it is possible to portray and to predict economic behavior accurately without direct examination of the production function, so much the better. This principle, which sets the tone for much of the following discussion, underlies the intense interest that recent developments in duality theory have aroused.

1.1 The production function defined

Our most basic assumption is that there exists a relationship between inputs and outputs that can be written in a convenient mathematical form. At a relatively general level, it is assumed there exists a function

$$Y(z) = 0. \tag{1.1}$$

Here, z is a real-valued, m-dimensional vector containing both inputs used and outputs produced in a given time period. It is usually more convenient, perhaps more intuitive, and always more restrictive to separate inputs and outputs into separate categories and rewrite Equation (1.1) as

$$Y(y, x) = 0, \tag{1.2}$$

---

[1] Readers interested in a thorough introduction to the genealogy of the production function should consult the interesting discussions of Schumpeter (1953) and Stigler (1965).

where x is an n-dimensional vector of nonnegative inputs and y is an $(m-n)$-dimensional vector of nonnegative outputs. Therefore, we explicitly exclude the possibility of negative output or negative inputs. Moreover, our representation is only concerned with those inputs that are in some sense economically scarce and over which the entrepreneur exercises effective control. Inputs, such as sunlight in the production of field crops, which are not under the effective control of the entrepreneur or are not economically scarce, are not unimportant. Indeed, they can be critical in determining the quantity and quality of output. But since they cannot be controlled by the entrepreneur, they do not enter as choice variables in the entrepreneurial decision, and it is the formulation and properties of economic choices in which we are mainly interested. Hence, such inputs are excluded from x and banished into the general structure of $Y(y, x)$.

Even (1.2) often proves to be a more general representation of the technology than actually needed. This chapter and those immediately following are only concerned with a single output; thus, y can now be treated as a scalar. Therefore, it is convenient to assume that there exists a solution to expression (1.2) that can be represented as

$$y = f(x). \tag{1.3}$$

For the sake of definiteness, it is important that $f(x)$ be single valued; that is, for any unique combination of inputs x, there corresponds a unique level of output. If this were not the case for any bundle of inputs, the entrepreneur would always have to choose between several output levels, and common sense suggests that he or she would always choose the highest available output. Therefore, in what follows, we always presume that the *production function* yields the maximum output for an arbitrary input vector. Hence, we specifically exclude the possibility of technical inefficiency. In passing, one might note that Shephard (1970) has shown that such a production function can be derived as a logical deduction from a relatively believable set of assumptions on the general technology. Such matters are far beyond the confines of this chapter (however, see Chapter 7).

1.2   Properties of the production function

Unfortunately, assuming that the production function yields the maximum obtainable output from a given input vector does not provide a sufficient basis to support the construction of a theory that successfully approximates the stylized facts of economic behavior that neoclassical economists generally agree characterize the real world. Therefore, we shall find it necessary to utilize a variety of further restrictions on $f(x)$. These are summarized next, but before they are presented, let us first emphasize that they do not represent a set of hypotheses to be maintained universally. (Indeed, some are contradictory or competing assumptions.) Rather, they represent a relatively complete catalog of assumptions that will be convenient to employ at various points in the presentation.

Properties of $f(x)$ (1A):

1. (a) if $x' \geq x$, then $f(x') \geq f(x)$ (monotonicity);
   (b) if $x' > x$, then $f(x') > f(x)$ (strict monotonicity)[2];
2. (a) $V(y) = \{x: f(x) \geq y\}$ is a convex set (quasi-concavity);
   (b) $f(\theta x^0 + (1-\theta)x^*) \geq \theta f(x^0) + (1-\theta)f(x^*)$ for $0 \leq \theta \leq 1$ (concavity);
3. (a) $f(0_n) = 0$, where 0_n is the null vector (weak essentiality);
   (b) $f(x_1, \ldots, x_{i-1}, 0, x_{i+1}, \ldots, x_n) = 0$ for all x_i (strict essentiality);
4. the set $V(y)$ is closed and nonempty for all $y > 0$;
5. $f(x)$ is finite, nonnegative, real valued, and single valued for all nonnegative and finite x;
6. (a) $f(x)$ is everywhere continuous; and
   (b) $f(x)$ is everywhere twice-continuously differentiable.

Properties 1A.1a and 1A.1b imply that additional units of any input can never decrease the level of output. In the case of a differentiable production function, this is equivalent to saying that all marginal productivities are positive. Although this assumption is almost universally maintained in production analysis, there are obvious exceptions to it. For example, one can consider the production of potatoes on a parcel of ground that is sufficiently small so that the addition of more units of labor leads to such overcrowding that the workers, by getting in one another's way, produce less. However, it seems reasonable that even though this is a technical possibility, one will not usually observe such behavior if individuals are rational. To believe otherwise would imply that individuals would purposely use a scarce input, thus increasing their cost of production, to reduce output. Of course, ex post, such things might happen in a world where there is a degree of uncertainty about the effect of the addition of

---

[2] In what follows, vector inequalities shall always follow the following conventions: $x^1 > x$ means that every element of x^1 is strictly greater than the corresponding element of x; $x^1 \geq x$ means that every element of x^1 is at least as large as the corresponding element in x and that at least one element of x^1 is strictly greater than the corresponding element of x.

an extra unit of an input, but we do not address the case of uncertainty. Certainly, the proposition would apply in an ex ante sense even if the producers had inexact knowledge of $f(x)$. The reader should note, however, that properties 1A.1a and 1A.1b both explicitly exclude the possibility of the existence of a third stage of production a la Cassels (see the discussion later of the law of variable proportions), where the marginal product is negative. Indeed, however, one might use Cassels's demonstration (repeated in almost every book on intermediate microeconomics) that the third region is one of economic infeasibility to justify either 1A.1a or 1A.1b.

Property 1A.2a implies that the *input requirement set* (all input combinations capable of producing output level y), there *defined as* $V(y)$, is convex. As we shall see later, this is essentially equivalent to assuming that the law of the diminishing marginal rate of technical substitution holds. But one can also motivate 1A.2a intuitively from a slightly different perspective; 1A.2a implies that if x^1 and x^2 are both elements of $V(y)$, then their convex combination $x^3 = \theta x^1 + (1-\theta)x^2$ is also an element of $V(y)$, that is, capable of producing y. More simply, convexity of $V(y)$ implies that if x^1 and x^2 can produce y, then any weighted average of these two input bundles also can. Panel (a) in Figure 1.1 presents a convex $V(y)$ for the case of a two-input production process, whereas panel (b) illustrates the case of a nonconvex $V(y)$. If $V(y)$ is a strictly convex set, $f(x)$ is said to be *strictly quasi-concave*.

Property 1A.2b is a mathematical restatement of a version of the famous "law of diminishing marginal productivity" that, once postulated, has been accepted rather uncritically ever since. Rather imprecisely put, this property says that as the utilization of a particular input rises, holding all other inputs fixed, the associated marginal increment in output must never increase. When $f(x)$ is twice-continuously differentiable, property 1A.2b implies that the Hessian matrix of $f(x)$ is negative semidefinite, implying in turn that its diagonal elements $[\partial^2 f(x)/\partial x_i^2]$ are nonpositive. As an example, consider the case of a farmer and his utilization of a single input, say, fertilizer. From common observation, the first application of fertilizer is likely to enhance dramatically the output of a particular bundle of inputs. But as the utilization of fertilizer is increased, holding all other inputs constant, one would not be surprised to see the successive increases in production become smaller. Indeed, too heavy use of chemical fertilizer with too little water could actually decrease production.

Observations like the fertilizer example have made the phenomenon modeled by property 1A.2b seem so self-evident that many famous economists tried to deduce it as a fact of nature. Hence, several proofs of this

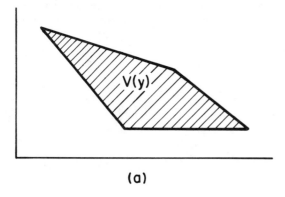

(a)

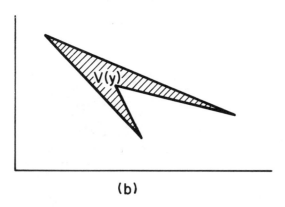

(b)

Figure 1.1 Convex and nonconvex sets.

"law" have been offered, but as clearly demonstrated by Menger (1954) and Shephard (1970), this law is indeed an assumption. This does not mean that it cannot be derived from a set of restrictions on the technology. Shephard provides a derivation of a related version of the law of diminishing marginal productivity on the basis of a relatively weak set of regularity conditions for $V(y)$. But for our purposes, it is interesting to note that when properties 1A.1b and 1A.2a are combined with the further assumption that $f(x)$ is positively linearly homogeneous, that is, $f(kx) = kf(x)$, $k > 0$ for all x, property 1A.2b is implied. To see this point, consider the following argument: If $f(x)$ is positively linearly homogeneous, then for any scalar $y > 0$, $f(x^0) > 0$, and $f(x^*) > 0$, one can easily see that

$$f(x^0 y / f(x^0)) = f(x^* y / f(x^*)) = y$$

so that the input combinations $x^0 y / f(x^0)$ and $x^* y / f(x^*)$ are elements of $V(y)$. Convexity of $V(y)$ then implies that any weighted average of $x^0 y / f(x^0)$ and $x^* y / f(x^*)$ should also be an element of $V(y)$. In particular, consider the weighting factor

$$\theta = f(x^0) / [(f(x^0) + f(x^*)]$$

defining

$$\theta x^0 y / f(x^0) + (1 - \theta) x^* y / f(x^*) = \{ y / [f(x^0) + f(x^*)] \} (x^0 + x^*).$$

Since this input combination belongs to $V(y)$ and $f(x)$ is linearly homogeneous, one obtains

$$f(\{ y / [f(x^0) + f(x^*)] \} (x^0 + x^*)) \geq y.$$

Then

$$f(x^0 + x^*) \geq f(x^0) + f(x^*).$$

Because this inequality, which implies that $f(x)$ is *superadditive*, applies for any arbitrary x^0 and x^* yielding positive output,

$$f(\lambda x' + (1 - \lambda) x'') \geq f(\lambda x') + f((1 - \lambda) x'')$$
$$= \lambda f(x') + (1 - \lambda) f(x''),$$

where the last equality follows by the linear homogeneity of $f(x)$ and demonstrates concavity. (One can, in fact, show that any linearly homogeneous and superadditive function is concave.) Accordingly, the law of diminishing marginal productivity is derivable from a set of maintained hypothesis even though it is apparently not deducible as a fact of nature.

Before closing the discussion of 1A.2b, one should note that this is a restrictive version of this law, for when applied to $f(x)$ globally, it rules out increasing marginal productivity and, hence, the so-called first region of production. This may be partially justified on the basis of Cassels's demonstration that the first region is not economically feasible. However, typically, classical economists assumed that 1A.2b only applied over a certain region of $f(x)$; there never was an assertion that it applied everywhere.

Property 1A.3a is easily explained and seems quite self-evident. Namely, production of a strictly positive output without the committal of scarce resources is ruled out. This does not mean that it is not physically possible to produce output without economically scarce resources, for there

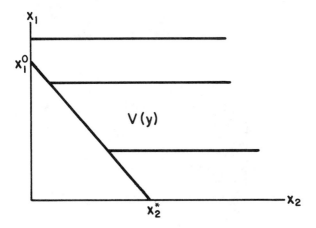

Figure 1.2 Nonessential inputs.

are many real-world examples to the contrary. Rather, such instances are not considered here as they do not present a truly economic problem; when an entrepreneur can produce positive output levels using only free resources, there is no limit to output. Property 1A.3b, however, is somewhat less intuitive and certainly more restrictive than 1A.3a. To examine its plausibility, it is perhaps best to introduce first the concept of an *essential input*. An input is essential to the production of output if a positive amount of output cannot be produced without a strictly positive utilization of that input. Good examples are coffee beans or tea leaves (in some processed form) in the production of their respective drinks. Property 1A.3b implies that all inputs are essential to the production process; that is, production requires the utilization of positive amounts of all inputs. Of course, the reader can likely think of many production processes that violate this condition in the real world. One example is the production of field crops without the use of fertilizer. Fertilizer obviously enhances production but in most instances is not essential. Geometrically, 1A.3b is interpretable as implying that no input requirement set intersects either of the axes. For example, the input requirement set $V(y)$ in Figure 1.2 is not consistent with 1A.3b since production is possible with no utilization of x_1 if at least x_2^* units of x_2 are committed or with no utilization of x_2 if more than x_1^* units of x_1 are utilized.

The nonemptiness part of property 1A.4 simply implies that it is always possible to produce any positive output; that is, it is a feasibility assumption. The closedness assumption is usually made to rule out the possibility of "holes" in the boundary of $V(y)$. To see what is meant by "holes," consider the input requirement set given by

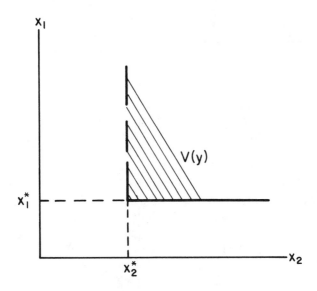

Figure 1.3 Open-input requirement set.

$$V(y) = \{x_1, x_2 : x_1 \geq x_1^* \text{ and } x_2 > x_2^*\}.$$

This particular production technology is represented graphically in Figure 1.3, where the broken vertical line is taken to represent the boundary of $V(y)$. Now for any x_2^0 that is arbitrarily close to x_2^* but is still greater than x_2^*, $x_2^0 \in V(y)$ so long as $x_1 \geq x_1^*$. But since $x_2^* \notin V(y)$, there must be a gap, or hole, in $V(y)$ where the technology discontinuously changes from being able to produce y to not being able to produce y. Property 1A.4, therefore, can be viewed as a technical assumption made to rule out such cases. It is mainly of use in guaranteeing the existence of well-defined constrained maxima and minima in what follows.

Property 1A.5 is virtually self-explanatory while property 1A.6a is simply made to rule out discontinuous jumps in the technology. Property 1A.6b will be utilized extensively in our presentation since it permits the use of differential calculus in the analysis. An example of a technology that is neither continuous nor everywhere differentiable is

$$f(x) = \begin{cases} 0 & 0 \leq x < 1 \\ 1 & 1 \leq x < 2 \\ \vdots & \\ n & n \leq x < n+1. \end{cases}$$

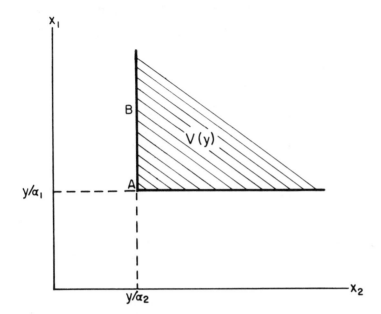

Figure 1.4 $V(y)$ for Leontief production function.

Example 1.1. Leontief and Cobb–Douglas production functions. Two of the best known production functions utilized by economists are the so-called Leontief and Cobb–Douglas functions. These functions are named after the individuals mainly responsible for their popularization in the economics literature. From a historical perspective, they are interesting because they have been widely used in both theoretical and empirical production analyses and other fields of economics. However, their widespread use in theoretical analysis only came about after their extensive use in empirical analysis. As such, it represents an excellent example of applied production analysts crystallizing a means of research for the entire economics profession. We shall briefly consider the properties of these functions in turn.

The Leontief function is often written as

$$f(x) = \min\{\alpha_1 x_1, \ldots, \alpha_n x_n\},$$

where $\alpha_1, \alpha_2, \ldots, \alpha_n$ are positive parameters. In words, this production function equates the output level with the smallest possible $\alpha_i x_i$. Thus, for example, if there are only two inputs (x_1, x_2), and $\alpha_1 x_1 = 2$ and $\alpha_2 x_2 = 3$, output would equal two units. The input requirement set for the Leontief function can be represented in the two-input case as in Figure 1.4, where

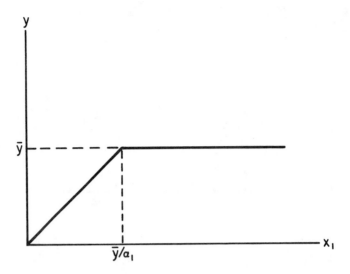

Figure 1.5 Leontief production.

the boundary on the x_i axis of $V(y)$ is given by y/α_i, which is in fact the minimum input of x_i consistent with the production of y.

In considering the Leontief function, it is interesting to see how its properties correlate with those listed here. Clearly, the Leontief satisfies 1A.1a but does not satisfy 1A.1b. To illustrate, consider points A and B in Figure 1.4. At B, x_1 is strictly greater than y/α_1, but the level of output remains at y. Therefore, the Leontief function is not everywhere increasing in x. Property 1A.2a is satisfied because $V(y)$, which is graphically represented by the shaded area in Figure 1.4, is convex. Property 1A.2b is also satisfied, and the easiest way to demonstrate this result is to recall our earlier result that linearly homogeneous, quasi-concave functions are concave. We have already seen that the Leontief function is quasi-concave; all that remains is to show that it satisfies linear homogeneity, that is, $kf(x) = f(kx)$. But this is easy; for any vector $x > 0$, let the subvector $\hat{x}$ represent those inputs for which the equality $y = \alpha_i \hat{x}_i$ holds. Then since multiplying x by a positive scalar cannot change the relative input levels (i.e., input proportions are held constant), we must have $f(kx) = k\alpha_i \hat{x}_i = kf(x)$ for all $x_i \in \hat{x}$, thus establishing the requisite linear homogeneity. This result is easily visualized with the aid of Figure 1.5, which demonstrates a particularly important point. In Figure 1.5, the value of the Leontief function depicted in Figure 1.4 has been graphed in x_1 space while holding x_2 constant at the level $x_2 = \bar{y}/\alpha_2$. From Figure

1.5, the Leontief function is concave in x_1 but the law of diminishing marginal productivity takes a particularly severe form. Over the range zero to $\bar{y}/\alpha_1$, additional increments of x_1 yield smooth increases in output but at a constant rate. In fact, over this range, the function is both concave and convex in x_1. But at the point y/α_1, any additional increments in x_1 cause no further increases in output as long as x_2 is held constant at $\bar{y}/\alpha_2$. Thus, the marginal productivity of x_1 drops to zero.

Since properties 1A.4 and 1A.5 are rather technical in nature, we shall not discuss them in detail; instead, their verification (or disproof) is left to the more advanced reader. This leaves us with properties 1A.6a and 1A.6b. These are most usefully discussed with the aid of Figure 1.5, from which it is apparent that property 1A.6a holds for x_1. The verification for x_2 can be carried out in a similar manner. Moreover, property 1A.6b holds for x_1 over the range of zero to y/α_1 but is violated at that point since no partial derivative with respect to x_1 is defined there.

This leads us to the Cobb–Douglas function in its most general form:

$$f(x) = A \prod_{i=1}^{n} x_i^{\alpha_i}, \quad \alpha_i > 0, \ i = 1, 2, \ldots, n.$$

Both properties 1A.1a and 1A.1b are satisfied for any $x > 0$, which as we shall see later is the only plausible case. This is demonstrated most simply by partial differentiation with respect to x_j:

$$\frac{\partial f(x)}{\partial x_j} = \alpha_j \frac{A \prod_{i=1}^{n} x_i^{\alpha_i}}{x_j}$$

which is strictly positive for $x > 0$. Property 1A.2b is not valid without further restrictions on the parameters α_i. To illustrate, differentiate our earlier expression for the marginal productivity of x_j to obtain

$$\frac{\partial^2 f(x)}{\partial x_j^2} = \frac{\alpha_j(\alpha_j - 1)}{x_j^2} A \prod_{i=1}^{n} x_i^{\alpha_i},$$

which is negative if $\alpha_j < 1$. Since diminishing marginal productivity is associated in twice-continuously differentiable functions with the diagonal elements of the Hessian matrix (the second partial derivative in the preceding equation) being negative, a necessary condition for the Cobb–Douglas function to satisfy 1A.2b is that $\alpha_j \leq 1$ for all j. The reader should further ascertain necessary or sufficient conditions for 1A.2b as an exercise.

Property 1A.3a is obviously satisfied, as is property 1A.3b. Thus, the Cobb–Douglas technology requires that all inputs be essential in production: All must be used in strictly positive amounts to obtain a positive output. Hence, the input requirement sets associated with the Cobb–Douglas function do not intersect the axis.

It is again left to the reader to verify properties 1A.4 and 1A.5, while it is obvious from the previous discussion that properties 1A.6a and 1A.6b hold for $x > 0$ and $\alpha_i > 0$.

> **Exercise 1.1. Arrow–Chenery–Minhas–Solow (ACMS) Function.** Along with the Cobb–Douglas and Leontief functions, perhaps the most ubiquitous function used in economic analysis is the ACMS, or constant elasticity of substitution (CES), function. Similar to the Cobb–Douglas and Leontief functions, it was originally introduced to the economics literature in the course of an empirical study. In the two-input case, it can be written as
>
> $$f(x) = \beta [a_1 x_1^{(\sigma-1)/\sigma} + a_2 x_2^{(\sigma-1)/\sigma}]^{\sigma/(\sigma-1)}.$$
>
> Decide whether or not the ACMS function satisfies properties 1A.1–1A.6.

1.3   Single-input variation

In this section, formal definitions and brief discussions of the two most popular measures of single-input variation are presented. Our first concept is the *average product of x_i*:

$$(AP)_i = f(x)/x_i. \tag{1.4}$$

The second concept is the *marginal productivity of x_i* (which we have already used extensively in our previous discussion). The marginal productivity of x_i is the change in output associated with a small change in the utilization of x_i. As usual, we define the *marginal productivity* of x_i when $f(x)$ is differentiable as the partial derivative of $f(x)$ with respect to x_i:

$$(MP)_i = \frac{\partial f(x)}{\partial x_i}. \tag{1.5}$$

From properties 1A.1a and 1A.1b, the marginal productivity of an input is always nonnegative. A unit-free measure of the marginal productivity, which shall prove especially useful in later discussions, is the *elasticity of output with respect to x_i*, denoted as ϵ_i and defined as

$$\epsilon_i \equiv \frac{\partial f(x)}{\partial x_i} \frac{x_i}{y}, \tag{1.6}$$

where ϵ_i is the percentage change in output associated with a 1 percent change in input i.

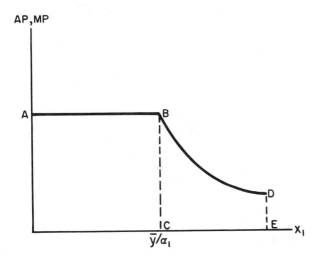

Figure 1.6 Average and marginal products for Leontief production function.

Example 1.2. Average and marginal products for Leontief production function. The concepts of marginal and average products can be usefully illustrated using the Leontief technology described in Figures 1.4 and 1.5. This simple illustration serves to underline an important point that is sometimes forgotten – average products and marginal productivities are not parameters and their values depend on where they are evaluated. In Figure 1.6, we present a graphic representation of the average product and marginal productivity of x_1 with x_2 held constant at $\bar{y}/\alpha_2$. For input levels less than $\bar{y}/\alpha_1$, the average product and marginal productivities coincide and are equal to α_1. However, once input level $\bar{y}/\alpha_1$ is reached, output cannot increase for the Leontief technology unless x_2 is simultaneously increased. Therefore, additional units of x_1 do not serve to increase output, and hence, the marginal productivity of x_1 jumps down discontinuously from α_1 to zero. Marginal productivity is therefore given by the distinct line segments AB and CE. On the other hand, even though output cannot increase once x_1 reaches y/α_1, it does not fall, so that average product does not jump but rather falls smoothly along BD.

To see the dependence of $(AP)_i$, and $(MP)_i$, on the level of utilization of x_2, consider the possibility of decreasing x_2 to $x_2^* < \bar{y}/\alpha_2$. In this instance, utilization of additional units of x_1 only increase output until the

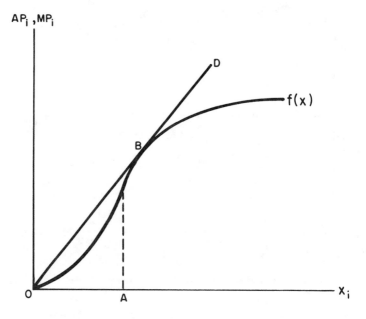

Figure 1.7 Law of variable proportions.

level $x_1^* = (\alpha_2/\alpha_1)x_2^* < \bar{y}/\alpha_1$ is reached. Hence, points B and C in Figure 1.6 move to the left in this instance.

1.4   Law of variable proportions

In this section, assume that property 1A.6b (twice differentiability) holds. This permits thinking of $(AP)_i$ and $(MP)_i$ as smooth curves, which in turn allows us to consider briefly the classical treatment of the interrelationship between $(MP)_i$ and $(AP)_i$ offered by Cassels. As commonly understood, the law of variable proportions, which is essentially a restatement of the law of diminishing marginal productivity, states that if the quantity of one input is successively increased by equal increments, holding all other inputs fixed, the resulting product increment will first increase and then decrease. Hence, diminishing marginal productivity only sets in for sufficiently large input bundles, whereas increasing marginal productivity is expressly permitted.

The relationship between output, $(MP)_i$, and $(AP)_i$ implied by the law of variable proportions is presented graphically in Figure 1.7. This representation is somewhat different from that usually seen in most microeconomic texts because we explicitly assume weak monotonicity, which rules out the possibility of negative marginal productivities. Hence, the graph of $f(x)$ on x_i never bends downward. Further, x_i is assumed to be essential to the production of output, and accordingly, the graph emanates from the origin.

Geometrically, the average product of x_i at x_i^*, say, is equivalent to the slope of the ray connecting the origin and the point on $f(x)$ associated with x_i^* (other inputs fixed). It is then an easy matter to establish that average product is maximized when $(AP)_i = (MP)_i$ since partial differentiation of Equation (1.4) with respect to x_i yields

$$\frac{\partial (AP)_i}{\partial x_i} = \frac{1}{x_i}\left(\frac{\partial f}{\partial x_i} - \frac{y}{x_i}\right),$$

which equals zero when $(AP)_i = (MP)_i$. Thus, in Figure 1.7, $(AP)_i$ is maximized when the ray connecting the origin and $f(x)$ is just tangent to $f(x)$, as is the case with $0D$.

In Figure 1.7, the technology represented exhibits increasing marginal productivity in the neighborhood of the origin, implying that

$$\frac{\partial^2 f(x)}{\partial x_i^2} \geq 0,$$

but at input level $x_i = A$, the graph of $f(x)$ reaches an inflection point that corresponds to the maximum marginal productivity. After point A, diminishing marginal productivity exists for x_i. In a classic discussion of these curves, Cassels has denoted the region of input utilization given by $0B$ as the "first stage of production," whereas the region beyond B is the "second stage of production," or the economic stage of production. He also defines a third stage where the marginal productivity is negative and then goes on to argue with the use of a cross-classification cum isoquant diagram that economically rational individuals will only operate in the second stage. The reader should note that B is often referred to as the "extensive margin" of production.

1.5   Measure of simultaneous input variation: elasticity of scale

In preceding sections, we considered two measures of how output responds to variations in single inputs holding all other inputs constant. Here we concern ourselves for the first time with a scalar-valued measure of how output changes in response to simultaneous input variation. The measure is the *elasticity of scale*, which, like many other terms in economics, has several aliases. It has been called variously the "function coefficient" and the "passuss coefficient" and was introduced into the economics

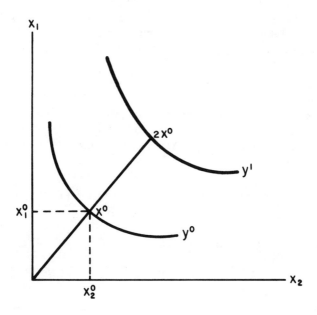

Figure 1.8 Scale elasticity.

literature by Johnson (1913) as the elasticity of production. For convenience, continue to assume that $f(x)$ is differentiable and strictly increasing for the following discussion. The *elasticity of scale* (ϵ) is then defined as

$$\epsilon \equiv \left. \frac{\partial \ln f(\lambda x)}{\partial \ln \lambda} \right|_{\lambda = 1}. \tag{1.7}$$

Hence, ϵ measures how output varies as a particular input bundle x is multiplied by a scalar. Considering that λx ($\lambda > 0$) is the formula for a ray through the origin in n-space, ϵ is thus an elasticity measure of how output changes along a ray from the origin. Here simultaneous input variation is therefore restricted to variations that do not change relative input utilizations; that is, the ratios (x_i/x_j) are constant for all i and j. Since the production function is strictly increasing in all its arguments, ϵ is positive for $\lambda \geq 1$.

Consider Figure 1.8, where, without loss of generality, we suppose that the original input combination is $x^0 = (x_1^0, x_2^0)$ at output level y^0. Multiply x^0 by $\lambda = 2$ to obtain the new input combination $2x^0$. In this case, the percentage change in λ is equal to 100. Note, however, that the Euclidean distance between x^0 and $2x^0$ is

$$d(2x^0, x^0) = [x_1^{0^2} + x_2^{0^2}]^{1/2},$$

which exactly equals $d(x^0, 0)$, the distance of x^0 from the origin. Thus, the percentage increase in the distance from the origin equals the percentage change in λ. Since we are dealing with scalar y, the percentage change in y reflected by the movement from y^0 to y' just equals the percentage change in output's distance from zero. Thus, ϵ is interpretable as measuring how accurately the distance between isoquants in input space reflects the distance in output space.

The elasticity of scale delineates three important characterizations of production functions. If $\epsilon = 1$, the production function exhibits *constant returns to scale*, and at x, $f(\lambda x) = \lambda f(x)$ $(\lambda \geq 1)$; multiplying all inputs by the same scalar multiplies output by the same scalar. When $\epsilon = 1$, isoquants are evenly spaced.

If $\epsilon < 1$, the production function exhibits *decreasing returns to scale*, and the distance between isoquants in input space overestimates the distance in output space; isoquants spread out as one moves out along a ray from the origin. Thus, it follows that at x, $f(\lambda x) \leq \lambda f(x)$ $(\lambda \geq 1)$. Decreasing returns to scale is a distinctly different concept than diminishing marginal productivity even though the two are frequently confused. Diminishing marginal productivity is a measure of output variation in response to changes in a single input, whereas, as emphasized above, decreasing returns to scale is associated with a simultaneous change in all inputs. Much more will be said about this presently. Finally, if $\epsilon > 1$, the distance in input space underestimates the distance in output space, and the production function exhibits *increasing returns to scale*. Isoquants, therefore, tend to be more crowded together as one moves along a ray from the origin.

The preceding description of the notions of constant, decreasing, and increasing returns to scale is pretty much the standard stuff of microeconomic texts. But one might fairly ask why an economist should be interested in such technical relationships? Fortunately, however, each of these concepts has an intrepretation that, although inexact almost to the point of error, is somewhat more digestible for economists. Let us start with the fact that decreasing returns to scale implies that for a given vector x, $f(\lambda x) \leq \lambda f(x)$ $(\lambda \geq 1)$, and then suppose that an entrepreneur has a given endowment of inputs denoted by $\bar{x}$ with which he or she wants to produce as much output as possible. Suppose further that he or she is deciding whether or not it would be better to split up the resource endowment equally into m separate operations or to produce everything in one large operation. For convenience, suppose that both alternatives are equally costly. If the available technology is characterized by decreasing returns to scale, it is better to split up the operation. To illustrate, let $x^* = \bar{x}/m$ and then use the fact of decreasing returns to find that $f(mx^*) = f(\bar{x}) \leq mf(x^*)$, where $f(\bar{x})$ is what can be produced in one central operation whereas $f(x^*)$ is what can be produced in each decentralized unit. Accordingly, there is no incentive to centralize the operation, and there is every incentive to decentralize the operation. And since centralization is usually associated with building a larger "scale" plant, so to speak, one might then say the entrepreneur faces *diseconomies of scale*. Exactly analogous arguments show that when $\epsilon = 1$, the entrepreneur is indifferent between centralization and decentralization, and when $\epsilon > 1$, he or she prefers centralization.

Before proceeding further, it is important to emphasize that ϵ, like all measures involving the differential calculus, is a local measure (here, the source of imprecision) and measures what happens to output in a small neighborhood of input space. This is often confusing, since it is common (as I have done) in economics for one to refer rather cavalierly to production being characterized by decreasing or constant returns to scale. In general, this involves the assumption that $\epsilon \leq 1$ over the entire feasible input space. However, as will become clear, a production function alternately can be characterized in certain regions by either constant or decreasing returns to scale. Properly speaking, therefore, ϵ should be explicitly recognized as depending on x and y, that is, $\epsilon(x, y)$. However, where there can be no confusion, we use the simpler ϵ notation.

For computational purposes, formula (1.7) can be directly evaluated to obtain

$$\frac{\partial \ln f(\lambda x)}{\partial \ln \lambda}\bigg|_{\lambda=1} = \sum_{i=1}^{n} \frac{\partial f}{\partial x_i} \frac{x_i}{y} = \sum_i \epsilon_i. \tag{1.8}$$

Thus, the elasticity of scale is the sum of the output elasticities. This fact has an interesting geometric implication for the marginal productivities. By (1.8), ϵ is the sum of the ratios of marginal to average products. If property 1A.1a holds, all marginal and average products are nonnegative. Therefore, decreasing (constant) returns to scale implies that each ϵ_i is less than (less than or equal to) 1 since their sum must be less than (equal to) 1. For a production function to exhibit decreasing (constant) returns to scale, it is necessary that all marginal products be less (no greater) than the corresponding average products, that is, they be in stage 2 of the production process, as depicted in Figure 1.7. This implies that production functions characterized by decreasing returns are also characterized by downward-sloping average product curves. These results demonstrate that for production functions characterized by decreasing returns to scale over the entire input space, the marginal contribution of an input to an output is always less than its average contribution. Output must be increasing at a slower rate than inputs if there are decreasing returns. But this suggests that $\partial^2 y/\partial x_i^2 \le 0$, or diminishing marginal productivity. Although decreasing returns is not the same as diminishing marginal productivity, it is apparently not inconsistent with it. We now turn to a more thorough discussion of this issue.

1.6 Elasticity of scale and law of variable proportions

One way to investigate further the relationship between returns to scale and the law of diminishing marginal productivity or the law of variable proportions is to consider the profile of $f(\lambda x)$ or the graph of $f(\lambda x)$ on λ. Before doing this, however, it is convenient to define two concepts that will make the parallel clearer. The *ray average product* (RAP) is defined by

$$\text{RAP} = f(\lambda x)/\lambda,$$

where λ is now an arbitrary and strictly positive scalar. To proceed, note that the slope of $f(\lambda x)$ for a given x, which we define as the *ray marginal productivity* (RMP), is

$$\frac{\partial f(\lambda x)}{\partial \lambda} = \sum_j \frac{\partial f(\lambda x)}{\partial x_j} x_j, \tag{1.9}$$

so that the elasticity of scale is the ratio of the ray marginal productivity to the ray average product evaluated at the point $\lambda = 1$. Differentiating (1.9) with respect to λ yields

$$\frac{\partial^2 f(\lambda x)}{\partial \lambda^2} = \sum_i \sum_j \frac{\partial f(\lambda x)}{\partial x_j \, \partial x_i} x_j x_i,$$

which is a quadratic form in the Hessian of $f(x)$ evaluated at λx. Hence, if the production function is concave at that point, it will exhibit diminishing ray marginal productivity, whereas if it is convex, it will exhibit increasing ray marginal productivity. Finally, differentiating the RAP with respect to λ yields

$$\frac{\partial(\text{RAP})}{\partial \lambda} = \frac{1}{\lambda} \left[\frac{\partial f(\lambda x)}{\partial \lambda} - \frac{f(\lambda x)}{\lambda} \right].$$

Thus, the ray average product reaches a maximum when the ray average product equals the ray marginal productivity, or when

$$\partial \ln f(\lambda x)/\partial \ln \lambda = 1.$$

Together these points suggest a simple geometric synthesis of the law of variable proportions and returns to scale. Suppose, in fact, that at

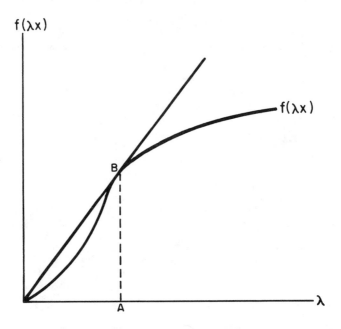

Figure 1.9 Law of variable proportions and elasticity of scale.

different points along the ray λx, $f(\lambda x)$ is variously convex and concave. Then one might represent the graph of $f(\lambda x)$ as in Figure 1.9, which is exactly analogous to Figure 1.7 except that it depicts output changes in response to simultaneous input variation. The profile emanates from the origin by maintaining weak essentiality. The ray average product at $f(\lambda x)$ is represented geometrically by the slope of the ray connecting $f(\lambda x)$ and the origin. As demonstrated, the ray average product is maximized at point B where the ray connecting $f(\lambda x)$ and the origin is just tangent to $f(\lambda x)$. From the geometry, several results are apparent. First, if $\lambda = 1$ is at point A in Figure 1.9, the production function exhibits constant returns to scale at x since, at A

$$\frac{\partial \ln f(\lambda x)}{\partial \ln \lambda} = 1$$

regardless of the value of λ. Second, if $\lambda = 1$ is to the right of A in Figure 1.9, $f(x)$ exhibits decreasing returns to scale at x since any ray from the origin to $f(\lambda x)$ for $\lambda > A$ will cut $f(\lambda x)$ from below, indicating that the ray average product is greater than the ray marginal productivity; thus, $\epsilon < 1$. Third, if $\lambda = 1$ is to the left of A, $f(x)$ exhibits increasing returns to scale at x. Moreover, it is obvious from Figure 1.9 that strict convexity of $f(x)$ is inconsistent with decreasing returns to scale since any ray from the origin will cut a convex $f(\lambda x)$ (emanating from the origin) from above. The converse is true for any strictly concave function.

That decreasing or constant returns to scale is consistent with concavity of $f(x)$ can also be seen by a straightforward algebraic argument using property 1A.1a. For any strictly positive input bundle q, decreasing returns to scale implies, by expression (1.8), that $f(q) \geq \sum q_i \, \partial f(q)/\partial x_i$. On the other hand, a differentiable $f(x)$ is concave on R^n if for any q, $z \in R_+^n$, $f(z) \leq f(q) + \sum_i [\partial f(q)/\partial x_i](z_i - q_i)$ (see Appendix). Without loss of generality, let $z = 0$, and we see that concavity requires $\sum_i [\partial f(q)/\partial x_i] q_i \leq f(q)$; thus, concavity ensures at least nonincreasing returns.

Example 1.3. Consider the *generalized power production function* introduced by de Janvry (1972):

$$f(x) = A \prod_{i=1}^{n} x_i^{f_i(x)} \exp g(x).$$

This function is a generalized version of the Cobb–Douglas; when $f_i(x) = \alpha_i$ and $g(x) = 0$, the Cobb–Douglas is obtained. Moreover, if $f_i = \alpha_i$ and $g(x) = \sum_i \gamma_i x_i$, this production function becomes the so-called *transcendental function*, which is a progenitor of the transcendental logarithmic function that is becoming increasingly popular in applied production research. Direct computation reveals that the elasticity of scale for the generalized power production function is

$$\epsilon = \sum_{i=1}^{n} \left(\sum_{j=1}^{n} x_j \frac{\partial f}{\partial x_j} + f_i(x) + \frac{\partial g}{\partial x_i} \right) x_i.$$

1.7   Measures of input substitutability

We have encountered several production functions each having quite different characteristics. One of these, the Leontief, has the property that if production occurs at $f(x) = \alpha_1 x_1 = \alpha_2 x_2 = \cdots = \alpha_n x_n$, a decrease in the utilization of any input implies that output will fall, no matter what happens to the utilization of other inputs. However, it has been long observed that decreased utilization of one input may be compensated for by increased utilization of another input. One example is the production of field crops where the introduction of and increased utilization of herbicides and pesticides greatly decreased the amount of labor that must be devoted to tending the crop in the form of, for example, weeding. As early as 1820–30, Von Thuenen (perhaps the first modern applied economist) was collecting evidence from his farming operation in Germany that suggested that this ability of one input to compensate for another was significant. Based on his observations, Von Thuenen postulated what has come to be known as the "principle of substitutability." In short, this principle suggests that it is possible to produce a constant output level with a variety of input combinations. In other words, if an entrepreneur decreases the utilization of one input, he or she can *substitute* increased utilization of another input or inputs to maintain the same level of output.

As is obvious from the Leontief function, which is most familiarly characteristic of such things as cake recipes, however, the principle of substitutability is not an economic law. There are well-defined production functions for which inputs are not substitutable. However, for those functions where inputs are substitutable, the degree to which inputs can substitute for one another is an important technical relationship for economic decision makers. Suppose, for example, that a tomato grower is trying to decide whether to custom-harvest the crop mechanically, to harvest it manually by hiring pickers, or to use a combination of both techniques. Then, the choice between the three alternatives will be affected by relative input costs as well as relative input substitutability (e.g., in the Leontief case, he or she would face no such choice). It also seems apparent that the grower could benefit immensely from the use of a clearly defined and accurate measure of input substitutability. The rest of this section discusses various measures of input substitutability that have been particularly valuable to production economists.

To help conceptualize whether one input is capable of substituting for another, it is convenient to introduce some further definitions. An input is said to be *limitational* if an increase in its usage is a necessary but not sufficient condition for output to increase. In terms of the Leontief technology, both inputs can be viewed as limitational at point A in Figure 1.4 since, for example, increasing x_1 to B in the figure results in no change in output. However, at point B, only x_1 is limitational since an increase in x_2 will lead to an output increase. At B, x_1 equals, say, $x_1^* = y\alpha^1$, so that increasing x_2 to $x_2^* = y\alpha_2$ means output must go up to $y^* = \min\{\alpha_1 x_1^*, \alpha_2 x_2^*\} > y$.

In the following discussion, we shall find it convenient to presume that properties 1A.1b, 1A.2a, and 1A.6b hold everywhere. This enables us to consider the most traditional means of depicting input substitutability. We start by considering the lower boundary of $V(y)$ defined by the level set $\bar{V}(y) = \{x: f(x) = y\}$. By strong monotonicity, the partial derivatives of $f(x)$ do not vanish, and the implicit function theorem implies that

$f(x) = y$ can be solved for x_i in terms of all the other inputs and y. Denote this solution as

$$x_i^* = x_i(x_i, x_2, \ldots, x_{i-1}, \ldots, x_n).$$

Substitution of x_j into $f(x)$ while evaluating all other x_j at the values that are consistent with $\bar{V}(y)$ preserves $\bar{V}(y)$:

$$y = f(x_i, \ldots, x_{i-1}, x_i^*, x_{i+1}, \ldots, x_n). \tag{1.10}$$

To determine how x_i adjusts to changes in the level of x_j while maintaining a constant output, partially differentiate (1.10) with respect to x_j to obtain

$$\frac{\partial f}{\partial x_i} \frac{\partial x_i}{\partial x_j} + \frac{\partial f}{\partial x_j} = 0,$$

which implies

$$\frac{\partial x_i}{\partial x_j} = -\frac{\partial f/\partial x_j}{\partial f/\partial x_j}. \tag{1.11}$$

The adjustment in x_i necessary to preserve $\bar{V}(y)$ after x_j changes equals minus the ratio of the marginal products. This ratio is called the *marginal rate of technical substitution* between x_i and x_j. Expression (1.10) represents the slope of the level set $\bar{V}(y)$ when projected into x_i, x_j space. The graph of the level set is often termed the *isoquant* and can be represented in the two-input case as the lower boundary of $V(y)$ (see Figure 1.10). It is negatively sloped because (1.10) is minus the ratio of two positive marginal products and is drawn as convex to the origin because $V(y)$ is convex. The shape of the isoquant has further economic implications. Since it is convex to the origin, it exhibits a diminishing rate of technical substitution. That is, as x_j is substituted for x_i in the production of y, the marginal rate of technical substitution declines. In Figure 1.10, moving down to the right from point A, it becomes more difficult to substitute x_1 for x_2 in the production of y while maintaining output y. This depiction recognizes that one cannot simply replace one unit of x_2. Since they are different inputs, one expects there to be some friction in the substitution process.

The importance of input substitutability has led to the definition of various *elasticities of substitution* providing unit-free measures of the substitutability between inputs. In discussing elasticities of substitution, it is convenient (and intuitive) to start with the case where x is a two-dimensional vector. In a classic work, Hicks (1963) offered the following definition of *elasticity of substitution* (σ) between inputs x_1 and x_2:

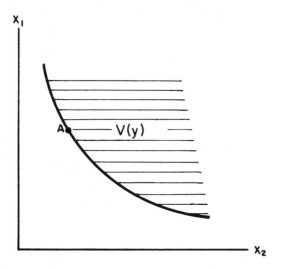

Figure 1.10 Isoquant.

$$\sigma \equiv \frac{d(x_2/x_1)}{d(f_1/f_2)} \frac{f_1/f_2}{x_2/x_1}, \tag{1.12}$$

where σ is the elasticity of the input ratio with respect to the marginal rate of technical substitution.

To conceptualize this measure, consider Figure 1.11; the original input ratio is given by the ray from the origin labeled $0AC$, whereas the corresponding marginal rate of technical substitution is given by the slope of the line segment tangent to the isoquant at point C. Suppose the input ratio changes to that associated with the ray $0BD$ from the origin. The marginal rate of technical substitution is now given by the slope of the line segment tangent to the isoquant at D. Thus, σ is a measure of the curvature of the isoquant where $d(x_2/x_1)/d(f_1/f_2)$ is given by the ratio Δ^k/Δ^l.

Example 1.4. By way of an example, suppose production is characterized by the linear function

$$f(x) = \gamma_1 x_1 + \gamma_2 x_2.$$

The isoquant associated with this production function has a constant slope equal to $-\gamma_2/\gamma_1$ and can be represented by a line segment in 2-space. Since its slope is constant, $d(f_1/f_2) = 0$ and $\sigma = \infty$. Any change in the usage of x_1 can be completely compensated by a change in the usage of

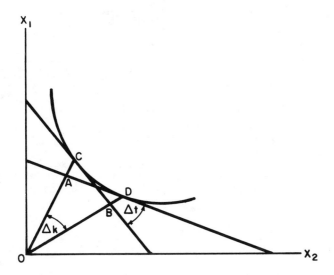

Figure 1.11 Elasticity of substitution.

x_2. In this instance, the inputs are considered perfect substitutes and, as should be clear from the preceding, exhibit constant and not a diminishing marginal rate of technical substitution. On the other hand, consider the Leontief technology. Obviously, here, inputs are not substitutable and $\sigma = 0$. Finally, consider the case of the two-input Cobb–Douglas function:

$$f(x) = A x_1^{\alpha_1} x_2^{\alpha_2}.$$

The marginal rate of technical substitution is given by

$$\frac{f_1}{f_2} = -\frac{\alpha_1}{\alpha_2} \frac{x_2}{x_1},$$

from which it follows that $\sigma = 1$.

Exercise 1.2. An equivalent representation of σ is

$$\sigma = \frac{-f_1 f_2 (x_1 f_1 + x_2 f_2)}{x_1 x_2 (f_{11} f_2^2 - 2 f_{12} f_1 f_2 + f_{22} f_1^2)}, \tag{1.13}$$

where $f_i \equiv \partial f / \partial x_i$ and $f_{ij} \equiv \partial^2 f / \partial x_i \partial x_j$.

The reader should verify this result. Now for the ACMS function introduced in Exercise 1.1, derive the associated elasticity of substitution. For the transcendental function in Example 1.3 with two inputs, calculate σ.

Expression (1.13) can be rewritten using matrix notation as

$$\frac{x_1 f_1 + x_2 f_2}{x_1 x_2} \frac{F_{12}}{F},$$

(1.14)

where F is the determinant of the bordered Hessian of the production function,

$$F = \begin{vmatrix} 0 & f_1 & f_2 \\ f_1 & f_{11} & f_{12} \\ f_2 & f_{12} & f_{22} \end{vmatrix},$$

and F_{12} is the associated cofactor of f_{12}. Since $f(x)$ is twice-continuously differentiable in its arguments, Young's theorem implies that $f_{12} = f_{21}$. Hence, the measure σ is symmetric in that

$$\frac{d \ln(x_2/x_1)}{d \ln(f_1/f_2)} = \frac{d \ln(x_1/x_2)}{d \ln(f_2/f_1)}.$$

Furthermore, for a quasi-concave production function with two inputs, σ is always positive.

The reason that σ is always positive in the two-input case can be easily understood by reference to Figure 1.11. Suppose initially that we are at point C on the isoquant. Consider moving to point D. Moving in this direction decreases the ratio x_1/x_2, but because of the presumption of a diminishing marginal rate of technical substitution, the ratio f_2/f_1 increases. Hence, σ has to be positive when $V(y)$ is convex because the ratio of inputs and the marginal rate of technical substitution move in opposite directions as one moves along the isoquant.

However, we usually are interested in multiple- (more than two) input production functions. As shown, any two inputs are substitutes as long as only they are permitted to vary. In general, however, we are interested in ascertaining how all inputs adjust to a change in the employment of a single input since in most practical situations, individuals face a wide array of production alternatives. As an example, consider a production function with three inputs $y = f(x_1, x_2, x_3)$. In this context, one can conceptualize at least three separate isoquants: the isoquant describing the relationship between x_2 and x_1 holding x_3 constant,

$$\frac{\partial x_2}{\partial x_1} = \frac{-f_1(x_1, x_2, x_3)}{f_2(x_1, x_2, x_3)};$$

the isoquant between x_2 and x_3 with x_1 constant,

$$\frac{\partial x_2}{\partial x_3} = \frac{-f_3(x_1, x_2, x_3)}{f_2(x_1, x_2, x_3)};$$

and the isoquant describing the relationship between x_3 and x_1 with x_2 constant,

$$\frac{\partial x_3}{\partial x_1} = \frac{-f_1(x_1, x_2, x_3)}{f_3(x_1, x_2, x_3)}.$$

These isoquants are represented graphically in Figure 1.12. Suppose we are originally at points $1a$, $1b$, and $1c$, respectively. What happens if the level of x_2 is increased? In panels (a) and (b), this is reflected by a movement along the isoquant to, say, points $2a$ and $2b$; x_2 is substituted for the other two inputs. However, in panel (c), the isoquant shifts back toward the origin because it now requires less of both x_1 and x_3 to produce a given level of y. Also, as the usage of x_1 is decreased, the level of x_3 shifts the isoquant in panel (a) outward. It is entirely possible that as a result of these interactions, one might end at a point like $3a$ in panel (a), that uses more of x_1 than originally. In such a case, inputs x_1 and x_2 are called *complements*.

Such arguments must make one wonder what is the most appropriate measure of the degree of substitutability between any two inputs. Unfortunately, like many other problems in economics, there is no one correct answer. Several alternatives exist, each of which is, generally speaking, based on some generalization of the formulas expressed here. The first definition that we consider is perhaps the most natural: the *direct elasticity of substitution*, defined by (1.12) with (i, j) replacing $(1, 2)$ and all x_k ($k \neq i$, $k \neq j$) held constant. This elasticity is denoted as σ_{ij}^D and can be interpreted as a short-run elasticity since it measures the degree of substitutability between input i and input j while all other inputs are fixed.

A second definition of the elasticity of substitution is based on a generalization of expression (1.14). The *Allen partial elasticity of substitution* (σ_{ij}) is defined by

$$\sigma_{ij} = \frac{\sum_i x_i f_i}{x_i x_j} \frac{F_{ji}}{F}, \tag{1.15}$$

where F is the bordered Hessian determinant

$$F = \begin{vmatrix} 0 & f_1 & f_2 & \cdots & f_n \\ f_1 & f_{11} & f_{12} & \cdots & f_{nn} \\ f_2 & \cdots & \cdots & & f_{nn} \\ \vdots & \vdots & \vdots & & \vdots \\ f_n & f_{1n} & \cdots & \cdots & f_{nn} \end{vmatrix},$$

and F_{ij} is the cofactor associated with f_{ij}. Both σ_{ij}^D and σ_{ij} are symmetric measures of the degree of substitutability between two inputs.

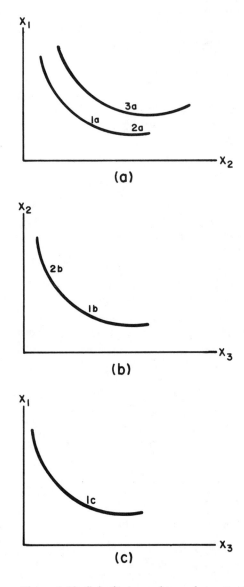

Figure 1.12 Substitutes and complements.

Furthermore, in the special case of a two-input production function, $\sigma_{ij} = \sigma_{ij}^{D}$. In both cases, goods are complements if the elasticity of substitution is negative and substitutes if the elasticity is positive.

Since σ_{ij} has received a great deal of attention, it is worthwhile to discuss further its properties. Denoting $K_i = x_i f_i / \sum x_i f_i$ and using the preceding facts and Cramer's rule, we obtain, in turn,

$$K_i \sigma_{ri} = \frac{f_i F_{ri}}{x_r F}$$

and

$$\sum_{i=1}^{n} K_i \sigma_{ri} = \frac{1}{x_r F} \sum_{i=1}^{n} f_i F_{ri} = 0,$$

where the second equality follows by expanding the first row (column) of the bordered Hessian consisting of marginal products by a set of alien cofactors. Hence,

$$K_r \sigma_{rr} = -\sum_{i \neq r} K_i \sigma_{ri} = \frac{f_r F_{rr}}{x_r F}.$$

If $f(x)$ is concave (i.e., property 1A.2b holds), the principal minors of the bordered Hessian of $f(x)$ alternate in sign, and this implies (see Allen 1938, 501–2) that $F_{rr}/F < 0$. Since we have assumed $f_r > 0$, σ_{rr} is negative. Thus, $\sum_{i \neq r} K_i \sigma_{ri} > 0$, from which we conclude that at least one σ_{ri} must be positive. In words, a factor of production cannot be a complement for all other factors in terms of the Allen measure. Of course, this is intuitively appealing since, in the two-input case, factors are always substitutes and one expects there to be some evidence of similar qualitative behavior in the n-input case.

The final elasticity of substitution to be considered here is the *Morishima elasticity of substitution*, which can be written as

$$\sigma_{ij}^M = \frac{f_j}{x_i} \frac{F_{ij}}{F} - \frac{f_j}{x_j} \frac{F_{ij}}{F}. \tag{1.16}$$

Using this definition, it is easy to relate σ_{ij}^M directly to the corresponding σ_{ij}. In particular, (1.16) can be rewritten as

$$\sigma_{ij}^M = \frac{f_j x_j}{f_i x_i} (\sigma_{ij} - \sigma_{jj}). \tag{1.16'}$$

This alternative formulation highlights two important facts. First, σ_{ij}^M is not symmetric since $\sigma_{ij}^M \neq \sigma_{ji}^M$. Second, a pair of goods can be complements in terms of Allen elasticities ($\sigma_{ij} < 0$), whereas the corresponding Morishima measure could class them as substitutes ($\sigma_{ij}^M > 0$). To see why this is possible, note that by our earlier results, $\sigma_{jj} \leq 0$. Thus, if $|\sigma_{ij}| < |\sigma_{jj}|$, σ_{ij}^M will always be positive even if $\sigma_{ij} < 0$. On the other hand, if two goods are substitutes according to the Allen measure, they are always substitutes according to the Morishima measure. Suppose, however, that $|\sigma_{ii}| > |\sigma_{ij}| > |\sigma_{jj}|$ and further that $\sigma_{ij} < 0$. From (1.16'), it follows that

$\sigma_{ij}^M < 0$, and we would usually refer to the two inputs as complements. But it also follows that $\sigma_{ji}^M > 0$. From this perspective, the two goods are substitutes. The asymmetry of the Morishima measure has important implications for the classification of inputs as substitutes and complements and highlights the somewhat arbitrary nature of any elasticity of substitution in the many-input case.

> **Exercise 1.3.** For the generalized power production factor with $f_i(x) = bx_i$, $g(x) = \sum_{i=1}^n \gamma_i x_i$, and $n = 3$, calculate the Allen partial elasticity of substitution and the Morishima elasticity of substitution.

1.8   Structure of production functions

We have outlined several basic properties that production functions possess. Although these restrictions are often adequate for theoretical analysis (mainly the basic qualitative results of the theory of the firm), they are not restrictive enough in most cases for applied production analysis – analysis based on a given data set or on a given microeconomic context. As all economists know, there always exists a trade-off between generality of the model and analytical or empirical tractability. (Note: Almost all empirical investigations actually require the specification of exact functional forms.) Although the main attraction of the dual approach is that it greatly mitigates this trade-off, the trade-off exists and is a very real problem for most applied production analysts. It is an unfortunate (but inescapable) reality that the properties of $f(x)$ simply do not allow one to make the type of quantitative assessments required of applied economists. When all is said and done, the ability to tell an entrepreneur that he or she should supply "more" when price rises is not likely to impress many people. But the ability to say "how much more" just might. A certain start in this direction is to specialize further the production function already developed. This section highlights some of the more common assumptions that impose structure on the production function while recognizing how they are more restrictive than the previously maintained properties. Of course, it is usually assumed that previously stated properties hold. At present, we only add an additional layer in the hope that this facilitates later analysis.

1.8a   *Transforms of production functions*

Strangely enough, a starting point for the discussion of the structure of production functions is a generalization of the concept of a production function. A *transform* of a production function $f(x)$ is defined by

$$H(x) \equiv F(f(x)), \tag{1.17}$$

where $F(\cdot)$ is a twice-continuously differentiable, finite, nonnegative, and nondecreasing function of $f(x)$. If $F(f(x))$ goes to infinity as $f(x)$ goes to infinity and $F(0) = 0$, then $H(x)$ has the same basic properties of $f(x)$ [for a proof of this result, see Shephard (1970, 24–25)]. Thus, for our purposes, $H(x)$ can be viewed as a production function. The implication of this result is that whenever one can specify a valid production function, a whole family of production functions can be generated by appropriate definitions of $F(\ )$.

On an intuitive level, the best description of a transform is probably that offered by Shephard (1970). Clearly, one can always view the production function as taking a group of inputs and combining them in such a way as to produce output. Just as clearly, output is simply an amalgam of technology and the inputs, and therefore, one can think of $f(x)$ as an aggregate of all the inputs. Viewing $f(x)$ as an aggregate input then suggests that it is natural to view $F(f(x))$ as a production function, where $F(\ )$ is just a single-input production function.

An important property of transforms is that they preserve much of the substitute relationship between inputs for arbitrary x. The marginal rate of technical substitution between inputs i and j at input level x^* is the same for both $H(x^*)$ and $f(x^*)$. This follows from

$$\frac{\partial x_i}{\partial x_j} = \frac{-\partial H/\partial x_j}{\partial H/\partial x_i} = \frac{-F'\,\partial f/\partial x_j}{F'\,\partial f/\partial x_i} = \frac{-\partial f/\partial x_j}{\partial f/\partial x_i}, \quad \forall i, j,$$

where F' is the derivative $F(f(x))$ with respect to $f(x)$. Thus, we determine completely the curvature, although not the exact positioning, of the isoquants of $H(x)$ directly from knowledge of $f(x)$.

1.8b   *Homothetic production functions*

Perhaps the most important special class of production functions is the class of transforms of linearly homogeneous production functions. A production function is *homothetic* if it can be represented:

$$F(f^*(x)) = f(x), \tag{1.18}$$

where F satisfies the properties outlined and $f^*(x)$ is consistent with properties 1A.1a, 1A.2a, 1A.3a, 1A.4, 1A.5, and 1A.6b and is linearly homogeneous, that is, $f^*(\lambda x) = \lambda f^*(x)$. By earlier results, therefore, there is no loss of generality in assuming that $f^*(x)$ is concave. Reverting to the interpretation of the argument of $F(\cdot)$ as an aggregate input, one thus sees why the family of homothetic functions is particularly important. It is the only class of transforms where proportional changes in all inputs are accurately reflected by the same proportional change in the aggregate input. Thus, increasing the scale of operation for each of the actual inputs is equivalent to increasing the scale of operation for the aggregate input, and where scale-type decisions must be made, no generality is lost in dealing only with the aggregate input.

It is sometimes more convenient to consider an alternative representation of homothetic production functions. If $F' \neq 0$, (1.18) can be rewritten as

$$h(y) = f^*(x), \tag{1.19}$$

where $h(y) = F^{-1}(y)$. Formulation (1.19) is particularly valuable because it allows us to establish easily that $f(x)$ is quasi-concave if it is homothetic, where $f^*(x)$ satisfies 1A.1b, 1A.2a, 1A.3a, 1A.4, 1A.5 and 1A.6b. By (1.19), $V(y) = \{x : f^*(x) \geq h(y)\}$. Now consider x' and $x'' \in V(y)$. Since $f^*(x)$ is concave, $f^*(\lambda x' + (1-\lambda)x'') \geq \lambda f^*(x') + (1-\lambda)f^*(x'') \geq h(y)$, where the last inequality follows by the fact that x' and $x'' \in V(y)$. Accordingly, $V(y)$ is convex, and $f(x)$ is quasi-concave.

Intuitively, $h(y)$ is the amount of the aggregate input required to produce an output of y. When only a single aggregate input exists, the input requirement set consists of all levels of the aggregate input exceeding $h(y)$. Put another way, the lower boundary of $V(y)$ in terms of the aggregate input is $h(y)$.

Homothetic production functions have some very interesting properties. For example, consider the marginal rate of technical substitution. From earlier results,

$$\frac{\partial x_i}{\partial x_j} = \frac{-\partial f^*/\partial x_j}{\partial f^*/\partial x_i}. \tag{1.20}$$

The right-hand side of (1.20) represents the ratio of partial derivatives of a linearly homogeneous function that by a basic property of homogeneous functions (see Appendix) is homogeneous of degree zero in x. Thus, if (1.20) is rewritten in the somewhat more suggestive form

$$\frac{\partial x_i}{\partial x_j} = \frac{-\partial f^*(x_1, \ldots, x_n)/\partial x_j}{\partial f^*(x_1, \ldots, x_n)/\partial x_i}, \tag{1.20'}$$

multiplying the arguments of f^* in the numerator and the denominator by a scalar does not change the value of (1.20'). The marginal rate of technical substitution is constant along any ray from the origin. In a sense, therefore, homotheticity implies a set of parallel isoquants.

Another important property of homothetic functions deals with how output varies along a ray from the origin in input space. Before investigating this behavior, a convenient way to characterize a ray in n-space is needed. One way is to normalize all inputs by, say, the jth input and look at the ratios. Another normalization is the Euclidean norm of the original input vector; denote the norm as $\|x\|$. A general representation of how output varies along a ray from the origin is as a function of the slope of the ray, the original input bundle, and the original output level:

$$f(\lambda x) = G(\lambda, x/\|x\|, f(x)).$$

Differentiate G with respect to λ and evaluate at $\lambda = 1$ to obtain the ray marginal productivity:

$$\left.\frac{\partial G(\lambda, x/\|x\|, f(x))}{\partial \lambda}\right|_{\lambda=1} = \sum_i \frac{\partial f}{\partial x_i} x_i,$$

so that the elasticity of scale can be written as

$$\epsilon = \left.\frac{\partial G(\lambda, x/\|x\|, f(x))/\partial \lambda}{G(\lambda, x/\|x\|, f(x))}\right|_{\lambda=1}.$$

Thus, in general, the elasticity of scale depends on the original input bundle, the slope of the ray, and the original output level.

Return to the definition of a homothetic production function in (1.19) and calculate the elasticity of scale using (1.10):

$$\epsilon = \frac{\sum_i \dfrac{\partial f^*}{\partial x_i} x_i}{h'(y)y} = \frac{h(y)}{h'(y)y}. \tag{1.21}$$

From (1.21), the elasticity of scale for a homothetic production is only a function of the level of output. Homothetic production functions, therefore, can be characterized by what is often referred to as the *generalized Euler equation* (McElroy, 1969)

$$\sum \frac{\partial f}{\partial x_i} x_i = \epsilon(y)y. \tag{1.22}$$

A special case of (1.22) is $\partial \epsilon/\partial y = 0$; $\epsilon(y)$ is thus a constant. In this instance, (1.22) is just the Euler equation, where $\epsilon(y)$ represents the degree of homogeneity. Thus, homogeneous functions are homothetic, and examining the properties of homothetic functions allows us to determine the properties of homogeneous functions.

Returning to our original definition of G, it is possible to characterize a wide range of behavior by choosing particular representations of G. In particular, a function is homogeneous of degree α if

$$G = \lambda^\alpha \cdot f(x).$$

If $f(x)$ is homothetic,

$$G = F(\lambda^{\alpha} \cdot \phi(x))$$

where $\phi(x) = F^{-1}(f(x))$ and F is a transform of the production function.

This representation can be used to characterize two further types of production functions: the *ray-homogeneous* production function and the *ray-homothetic* production function. A production function is ray homogeneous if

$$G = \lambda^{H(x/\|x\|)} \cdot f(x),$$

where $H(\cdot)$ is a strictly positive and bounded function. Using this definition of G, differentiating with respect to λ, and evaluating at $\lambda = 1$ yields

$$\sum_i \frac{\partial f}{\partial x_i} x_i = H(x/\|x\|) f(x). \tag{1.23}$$

Thus, one readily sees why this type of function is called ray homogeneous. Returns to scale, $H(x/\|x\|)$, vary with the input mix but are independent of output.

A production function is ray homothetic if

$$G = F(\lambda^{H(x/\|x\|)} \cdot \phi(x)).$$

The elasticity of scale for such a production function can be written as a function of both $x/\|x\|$ and the output level. Thus, along any ray, the production function is homothetic. It may perform differently along different rays (Färe and Shephard, 1977).

Example 1.5. Both the Cobb–Douglas and the ACMS functions are homothetic. To see that the Cobb–Douglas is homothetic, calculate the elasticity of scale to obtain

$$\epsilon = \sum_i \alpha_i,$$

which for constant α_i's is constant, implying the Cobb–Douglas is homogeneous and therefore homothetic. Moreover, any monotonic transformation of the Cobb–Douglas is also homothetic. Consider, for example,

$$f(x) = \exp\left(A \prod_{i=1}^{n} x_i^{\alpha_i}\right).$$

By direct calculation,

$$\frac{\partial \ln f(x)}{\partial \ln x_i} = \alpha_i A \prod_{i=1}^{n} x_i^{\alpha_i} = \alpha_i \ln y,$$

which yields

$$\epsilon = \ln y \sum_{i=1}^{n} \alpha_i,$$

so that the elasticity of scale is only functionally related to the level of output.

Exercise 1.4. Derive sufficient conditions for the generalized power production function to be homothetic.

1.8c   *Separability*

So far, we have characterized x as an n-dimensional vector, where n is presumedly a very large number. However, we have often found it convenient to depict results and definitions in terms of the two-input production model that is amenable to geometric exposition. The reason is that people find it much easier first to conceptualize simple special cases while trying later to extend such analyses to higher dimensional, more realistic problems. Perhaps the best evidence of this in the economics literature is the categorization by classical economists of only three types of inputs: capital, labor, and land. They realized, of course, that there were many more than three distinct inputs,[3] but out of analytical necessity, they usually reverted to the simpler models. If the number of inputs presented only analytical difficulties, one might be tempted to say that one role of applied production economics should be to resolve empirically as many of the ambiguities arising out of problems of higher dimensionality as possible. However, it is often only when one approaches applied production analysis that the dimensionality problem becomes truly severe. In the case of econometric production analysis, for example, a prerequisite for accurate research is the existence of a data set with sufficient, independent observations to afford a degree of confidence in the precision of the results. Unfortunately, however, when the number of inputs is very large (as it often tends to be), obtaining enough usable data to permit any (much less precise) estimation often proves to be an impossible task.

---

[3] An especially lucid demonstration of this fact can be found in Henry George's (1942) critique of classical theory, which contains an elaborate delineation of what type of input can be considered as land. George categorizes all inputs that would now be called natural resources as land.

This has led many economists to fall back on the classical device of defining the production process in terms of a smaller number of inputs while trying to find ways to justify such a procedure theoretically. Clearly, what is required if all inputs are to be accounted for is some way of aggregating inputs. In our discussion of transforms, we have seen that the production function itself serves just such a purpose since, for example, a homothetic function can always be viewed as a single-input production function.

One way to address the problems caused by the existence of many inputs is to ask the question "Can the production process be broken into stages so that at each stage some inputs are used to make an intermediate input that is then used with other intermediate inputs to produce the final product?" An example might be offered by car manufacturing, where, for example, many small parts are used to make an engine that is then used as a separate input in final assembly. The technology of constructing an engine is different from that of making a car door. From an analytical perspective, it may be appropriate to specify separate production functions for both the car door and the engine while specifying yet another production function describing how the door and engine are used in final assembly. If one can do just that (i.e., separate the technology into several stages), the technology is *separable*.

A visual notion of a separable technology is offered by Figure 1.13, which illustrates the style of automobile production described above. The figure has a tree shape. Each secondary branch describes the production of a major part of an automobile (the chassis, doors, engine, wheels, etc.). The main stem represents the final stage of assembly, where intermediate inputs are combined into the car.

In what follows, we examine the functional properties required to permit the construction of a separable production function. Not all technologies are separable, and the issue of separability is most easily described in the context of continuously differentiable technologies. Thus, in what follows, we assume that $f(x)$ is twice-continuously differentiable.

Separability hinges on how the marginal rate of technical substitution between two inputs responds to changes in another input. By definition, *inputs x_i and x_j are separable from x_k in $f(x)$ if*

$$\frac{\partial}{\partial x_k} \frac{\partial f / \partial x_i}{\partial f / \partial x_j} = 0. \tag{1.24}$$

In the following, we always presume that $i, j \neq k$. That is, an input is never separable from itself. The meaning of (1.24) is that the slope of an isoquant in i, j-space is not affected by what happens in k-space. This does not mean, however, that the isoquant in i, j-space is not affected. Only the slope remains unchanged.

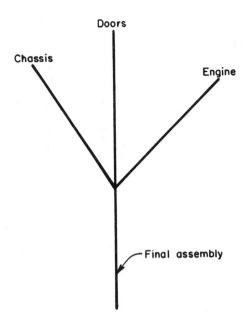

Figure 1.13 Separable technology.

Consider Figure 1.14, where panel (a) represents an isoquant map consistent with x_1 and x_2 separable from x_3. In that panel, changes in x_3, represented by shifting the isoquant from (y, x_3^0) to (y, x_3^1), do not change the rate at which x_1 and x_2 substitute for one another in the production of y. Panel (b), on the other hand, represents an isoquant map inconsistent with separability. Here, changes in x_3 evoke not only shifts in the isoquant but a rotation as well.

An equivalent representation of (1.24) is

$$\frac{f_{ik}x_k}{f_i} = \frac{f_{jk}x_k}{f_j} \tag{1.25}$$

and

$$\frac{\partial \ln f_i}{\partial \ln x_k} = \frac{\partial \ln f_j}{\partial \ln x_k}.$$

Separability requires that the elasticity of the marginal product of x_i with respect to x_k equal the elasticity of the marginal product of x_j with respect to x_k.

To proceed to input aggregation, it proves convenient to introduce some further notation. Let **I** denote the set of indices of the input vector **I** =

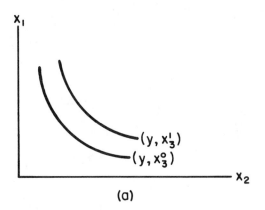

(a)

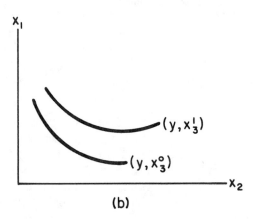

(b)

Figure 1.14 Separability.

$\{1, 2, \ldots, n\}$. Now partition $\mathbf{I}$ into subsets (each subset is denoted by $\mathbf{I}^k$) to define the partition of $\mathbf{I}$, $\hat{\mathbf{I}} = \{\mathbf{I}^1, \mathbf{I}^2, \ldots, \mathbf{I}^m\}$. The partition $\hat{\mathbf{I}}$ defines a corresponding partition in the input vector $\hat{x} = (x^1, x^2, \ldots, x^m)$, where each x^j is a subvector of the n-dimensional vector x.

Using these definitions, we can delineate several distinct types of separability. The production function is *weakly separable* in the partition $\hat{\mathbf{I}}$ if

$$\frac{\partial}{\partial x_k} \frac{\partial f(x)/\partial x_i}{\partial f(x)/\partial x_j} = 0, \quad i, j \in \mathbf{I}^r, \ k \notin \mathbf{I}^r. \tag{1.26}$$

In words, $f(x)$ is weakly separable in the partition $\hat{\mathbf{I}}$ if the marginal rate of technical substitution between x_i and x_j, each of which are elements of the same subvector, is independent of all inputs that are not elements of their respective subvector. Assuming that $f(x)$ satisfies strict monotonicity and strict quasi-concavity, it can be shown that (1.26) is equivalent to being able to write (see Goldman and Uzawa 1964)

$$f(x) = F(f^1(x^1), f^2(x^2), ..., f^m(x^m)), \tag{1.27}$$

where F is strictly increasing and quasi-concave and each $f^i(x^i)$ satisfies properties 1A.1b and 1A.2a. The intuitive interpretation of the functions $f^i(x^i)$ is now clear. Each can be interpreted as an aggregate input that is constructed from a subset of the inputs. Moreover, since each $f^i(x^i)$ possesses some of the basic properties of a production function, it can also be thought of intuitively as a production function itself. Apparently, therefore, when the production function is weakly separable, it is legitimate to think of production occurring in two logical stages. In the first stage, the inputs in subvector x^i are used to produce an aggregate input via the *micro-production function* $f^i(x^i)$. In the second stage, these aggregate inputs are then used to produce the resulting output via the *macro-production function* $F(\cdot)$, which is increasing and quasi-concave. If we denote the aggregate inputs as $X^i = f^i(x^i)$, it is legitimate to think of a general production function in terms of them alone,

$$F(X^1, X^2, ..., X^m),$$

where this production function now satisfies the same general properties as previously imposed. The same can be said for the construction of each of the aggregate inputs $f^i(x^i)$.

Although it seems reasonable to think of production as proceeding in two stages, there is an important point that is easily overlooked and, therefore, bears emphasizing. If we use (1.27) in (1.26), we find that separability of this type requires

$$\frac{\partial}{\partial x_k} \frac{\partial f^r(x^r)/\partial x_i}{\partial f^r(x^r)/\partial x_j} = 0, \quad i, j \in \mathbf{I}^r, \ k \notin \mathbf{I}^r.$$

That is, it is not enough that there exist a two-stage process. Rather, it is required that in the first stage the micro-production functions be independent of one another. In the automobile production example, this would imply, say, that the production of doors could proceed completely independently of the production of windshield wipers. In many cases, this may be true, but in others, it may not be true, especially where the overall production process requires the utilization of the same entrepreneurial input at multiple points in the production process.

A stronger form of separability exists: When the production function is *strongly separable* in the partition $\hat{\mathbf{I}}$, it satisfies

$$\frac{\partial}{\partial x_k} \frac{\partial f(x)/\partial x_i}{\partial f(x)/\partial x_j} = 0, \quad i \in \mathbf{I}^r, \, j \in \mathbf{I}^v, \, k \notin \mathbf{I}^v \cup \mathbf{I}^r. \tag{1.28}$$

Expression (1.28) is somewhat more restrictive than (1.26) because it implies that the marginal rate of technical substitution between any two inputs (regardless of which subvectors they belong to) is independent of the utilization of any input that is not an element of either subvector. By (1.28), if a function is strongly separable, it is also weakly separable. If the production function is strongly separable, it can be written as

$$f(x) = F^*\left(\sum_i^m f^i(x^i) \right), \tag{1.29}$$

where, to avoid confusion, we explicitly state that the $f^i(x^i)$ are not necessarily the same functions as in (1.27). If $f(x)$ satisfies 1A.1b and 1A.2a, then F^* and each $f^i(x^i)$ will also. In other words, we can continue to interpret each $f^i(x^i)$ as an aggregate input. Here, however, the relationship is more restrictive because (1.29) implies that the level sets of $F(\cdot)$ in terms of the aggregate inputs are straight lines. Thus, the aggregate inputs are perfectly substitutable for one another in the production of output. This can be most easily seen by noting that

$$\frac{\partial X^i}{\partial X^j} = -\frac{\partial F^*(X^1 \cdots X^m)/\partial X^j}{\partial F^*(X^1 \cdots X^m)/\partial X^i} = -1$$

in the case of a strongly separable production function. Of course, it also follows from (1.29) that a strongly separable production function is also homothetic in the aggregate inputs since $\sum_{i=1}^m X^i$ is linearly homogeneous in X^i.

Finally, if $m = n$, each subvector contains only one element, and $f(x)$ is also strongly separable in the partition, $f(x)$ is said to be *factor-wise separable*. Put another way, $f(x)$ is *factor-wise separable* if

$$\frac{\partial}{\partial x_k} \frac{\partial f(x)/\partial x_i}{\partial f(x)/\partial x_j} = 0, \quad k \neq i, \, k \neq j, \tag{1.30}$$

which, using (1.29), implies that the production function assumes the form

$$f(x) = F^*\left(\sum_{i=1}^n g^i(x_i) \right);$$

and since $g^i(x_i)$ only depends on x_i, there appears to be relatively little loss of generality in redefining x_i (e.g., respecifying units) so that it actually corresponds to $g^i(x_i)$. If this is done, the production function is of the general form

$$f(x) = F\left(\sum_{i=1}^{n} x_i\right). \tag{1.31}$$

The form of (1.29) and (1.30) is interesting because it illustrates cases where particular inputs (aggregate or micro as the case might be) may be nonessential in the production of output. Say, for example, that $X^j = 0$ for all $j \neq i$; then we can rewrite (1.29) as

$$F(x) = F^*(X^i) = F^*(f^i(x^i)),$$

so that, in this instance, output is nonzero even though there is zero utilization of all x_j for $j \notin \mathbf{I}^i$.

Example 1.6. The Cobb–Douglas function is factor-wise separable, as can be verified from the fact that the marginal rate of technical substitution between x_i and x_j can be written as

$$\frac{\partial x_i}{\partial x_j} = -\frac{x_i}{x_j}\frac{\alpha_j}{\alpha_i},$$

which is, of course, independent of x_k, where $k \neq i$, $k \neq j$. This implies that a Cobb–Douglas function defined in terms of aggregate inputs will be strongly separable. As an example, suppose we specify a generalized Cobb–Douglas of the form

$$f(x) = A\prod_{i=1}^{m}(X^i)^{\alpha_i} = A\prod_{i=1}^{m} f^i(x^i)^{\alpha_i}.$$

Then this function will be strongly separable since one can verify that, for $i \in \mathbf{I}^r$,

$$\frac{\partial f(x)}{\partial x_i} = \frac{\alpha_r}{f^r(x^r)}\frac{\partial f^r(x^r)}{\partial x_i} A\prod_{i=1}^{m} f^i(x^i)^{\alpha_i},$$

which, for $j \in \mathbf{I}^k$, gives

$$\frac{\partial x_i}{\partial x_j} = \frac{\alpha_k}{\alpha_r}\frac{f^r(x^r)}{f^k(x^k)}\frac{\partial f^k/\partial x_j}{\partial f^r/\partial x_i},$$

which only depends on the elements of x^r and x^k.

Perhaps the most interesting aspect of the foregoing discussion is that assuming separability imposes structure on $f(x)$. Thus, as is the case with homotheticity, if we are willing to accept the restrictions implied by separability, we can greatly narrow the class of candidate functions for the production function. This ability is especially valuable in applied or econometric production analysis where modern econometric techniques usually require a specific functional relationship. Separability suggests a family of such functions; but as we will see, there is a cost associated with this capability. However, separability, especially in the form of strong separability, can greatly economize on the number of parameters to be estimated in applied analysis. In fact, many functions commonly used in empirical analysis are both strongly separable and homothetic.

Bibliographical notes

Some of the material is readily available in most standard texts on production theory. Excellent sources on the properties of the production function and related issues are Ferguson and Shephard (1970). Much of the discussion concerning the elasticity of scale appears to be a relatively novel way of viewing this concept. However, the relationship between the law of variable proportions and returns to scale is implicit in the work of Carlson (1939), which appeared shortly after the classic study of Cassels (1936). The discussion of separability essentially follows that contained in Blackorby, Primont, and Russell (1978). There are differences both in the level of the mathematics required and in the terminology. Blackorby et al. refer to what we have called weak separability as separability in the partition of x and to strong separability as complete separability. The discussion of the various forms of the elasticity of substitution and the homotheticity are derived from a wide variety of sources that include (but are not restricted to) Shephard (1953, 1970), Fuss and McFadden (1978), Mundlak (1968), and Allen (1938).

CHAPTER 2

Cost functions

The cost function is not a new concept. However, the past 10–15 years have witnessed such a heightened interest in its properties that the uninitiated might easily be convinced that it was discovered intact in the late 1960s or early 1970s. For example, Ferguson's (1969) definitive exposition of the neoclassical theory of cost and production only contains one reference in its index to the subject of cost functions. But by 1980, almost all working economists had realized that the complete, neoclassical theory of cost could be cast solely in terms of the cost function. What is striking, however, is that it took the economics profession so long to realize the ability of the cost function to characterize completely cost-minimizing behavior since this was clearly outlined in Samuelson's (1948) *Foundations of Economic Analysis* and exhaustively investigated in Shephard's (1953) classic exposition of duality.

This chapter provides an analysis of cost-minimizing behavior that emphasizes indirect or dual analytical methods almost exclusively. Consequently, the more traditional approach to comparative statics is practically ignored. There are two reasons for this: First, it is not possible to improve on the definitive expositions given by Samuelson and later Ferguson; second, since the two approaches are basically different roads to the same destination, it seems best to choose one and stick to it rather than trying to proceed along both simultaneously. That is not to say that the more traditional approach should be neglected. As one first trained in that approach, I would be the first to admit its many advantages. However, there are places where the dual or indirect approach is easier, and the subject matter of this chapter clearly falls in that category.

So far, I have referred rather cavalierly to the dual approach, duality, and so on, without really providing an explanation of what these concepts mean. The most succinct definition of duality that I have come across is that offered by Gorman (1976): "Duality is about the choice of the independent variables in terms of which one defines a theory." The essence of the dual approach is that technology (or in the case of the consumer problem, preferences) constrains optimizing behavior of individuals. One should therefore be able to use an accurate representation of optimizing behavior to study the technology. The basic idea is deceptively simple:

Since the technology conditions the producer's response to market phenomena, examining these conditioned responses should enable us to say
something about the technology.

Since the cost function is a mathematical representation of the cost-
minimizing problem, it is, in a sense, a statistic combining in one form
relatively disparate pieces of information. In fact, McFadden (1978a) has
termed it a "sufficient statistic" for the technology (more on this later).
Thus, the cost function (and its related concepts, e.g., the profit function) provides a natural basis for investigation of the technology. But
before one uses the cost function for such analyses, a firm grasp of the
theory underlying the cost function is required. This is the purpose of
this chapter – to provide the "why" and "how come" the cost function
is a "sufficient statistic."

In the following, we first derive the basic properties of cost functions
in a modern fashion that relies only slightly on the properties of the underlying production function. These properties of the cost function are
shown to characterize exhaustively the comparative static behavior of
cost-minimizing demands. Then a motivation for the use of dual techniques is offered, that is, the ability to extract important characteristics
of the technology from observed economic behavior in the form of costs,
prices, and input demands. This section provides the foundation for most
of the empirical research using cost functions and provides a succinct,
but hopefully revealing, discussion of the basic issues involved in establishing the existence of a duality between costs and technology. No actual
proof of duality is offered. Although it would be ideal if all had a complete grasp of the mathematical intricacies underlying duality, this does
not appear essential to the conduct of high-quality empirical research involving cost functions.

2.1   The cost function defined

The cost function is defined as

$$c(w, y) = \min_{x \geq 0}\{w \cdot x : x \in V(y)\}, \tag{2.1}$$

where w is a vector of strictly positive input prices and $w \cdot x$ is the inner
product $(\sum_i w_i x_i)$. In words, the cost function is the minimum cost of
producing a given output level during a given time period expressed as a
function of input prices and output. The representation in (2.1) assumes
that input prices are exogenous to the producer. In what follows, we shall
generally presume that producers are atomistic competitors in the sense
that they take input (and other) prices as given. Moreover, in the spirit
of Chapter 1, we rule out the existence of inputs with zero prices.

Before proceeding to an examination of the properties of the cost function, a few comments about $c(w, y)$ as defined in (2.1) seem appropriate. First, $c(w, y)$ depends on the technology since the only constraint to the minimization problem in (2.1) is that x be capable of producing at least output y. Apparently, therefore, the more a priori restrictions that are placed on the technology, the more constrained producers will be in solving the minimum-cost problem. This is perhaps best illustrated by the fact that without at least some assumptions on $V(y)$, the cost function will not even be well defined. As is well known, the minimum value of an unconstrained linear function is minus infinity. Therefore, in what follows, it is necessary to utilize some of the properties of $f(x)$ outlined in Chapter 1. However, as a general rule, the imposition of restrictions will be as parsimonious as possible within the mathematical confines of the present text. The goal is to place as few restrictions as possible on the a priori behavior of economic agents so as to permit the derivation of as general a behavioral response pattern as possible.

2.2 Properties of cost functions

The first order of business is to ascertain that the cost function defined in (2.1) exists. To do so, the range of feasible input combinations must be restricted further; that is, some restrictions have to be placed on $V(y)$. For the remaining discussion of cost functions, assume that $V(y)$ is nonempty and closed, that is, property 1A.4 applies. Then, following McFadden (1978a), there must exist an $x' \in V(y)$ (by nonemptiness), and the problem in (2.1) can be reformulated as

$$\min_{x \geq 0} \{w \cdot x : w \cdot (x - x') \leq 0; x \in V(y)\}.$$

This reformulation is appropriate because if x' can produce y, the minimum cost of producing y must be no larger than wx'. Hence, the feasible region from which the cost-minimizing bundle can be chosen is given by the intersection of the half-space $w(x - x') \leq 0$ and the input requirement set. The resulting region is illustrated graphically by the shaded area in Figure 2.1. Since property 1A.4 holds, this region is both closed and bounded. Hence, the Weierstrass theorem (see Appendix) can be applied to demonstrate the existence of a minimum since $w \cdot x$ is continuous. Although only discussed briefly in Chapter 1, property 1A.4 proves to be the most basic assumption in our analysis. If the production function satisfies properties 1A.1a (monotonicity), 1A.3a (weak essentiality), 1A.4 (nonemptiness of $V(y)$), and 1A.5 (finite, nonnegative, real valued for all nonnegative and finite x), the cost function defined by (2.1) will satisfy the following.

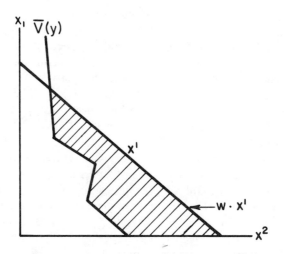

Figure 2.1 Feasible solutions to least cost problem.

Properties of $c(w, y)$ (2B):

1. $c(w, y) > 0$ for $w > 0$ and $y > 0$ (nonnegativity);
2. if $w' \geq w$, then $c(w', y) \geq c(w, y)$ (nondecreasing in w);
3. concave and continuous in w;
4. $c(tw, y) = tc(w, y)$, $t > 0$ (positively linearly homogeneous);
5. if $y \geq y'$, then $c(w, y) \geq c(w, y')$ (nondecreasing in y); and
6. $c(w, 0) = 0$ (no fixed costs).

Nonnegativity: Property 2B.1 simply says that it is impossible to produce a positive output at zero cost. To demonstrate this result, note that weak essentiality of the production function requires the utilization of a strictly positive amount of at least one input to produce a positive output level. As long as input prices are all strictly positive, the cost of producing a positive output must also be positive.

Nondecreasing in w: Property 2B.2, which indicates that increasing any input price must not decrease cost, is also quite self-evident and easy to prove. Consider the two input price vectors w^1 and w^2 such that $w^1 \geq w^2$. Let x^1 and x^2 be the corresponding cost-minimizing input bundles. Since changing w does not affect the set of feasible input choices, x^1 potentially could be cost minimizing when input prices are w^2. But since it is not chosen, the following inequality must hold: $w^2 x^2 \leq w^2 x^1$. However, since $w^1 \geq w^2$, it must also be true that $w^1 x^1 \geq w^2 x^1$. Putting

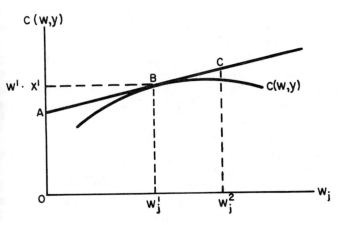

Figure 2.2 Graphical demonstration of Shephard's lemma and concavity of $c(w, y)$.

these inequalities together yields $c(w^1, y) = w^1 x^1 \geq w^2 x^2 = c(w^2, y)$, which is the desired inequality.

The basic idea behind the proof of property 2B.2 can be used to reveal a fundamental fact about the response of cost-minimizing input bundles to changes in input prices. By an analogous argument, $w^1 x^1 \leq w^1 x^2$, which when added to $w^2 x^2 \leq w^2 x^1$ yields the *fundamental inequality of cost minimization*:

$$(w^1 - w^2)(x^1 - x^2) \leq 0. \tag{2.2}$$

To gain some intuitive insight into expression (2.2), consider the case where only the ith element of w^1 and w^2 differ. Expression (2.2) then implies

$$(w_i^1 - w_i^2)(x_i^1 - x_i^2) \leq 0,$$

or, in words, single-input price changes evoke opposite direction changes in input utilization. Hence, expression (2.2) is a generalization of the familiar principle that derived-demand curves are downward sloping and underlies most of the comparative static properties of derived demand to be developed later in this chapter.

Concavity and continuity: Property 2B.3, which is a direct consequence of expression (2.2), may not seem immediately intuitive but is easily motivated with the aid of Figure 2.2, which illustrates the relationship between cost and any single-input price. The line segment emanating from point A through point B represents how cost changes in response to changes in w_j if the input vector is held fixed at x^1. Suppose that $x^1 \in V(y)$ and further that when input prices are given by w^1, x^1 (which corresponds to B) is the least cost input bundle. Consider an increase in w_j to something like w_j^2 in Figure 2.2. Since $V(y)$ is independent of w, x^1 can still be used. If it is, costs rise too. On the other hand, moving to point C on this line segment need not be optimal. Moreover, the optimal response to the change in w_j can never result in a level of cost higher than that associated with C. Otherwise, the producer would simply move to C. Accordingly, the cost function when graphed over w_j can never lie above this line segment, suggesting that $c(w, y)$ assumes the shape of an upturned bowl, as illustrated in Figure 2.2.

From these arguments, it is now fairly obvious and intuitive why $c(w, y)$ should be concave in w. At worst, $c(w, y)$ would be linear, and this is the case when the input bundle is absolutely fixed; that is, there are no substitution possibilities. But if inputs can be substituted for one another, the substitution of now relatively cheaper inputs for x_j in production should mitigate the cost rise associated with the increase in w_j. Otherwise, the firm would not substitute inputs.

Now to a formal proof of property 2B.3. Consider two vectors of input prices w^1 and w^{11}. Let x^1 and x^{11} be the cost-minimizing bundles for w^1 and w^{11}, respectively. Define the convex combination of w^1 and w^{11}:

$$w^0 = \theta w^1 + (1-\theta)w^{11}, \quad 0 \le \theta \le 1.$$

Our problem is to show that $c(w^0 y) \ge \theta c(w^1, y) + (1-\theta)c(w^{11}, y)$ to establish concavity. Let x^0 be the cost-minimizing input bundle associated with w^0. By definition, $x^0 \in V(y)$. By cost minimization,

$$w^1 \cdot x^0 \ge w^1 \cdot x^1 \quad \text{and} \quad w^{11} \cdot x^0 \ge w^{11} \cdot x^{11}$$

since x^1 and x^{11} are cost-minimizing input bundles. Therefore, we can write

$$c(w^0, y) = w^0 \cdot x^0$$
$$= [\theta w^1 + (1-\theta)w^{11}] \cdot x^0$$
$$= \theta w^1 \cdot x^0 + (1-\theta)w^{11} \cdot x^0$$
$$\ge \theta c(w^1, y) + (1-\theta)c(w^{11}, y),$$

which establishes the desired concavity.

Combining properties 2B.1–2B.3 suggests that $c(w, y)$ can be represented graphically by something like panel (a) in Figure 2.3. Note in particular that this representation is increasing, concave, and continuous in

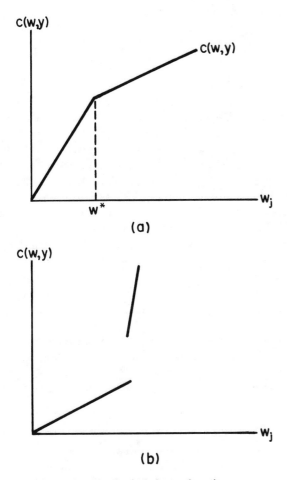

Figure 2.3 Properties of cost functions.

w but not everywhere differentiable. Moreover, these same properties rule out the existence of cost functions of the type illustrated in panel (b) of Figure 2.3, which is neither concave nor continuous in w.

Positive linear homogeneity: Property 2B.4 is a restatement of the familiar principle that only relative prices matter to economically optimizing agents. Or, as long as input prices only vary proportionately, the cost-minimizing choice of inputs will not vary. To demonstrate this property, consider the following argument:

$$c(tw, y) = \min_{x \geq 0}\{(tw) \cdot x : x \in V(y)\}$$

$$= t \min_{x \geq 0}\{w \cdot x : x \in V(y)\}$$

$$= tc(w, y).$$

Property 2B.5 also is somewhat self-evident and simply means that increasing output cannot decrease the costs. To demonstrate it formally note that for $y' \geq y$, monotonicity of the production function implies that $V(y') \subseteq V(y)$; that is, any input combination that can be used to produce y' can also produce y. Therefore, since the input requirement set for y' is contained within that for y, any minimum achieved on $V(y')$ can also be achieved on $V(y)$. Hence, minimum costs cannot decrease as output expands. Note further that we have said nothing about $c(w, y)$ being continuous in y. Thus, if we replaced w_i with y on the vertical axis in panel (b) of Figure 2.3, the resulting figure would presumedly be a valid representation of cost behavior in terms of output.

No fixed costs: Property 2B.6, which says that it is costless to produce zero output, is a direct consequence of weak essentiality. It is important, however, because it also highlights a fact not discussed explicitly to this point. That is, the present discussion only deals with cases in which all inputs are perfectly variable. There are no costs the entrepreneur must incur regardless of the amount of output produced. Later we will see that this is tantamount to assuming that we are dealing with a perfectly long-run problem.

Shephard's lemma: So far, nothing has been said about the possible differentiability of the cost function in input prices. We know that it is continuous in w, but, for example, points such as w^* in panel (a) of Figure 2.3 are perfectly legitimate representations of cost behavior. However, when the cost function is differentiable, it possesses a very useful property that has provided the foundation for much recent applied research. Namely, the cost function satisfies property 2B.7:

7. If the cost function is differentiable in w, then there exists a unique vector of cost-minimizing demands that is equal to the gradient of $c(w, y)$ in w. That is, if $x_i(w, y)$ is the ith, unique, cost-minimizing demand, then $x_i(w, y) = \partial c(w, y)/\partial w_i$ (*Shephard's lemma*).

Before proving property 2B.7, let us first comment on its implications. Quite obviously, if the cost function is differentiable, then one can easily obtain an expression for the cost-minimizing demands by simple calculus manipulation. Less obviously, but more important, is the implication that the behavior of the derived demands is determined by the properties of the cost function. Thus, for example, properties 2B.1–2B.6 of the cost function place implicit (and, as we shall see, exhaustive) conditions on the cost-minimizing demands. From an empirical perspective, the import of this result is enormous since it suggests that one can systematically characterize derived-demand behavior by examining empirical properties of cost functions. We shall say a good more about this later, but for now, we turn to a demonstration of this result. In what follows, we demonstrate that the gradient of a differentiable cost is the cost-minimizing input vector. The demonstration of uniqueness requires a mathematical argument that goes beyond the confines of this text.

As some readers probably recognize, part of Shephard's lemma is a special case of the envelope theorem developed in the Appendix. However, its centrality to modern producer theory merits a separate discussion, apart from mechanical application of a lemma developed in the Appendix. To proceed let us recycle Figure 2.2 and look at it from a slightly different perspective. For input prices w^1, let the cost-minimizing choice be $w^1 x^1$ and let point B in Figure 2.2 correspond to the level of total cost associated with w_j^1. The line segment running from A through B then represents how total costs would vary in response to changes in w_j if the input bundle were held constant at x^1 with all $w_k \neq w_j$ also held constant. By our proof of concavity, the cost function must not lie above this line segment while it must share at least point B in common with the line segment. Since $c(w, y)$ cannot intersect the line segment but must have at least one point in common with the line segment, $c(w, y)$ and the line segment must be tangent at B. Hence, the slope of $c(w, y)$ in w_j space at B must equal the slope of its tangent at B. But the derivative of this line segment with respect to w_j is simply x_j^1, the cost minimizing demand. Accordingly, we have demonstrated graphically property 2B.7.

A more formal proof of property 2B.7 is offered by a simple, but instructive, argument. By definition of the cost function, for input prices w^0, the cost-minimizing bundle x^0 defines $w^0 x^0 = c(w^0, y)$. Since $V(y)$ is independent of w, x^0 is feasible for any other price vector but is not necessarily cost minimizing for other input prices (i.e., for $w \neq w^0$),

$$w \cdot x^0 \geq c(w, y).$$

This, of course, is a restatement of the inequality utilized to derive the fundamental inequality of cost minimization. Here, however, this inequality implies that the function

$$L(w, x^0, y) = wx^0 - c(w, y)$$

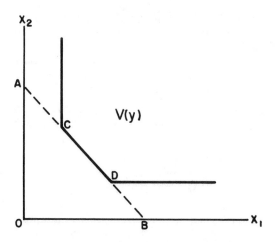

Figure 2.4 Cost minimization for $f(x)$ that is not strictly convex.

achieves a minimum at w^0 when $L(w^0, x^0, y) = 0$. For twice-continuously differentiable $c(w, y)$ the first-order conditions for this problem require

$$\frac{\partial L(w^0, x^0, y)}{\partial w_i} = x_i^0 - \frac{\partial c(w^0, y)}{\partial w_i} = 0,$$

which establishes the desired result. Moreover, second-order conditions require that the matrix with typical element $\{\partial^2 c(w^0, y)/\partial w_i\, \partial w_j\}$ be negative semidefinite. By a fundamental result on differentiable functions, this implies that $c(w, y)$ must be concave in w (see Appendix). Thus, as is apparent from Figure 2.2, Shephard's lemma and the concavity property are closely related phenomena and can be viewed intuitively as manifestations of the same basic characteristics of producers' behavior. More will be said about this later. For now, we turn to a brief (but hopefully intuitive) discussion of conditions sufficient for Shephard's lemma to hold.

Shephard's lemma will hold if $V(y)$ is a strictly convex set; this condition is sufficient to imply the existence of a unique cost-minimizing bundle. Intuitively, this fact is perhaps best demonstrated with the aid of Figures 2.4 and 2.5. Figure 2.4 represents the cost-minimizing solution for an input requirement set that is not strictly convex. As the reader undoubtedly knows from standard neoclassical theory, cost minimization requires (for an interior solution) equating the marginal rate of technical substitution to the negative of the ratio of input prices. But if the input price ratio happens to be given by the slope of the line segment AB in

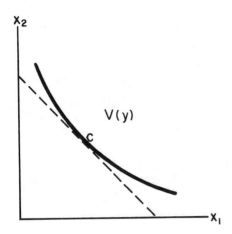

Figure 2.5   Cost minimization with $f(x)$ strictly quasi-concave.

Figure 2.4, there are an infinity of input pairs between points C and D on the isoquant for which this equality holds. Therefore, one cannot expect to be able to recapture a unique cost-minimizing input bundle from the cost minimization problem by traditional means (for an explicit illustration of this phenomenon, see Example 2.1).

Figure 2.5 illustrates the case of a strictly quasi-concave production function, and it is immediately apparent that there exists a unique cost-minimizing input bundle at point E.

Example 2.1. Cost functions for the Leontief and linear technologies. From Chapter 1, the Leontief technology can be written as

$$f(x) = \min\{\alpha_1 x_1, \alpha_2 x_2, \ldots, \alpha_n x_n\},$$

which implies that the associated cost function is

$$c(w, y) = \min_{x}\{w \cdot x : y = \min(\alpha_1 x_1, \alpha_2 x_2, \ldots, \alpha_n x_n)\}.$$

Geometrically, it is clear that the most efficient input utilization regardless of the cost of inputs will come at the vertex in n-space consistent with $y = \alpha_1 x_1 = \alpha_2 x_2 = \cdots = \alpha_n x_n$. At this point only, all inputs are limitational, and no input can be decreased without lowering output while increasing any subset of the inputs can only raise costs but not output. The ith cost-minimizing demand must then be given by $x_i(w, y) = y/\alpha_i$, which is in fact independent of input prices. The associated cost function can, therefore, be written as

$$c(w, y) = y \sum_{i=1}^{n} \frac{w_i}{\alpha_i},$$ (2.3)

which is represented geometrically as a plane in n-dimensional space.

It is instructive to establish that (2.3) satisfies properties 2B. To see that it is nondecreasing in w_i, simply differentiate expression (2.3) with respect to w_i to obtain

$$\frac{\partial c(y, w)}{\partial w_i} = \frac{y}{\alpha_i},$$

which by the properties of the Leontief function is strictly positive for $y > 0$. Moreover, this expression also serves to establish that $c(w, y)$ is continuous while satisfying Shephard's lemma.

Expression (2.3) is not strictly concave in w since linearity implies

$$c(\theta w^0 + (1-\theta)w^*, y) = y \sum_{i=1}^{n} \frac{\theta w_i^0}{i} + y \sum_{i=1}^{n} \frac{(1-\theta)w_i^*}{y}$$

$$= \theta c(w^0, y) + (1-\theta)c(w^*, y).$$

Hence, (2.3) is both concave and convex. Since it is linear in each w_i, it is obviously linearly homogeneous as required. Moreover, properties 2B.5 and 2B.6 are also easily verified.

Before we turn to a discussion of the linear technology, it is perhaps worthwhile to note that the usual approach of dealing with the cost minimization problem of inverting first-order conditions would not have worked for the Leontief function. The more indirect approach of utilizing the cost function, however, has yielded useful results.

Now consider the linear technology given by

$$f(x) = \sum_{i=1}^{n} \beta_i x_i,$$

where each $\beta_i > 0$. In the two-dimensional case, the level set of this technology is illustrated in Figure 2.6 as the line segment AD with the slope given by the constant $-\beta_1/\beta_2$ that intersects each axis. Common sense, therefore, indicates that since neither input is essential, only the cheapest effective input will ever be used. An effective input is defined as $\beta_i x_i$. Thus, in the case of Figure 2.6, input 1 is utilized if

$$w_1 y/\beta_1 < w_2 y/\beta_2;$$

only input 2 is utilized if this inequality is reversed; and in the case where

$$w_1 y/\beta_1 = w_2 y/\beta_2,$$

it is not clear whether input 1 or input 2 is utilized. In the last instance, minus the slope of the price ratio is just equal to the constant marginal

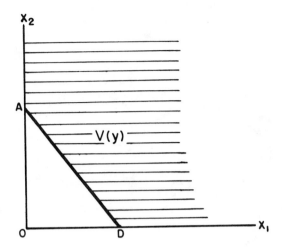

Figure 2.6 Input requirement set for linear technology.

rate of technical substitution, and the situation is very similar to that depicted in Figure 2.4.

By natural extension, these arguments imply that the associated cost
function is

$$c(w, y) = \min\left\{\frac{w_1 y}{\beta_1}, \frac{w_2 y}{\beta_2}, \ldots, \frac{w_n y}{\beta_n}\right\}$$

$$= y \min\left\{\frac{w_1}{\beta_1}, \frac{w_2}{\beta_2}, \ldots, \frac{w_n}{\beta_n}\right\}, \tag{2.4}$$

which is obviously a Leontief function in input prices. Hence, we reach the
interesting conclusion that the cost function associated with a Leontief
production function is linear in input prices, whereas the cost function associated with a linear production function is Leontief. Notice further that
it is now an easy matter to extend the arguments of Chapter 1 to establish
that the cost function in (2.4) satisfies properties 2B.1–2B.6. However, it
is equally obvious that property 2B.7 will not hold everywhere since, by
analogy with earlier arguments, expression (2.4) in the two-input case implies that the cost function as a function of w_1 can be represented as in Figure 2.7. Clearly this function is not differentiable at point B, so that 2B.7
cannot apply. Thus, we affirm our earlier statement that functions with an
$f(x)$ that is not strictly quasi-concave will not be everywhere differentiable. Notice, however, that to the left of B, this function is differentiable in
w_1, and similarly to the right of B, the function is also differentiable in w_1.
But at B, $w_1/\beta_1 = w_2/\beta_2$, and the level of derived demand is indeterminate.

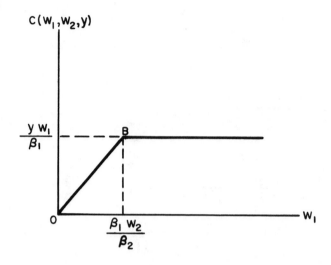

Figure 2.7 Cost function for linear technology.

Example 2.2. The Cobb–Douglas production function

$$f(x) = Ax_1^a x_2^b$$

was introduced in Chapter 1. This example uses the Cobb–Douglas production function to illustrate the primal approach to solving the cost minimization problem. The exercise that follows is designed to demonstrate that the resulting cost function satisfies properties 2B, which were derived by more direct methods. First, form the Lagrangian expression

$$L = wx + l(y - Ax_1^a x_2^b),$$

where l is a Lagrangian multiplier. By usual results in the theory of nonlinear programming, the solution to the unconstrained minimization of L solves the cost minimization problem in (2.1), when the technology is Cobb–Douglas. Since the Cobb–Douglas function is characterized by strict essentiality (property 1A.3b), we can restrict ourselves to considering interior solutions, that is, those that require $x > 0$. Hence, the first-order conditions require

$$\frac{\partial L}{\partial x_1} = w_1 - laAx_1^{a-l}x_2^b = 0,$$

$$\frac{\partial L}{\partial x_2} = w_2 - lbAx_1^a x_2^{b-l} = 0,$$

and

$$y - Ax_1^a x_2^b = 0.$$

Solving these equations simultaneously for x_1, x_2 and l yields

$$x_1 = \left(\frac{y}{A}\right)^d \left(\frac{w_2}{w_1}\right)^{b/d} \left(\frac{a}{b}\right)^{b/d},$$

$$x_2 = \left(\frac{y}{A}\right)^d \left(\frac{w_1}{w_2}\right)^{a/d} \left(\frac{a}{b}\right)^{a/d},$$

where $d = a + b$. Substituting these equations into the definition in (2.1) yields the associated cost function.

> **Exercise 2.1.** Use the cost-minimizing derived demands from Example 2.2 to form the cost function for the Cobb–Douglas production function. Verify that it satisfies properties 2B.

> **Exercise 2.2.** Derive the cost function for the production function
>
> $$f(x) = \begin{cases} a_1 x_1, & x_1 < x_1^*; \\ x_2 a_2 + a_1 x_1^*, & x_1 \geq x_1^*. \end{cases}$$
>
> Does this cost function satisfy properties 2B?

2.3   Comparative statics from the cost function

Traditionally, one of the main reasons for considering the cost minimization problem in a formal mathematical manner was to enable economists to answer systematically such questions as "What happens to input utilization if the ith input price rises?" and "What happens to input utilization and costs if output increases?" In this section, such issues are addressed solely in terms of the cost function. The principal conclusion is that the cost function approach offers considerable computational economies by removing the need for complex matrix inversion procedures that characterize the more traditional approach to comparative statics. After all, for most people, taking partial derivatives is easier than inverting a matrix. In what follows, we first consider input price variation and then output variation. The cost function is presumed to be at least twice-continuously differentiable in all its arguments.

2.3a   *Comparative statics of input price changes*

The question this section answers is how cost and derived demands respond to changes in input prices? To some extent, this question has already been addressed in the earlier discussion of the fundamental inequality of cost minimization. There, it was seen that a rise in any input price evokes a decline in the use of that input. Thus, at a minimum, cost-minimizing derived-demand curves must be downward sloping. Fortunately, however, the properties of $c(w, y)$ enable one to say quite a bit more about derived-demand behavior.

Consider the simultaneous increase in all input prices that results from multiplying the input price vector by a positive scalar. By linear homogeneity, costs increase in the same proportion. Applying Shephard's lemma yields

$$\frac{\partial x_i(w, y)}{\partial w_j} = \frac{\partial^2 c(w, y)}{\partial w_i \, \partial w_j}. \tag{2.5}$$

All derived-demand responses to input prices can be computed directly from the Hessian matrix of the cost function. Linear homogeneity of the cost function then implies that the derived demands are homogeneous of degree zero in input prices since the partial derivatives of a function homogeneous of degree k are homogeneous of degree $k-1$ (see Appendix). Mathematically, this fact is expressed as

$$x_i(tw, y) = x_i(w, y), \quad i = 1, 2, \ldots, n,$$

which by Euler's theorem implies

$$\sum_j \frac{\partial x_i(w, y)}{\partial w_j} w_j = 0. \tag{2.6}$$

Utilizing (2.5) and (2.6) together gives

$$\nabla_{ww} c(w, y) \cdot w = 0, \tag{2.7}$$

where $\nabla_{ww} c(w, y)$ is the matrix with typical element given by expression (2.5). Since expression (2.5) implies that $\nabla_{ww} c(w, y)$ delimits the comparative static behavior of derived demands in factor prices, it is worthwhile to investigate its properties thoroughly. Concavity and twice-continuous differentiability of $c(w, y)$ imply that $\nabla_{ww} c(w, y)$ is negative semidefinite. This fact translates into the following restrictions on derived-demand behavior:

$$\frac{\partial x_i(w, y)}{\partial w_i} \leq 0, \tag{2.8}$$

$$\frac{\partial x_i(w, y)}{\partial w_j} = \frac{\partial x_j(w, y)}{\partial w_i}. \tag{2.9}$$

Given the earlier discussion of expression (2.2), expression (2.8) is not surprising. It is simply a restatement of (2.2) for the case of continuously differentiable derived demands. Since the reader is likely already familiar with results such as (2.9), often referred to as *reciprocity* or *symmetry conditions,* there probably is no surprise here either. However, the economic intuition behind (2.2) and (2.8) is obvious – as something becomes more dear, you buy less. On the other hand, the economic intuition behind (2.9) is not very transparent, and (2.9) apparently only follows as a mechanical implication of the presumed differentiability properties of derived demands and the cost function.

Before closing this discussion, two further topics are conveniently addressed: unit-free measures of (2.5) and input price effects on marginal cost. The most obvious unit-free measure of (2.5) is the *derived-demand elasticity:*

$$\epsilon_{ij} \equiv \frac{w_j}{x_i(w, y)} \frac{\partial x_i(w, y)}{\partial w_j}. \tag{2.10}$$

Using (2.6) and (2.10) together gives

$$\sum_j \epsilon_{ij} = 0, \tag{2.11}$$

whereas (2.8) and (2.10) imply

$$\epsilon_{ii} \leq 0. \tag{2.12}$$

Notice, in particular, that these derived-demand elasticities are not symmetric, that is, $\epsilon_{ij} \neq \epsilon_{ji}$ unless suitably normalized. However, it can be shown easily that

$$\epsilon_{ij} = \frac{S_j}{S_i} \epsilon_{ji},$$

where $S_k = w_k x_k(w, y)/c(w, y)$. As later developments show, this last result provides for the symmetry of Allen partial elasticities of substitution. For the moment, however, noting that the matrix of derived-demand elasticities is singular with negative diagonal elements suffices.

Discussing marginal cost behavior anticipates the next section because it obviously necessitates a brief discussion of how cost varies with output. But for the sake of completeness, we take it up here. To start, define "marginal cost" as the partial derivative of the cost function with respect to output. Because $c(w, y)$ is nondecreasing in y, marginal cost is always nonnegative. We now want to determine how marginal cost varies with input price changes. The most important result that can be isolated is that marginal cost is linearly homogeneous in input prices,

$$\frac{\partial c(tw, y)}{\partial y} = t \frac{\partial c(w, y)}{\partial y}, \quad t > 0. \tag{2.13}$$

Differentiating marginal cost with respect to each w_i implies

$$\sum \frac{\partial^2 c}{\partial y \, \partial w_i} w_i = \sum_i \frac{\partial^2 c}{\partial w_i \, \partial y} w_i$$

$$= \frac{\partial}{\partial y} \sum_i \frac{\partial c}{\partial w_i} w_i$$

$$= \frac{\partial c(w, y)}{\partial y},$$

which by Euler's theorem establishes linear homogeneity. The first equality follows by the twice-continuous differentiability of $c(w, y)$, and the third equality follows by the linear homogeneity of $c(w, y)$. Intuitively, this result says that an equiproportional increase in all input prices shifts the marginal-cost curve in a parallel fashion. Again, it is a consequence of the general principle that in economics only relative prices matter.

Summarizing results yields

$$\frac{\partial x_i(w, y)}{\partial w_j} = \frac{\partial x_j(w, y)}{\partial w_i}, \qquad \frac{\partial x_i(w, y)}{\partial w_i} \le 0;$$

$$\sum_j \frac{\partial x_i(w, y)}{\partial w_j} w_j = 0;$$

$$\frac{\partial c(tw, y)}{\partial y} = \frac{t \, \partial c(w, y)}{\partial y}.$$

These results provide exhaustive general conditions on the comparative static behavior of cost-minimizing derived demands. The interested reader should also note that the first three equations are identical to the results characterizing Hicksian-compensated demand behavior in the consumer problem. In fact, problem (2.1) is equivalent mathematically to minimizing the consumer expenditure required to achieve a given utility level. With an appropriate change of notation, $c(w, y)$ can be interpreted as a consumer expenditure function, and the results detailed in this section provide a complete theory of consumer demand.

Example 2.3. Using the properties of the cost function in applied production analysis. Perhaps the most compelling consequence of Shephard's lemma is that it indicates clearly that systematic investigations of cost-minimizing firms can be carried out solely in terms of the cost function. For example, if one can specify a function satisfying properties 2B, the associated derived demands generated by Shephard's lemma will exhibit all of the properties characteristic of cost-minimizing demands. Thus, an obvious avenue to pursue in econometric research of cost-minimizing firms is the specification of a function satisfying properties 2B and the consequent utilization of this cost function to generate a system of well-behaved derived-demand equations on which estimation can be based.

Apparently, the first person to realize the advantages of this procedure was Nerlove (1963), who used an approximation of it in an examination of economies of scale in electricity generation. Nerlove's basic approach was to use a Cobb–Douglas cost function and the associated system of derived demands to model behavior of firms in that industry.

To illustrate, consider the following Cobb–Douglas cost function in log-linear form:

$$\ln c(w, y) = 0.5 \ln y + 0.32 \ln w_L + 0.28 \ln w_k + 0.40 \ln w_M, \tag{2.14}$$

where we assume the existence of three inputs: labor (x_L), capital (x_K), and raw materials (x_M). Equation (2.14) exhibits properties 2B.1–2B.5, as the reader has already ascertained for the two-input case in Exercise 2.1. Using Shephard's lemma, the cost-minimizing derived demands are

$$x_L(w, y) = 0.32 (y^{0.5} w_L^{0.32} w_K^{0.28} w_M^{0.40})/w_L,$$

$$x_K(w, y) = 0.28 (y^{0.5} w_L^{0.32} w_K^{0.28} w_M^{0.40})/w_K, \tag{2.15}$$

$$x_M(w, y) = 0.40 (y^{0.5} w_L^{0.32} w_K^{0.28} w_M^{0.40})/w_M.$$

The corresponding marginal-cost function is

$$\frac{\partial c(w, y)}{\partial y} = 0.5 (y^{0.5} w_L^{0.32} w_K^{0.28} w_M^{0.40})/y. \tag{2.16}$$

Given the structure of (2.14)–(2.16), the most convenient method of investigating the comparative statics behavior of derived demands is by the use of the derived-demand elasticities. Direct calculation establishes

$$\begin{bmatrix} \epsilon_{LL} & \epsilon_{LK} & \epsilon_{LM} \\ \epsilon_{KL} & \epsilon_{KK} & \epsilon_{KM} \\ \epsilon_{ML} & \epsilon_{MK} & \epsilon_{MM} \end{bmatrix} = \begin{bmatrix} -0.68 & 0.28 & 0.40 \\ 0.32 & -0.72 & 0.40 \\ 0.32 & 0.28 & -0.60 \end{bmatrix},$$

which satisfies restrictions (2.11) and (2.12). For this example, each input is more responsive to changes in its own price than to changes in other input prices. Moreover, capital utilization is the most own-price elastic of the three inputs.

Finally, to verify the validity of (2.13), notice that (2.16) can be re-written as

$$\frac{\partial c(w, y)}{\partial y} = 0.5 y^{-0.5} w_L^{0.32} w_K^{0.28} w_M^{0.40},$$

so that

$$\frac{\partial c(tw, y)}{\partial y} = 0.5y^{-0.5}(tw_L)^{0.32}(tw_K)^{0.28}(tw_M)^{0.40}$$

$$= 0.5y^{-0.5}t^{0.32}w_L^{0.32}t^{0.28}w_k^{0.28}t^{0.40}w_M^{0.40}$$

$$= t^{(0.32+0.28+0.40)}(0.5y^{-0.5})w_L^{0.32}w_K^{0.28}w_M^{0.40}$$

$$= t(0.5y^{-0.5})w_L^{0.32}w_K^{0.28}w_M^{0.40} = t\frac{\partial c(w, y)}{\partial y},$$

where the third equality follows by the law of exponents.

Example 2.4. By earlier results, the cost function associated with the Leontief technology assumes the general form

$$c(w, y) = y \sum \frac{w_i}{a_i}.$$

By Shephard's lemma, therefore, the derived demands associated with the technology are $x_i(w, y) = y/a_i$, which are independent of the input price level. Hence, the matrix of the price derivatives of derived demands is the null matrix that trivially satisfies the negative semidefiniteness property previously isolated.

Exercise 2.3. Determine the comparative static properties of the derived demands associated with a linear production function.

2.3b   *Comparative statics and changes in output*

Cost flexibility and elasticities of size and scale: Traditionally, the lion's share of economists' attention has been devoted to the effect of output on costs. The classic treatment is that of Viner (1931). This section first considers derived-demand response to output variation and then provides an in-depth treatment of the effect of output changes on cost.

By Shephard's lemma, the effect of a change in output on the derived demand for x_i is

$$\frac{\partial x_i(w, y)}{\partial y} = \frac{\partial^2 c(w, y)}{\partial w_i \, \partial y}$$

$$= \frac{\partial^2 c(w, y)}{\partial y \, \partial w_i}$$

$$= \frac{\partial[\partial c(w, y)/\partial y]}{\partial w_i}, \tag{2.17}$$

where the second equality follows by the symmetry of partial derivatives. Hence, the response of the ith input to changes in output equals the change in marginal cost caused by a change in w_i. Unfortunately, ascertaining unambiguously whether (2.17) is positive or negative is not possible. When (2.17) is negative, the ith input is defined to be *inferior* or *regressive*; when (2.17) is positive, the ith input is said to be *normal*.

Although expression (2.17) cannot be signed unambiguously, all inputs cannot be regressive. The easiest way to show this result is by the linear homogeneity of marginal cost, which yields

$$\sum_i w_i \frac{\partial x_i(w, y)}{\partial y} = \sum_i \frac{\partial^2 c(w, y)}{\partial y \, \partial w_i} w_i = \frac{\partial c(w, y)}{\partial y}.$$

Since $w_i > 0$ for all i and $\partial c(w, y)/\partial y \geq 0$ (property 2B.5), not all of the $\partial x_i(w, y)/\partial y$ terms can be negative. Of course, this makes good intuitive sense. Suppose the opposite; that is, each $\partial x_i(w, y)/\partial y < 0$. An immediate consequence of this supposition is that output can be increased or at worst maintained while decreasing the utilization of all inputs. But this violates weak monotonicity of the production function.

We now turn to an investigation of how output affects the level of cost. One might think it sufficient to have noted that marginal cost is nonnegative. However, there are other important issues that can be addressed in the context of cost and output changes. To initiate our discussion, we define the *cost flexibility* as the ratio of marginal cost divided by average cost, where, of course, average cost is $c(w, y)/y$:

$$n(w, y) = \frac{[\partial c(w, y)/\partial y] y}{c(w, y)} = \frac{\partial \ln c(w, y)}{\partial \ln y}.$$

Often, $n(w, y)$ is also referred to as the elasticity of cost with respect to output as well as several other terms. But we use the flexibility terminology to remind the reader that $n(w, y)$ represents the percentage change in something denominated in monetary units attributable to a percentage change of something denominated in quantity units. Moreover, this terminology hopefully avoids confusing $n(w, y)$ with its reciprocal, which we hereafter refer to as the *elasticity of size*.

The importance of $n(w, y)$ seems well illustrated by an argument similar to that utilized in Chapter 1 in the discussion of economies of scale. Suppose, for example, that a public utility (say, an electricity company) is obligated to produce and sell a given output level y at a regulated price. Because its revenues are fixed, the utility maximizes profit by minimizing the cost of producing that output. Suppose further, however, that the manager of the utility is considering two ways of producing that output level: producing y in m separate but identical operations each producing $y^* = y/m$ units of output or producing y in a single operation. Assuming that the same technology would be used in both instances, the utility manager needs to compare $c(w, y)$ with $mc(w, y^*)$. If $c(w, y) > mc(w, y^*)$, it is to the firm's advantage to produce in m separate operations. The converse holds if $c(w, y) < mc(w, y^*)$. The magnitude of $n(w, y)$ is an indicator of when such decisions would be profitable. The argument is as follows: For any strictly positive m, there exists a function $\zeta(m, y^*, w)$ such that

$$c(w, y) = c(w, my^*) = m^{\zeta(m, y^*, w)} c(w, y^*). \tag{2.18}$$

If $\zeta(m, y^*, w) > 1$, $c(w, my^*) > mc(w, y^*)$, whereas if $\zeta(m, y^*, w) < 1$, the converse is true. Hence, the magnitude of $\zeta(m, y^*, w)$ reveals the relative profitability of the two alternatives. However,

$$\lim_{m \to 1} \zeta(m, y^*, w) = n(y^*, w).$$

This result is demonstrated by first taking natural logarithms of both sides of (2.18) and solving to obtain

$$\zeta(m, y^*, w) = \frac{\ln c(w, my^*) - \ln c(w, y^*)}{\ln m}.$$

Both the numerator and the denominator of this expression approach zero as $m \to 1$, and thus l'Hopital's rule implies

$$\lim_{m \to 1} \zeta(m, y^*, w) = \left. \frac{\partial \ln c(w, my^*)/\partial m}{\partial \ln m/\partial m} \right|_{m=1}$$

$$= \frac{\partial \ln c(w, y^*)}{\partial \ln y^*} = n(y^*, w). \tag{2.19}$$

Thus, the cost flexibility is a potentially important ingredient for this type of decision. If $n(y^*, w) > 1$, there are apparently no cost advantages to be reaped from centralizing production. Accordingly, we say that the firm exhibits *diseconomies of size* because apparently smaller sized (where size is measured in terms of output) operations are more cost-effective. If $n(y^*, w) < 1$, the firm exhibits *economies of size* because there are cost advantages to larger sized operations. When $n(y^*, w) = 1$, there are no economies or diseconomies of size, and analogous to the earlier discussion on scale economies, we say that the firm is characterized by constant returns to size.

Before proceeding, an important *caveat* should be added to the previous discussion, which for the sake of easy intuition has eschewed some important aspects of real-world decision making. Implicitly, we have assumed that there are no separate costs associated with setting up m separate operations. Obviously, this is not the case, and to be empirically appealing, our results need to take this type of problem into account. At present, we content ourselves with noting the problem and defer further discussion of it until we address the related problem of the short-run cost function.

The reader has probably already realized that $n(y, w)$ is closely related to $\epsilon(x, y)$ the (elasticity of scale) defined in Chapter 1. The examples used to illustrate both of these concepts were chosen to reinforce the reader's intuitive melding of these concepts. For, in fact, at cost-minimizing points, $n(y, w)$ is the reciprocal of $\epsilon(x, y)$. To prove this, consider the Lagrangian function associated with problem (2.1),

$$L(x, y, \lambda) = w \cdot x + \lambda[y - f(x)], \qquad (2.20)$$

where λ is a nonnegative Lagrangian multiplier. If attention is restricted to the case where $f(x)$ satisfies property 1A.1b (i.e., it is strictly increasing in x and it is further presumed that $x > 0$), the solution to the cost-minimizing problem is given by (see Appendix)

$$\frac{\partial L(x, y, \lambda)}{\partial x_i} = w_i - \lambda \frac{\partial f(x)}{\partial x_i} = 0, \quad i = 1, 2, \dots, n,$$

$$\frac{\partial L(x, y, \lambda)}{\partial \lambda} = y - f(x) = 0. \qquad (2.21)$$

An application of the envelope theorem to the Lagrangian expression in (2.20) (see Appendix) implies that the optimal value of the Lagrangian multiplier λ equals marginal cost. This can be seen more directly by exploiting conditions (2.21). Differentiating the second equation in (2.21) yields

$$dy = \sum \frac{\partial f(x)}{\partial x_i} dx_i,$$

which, making use of the first equation in (2.21), gives

$$\lambda dy = \sum w_i dx_i.$$

This last equality establishes the desired result because the term on the right-hand side is the change in cost caused by changing output while holding factor prices fixed. Using this result and the first equality in (2.21) again gives

$$\sum_i w_i x_i(y, w) = \lambda(w, y) \sum_{i=1}^{n} \frac{\partial f[x(w, y)]}{\partial x_i} x_i(w, y),$$

which, upon substitution of the calculating formula for the elasticity of scale, yields

$$\sum_{i=1}^{n} w_i x_i(w, y) = \lambda(w, y)\epsilon(y, x(w, y))y.$$

Solving yields

$$\epsilon(y, x(w, y)) = \sum_{i=1}^{n} \frac{w_i x_i(w, y)}{\lambda(w, y)y}$$

$$= \frac{c(w, y)}{(\partial c(w, y)/\partial y)y}$$

$$= n(y, w)^{-1}$$

$$= \epsilon^*(y, w), \tag{2.22}$$

which illustrates the desired result. In what follows, we shall denote $\epsilon^*(y, w)$ as the elasticity of size.

At cost-minimizing points, a firm exhibits increasing returns to scale $\epsilon(y, x) > 1$ if and only if it simultaneously exhibits increasing returns to size $\epsilon^*(y, w) > 1$, whereas it exhibits decreasing returns to scale if and only if it exhibits simultaneously decreasing returns to size. Thus, the concepts of returns to scale and returns to size are very closely related. One might well question why it is necessary to distinguish between economies of scale and economies of size. Many discussions use the terminology of "increasing (decreasing) returns to scale" and "returns to size" interchangeably. However, they are not the same thing even though the most convenient measures of these phenomena coincide at cost-minimizing points. As discussed in Chapter 1, the elasticity of scale measures how output responds as one moves out along a scale line from the origin in input space. The elasticity of size measures the cost response associated with movements along the locus of cost-minimizing points in input space, that is, the *expansion path*. By necessity, therefore, the two measures are generally based on different input combinations.

Homotheticity and elasticity of size: To fix ideas somewhat, consider Figuse 2.8, where the solution to (2.21) is originally represented by point A. If input prices remain constant but output expands, the solution moves to a point such as B on the next isoquant. The elasticity of size is a measure of how costs change in the move from A to B. On the other hand, the elasticity of scale is a percentage measure of the movement from A along a scale line to the next isoquant, (i.e., point C). Hence, the measures should only correspond when the next cost-minimizing point is on the scale line. In what follows, it will be shown that this is true in the case of homothetic $f(x)$.

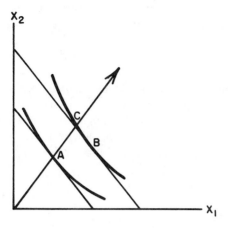

Figure 2.8 Elasticities of scale and size.

The best way to demonstrate formally the differences between the two concepts is to examine how the elasticity of size and the elasticity of scale vary with output changes. Differentiation of (2.22) gives

$$\frac{\partial \epsilon^*(y, w)}{\partial y} = \frac{\partial \epsilon(y, x(w, y))}{\partial y} + \sum_j \frac{\partial \epsilon}{\partial x_j} \frac{\partial x_j}{\partial y}. \qquad (2.23)$$

Hence, the total effect of the change in y on $\epsilon^*(y, w)$ can be decomposed into two separate effects. First, there is the direct effect, which is identical to the effect of a change in output on the elasticity of scale. Geometrically, this is the movement from A to C. Second, there is an effect associated with the reallocation of the cost-minimizing input bundle caused by the output change. This is measured by the movement from C to B. The only time that the second effect disappears is when the elasticity of scale is independent of x. But as seen in Chapter 1, this implies that the production function exhibits homotheticity. Hence, expression (2.23) suggests that homothetic production functions generate cost functions with the property that the elasticity of size and the elasticity of scale are always equivalent. And this is indeed the case, since if $f(x)$ is homothetic,

$$c(w, y) = \min_{x > 0} \{w \cdot x : h(y) \leq f^*(x)\}$$

$$= \min_{x > 0} \{w \cdot x : 1 \leq f^*(x/h(y))\}$$

$$= \min_{z > 0} \{h(y)w \cdot z : 1 \leq f^*(z)\}$$

$$= h(y) \min_{z > 0} \{w \cdot z : 1 \leq f^*(z)\}$$

$$= h(y)c(w), \qquad (2.24)$$

where the second equality follows from the linear homogeneity of f^*, $z = x/h(y)$, and $c(w)$ is a function that satisfies properties 2B.1–2B.4. By direct calculation,

$$\epsilon^*(y, w) = h(y)/yh'(y) = \epsilon(y, x). \tag{2.25}$$

Expression (2.25) also implies that $\epsilon^*(y, w)$ generated by a homothetic technology is independent of input prices. This is an if-and-only-if proposition; that is, the elasticity of size is independent of w if and only if $c(w, y)$ is consistent with that generated by a homothetic production function. If the elasticity of size is independent of input prices,

$$\frac{\partial \ln c(w, y)}{\partial \ln y} = g(y) \quad \text{and} \quad \frac{\partial \ln c(w, y)}{\partial y} = \frac{g(y)}{y}.$$

Integrating this last expression yields

$$\ln c(w, y) = \int g(y)\, d \ln y$$

$$= m(y) + \theta(w),$$

where $\theta(w)$ is a constant of integration. Hence,

$$c(w, y) = \exp[m(y) + \theta(w)]$$

$$= \exp[m(y)] \exp[\theta(w)]$$

$$= h(y) c(w),$$

as required.

The fact that homothetic production implies a cost function such as (2.24) has other interesting implications besides enabling one to measure accurately economies of scale by only considering the properties of the cost function. In fact, if this were all it were to imply, homothetic technologies would be of relatively little interest to economists. Presumedly, economists are more interested in the potential existence of size economies than scale economies since the latter usually do not correspond to economically relevant choices. But homotheticity has other interesting implications. For example, homotheticity implies that all inputs are *normal,* that is, nondecreasing in output. This is most easily seen by using (2.24) to calculate the *elasticity of derived demand with respect to output:*

$$\xi_i = \frac{\partial \ln x_i(w, y)}{\partial \ln y} = \frac{h'(y)y}{h(y)} = n(y, w).$$

Since output increases always increase cost, this expression must be positive, as required by normality. Moreover, since all derived demands exhibit the same elasticity with respect to output, all optimal input ratios are independent of output. This, of course, is quite similar to the finding that homotheticity implies that marginal rates of technical substitution only depend on relative inputs. To show this result formally, apply Shephard's lemma to (2.24) and take ratios:

$$\frac{x_i(w, y)}{x_j(w, y)} = \frac{\partial c(w)/\partial w_i}{\partial c(w)/\partial w_j}. \tag{2.26}$$

Furthermore, expression (2.26) is easily motivated intuitively by using expression (2.21) for homothetic $f(x)$. Consider, for example, the case of two inputs where $f(x)$ is homothetic. By (2.21),

$$\frac{\partial f(x)/\partial x_1}{\partial f(x)/\partial x_2} = \frac{\partial f^*(x)/\partial x_1}{\partial f^*(x)/\partial x_2} = \frac{w_1}{w_2}.$$

Because $f^*(x)$ is linearly homogeneous, the left-hand side of this expression is only a function of the input ratio; call it $g(x_1/x_2)$. Now invert to solve for the input ratio solely in terms of w_1/w_2.

Another way of expressing (2.26) is

$$\frac{\partial}{\partial y} \frac{\partial c(w, y)/\partial w_i}{\partial c(w, y)/\partial w_j} = 0, \tag{2.27}$$

which indicates that homotheticity is sufficient for output to be separable from input prices in $c(w, y)$. By results in Chapter 1, (2.27) means that, at a minimum, one can write

$$c(w, y) = c^*(y, g(w)). \tag{2.28}$$

However, it is easy to demonstrate that (2.28) is equivalent to (2.24). Thus, whenever output is separable from input prices, the cost function is consistent with homotheticity of $f(x)$. To illustrate, notice that the linear homogeneity of $c(w, y)$ and (2.28) imply that

$$\frac{\partial c(w, y)/\partial w_i}{\partial c(w, y)/\partial w_j} = \frac{\partial g(w)/\partial w_i}{\partial g(w)/\partial w_j}, \quad \forall i, j, \tag{2.29}$$

is homogeneous of degree zero in w. By results due to Lau (see Appendix), $g(w)$ must therefore be homothetic in w, and hence,

$$g(w) = G(g^*(w)),$$

where $g^*(w)$ is linearly homogeneous. Now rewrite (2.28),

$$c(w, y) = c^*(y, G(g^*(w))) = \hat{c}(y, g^*(w)).$$

If all input prices are multiplied by the positive scalar t, one finds that $\hat{c}(y, g^*(tw)) = \hat{c}(y, tg^*(w))$ by the linear homogeneity of $g^*(w)$. But by the linear homogeneity of the cost function, one must also have

$$c(tw, y) = \hat{c}(y, g^*(tw)) = tc(w, y) = t\hat{c}(y, g^*(w)).$$

Combining these results implies

$$\hat{c}(y, tg^*(w)) = t\hat{c}(y, g^*(w)).$$

Therefore, c is positively linearly homogeneous in $g^*(w)$. As a consequence, one can write

$$c(w, y) = g^*(w)\hat{c}(y, 1) = h(y)c(w), \tag{2.30}$$

as required.

Heuristically, the ability to write $c(w, y)$ as in (2.24) and (2.30) is easily explained for homothetic $f(x)$. Since homotheticity is equivalent to the ability to construct an aggregate input, $f^*(x)$, one can always interpret $h(y)$ as the inverse mapping of a single-input production function, that is, the exact amount of the aggregate input required to produce output y. Cost should therefore be the product of this aggregate input and an aggregate price index. But the function $c(w)$ serves exactly this latter role. One obvious consequence, therefore, of the equivalence of (2.24) and (2.28) is that when output is separable from w in $c(w, y)$, $c(w, y)/c(w)$ can be thought of as an aggregate input index.

Bringing arguments together, it is easy to see why the class of homothetic technologies has been peculiarly important in applied production analysis. First, they are particularly convenient to use in measuring economies of scale. Second, homotheticity implies a reasonably tractable form of the cost function. Finally, any time output is separable from input prices, the cost function is consistent with a homothetic $f(x)$.

To close this section, we remind the reader that any homogeneous function is also homothetic; therefore, all results developed for homothetic functions also apply for homogeneous functions. In particular, if $f(x)$ is homogeneous of degree k, it is always possible to write

$$f(x) = [g(x)]^k,$$

where $g(x)$ is linearly homogeneous. Hence, one can then write the level set associated with a particular y as $y^{1/k} = g(x)$. The associated cost function assumes the general form

$$c(w, y) = y^{1/k}c(w). \tag{2.31}$$

Example 2.5. The Leontief and linear technologies and output variation.
The cost functions associated with the Leontief and linear technologies have been shown to be of the general forms, respectively,

$$c(w, y) = y \sum_{i=1}^{n} \frac{w_i}{\alpha_i},$$

$$c(w, y) = y \min_{w} \left\{ \frac{w_1}{\beta_1}, \frac{w_2}{\beta_2}, \dots, \frac{w_n}{\beta_n} \right\}.$$

Presumedly, therefore, both the Leontief and linear technologies exhibit constant returns to scale since the cost flexibility identically equals 1. Hence, both cost functions are also consistent with a homothetic technology. Both, however, are not twice-continuously differentiable, and therefore, all of the results developed in the previous section may not apply. To underline the importance of the differentiability assumptions to the preceding analysis, consider the cost function associated with the linear technology. Let $w_i/\beta_i < w_j/\beta_j$ for all $j \neq i$. Then,

$$\frac{\partial c(w, y)}{\partial w_i} = \frac{y}{\beta_i}$$

is the cost-minimizing derived demand, whereas for all other inputs (see Figure 2.7),

$$\frac{\partial \ln c(w, y)}{\partial \ln y} \neq \frac{\partial \ln x_j(w, y)}{\partial \ln y},$$

as would be required in the twice-continuously differentiable case. The technology associated with the Leontief technology, however, satisfies the condition that

$$\frac{\partial \ln c}{\partial \ln y} = \frac{\partial \ln x_i(w, y)}{\partial \ln y},$$

which, in this case, equals 1.

> **Exercise 2.4.** For the Cobb–Douglas technology outlined in Example 2.2, calculate the cost flexibility and determine whether there exists any economies of size.

> **Exercise 2.5.** For the technology in Exercise 2.2, decide whether or not the cost function is consistent with a homothetic technology.

2.3c *Average cost, marginal cost, and cost flexibility*

The cost flexibility is the ratio of marginal to average cost. Thus, as with the elasticity of scale, there is an easy geometric interpretation of the cost flexibility that is closely related to the law of variable proportions. Before discussing the geometry, however, it is useful to pursue this analogy a little further analytically. In Chapter 1, increasing returns to scale were shown to be inconsistent with strict concavity of the production function, and decreasing returns to scale were shown to be inconsistent with strict convexity in the neighborhood of the origin if the production function satisfies weak essentiality. We now show that concavity of $f(x)$ implies

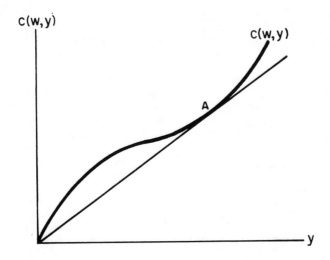

Figure 2.9 Total cost, average cost, marginal cost, and cost flexibility.

that the cost function is convex in output. Denote the cost-minimizing bundles associated with outputs y^1 and y^0 as x^1 and x^0, respectively. Since the production function is concave,

$$f(\theta x^1 + (1-\theta)x^0) \geq \theta f(x^1) + (1-\theta)f(x^0)$$
$$\geq \theta y^1 + (1-\theta)y^0,$$

where the second inequality follows because $x^1 \in V(y^1)$ and $x^0 \in V(y^0)$ and implies that $\theta x^0 + (1-\theta)x^1 \in V(\theta y^1 + (1-\theta)y^0)$. Since this weighted input average can produce the weighted average of outputs, cost minimization implies

$$w \cdot [\theta x' + (1-\theta)x^0] \geq c(\theta y' + (1-\theta)y^0, w).$$

But the left-hand side of this inequality is, by definition,

$$\theta c(y', w) + (1-\theta)c(y^0, w),$$

and the demonstration is complete.

Hence, if costs emanate from the origin while passing first through a concave configuration and then through a convex configuration (see Figure 2.9), the first segment cannot be associated with diminishing marginal productivity. Therefore, one might identify this first region with some or all inputs exhibiting increasing marginal productivity. When the cost function is concave, costs rise at a decreasing rate. Intuitively, this can be explained by recognizing that increasing marginal productivity means that each extra unit of input purchased is more effective in expanding output than the last unit purchased. Thus, although costs rise with the expansion of output, each increment in output is associated with falling marginal costs because of the increased marginal productivity of inputs. On the other hand, when marginal productivity is decreasing, a similar argument establishes that it is plausible to think of marginal cost as increasing as output rises.

Now turn to the graphic analysis of the relationship between the cost flexibility and average and marginal costs. By definition, the cost flexibility is the ratio of marginal cost to average cost. Because marginal cost is the slope of the cost function in output space, in terms of Figure 2.9, the cost flexibility at any output is the ratio of the slope of the tangent line to the slope of the ray connecting the origin and the corresponding point on the cost function (the slope of this latter ray measures average cost). If the ray from the origin cuts the tangent from below, the slope of the ray exceeds that of the tangent: Average cost exceeds marginal cost, and the cost flexibility is less than 1. The converse is true if the ray from the origin cuts the tangent from above. Hence, when the cost function is strictly concave and emanates from the origin, the cost flexibility must be less than 1; there must be increasing returns to size. If the cost function is strictly convex and emanates from the origin, the cost flexibility must exceed 1; there are decreasing returns to size.

We now turn to a calculus derivation of the arguments illustrated in Figure 2.9. I shall first demonstrate that any cost function that emanates from the origin in output space (i.e., any cost function without fixed costs) exhibits constant returns to size in the neighborhood of the origin. Next I demonstrate that a convex cost function emanating from the origin exhibits decreasing returns to size locally. To accomplish the first task, recall that the cost flexibility is defined as

$$n(w, y) = \frac{\partial c(w, y)/\partial y}{c(w, y)/y}.$$

Both the numerator and the denominator of average cost approach zero as output goes to zero. So, using l'Hopital's rule gives

$$\lim_{y \to 0} \frac{c(w, y)}{y} = \frac{\partial c(w, 0)}{\partial y}.$$

Substituting this last result into the definition and evaluating at zero output establishes that in the neighborhood of the origin, there exist constant returns to size.

Demonstrating that convexity and no fixed costs implies decreasing returns to size locally requires the recognition that a Taylor series approximation to the first order always underestimates a convex function (see Appendix). Hence, for any y^* and y',

$$c(w, y^*) \geq c(w, y') + \frac{\partial c(w, y')}{\partial y}(y^* - y').$$

Then letting y^* go to zero and remembering that there are no fixed costs establishes that marginal cost exceeds average cost at y'. The cost flexibility must be greater than 1.

Economists often think of average-cost curves as U-shaped when they are pictorially represented in output space. In terms of the calculus, a U-shape means that the average-cost curve must attain a critical value where its slope is zero and where the second derivative is positive. The earlier discussion of the scale elasticity showed that ray average product is maximized where ray average product equaled ray marginal product. By analogy, one might expect average costs to reach a critical point where average cost equals marginal cost and where the cost flexibility equals 1. This intuition is illustrated in Figure 2.9; average cost is minimized at point A, where a ray from the origin is just tangent to the cost curve. At this point, the cost flexibility is 1 by definition. Therefore, the cost flexibility is apparently an important determinant of whether the average-cost curve assumes the familiar U-shape.

To examine this issue more formally, define an average-cost curve as U-shaped if a y^* exists such that

$$\frac{\partial[c(w, y^*)/y^*]}{\partial y} = 0 \quad \text{and} \quad \frac{\partial^2[c(w, y^*)/y^*]}{\partial y^2} \geq 0. \qquad (2.32)$$

Calculating the first expression in (2.32) yields

$$\frac{\partial c(w, y)/y}{\partial y} = \frac{1}{y}\left[\frac{\partial c(w, y)}{\partial y} - \frac{c(w, y)}{y}\right]$$

$$= \frac{c(w, y)}{y^2}[n(w, y) - 1]. \qquad (2.33)$$

Hence, as suggested by the graphic analysis, average costs are minimized at the point where there are constant returns to size and scale. Using (2.33) to evaluate the second term in (2.32) at y^* gives

$$\frac{\partial^2[c(w, y^*)/y^*]}{\partial y^2} = \frac{c(w, y^*)}{y^2}\frac{\partial n(w, y^*)}{\partial y}$$

so that the average-cost curve is only U-shaped if $n(w, y)$ is increasing in y at y^*. But since $n(w, y) = 1/\epsilon^*(w, y)$, $\partial n(w, y)/\partial y > 0$ implies that $\partial \epsilon^*(w, y)/\partial y < 0$. If average costs are U-shaped, the elasticity of size must be decreasing in y. This result reinforces our earlier conclusion that the elasticities of size and scale convey different information. Combining this result with (2.23) reveals, for example, that restricting $\partial \epsilon(x, y)/\partial y$ to be

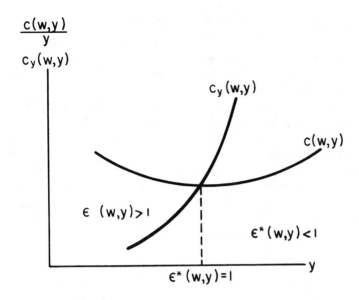

Figure 2.10 U-shaped average cost and returns to size.

negative does not guarantee the existence of the U-shaped average-cost curve.

Summarizing results, average costs and marginal costs can be depicted as in Figure 2.10 if there exists a y^* such that $\epsilon^*(y^*, w) = 1$, and

$$\frac{\partial \epsilon^*(y^*, w)}{\partial y} \leq 0.$$

Or equivalently, the cost function must be convex at a y^* satisfying $\epsilon^*(y^*, w) = 1$ [a sufficient condition is that $f(\cdot)$ be concave]. From Figure 2.10, one sees that at points to the left of minimum average cost, there exist increasing returns to size since marginal cost is less than average cost. This is verified further by reference to the convex portion of $c(w, y)$ in Figure 2.9. At points to the right of minimum average costs in Figure 2.10, there are decreasing returns to size. Intuitively, for a convex cost function, increasing returns to size are associated with decreasing average cost, whereas decreasing returns to size are associated with increasing average cost. Returning to our utility example, it is easy to see why the entrepreneur facing convex costs and decreasing returns to size would benefit by decentralization. Decentralization means producing less in each plant, thereby reducing average costs while increasing profit.

2.4   Duality between cost and production functions

Previous developments demonstrated that restricting the production function restricts the cost function. As general examples, assuming the closedness and nonemptiness of $V(y)$ implies the existence of a solution to problem (2.1) and imposing homotheticity implies that the cost function assumes the form $h(y)c(w)$. Hence, technological restrictions are manifested in the economic behavior of optimizing agents. A logical question then seems to be: Can the process be reversed? Or put another way, can we use exclusively economic phenomena to reconstruct and study the properties of the technology? The dual approach is an attempt to isolate circumstances in which this is possible. Contributions to this theory are widespread, with many economists possessing valid claims as progenitors of the dual approach. However, ultimate credit must be given to Shephard (1953), whose early contribution represents the first systematic attempt to accomplish such a result, that is, a description of the technology solely in terms of the cost function.

The implication of being able to use the cost function to describe accurately the technology is that the specification of a well-behaved cost function is equivalent to the specification of a well-behaved production function. In McFadden's (1978a) terminology, the cost function is a "sufficient statistic" for the technology since all economically relevant information about the technology can be gleaned from the cost function. More will be said later about what constitutes "economically relevant information."

This section contains a mainly heuristic discussion of the dual relationship between cost and production functions and aims only to convince the reader that it is plausible that such a relationship may exist. A duality is not explicitly demonstrated. Inveterate skeptics are referred to any of the many duality proofs in the literature (e.g., Shephard 1953, 1970; McFadden 1978a; Diewert 1971).

By way of outlining what follows, I first try to motivate the existence of a duality utilizing arguments [apparently originally due to Uzawa (1962)] similar to those used in the revealed preference literature. Although Shephard's original demonstration (1953) of a duality relied on the properties of the distance function, Uzawa's approach strikes me as more geometrically appealing. This section closes with a further geometric interpretation of dual relationships.

2.4a   *Duality and the input requirement set*

Uzawa (1962) generalized Shephard's (1953) results by showing that the cost function could be used to reconstruct the input requirement set from

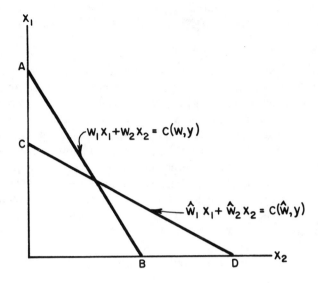

Figure 2.11 Minkowski's theorem and duality.

which it was generated. [Later contributions are Friedman (1972), Mc-Fadden (1978a), and Shephard (1970); see also Appendix, pp. 303–8.]

By Minkowski's theorem (see Appendix), every closed, convex set in $\mathbb{R}^n$ can be characterized by the intersection of its supporting half-spaces. A half-space $H(m, k)$ is defined as

$$H(m, k) = \{x : m \cdot x \leq k\},$$

where $m \in \mathbb{R}^n$ and $k \in \mathbb{R}$. This definition suggests that the cost function can define a half-space. For example, evaluate $c(w, y)$ at a particular w and y and define

$$N(w, y) = \{x : w \cdot x \leq c(w, y)\}.$$

Because $c(w, y)$ is the minimum cost of producing y no $x \in N(w, y)$ can, by definition, represent a strictly cheaper way of producing y than $c(w, y)$. Put another way, if the cost-minimizing input bundle for w and y belongs to $N(w, y)$, it lies on the hyperplane $w \cdot x = c(w, y)$. Consider Figure 2.11, where the hyperplane consistent with $w_1 x_1 + w_2 x_2 = c(w_1, w_2, y)$ is labeled AB. By the preceding argument, the cost-minimizing bundle associated with output y and prices w_1 and w_2 cannot be below this line segment. Thus, the half-space above AB should contain $V(y)$. If there exists an $x \in V(y)$ that is below AB, it represents a strictly cheaper way of producing y than $c(w_1, w_2, y)$. But this means $c(w, y)$ is not cost minimizing.

However, since at least one point on AB has to be able to produce y, $V(y)$ and AB share a point in common. Now consider the half-space defined by

$$N(w^1, y) = \{x : w^1 \cdot x \le c(w^1, y)\},$$

where $w \ne w^1$. The elements of this set again cannot represent strictly cheaper ways of producing y than the cost function. Furthermore, by arguments similar to the above, if the hyperplane $w^1 \cdot x = c(w^1, y)$ is represented by CD in Figure 2.11, the area above CD must contain $V(y)$, whereas CD shares at least one point in common with $V(y)$. At the same time, $V(y)$ must lie above both CD and AB; the region that must be searched to identify $V(y)$ has been considerably narrowed. If this approach is followed for all possible price vectors, the lower boundary of the intersection of these half-spaces starts to assume a shape similar to that of the familiar neoclassical isoquant. Thus, by examining infinitely many price vectors, one should be able to provide at least a lower bound for $V(y)$.

The geometric arguments presented suggest that

$$V^*(y) = \{x : w \cdot x \ge c(w, y) \ \forall w > 0\} \tag{2.34}$$

might closely approximate the original input requirement set that generated $c(w, y)$. The essence of duality theory is to demonstrate that, in fact, $V^*(y) = V(y)$; that is, the original technology can be resurrected directly from the cost function. If this is to be true, however, at a minimum, $V^*(y)$ should exhibit those properties of $V(y)$ utilized in developing $c(w, y)$, that is, properties 1A.1a (monotonicity), 1A.3a (weak essentiality), and 1A.4 (nonemptiness of the input requirement set).

One must establish that $V^*(y)$ possesses these properties as a first step to demonstrating that there exists a duality. If it does, then $V^*(y)$ certainly represents a valid production technology, in the sense that $V^*(y)$ can generate a well-behaved cost function. All that then remains is to establish that the "inversion" process described by (2.34) is unique; that is, it isolates exactly the original $V(y)$. Unfortunately, a formal demonstration of all of these facts goes well beyond the mathematical confines of this book. However, we can stay within these mathematical limits and still convince the reader that $V^*(y)$ satisfies properties 1A.1a, 1A.3a, as well as 1A.2a (quasi-concavity).

To demonstrate monotonicity (1A.1a), notice that an equivalent way of writing this property in terms of input requirement sets is: For any $x \in V(y)$, $x' \ge x$ implies that $x' \in V(y)$ since $f(x') \ge f(x) \ge y$ by 1A.1a. To establish 1A.1a for $V^*(y)$, one must therefore show that if $x \in V^*(y)$, then for any $x' \ge x$, $x' \in V^*(y)$. But this is easy since, for x to belong to $V^*(y)$, $w \cdot x \ge c(w, y)$, and if $x' \ge x$, the positivity of w implies $w \cdot x' \ge w \cdot x \ge$

$c(w, y)$. Hence, $x' \in V^*(y)$. An alternative means of expressing 1A.3a, is $0_n \in V(0)$ but $0_n \notin V(y)$ for any $y > 0$. By property 2B.6, $c(w, 0) = 0$ so that $w \cdot 0_n = 0 = c(w, 0)$ and $0_n \in V^*(0)$. But for any $y > 0$, property 2B.1 requires $c(w, y) > 0$ for $y > 0$. Here, 0_n cannot be an element of $V^*(y)$ for any $y > 0$. Accordingly, the technology described by (2.34) satisfies both the weak monotonicity and weak essentiality requirements. A demonstration of property 1A.4 can be found in McFadden (1978a).

The *implicit input requirement set, $V^*(y)$*, is always convex (property 1A.2a) regardless of whether or not $V(y)$ is convex and is therefore consistent with a quasi-concave production function. Thus, a cost function satisfying properties 2B defines an implicit requirement set exhibiting a diminishing marginal rate of technical substitution, nonnegative marginal productivity, and weak essentiality. Intuitively, the reader should have little difficulty accepting $V^*(y)$ as an input requirement set for a technology exhibiting isoquants convex to the origin, with isoquants further from the origin representing higher levels of output.

That $V^*(y)$ is convex is clear from Figure 2.11 and the accompanying discussion. To demonstrate this result formally, one needs to show that if x^0 and $x' \in V^*(y)$, $x^2 = \theta x^0 + (1-\theta)x' \in V^*(y)$ for $0 \le \theta \le 1$. This requires that $w \cdot x^2 = w \cdot [\theta x^0 + (1-\theta)x'] = \theta w \cdot x^0 + (1-\theta)w \cdot x' \ge c(w, y)$. But this follows since by the definition of $V^*(y)$, $w \cdot x^0$ and $w \cdot x'$ are both greater than $c(w, y)$.

The most important facet of this result is that $V^*(y)$ is always convex regardless of the shape of $V(y)$. Although not internally contradictory [it was not necessary to use the shape of $V(y)$ in deriving the properties of $c(w, y)$], this finding may seem surprising at first glance. But there is a sound economic reason for this result that is easily demonstrated. Consider Figure 2.12, which illustrates cost minimization for a nonconvex $V(y)$ [$\bar{V}(y)$ is given by the heavy kinked line $ABCDE$]. Suppose relative input prices are given by the slope of the line segment AB: The cost-minimizing bundle is not unique but lies somewhere along AB. Similarly, when relative input prices are given by the slope DE, the cost-minimizing input bundle lies somewhere along DE. As long as either of these price ratios is effective, points on the nonconvex part of $\bar{V}(y)$ (BCD) cannot be observed. Suppose now that relative prices are given by the slope BC, costs are minimized at D (note HI is parallel to BC), whereas if relative input prices are given by CD, costs are minimized at B (FG is parallel to CD). Thus, points along the nonconvex part of $\bar{V}(y)$ are never cost minimizing. In fact, a cost function cannot replicate nonconvexities in $V(y)$ because a competitive cost minimizer never utilizes such input combinations. Here, $V^*(y)$ corresponds to $ABDE$, where the dashed line segment BD replaces the nonconvex BCD. An input requirement set with lower boundary

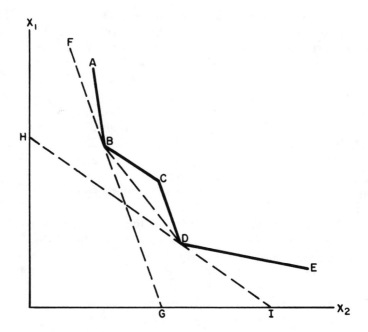

Figure 2.12 Why $V^*(y)$ is convex.

$ABDE$ is observationally equivalent to that given by $ABCDE$ under cost minimization. That is, the cost function associated with $ABCDE$ is the same as that associated with $ABDE$. A natural implication of this result is that if a duality exists between $V(y)$ and $c(w, y)$, $V(y)$ should not possess nonconvex configurations like those illustrated in Figure 2.12.

Putting these informal arguments together, one sees that it is possible to reconstruct input requirement sets directly from any cost function. And since input requirement sets are alternative representations of the technology, the cost function can be used to construct technologies. Hence, specification of a cost function satisfying properties 2B.1–2B.6 automatically guarantees the ability to calculate, in principle, a derived technology that satisfies properties 1A.1a, 1A.2a, 1A.3a, and 1A.4. And if the original technology is convex (1A.2a), this derived technology is the original technology that generated $c(w, y)$. However, when $f(x)$ does not satisfy 1A.2a, the technology derived via (2.34) does not yield any information about the nonconvex region. But as illustrated, these nonconvexities are meaningless from an economic standpoint since they are never utilized by cost-minimizing firms. Ignoring them, therefore, results in no loss of economically relevant information. In applied production analysis based on the behavior of cost-minimizing firms, there is no loss of generality in assuming that $V(y)$ is convex. Even if it is not, there exists a convex $V^*(y)$ that is observationally equivalent to $V(y)$ in the sense that the cost function derived from $V^*(y)$ is the same as that derived from $V(y)$.

Example 2.6. $V^*(y)$ for a linear cost function. Suppose that

$$c(w, y) = y \sum_{i=1}^{n} \gamma_i w_i, \tag{2.35}$$

where $\gamma_i > 0$ for all i. By the results of Example 2.1, one would suspect that the cost function in (2.35) is closely related to that associated with a Leontief technology where $\alpha_i = 1/\gamma_i$. This suspicion is easy to confirm formally. Applying (2.34) to (2.35) yields

$$V^*(y) = \left\{ x: \sum_{i=1}^{n} w_i x_i \geq y \sum_{i=1}^{n} \gamma_i w_i; \ \forall w > 0 \right\}.$$

Equivalently, therefore, $x \in V^*(y)$ if it satisfies the inequality

$$\sum_{i=1}^{n} w_i (x_i - y\gamma_i) \geq 0$$

for any arbitrary $w > 0$. But this in turn suggests that for $x_i \in V^*(y)$,

$$x_i \geq y\gamma_i \quad \forall i.$$

Geometrically, this inequality is equivalent to the representation of $V^*(y)$ by right-angled isoquants so that expression (2.35) is apparently generated by a Leontief technology of the general form

$$f(x) = \min_{x} \{ x_1/\gamma_1, x_2/\gamma_2, \dots, x_n/\gamma_n \}.$$

Exercise 2.6. Construct $V^*(y)$ for the cost function

$$c(w, y) = \min_{w} \{ \gamma_1 w_1, \gamma_2 w_2, \dots, \gamma_n w_n \}.$$

Verify that $V^*(y)$ is convex.

Exercise 2.7. Construct $V^*(y)$ for the cost function

$$c(w, y) = \begin{cases} y\left(\dfrac{w_1}{\beta_1} + \dfrac{w_2}{\beta_2} \right), & \dfrac{w_1}{w_2} \leq a > 0; \\[2mm] y\left(\dfrac{w_2}{\alpha_1} + \dfrac{w_2}{\alpha_2} \right), & \dfrac{w_1}{w_2} > a > 0. \end{cases}$$

Is $V^*(y)$ convex?

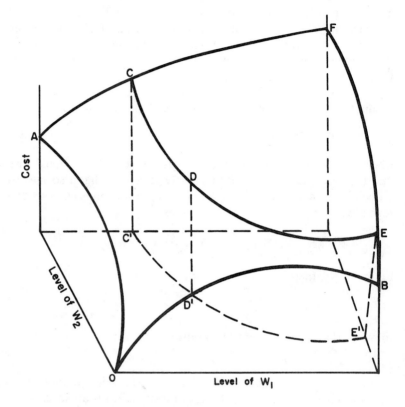

Figure 2.13   Cost as function of factor prices.

2.4b   *More geometry of duality*

Previous results indicate that the cost and production functions are in many ways very similar, which suggests that similar methods can be used to analyze them geometrically. Consider the simplest case of two inputs with the cost function given by $c(w_1, w_2, y)$. For constant y, this function is depicted graphically in Figure 2.13 by the surface $0AFB$. Consider that portion of this surface consistent with a constant level of cost, say, $c(w, y) = 1$. Graphically, this set is represented by the contour on the cost surface given by CDE. If these points are projected directly into price space, the locus of input prices, $C'D'E'$, is obtained.

What are the properties of the locus of points $C'D'E'$? Here, $C'D'E'$ is a representation of the level set $\{w : c(w, y) = 1\}$, which in turn is the lower boundary of the upper contour set of $c(w, y)$:

$$R(y) = \{w : c(w, y) \geq 1\}.$$

Since $c(w, y)$ is concave (and thus quasi-concave), $R(y)$ must be convex. Hence, its boundary is convex to the origin as drawn in Figure 2.13. Here, $R(y)$ is referred to as the *factor price requirement set* in analogy with $V(y)$, and the level set $\{w : c(w, y) = 1\}$ is the *factor price frontier*; the factor price frontier is also often referred to as the isocost or unit isocost curve.

To see how one input price responds to a change in another input price to maintain costs constant, solve for w_i as a function of the other input prices and output (assume the implicit function theorem applies):

$$w_i^* = w_i(w_1, \ldots, w_{i-1}, w_{i+1}, w_{i+2}, \ldots, w_n). \tag{2.36}$$

Substituting (2.36) into the equality $c(w, y) = 1$ and differentiating with respect to w_j obtains

$$\frac{\partial w_i}{\partial w_j} = \frac{\partial c(w, y)/\partial w_j}{\partial c(w, y)/\partial w_i} = -\frac{x_j(w, y)}{x_i(w, y)} \tag{2.37}$$

as the slope of the factor price frontier in (i, j)-space. The second equality follows by Shephard's lemma. Thus, the rate at which w_i must be adjusted to compensate for a change in w_j is minus the ratio of the optimal inputs. As long as only two input prices change, an increase in one input price must lead to a decrease in the other if cost is to remain constant. The slope of the factor price frontier in (i, j)-space must, therefore, be negative, as represented in Figure 2.13.

Expression (2.37) has another, perhaps more important, implication. From Chapter 1, the slope of the isoquant is minus the ratio of marginal productivities, which under cost minimization requires

$$\frac{\partial x_i}{\partial x_j} = -\frac{w_j}{w_i}. \tag{2.38}$$

Comparing (2.38) with (2.37) emphasizes the unique relationship between the cost and production functions. Expression (2.38) implies that obtaining an accurate representation of the isoquant only requires looking in input price space whereas (2.37) says the converse is also true. Consider Figure 2.14, where the factor price frontier is represented graphically. From (2.37), the slope of this curve equals $-x_2/x_1$. Consider, however, that the ray from the origin through point A on the factor price frontier gives the associated input price ratio. By (2.38), however, the slope of this ray equals the corresponding marginal rate of technical substitution. Hence, one can obtain both the slope of the isoquant and relative input utilization directly from the factor price frontier. If all points on the factor price frontier were examined in this manner, one could eventually

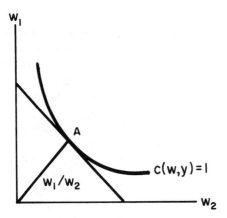

Figure 2.14 Dual relationship between factor price frontier and isoquant.

trace out the associated isoquant. This geometric representation underlines the results contained in the preceding discussion. If one has the cost function, he or she possesses enough information to trace out isoquants in input space.

Consider Figure 2.14 a little closer. Suppose the elasticity of the curvature of the factor price frontier is defined as

$$\rho = \frac{d\ln(w_1/w_2)}{d\ln(c_2/c_1)} = \frac{d\ln(w_1/w_2)}{d\ln(x_2/x_1)}.$$

By (2.38), therefore, $\rho = \sigma^{-1}$, and the curvature of the factor price frontier is integrally linked to the curvature of the isoquant. When $\rho = \infty$ (i.e., the factor price frontier is flat), $\sigma = 0$, which is a kink in the isoquant. Conversely, if $\rho = 0$, $\sigma = \infty$, and the kink in the factor price frontier is mirrored in a flat isoquant. These results are depicted graphically in Figure 2.15. But they are already implicit in the representations of the linear and Leontief cost functions. Since the cost function associated with the Leontief technology is

$$c(w, y) = y \sum_{j=1}^{n} \frac{w_j}{\alpha_j},$$

the slope of the factor price frontier in (w_i, w_j)-space is β_j/β_i, which is a constant. Hence, ρ assumes the value of $+\infty$. Similarly, the fact that the cost function associated with the linear technology is

$$c(w, y) = y \min_{w}\{w_1/\beta_1, w_2/\beta_2, \ldots, w_n/\beta_n\}$$

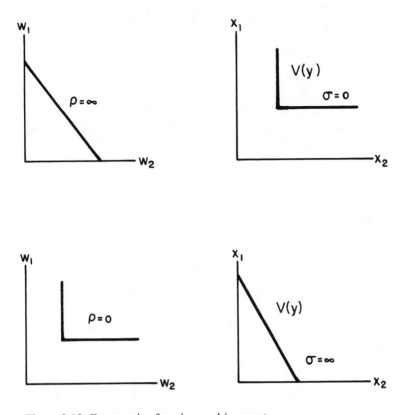

Figure 2.15 Factor price frontiers and isoquant.

implies that the factor price frontier in (w_i, w_j)-space is a right angle. And again the result is confirmed since $\rho = 0$.

Moreover, this result is important because it suggests a very natural way of generating self-dual functional forms, technologies for which the cost and the production function assume the same basic form. When the elasticity of substitution is constant and equal to σ, $\sigma \neq 0, \sigma \neq \infty$, the corresponding cost function should have a constant $\rho = 1/\sigma$. This result is pursued in the following example and exercise.

Example 2.7. The Cobb–Douglas as a self-dual function. If the elasticity of substitution is constant, the elasticity of the curvature of the factor price frontier (ρ) is also constant and equal to the reciprocal of the elasticity of substitution. Since the elasticity of substitution for the Cobb–Douglas production function equals 1, the elasticity of the curvature of the factor price frontier for the associated dual-cost function also equals 1. Using the definition of ρ then implies that the slope of the factor price frontier is always proportional to the input price ratio since, if $\rho = 1$,

$$d \ln\{c_1/c_2\} = d \ln(w_2/w_1),$$

where the subscripts on $c(w, y)$ denote partial vertical differentiation. Hence, using w^* to denote the price ratio (w_1/w_2), the slope of the factor price frontier must be $-Aw^*$, where A is a constant of integration.

To proceed, note that the linear homogeneity of $c(w, y)$ allows writing

$$c(w_1, w_2, y) = w_2 c(w_1/w_2, 1, y)$$

$$= w_2 c^*(w^*),$$

where the y subscript has been dropped for notational convenience. Using this result and the definition of w^* means that the slope of the factor price frontier can be written as

$$(c^* - c^{*\prime} w^*)/c^{*\prime} = -Aw^*,$$

where $c^{*\prime}$ is the derivative of c^*, and the equality is the consequence of ρ, as shown previously. This last equation is a first-order differential equation in w^* that can be integrated, using the fact that $c^{*\prime} w^*/c^*$ is the elasticity of c^* with respect to w^*, to get

$$c^*(w^*) = Bw^{*(1/(1-A))},$$

where B is a constant of integration depending on y. Substituting into the definition of c^* yields

$$c(w, y) = Bw_1^{1/(1-A)} w_2^{-A/(1-A)}.$$

Exercise 2.8. Use direct methods to show that the cost function associated with the ACMS–CES production function introduced in Chapter 1 is itself of the ACMS–CES form.

Bibliographical notes

The discussion of the properties of the basic cost function draws on numerous sources including (but not limited to) Shephard (1970), McFadden (1978a), Diewert (1971), and Mundlak (1968). The section on the elasticity of size relies heavily on Hanoch (1975). Obviously, the section on duality is taken almost directly from the work of Shephard (1970), McFadden (1978a), and Diewert (1971).

CHAPTER 3

Structure of cost functions and short-run cost functions

Chapter 2 concluded by demonstrating the existence of a duality between the production and cost functions. Thus, the cost function can be used to resurrect all the economically relevant information about the original technology. One expects the cost function to yield information about the technology that is of particular interest to economists. For example, Chapter 2 showed that the elasticity of scale is accurately measured at cost-minimizing points by the reciprocal of the cost flexibility, that is, the elasticity of size. But duality suggests that even more information about the technology is available from the cost function via the implicit input requirement set. To reinforce this point, the first part of this chapter shows that elasticities of substitution can be recaptured directly from the cost function.

In the previous chapter it was mentioned several times that the analysis presumed that all inputs were variable. However, as we know from the theory of the firm, many firms face binding constraints to the amount of inputs that can be used in any given time period. The second section of this chapter takes up the issue of input fixity in considering how the long- and short-run cost functions relate to one another.

This chapter concludes by discussing separable cost structures and how they relate to separable production structures. The analysis shows that separable cost structures are not equivalent, except in special circumstances, to separable production structures. Addressing the issue of functional structure in a completely rigorous fashion requires mathematical arguments that considerably exceed the prerequisites of the present book. Thus, formal arguments are virtually missing in this last section of the chapter. Readers wanting a more thorough and complete derivation of the results are referred to the excellent monograph by Blackorby, Primont, and Russell (1978) (especially Chapters 3 and 4).

3.1   Measuring elasticities of substitution with cost function

This section has two purposes: The first is to demonstrate that the elasticities of substitution presented in Chapter 1 can be derived directly from the cost function; the second, somewhat more polemical than the first, is to point out that although this result is interesting, it is not really very important for the purposes of applied production analysis.

The first-order conditions for cost minimization [Equations (2.21)] imply that the marginal rate of technical substitution between the ith and jth inputs equals the ratio of the ith to the jth input price. In the two-input case, the original definition of the elasticity of substitution therefore can be rewritten as

$$\sigma \equiv \frac{d\ln(x_2/x_1)}{d\ln(f_1/f_2)}$$

$$= \frac{d\ln(x_2/x_1)}{d\ln(w_1/w_2)}$$

$$= \frac{\hat{x}_2 - \hat{x}_1}{\hat{w}_1 - \hat{w}_2}$$

where the circumflex denotes percentage change [recall that the logarithmic derivative of x ($d\ln x$) equals $\hat{x}$]. Thus, σ can be interpreted as the elasticity of an input ratio with respect to an input price ratio. Because x_i and x_j are available from the cost function via Shephard's lemma, one can obtain accurate substitution measures from the cost function. But more than that, this result provides an intuitive basis for further consideration of elasticities of substitution; they provide information on relative input responsiveness to changes in relative input prices. Hence, they enable the economist to ascertain, for example, how the input mix might respond to a price rise. It is trying to understand such adjustments that primarily generates economists' interest in the curvature of the isoquant.

Before proceeding further with derivations, however, note that a ratio (α/δ) can change in any one of several ways. The value of α can change, the value of δ can change, or both α and δ can change simultaneously. This observation leads to the definition of several elasticities of substitution. In the following, *one-price–one-factor elasticities of substitution (OOES)* are those that can be expressed in the form $\hat{x}_i/\hat{w}_j$. Elasticities in the form $(\hat{x}_i - \hat{x}_j)/\hat{w}_j$ are called *two-factor–one-price elasticities of substitution (TOES)*. *Two-factor–two-price elasticities of substitution (TTES)* are those of the form $(\hat{x}_i - \hat{x}_j)/(\hat{w}_j - \hat{w}_i)$ (Mundlak, 1968).

Since the definitions of the various elasticities of substitution in Chapter 1 maintained twice-continuous differentiability of $f(x)$, in what follows, we maintain that same assumption. Differentiating the first-order conditions for the cost minimization problem in Equations (2.21) totally and rearranging yields

$$\lambda \begin{bmatrix} 0 & \nabla_x f(x)' \\ \nabla_x f(x) & \nabla_{xx} f(x) \end{bmatrix} \begin{bmatrix} \hat{\lambda} \\ dx \end{bmatrix} = \begin{bmatrix} dy \\ dw \end{bmatrix},$$

where ∇_x denotes the gradient of the function it modifies and ∇_{xx} denotes the Hessian matrix (the matrix of second derivatives), dx is an n-dimensional vector with typical element dx_i, and dw is defined similarly. Inverting this system yields

$$\begin{bmatrix} \hat{\lambda} \\ dx \end{bmatrix} = \lambda^{-1} \begin{bmatrix} B^{00} & B^{0i} \\ B^{i0} & B^{ij} \end{bmatrix} \begin{bmatrix} dy \\ dw \end{bmatrix},$$

where B^{ij} is an $n \times n$ matrix with typical element b_{ij}. These results imply

$$\frac{\partial x_i(w, y)}{\partial w_j} = \frac{b_{ij}}{\lambda},$$

which by the cofactor rule on matrix inversion can be rewritten as

$$\frac{\partial x_i(w, y)}{\partial w_j} = \frac{F_{ji}}{F\lambda}. \tag{3.1}$$

The notation used in Chapter 1 is followed, and F_{ji} is the cofactor of the (j, i) element of the bordered Hessian of the production function and F is the determinant of the bordered Hessian.

Expression (3.1), when combined with the definition of the Allen elasticity (repeated here for convenience),

$$\sigma_{ij} = \frac{F_{ji}}{F} \frac{\sum_{i=1}^{n} (\partial f(x)/\partial x_i) x_i}{x_i x_j},$$

yields

$$\sigma_{ij} = \epsilon_{ij}/S_j. \tag{3.2}$$

Here, S_j is the jth cost share $(w_j x_j/c(w, y))$. The Allen elasticity of substitution is therefore an OOES since it is a derived-demand elasticity divided by a cost share. We have established the first goal of this section with regard to the Allen elasticity of substitution. Now to the second goal.

Expression (3.2) apparently represents the most economically compelling reason for interest in the Allen elasticity. However, it is also a most compelling argument for ignoring the Allen measure in applied analysis. Consider the plight of a government policymaker whose staff economist has provided him with an Allen elasticity of substitution for the effect of an oil price rise on coal utilization. It is an open question whether this individual is better or worse off than he or she was in the absence of this information. The interesting measure is ϵ_{ij} – why disguise it by dividing by a cost share? This question becomes all the more pointed when the best reason for doing so is that it yields a measure that can only be interpreted intuitively in terms of ϵ_{ij} or in terms of highly nonlinear expressions involving second and first partial derivatives of the production function.

Using expression (3.2) and results from Chapter 1 yields

$$\sigma_{ij}^{M} = \epsilon_{ij} - \epsilon_{jj}. \tag{3.3}$$

The Morishima elasticity is a TOES since an equivalent representation of the right-hand side of (3.3) is

$$\epsilon_{ij} - \epsilon_{jj} = \partial \ln[x_i(w, y)/x_j(w, y)]/\partial \ln w_j.$$

In addition, the Morishima elasticity, which when initially defined was certainly no more intuitive than the Allen elasticity, turns out to be a much more economically relevant concept than the Allen elasticity since it is an exact measure of how the i, j input ratio responds to a change in w_j.

In comparing the usefulness of an OOES, like the Allen measure or ϵ_{ij}, with that of a TOES, it is practical first to define a notion of complementary or substitutive behavior. Inputs i and j are *Allen substitutes* if $\epsilon_{ij} > 0$ and *Allen complements* if the inequality is reversed. Inputs i and j are *Morishima substitutes* if $\sigma_{ij}^{M} > 0$ and *Morishima complements* if the inequality is reversed. Two inputs are Allen substitutes if an increase in the price of one leads to an increase in the utilization of the other. If inputs are Allen substitutes, an increase in w_j, say, increases the ratio $x_i(w, y)/x_j(w, y)$ since ϵ_{jj} is always negative. On the other hand, two inputs are Allen complements if an increase in the price of one leads to decreased utilization of the other. Examples of such inputs might be something like charcoal and charcoal lighter fluid in the production of cooking heat and cereal and milk in the production of breakfast nourishment. A priori, Allen complementary behavior is consistent with the input ratio $x_i(w, y)/x_j(w, y)$ rising or falling in response to a change in w_j.

By the homogeneity of input demands,

$$\sum_{i \neq j} \epsilon_{ji} = -\epsilon_{jj}. \tag{3.4}$$

Concavity of $c(w, y)$ implies that $\epsilon_{jj} \leq 0$, which in turn implies that the left-hand side of expression (3.4) must be nonnegative. Hence, no input can be an Allen complement for all other inputs. Finally, notice that even though $\epsilon_{ij} \neq \epsilon_{ji}$, $\text{sign}(\epsilon_{ij}) = \text{sign}(\epsilon_{ji})$ so that the classification of two inputs as Allen complements or Allen substitutes is invariant to whether ϵ_{ij} or ϵ_{ji} is used.

Inputs i and j are Morishima substitutes if and only if an increase in w_j causes the input ratio $x_i(w, y)/x_j(w, y)$ to rise. Hence, when inputs are Allen substitutes, they must also be Morishima substitutes. But the converse does not hold. Consider the case where $\epsilon_{ij} < 0$ but $|\epsilon_{ij}| < |\epsilon_{jj}|$. In this instance, the two inputs are Morishima substitutes since a rise in w_j leads to an increase in the ratio $x_i(w, y)/x_j(w, y)$ as the utilization of $x_j(w, y)$ is falling more quickly in percentage terms than the utilization of

$x_i(w, y)$. But as with the Allen measure, an input cannot be a Morishima complement for all other inputs since

$$\sum_i \sigma_{ji}^M = \sum_i (\epsilon_{ji} - \epsilon_{ii})$$

$$= -\sum_i \epsilon_{ii} \geq 0,$$

where the inequality is a consequence of the concavity of the cost function. Unfortunately, however, the Morishima elasticity is not sign symmetric, and the classification of inputs i and j as Morishima substitutes or complements depends critically on which input price changes.

Before leaving this discussion of elasticities of substitution, it is worthwhile to consider at least one TTES. Suppose, in fact, that two input prices (w_i and w_j) change. Then

$$\hat{x}_i(w, y) = \epsilon_{ii} \hat{w}_i + \epsilon_{ij} \hat{w}_j \quad \text{and} \quad \hat{x}_j(w, y) = \epsilon_{ji} \hat{w}_i + \epsilon_{jj} \hat{w}_j.$$

Subtraction then yields

$$\hat{x}_i(w, y) - \hat{x}_j(w, y) = (\epsilon_{ii} - \epsilon_{ji}) \hat{w}_i + (\epsilon_{ij} - \epsilon_{jj}) \hat{w}_j$$

$$= \sigma_{ij}^M \hat{w}_j - \sigma_{ji}^M \hat{w}_i.$$

This last result implies that the associated TTES is

$$\frac{\hat{x}_i(w, y) - \hat{x}_j(w, y)}{\hat{w}_j - \hat{w}_i} = \sigma_{ij}^M \frac{\hat{w}_j}{\hat{w}_j - \hat{w}_i} - \sigma_{ji}^M \frac{\hat{w}_i}{\hat{w}_j - \hat{w}_i}.$$

Not surprisingly, therefore, the class of TTES measures emerges as a weighted combination of the respective Morishima elasticities, each of which measures how input ratios respond to changes in single-input prices. Utilizing Shephard's lemma also gives

$$\hat{c}(w, y) = S_i \hat{w}_i + S_j \hat{w}_j.$$

If attention is restricted to movements along a given factor price frontier, one can define the *shadow elasticity of substitution* as the TTES evaluated at constant cost and by the above:

$$\sigma_{ij}^S = \frac{S_i}{S_i + S_j} \sigma_{ij}^M + \frac{S_j}{S_i + S_j} \sigma_{ji}^M. \tag{3.5}$$

Therefore, the shadow elasticity of substitution is a weighted average of two Morishima elasticities where the weights are given by the relative cost shares. Note, in particular, that this TTES is in fact symmetric in addition to providing a more complete measure of relative input responsiveness.

Example. Although the preceding arguments demonstrate analytically that there can be important differences among the various elasticities of

Table 3.1. *Allen partial elasticities of substitution* (σ_{ij}), *U.S. meat products industry, 1965*[a]

Item	Capital	Labor	Energy	Materials	Structures
Capital	−17.994	11.282	−14.671	−0.640	21.888
	(3.800)	(2.451)	(4.205)	(0.199)	(1.742)
Labor		−7646	14.790	0.327	4.131
		(1.237)	(2.352)	(0.138)	(4.354)
Energy			−163.621	−0.378	74.979
			(12.049)	(0.170)	(15.572)
Materials				−0.011	−0.493
				(0.008)	(0.341)
Structures					−131.235
					(24.494)

[a] Standard errors calculated treating estimated factor demands as nonstochastic are reported in parentheses.

substitution, an example based on empirical estimates from a study of the U.S. meat industry by Ball and Chambers (1982) may prove instructive. Since econometric issues are deferred until later, I will not address the matter of just how these elasticities were estimated. The purpose of the following discussion is to illustrate the asymmetries of the various elasticities. The study underlying these elasticities postulated the existence of five inputs into the production process: capital equipment (K), labor (L), energy (E), intermediate materials (M), and capital structures (S).

Allen elasticities of substitution are reported in Table 3.1. This table suggests that labor is an Allen substitute for all other inputs; capital equipment is an Allen complement for energy and materials. Morishima elasticities are reported in Table 3.2. Since the Morishima is a TOES, σ_{ij}^M measures relative input adjustment to single-factor price changes, whereas the σ_{ij} only measure how a single input adjusts to changes in a single-input price. Comparing the tables while keeping this point in mind reveals some interesting information. First, the nonsymmetric nature of the Morishima elasticities is clearly highlighted. Second, the evidence of complementary behavior using the Morishima measure is weaker than for the Allen measure. Consider, for example, the relationship between σ_{MK} and σ_{MK}^M. From Table 3.1, a rise in the price of capital leads to decreased utilization of materials ($\sigma_{MK} = -0.640$). On the other hand, the associated Morishima elasticity is positive ($\sigma_{MK}^M = 0.258$). This can be

Table 3.2. *Morishima elasticities of substitution* (σ_{ij}^M), *U.S. meat products industry, 1965*[a]

Item	Capital	Labor	Energy	Materials	Structures
Capital	0	1.383	0.782	−0.567	0.671
		(0.281)	(0.068)	(0.180)	(1.111)
Labor	0.436	0	0.934	0.305	0.593
	(0.076)		(0.069)	(0.135)	(0.223)
Energy	0.056	1.640	0	−0.331	0.904
	(0.098)	(0.218)		(0.145)	(0.00034)
Materials	0.258	0.582	0.854	0	0.573
	(0.053)	(0.143)	(0.065)		(0.114)
Structures	0.594	0.861	1.249	−0.434	0
	(0.092)	(0.111)	(0.109)	(0.314)	

[a] Standard errors calculated treating estimated factor demands as nonstochastic are reported in parentheses.

interpreted in the following way: As the price of capital increases, utilization of materials falls off – evidence of complementary behavior. At the same time, however, usage of capital also declines (as required by concavity) at such a rate that the ratio M/K actually falls. Now σ_{MK}^M and σ_{KM}^M have opposite signs. Thus, whereas materials and capital behave as Morishima substitutes when the price of capital rises, they behave as Morishima complements when the price of materials rises. Our evidence, therefore, suggests that capital equipment is more price responsive than materials to changes in either W_K or W_M.

Shadow elasticities of substitution corresponding to this technology are reported in Table 3.3. They show the percentage adjustment in input ratios to changes in factor price ratios. As such, they are closer intuitively to Hicks's definition of the elasticity of substitution. Using this measure, Table 3.3 indicates that when changes in the price ratio – as opposed to single price changes – are considered, all input prices act as if they were substitutes.

The fact that the differing elasticities do not give the same results when stratifying inputs into complements and substitutes does not mean that there is something inherently wrong with any of them. Rather, it highlights the difficulties pointed out in Chapter 1 with defining a meaningful measure of substitution relationships in the many-input case. The reader

Table 3.3. *Shadow elasticities of substitution* (σ_{ij}^S), *U.S. meat products industry, 1965*[a]

Item	Capital	Labor	Energy	Materials	Structures
Capital	0	0.597 (0.126)	0.593 (0.065)	0.245 (0.056)	0.653 (0.112)
Labor		0	0.981 (0.072)	0.562 (0.128)	0.608 (0.108)
Energy			0	0.848 (0.009)	1.061 (0.128)
Materials				0	0.568 (0.110)
Structures					0

[a] Standard errors calculated treating estimated factor demands as nonstochastic are reported in parentheses.

should bear in mind that each measures quite different, although related, phenomena. Thus, it seems apparent that applied production analysts might have occasion to be interested in all three concepts.

3.2   Short- and long-run costs

So far, all elements of x have been treated as freely variable. It is not uncommon, however, for producers to be faced with the existence of inputs that are only available in limited amounts. For example, at any one time, most farmers have available only a fixed amount of land on which to plant crops. Although they need not utilize all the available land, they cannot use more than what is available. Thus, they face additional constraints in their cost minimization decision. As time passes, however, the farmer is often able to purchase more land to use in the production of his crops, and the constraint can be relaxed.

Economists have created a mental tool to deal with such matters. They refer to *short-run* decisions as those that involve some fixity of inputs. *Long-run* decisions are those that involve no fixed inputs. Hence, the analysis so far has only encompassed long-run problems, and $c(w, y)$ should be explicitly interpreted as a long-run cost function. Not surprisingly, the solutions to the short-run and the long-run problems are not always the same. In turn, the behavior of costs in the short run is not the same as in the long run. This section provides a thorough, but concise, treatment of the relationship between long- and short-run cost minimization.

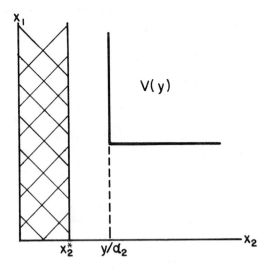

Figure 3.1 Input constraints and nonfeasibility.

Before proceeding, two points should be stressed. First, the decision to define the production function in terms of all inputs and not just those that are variable in the short run has the advantage of offering an explicit representation of just what the terminology "short run" means. By no means, however, is this a universal practice in economics. For example, Carlson's (1939) classic treatment of cost and production presumes the existence of some fixed inputs and defines the production function solely in terms of perfectly variable inputs. Second, the existence of fixed inputs, except in very limited circumstances, does not substantially alter the general properties of a variable-cost function. This fact should become clearer as the discussion progresses.

Short-run cost function: Suppose that the input vector is partitioned into two components, with x^1 containing perfectly variable inputs and x^2 containing those inputs that are fixed or subject to some availability constraint. Obviously, the availability of inputs is an important determinant of firm behavior. This fact is illustrated in Figure 3.1, which depicts a two-input Leontief technology when there is some constraint on the availability of x_2. If the amount of x_2 available to the producer in the short run is less than y/α_2, say, x_2^*, then production of output at y is not possible since the range of feasible input choices (given by the cross-hatched area) does not intersect $V(y)$. Thus, it makes no sense to consider the properties of a cost function when the situation is similar to that in Figure 3.1.

Define the *restricted input requirement set*

$$L(y, x^2) = \{x^1 : f(x^1, x^2) \geq y\},$$

where x^2 is now taken to be the maximum available amount of x^2. A minimum assumption on the technology is that $L(y, x^2)$ be nonempty to preclude outcomes like those illustrated previously. Of course, a similar assumption was required in the original definition of the cost minimization problem. In fact, if one defines

$$c(w^1, y, x^2) = \min_{x^1 \geq 0} \{w^1 x^1 : x^1 \in L(y, x^2)\}, \qquad (3.6)$$

where w^1 is the set of variable input prices as the *short-run variable-cost function,* then assuming that $f(\cdot)$ satisfies properties 1A.1a and 1A.3a in x^1 and that $L(y, x^2)$ is nonempty is sufficient to prove the existence of a well-defined short-run variable-cost function satisfying properties 2B.1–2B.6 in terms of w^1 and y. Further, if $c(w^1, y, x^2)$ is differentiable, it will also satisfy Shephard's lemma in w^1. Since the proof of this result only repeats previous arguments, it is left to the interested reader as an informal exercise. But the existence of a solution to (3.6) satisfying these properties affirms our earlier point that the inclusion or exclusion of the fixed-input vector in the representation of the technology does not affect significantly the formal derivation of the properties of cost in variable input prices and output.

However, in addition to properties 2B.1–2B.6, $c(w^1, y, x^2)$ satisfies the additional property that it is nonincreasing in x^2, that is,

$$x^2 \geq x^{2*} \text{ implies } c(w^1, y, x^2) \leq c(w^1, y, x^{2*}).$$

This fact is easily proved formally and is perhaps best illustrated by Figure 3.2, where the intersection of $V(y)$ and the constrained input set is given by the shaded area, which is, of course, equivalent to $L(y, x^2)$. Suppose now that the availability of x_2 is increased beyond x_2^*. The range of feasible choices for x_1 has increased so that new cost-minimizing opportunities, previously unavailable, are opened up. Hence, variable costs cannot increase since what is least cost now may not have been even feasible before the constraint was relaxed.

Long- and short-run costs and Le Chatelier–Samuelson principle: Expression (3.6) gives the variable costs associated with producing y. However, since the elements of x^2 are presumably not free, the *short-run total cost* associated with producing y is

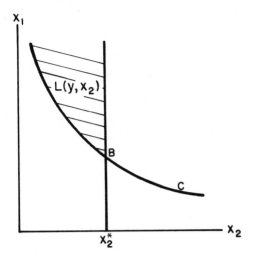

Figure 3.2 Why short-run variable costs are nonincreasing in constrained inputs.

$$c^s(w, y, x^2) = c(w^1, y, x^2) + w^2 x^2. \tag{3.7}$$

In what follows, it is convenient to assume that the constraint on x^2 is always binding so that all of x^2 available is utilized. It is presumed that $c(w, y)$ and $c(w^1, y, x^2)$ are twice-continuously differentiable in all arguments.

The relationship between $c^s(w, y, x^2)$ and $c(w, y)$ is the subject of a vast literature. The classic treatment is that of Viner (1931), which, although flawed in some minor technical respects, remains the standard by which contributions to production analysis might well be judged. From the definition of the long run, the main difference between $c(w, y)$ and $c^s(w, y, x^2)$ is that in (3.7) the fixed inputs do not necessarily minimize costs. However, by definition of $c(w^1, y, x^2)$, variable costs are minimized for any choice of x^2. Hence, if decision makers are rational,

$$c(w, y) = \min_{x^2} c(w^1, y, x^2) + w^2 x^2. \tag{3.8}$$

Although somewhat tautological, expression (3.8) is important because it provides a basis for the rest of our analysis. Moreover, the decomposition of the long-run problem into two components – that of minimizing variable costs given x^2 and then choosing x^2 – represents an analytical tactic that will be used heavily throughout this book. Hence, the manipulation that follows presages much of our remaining analysis.

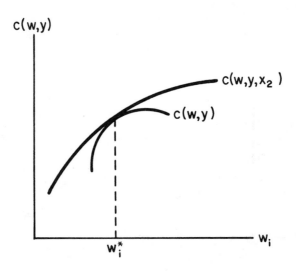

Figure 3.3   Long- and short-run costs and Le Chatelier–Samuelson principle.

From expression (3.8), it follows that

$$c(w, y) \le c^s(w, y, x^2) \quad \text{and} \quad c(w, y) = c^s(w, y, x^2(w, y)),$$

where $x^2(w, y)$ denotes the solution to (3.8). Together these expressions imply that $c(w, y)$ is the lower envelope of the respective $c^s(w, y, x^2)$ functions in both input price space and output space. That $c(w, y)$ is a lower bound is obvious from the first expression. The second expression, however, indicates that the long- and short-run cost functions will share some points in common – specifically those for which the relevant fixed-input bundle minimizes cost. But since the first expression implies that the two cost curves cannot intersect in either input price or output space, the envelope relationship must hold.

Now the fact that $c(w, y)$ is the lower envelope for the various short-run total cost curves in input price space has some very important economic content. Consider Figure 3.3, which illustrates this result graphically for the ith variable-input price. By the properties of cost functions, both $c(w, y)$ and $c^s(w, y, x^2)$ are concave in the variable-input prices. But if $c(w, y)$ and $c^s(w, y, x^2)$ are to be tangent at, say, w_i^*, then the fact that $c(w, y)$ must never be above $c^s(w, y, x^2)$ implies that $c(w, y)$ must be "more concave" than $c^s(w, y, x^2)$ at w_i^*, as illustrated. At w_i^*, however, the fixed-input bundle minimizes cost. Moreover, since the two curves are tangent,

$$\frac{\partial c(w, y)}{\partial w_i} = \frac{\partial c^s(w, y, x^2)}{\partial w_i},$$

which by Shephard's lemma implies

$$x_i(w, y) = x_i(w, y, x^2(w, y)).$$

That is, the long-run derived demand for the ith variable input equals the corresponding short-run derived demand evaluated at the fixed-input vector, which minimizes long-run cost. Now the fact that $c(w, y)$ is more concave in w_i here than $c^s(w, y, x^2)$ implies that

$$\frac{\partial x_i(w, y)}{\partial w_i} \leq \frac{\partial x_i(w, y, x^2(w, y))}{\partial w_i}. \tag{3.9}$$

In other words, long-run derived demand is more own-price elastic than short-run derived demand. Expression (3.9) is a manifestation of the well-known *Le Chatelier–Samuelson principle* that plays a prominent role in modern economics. As demonstrated, the Le Chatelier–Samuelson principle is a direct consequence of the envelope relationship and the concavity of the cost function. Since expressions such as (3.9) play such a central role in the theory of the firm, we now turn to a more thorough derivation (Otani, 1982).

By the envelope theorem and (3.8),

$$x_i(w, y) = \frac{\partial c(w, y)}{\partial w_i} = \frac{\partial c(w^1, y, x^2(w, y))}{\partial w_i}, \quad i \in N^1, \tag{3.10}$$

where N^1 is the set of indexes associated with the variable inputs and N^2 is the set associated with w^2, x^2. From (3.10), adjustments in either w^1 or y have two separate effects on long-run variable-input demand. The first is a direct effect associated with the change in the short-run derived demand due to a change in either w^1 or y holding x^2 constant. The second effect is associated with the short-run, variable-input demand adjusting to the changes in x^2 that long-run adjustment requires.

Differentiating (3.10) with respect to w_i ($i \in N^1$),

$$\frac{\partial x_i(w, y)}{\partial w_i} = \frac{\partial^2 c(w^1, y, x^2)}{\partial w_i^2} + \sum_{j \in N^2} \frac{\partial^2 c(w^1, y, x^2)}{\partial w_i \, \partial x_j} \frac{\partial x_j(w, y)}{\partial w_i}.$$

By the twice-continuous differentiability of $c(w, y)$ and Shephard's lemma, $\partial x_j(w, y)/\partial w_i$ ($i \in N^1, j \in N^2$) $= \partial x_i(w, y)/\partial w_j$ ($i \in N^1, j \in N^2$). But also by (3.10),

$$\frac{\partial x_i(w, y)}{\partial w_j} = \sum_{k \in N^2} \frac{\partial^2 c(w^1, y, x^2)}{\partial w_i \, \partial x_k} \frac{\partial x_k(w, y)}{\partial w_j}, \quad i \in N^1, j \in N^2.$$

Putting results together yields

$$\frac{\partial x_i(w, y)}{\partial w_i} = \frac{\partial^2 c(w^1, y, x^2)}{\partial w_i^2} + \sum_{j \in N^2} \sum_{k \in N^2} \frac{\partial^2 c(w^1, y, x^2)}{\partial w_i \partial x_k}$$

$$\times \left(\frac{\partial x_k(w, y)}{\partial w_j} \right) \frac{\partial^2 c(w^1, y, x^2)}{\partial w_i \partial x_j}, \quad i \in N^1, \qquad (3.11)$$

as the overall own-price effect on long-run variable demand. Since $c(w^1, y, x^2)$ is concave, the first term on the right of (3.11) is negative. The second term is that associated with the price-induced adjustment in x^2. But this term is a quadratic form in the principal submatrix of $\nabla_{ww} c(w, y)$ obtained by deleting rows and columns for each w_i ($i \in N^1$). Since $\nabla_{ww} c(w, y)$ is negative semidefinite, this principal submatrix is also negative semidefinite (see Appendix), and the second term is also negative. Thus, we have formally established (3.9). This result can be further illustrated graphically with the aid of Figure 3.2. Suppose that input prices are originally such that B is the long-run, cost-minimizing point. Let w_1 rise to such an extent that C becomes the long-run cost minimizer but cannot be attained because of the constraint on x_2. However, as the firm acquires x^2 over the long run, C eventually becomes feasible and the firm gradually decreases its utilization of x_1.

The Le Chatelier–Samuelson principle as outlined in (3.9) can be easily extended to encompass the successive relaxation of input constraints. Define a new partition of the input vector

$$x = (x^1, x^2, \ldots, x^k),$$

where x^1 remains the vector of perfectly variable inputs and x^i ($i > 1$) denotes a subvector of fixed inputs. Here, however, we assume that the constraints on the fixed inputs are relaxed successively, that is, the lower the index of x^i ($i > 1$), the sooner the constraint is relaxed. In effect, we are thinking of a series of short-run problems with each new short-run problem defined by the relaxation of an input constraint on one of the fixed-input bundles. In the shortest of runs, the variable-cost function is

$$c(w^1, y, x^2, \ldots, x^k) = \min_{x^1} \{ w^1 \cdot x^1 : x^1 \in L(y, x^2, \ldots, x^k) \}.$$

Once the constraint on x^2 is relaxed, the new short-run problem becomes

$$c(w^1, w^2, y, x^3, \ldots, x^k) = \min_{x^2} \{ c(w^1, y, x^2, \ldots, x^k) + w^2 x^2 \},$$

and by analogy, we determine that, in general,

$$c(w^1, \ldots, w^i, y, x^{i+1}, \ldots, x^k) = \min_{x^i} \{ c(w^1, \ldots, w^{i-1}, y, x^i, \ldots, x^k) + w^i x^i \}$$

and

$$c(w, y) = \min_{x^k}\{c(w^1, ..., w^{k-1}, y, x^k) + w^k x^k\}.$$

Defining

$$c^s(w, y, x^i, ..., x^k) = c(w^1, ..., w^{i-1}, y, x^i, ..., x^k) + \sum_{v=i}^{k} x^v w^v,$$

this nesting of minimization problems implies that

$$c(w, y) \le c^s(w, y, x^k) \le \cdots \le c^s(w, y, x^2, ..., x^k).$$

Exactly parallel arguments to those made earlier reveal that

$$\frac{\partial x_i(w, y)}{\partial w_i} \le \frac{\partial x_i(w, y, x^k)}{\partial w_i} \le \cdots \le \frac{\partial x_i(w, y, x^2, ..., x^k)}{\partial w_i}, \quad i \in N^1.$$

That is, as less and less inputs are fixed in the production process, the responsiveness of the perfectly variable inputs to changes in their own prices increase. Before closing this discussion of the Le Chatelier–Samuelson principle, note that these results have been developed without any reliance on the existence of a complementary or substitutive relationship between the various inputs. Thus, the principle must apply regardless of whether inputs are complements.

Exercise 3.1. In the preceding discussion, we demonstrated that the Le Chatelier–Samuelson principle implies a weak inequality between $\partial x_i(w, y)/\partial w_i$ and $\partial x_i(w, y, x^2)/\partial w_i$ ($i \in N^1$). By expression (3.11), this weak inequality becomes an equality if and only if

$$\sum_{j \in N^2} \sum_{k \in N^2} \frac{\partial^2 c(w^1, y, x^2)}{\partial w_i \, \partial w_h} \frac{\partial x_k(w, y)}{\partial w_j} \frac{\partial^2 c(w^1, y, x^k)}{\partial w_i \, \partial w_j}$$

equals zero. A sufficient condition for this result to hold is that $c(w^1, y, x^2)$ be expressible,

$$C_1(w^1, y) + C_2(x^2).$$

Derive the necessary conditions for the long-run and short-run effects to be equal.

Long- and short-run average costs: Parallel arguments reveal that the long-run average-cost curve is the lower envelope for the short-run average-cost curves, a relationship depicted graphically in Figure 3.4 under the presumption that $c(w, y)$ is convex in y. In Figure 3.4, the notation c^{s_i} is shorthand for c^s evaluated at the fixed-input bundle x^{2i}. It is in this context that one might grasp some further intuition on the notions of

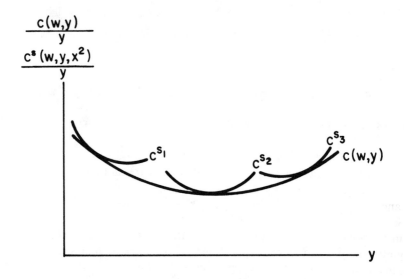

Figure 3.4 Long- and short-run average costs.

economies of size and scale. In a previous discussion, economies of size were motivated in terms of a decision on the number of identical operations to set up. Here, however, economies of size can be motivated in terms of long-run decision making. Each point on the long-run average-cost curve is also a point on an associated short-run average-cost curve where the fixed-input bundle is evaluated at its long-run cost-minimizing value. Hence, we may rephrase Viner (1931) and identify each separate fixed-input bundle as a *plant*, with the *size* of the plant measured by the output level for which that plant minimizes the long-run cost.

The existence of size economies implies that the producer can decrease long-run average cost by altering the plant in order to move down the long-run average-cost curve. One should be careful, however, to not identify movements along the long-run average-cost curve with plant expansion in the sense that all fixed inputs are increased. This need be the case only when there is a single fixed input. In the farm context used to illustrate the notions of long run and short run, economies of size imply that a farmer can successfully decrease average or unit costs by acquiring more land, that is, expanding his plant size, or perhaps more appropriately his farm size. In this context, the elasticity of size assumes particular importance. If one evaluates $\epsilon^*(y, w)$ and finds it to be less than 1, it implies that the firm involved can decrease average cost by decreasing production. The converse holds if $\epsilon^*(y, w) > 1$.

Besides offering further insight into some aspects of long-run decision making, expression (3.8) is also important because it details the effects of input fixity on a firm's decisions. The first-order conditions associated with (3.8) require that

$$\frac{\partial c(w^1, y, x^2)}{\partial x_j} + w_j = 0, \quad j \in N^2 \tag{3.12}$$

for an interior solution. Expression (3.12) implies that when fixed inputs are adjusted to their long-run values, the marginal decrease in short-run variable costs must equal minus the associated input price. In other words, in the long run, a fixed input is acquired just up to the point where the associated decrease in variable costs (i.e., the shadow price) is exactly balanced by the marginal-cost increment (i.e., w_j^2).

Second-order conditions for (3.8) require that the matrix with typical element $\{\partial^2 c(w^1, y, x^2)/\partial x_i \, \partial x_j\}$ ($i, j \in N^2$) be positive semidefinite. This requirement implies that the short-run variable-cost function must be convex in the fixed factors if it is to be consistent with long-run cost minimization. Since one can interpret the partial derivatives of $c(w^1, y, x^2)$ with respect to the elements of x^2 as shadow prices of the fixed factors, convexity of $c(w^1, y, x^2)$ in x^2 implies that the shadow prices approach zero as the endowment of fixed inputs becomes arbitrarily large. On an intuitive level, this result is the counterpart of the law of diminishing marginal productivity since the larger x^2 is, the smaller will be the decrease in the short-run variable costs that follows by augmenting x^2.

Exercise 3.2. Show that if $f(x)$ is strictly concave in x,

$$\frac{\partial^2 c(y, w)}{\partial y^2} \leq \frac{\partial^2 c^s(w, y, x^2)}{\partial y^2},$$

that is, long-run marginal cost is less steeply sloped than short-run marginal cost.

3.3   Structure of cost functions

As noted in Chapter 1, it is often necessary in applied or theoretical work to restrict the production function to allow the derivation of results or empirical investigation. Since restricting $f(x)$ alters the feasible input set for cost minimization, one can expect that such restrictions have direct consequences for the structure of the cost function. An excellent example is already available in the fact that the homotheticity of $f(x)$ implies that the cost function assumes the form $h(y)c(w)$.

Duality theorems discussed above, however, suggest that there is no reason to initiate the study of production problems with $f(x)$. A consequence of these results is that specification of a well-behaved cost function is equivalent to the specification of an implicit technology, $V^*(y)$, which satisfies all the properties necessary to generate a well-behaved cost function. Because analysis can start with the cost function, the structure of the cost function is of inherent interest. Moreover, arguments very similar to those marshalled in the discussion of aggregate inputs and separability of the production function are equally relevant for the cost function. Simply put, very often, a researcher finds it convenient (and perhaps even necessary) to aggregate input prices in some fashion. As already seen for homotheticity, it is legitimate to think of the cost function itself as an aggregate input price. Since output is really nothing more than an aggregate input, the cost function can be interpreted as the price of acquiring that aggregate input. Interestingly, this aggregate input price always depends on the amount of the aggregate input that is purchased. In the following, the notion of separability is used to consider less restrictive means of aggregating inputs. Attention is then turned to the possible equivalence of separable cost and separable production functions.

3.3a   *Separability of cost function*

Because the cost function is a mapping from $(n+1)$-space onto the real line whereas the production function is a mapping from n-space, some notational adjustments are necessary for discussing the separability of the cost function. These involve defining separability in terms of output as well as in terms of input prices. In what follows, always presume that $c(w, y)$ is at least twice differentiable. Define the set of input price indices as above $\mathbf{I} = \{1, 2, \ldots, n\}$ and the partition $\hat{\mathbf{I}} = \{\mathbf{I}^1, \mathbf{I}^2, \ldots, \mathbf{I}^m\}$. Also define the extended index set $_0\mathbf{I} = \{0, 1, 2, \ldots, n\}$ and the extended partition $_0\hat{\mathbf{I}} = \{0, \mathbf{I}^1, \mathbf{I}^2, \ldots, \mathbf{I}^m\}$, where 0 is the output index. The corresponding partition of w is $w = \{w^1, w^2, \ldots, w^m\}$.

Since separability of $f(x)$ revolves around ways marginal rates of technical substitution can be independent of certain inputs, it seems logical to define separability of the cost function in terms of the slope of the factor price frontier. Prices w_i and w_j are separable from w_k in $c(w, y)$ if

$$\frac{\partial}{\partial w_k} \frac{\partial c(w, y)/\partial w_i}{\partial c(w, y)/\partial w_j} = 0. \tag{3.13}$$

By Shephard's lemma, w_i and w_j are separable from w_k if and only if $\epsilon_{ik} = \epsilon_{jk}$ since an equivalent representation of (3.13) is

$$\frac{\partial x_i(w, y)/\partial w_k}{x_i(w, y)} = \frac{\partial x_j(w, y)/\partial w_k}{x_j(w, y)}.$$

Separability of the cost function, therefore, has more specific economic implications than separability of the production function. These expressions also make the restrictiveness of the separability assumption more graphic. Since the degree of Allen substitutability is defined by the derived-demand elasticities, maintaining separability here is equivalent to restricting severely the degree and direction of Allen substitution relationships. From the preceding discussion, if w_i and w_j are separable from w_k, inputs x_i and x_k can be Allen substitutes only if x_j and x_k are also Allen substitutes.

Weakly separable costs: The cost function is *weakly separable* in the partition $\hat{\mathbf{I}}$ if

$$\frac{\partial}{\partial w_t} \left(\frac{\partial c(w, y)/\partial w_j}{\partial c(w, y)/\partial w_i} \right) = 0, \quad i, j \in \mathbf{I}^k, \ t \notin \mathbf{I}^k.$$

Cost functions are weakly separable if the slope of the factor price frontier in (w_j, w_i)-space, where w_i and w_j are elements of the same subvector, is independent of all factor prices that are not elements of that same subvector. Weak separability, therefore, requires that the derived-demand elasticities for all inputs in a given group with respect to a price from a separate group are equal. As can easily be seen, such restrictions can have important econometric implications. Suppose, for example, that an individual is only interested in estimating derived-demand elasticities. If the function is weakly separable, the number of elasticities that must be directly estimated declines significantly.

A weakly separable cost function can be written as

$$c(w, y) = C^*(y, c^1(y, w^1), ..., c^m(y, w^m)),$$

where the function C^* is increasing and differentiable in w (see Blackorby, Primont, and Russell 1978, 112). The function C^* can also be chosen to be linearly homogeneous in the c^i functions. Each of the functions c^i can then be chosen so that it is nonnegative, nondecreasing in w, concave and continuous in w, positive linearly homogeneous, and nondecreasing in y, and each c^i is convex in y. In other words, each of the c^i functions itself possesses the properties of a cost function and can be thought of in those terms. Since the ability to write the cost function in this fashion is an important consequence of weak separability, a more thorough understanding of the principles underlying this result is worthwhile. From the weak separability results developed in Chapter 1 (1.27), weak separability implies that

$$c(w, y) = K(y, \phi^1(y, w^1), \ldots, \phi^m(y, w^m)).$$

We need to show that it is reasonable to think of the subfunctions ϕ^i as possessing the properties of a cost function. The first step is to note that the linear homogeneity of the cost function in w implies that the ratio of any two partial derivatives of $c(w, y)$ with respect to any two factor prices is itself homogeneous of degree zero. Hence, we obtain

$$\frac{\partial c(w, y)/\partial w_i}{\partial c(w, y)/\partial w_j} = \frac{\partial \phi^k(y, w^k)/\partial w_i}{\partial \phi^k(y, w^k)/\partial w_j}, \quad (i, j) \in \mathbf{I}^k,$$

which is homogeneous of degree zero in w^k. Consequently, Lau's lemma (see Appendix) implies that each ϕ^k must be homothetic in the respective w^k, whence

$$\phi^k(y, w^k) = \theta^k(c^k(y, w^k)),$$

where $c^k(y, w^k)$ is linearly homogeneous in w^k. A straightforward redefinition of the function then yields the desired expression. Now since each $c^k(\cdot)$ is linearly homogeneous, overall linear homogeneity requires that

$$c(tw, y) = C^*(y, c^1(y, tw^1), \ldots, c^m(y, tw^m))$$
$$= C^*(y, tc(y^1, w^1), \ldots, tc^m(y, w^m))$$
$$= tc(w, y).$$

But the last equality implies that $C^*(\cdot)$ itself must be linearly homogeneous in the c^i functions. Similar arguments will establish that it is reasonable to think of each $c^i(\cdot)$ as possessing the stated properties. Therefore, one can interpret each c^i (in a sense) as a sectoral cost function or as a composite or aggregate price. Separability permits one to construct composite prices using subvectors of input prices. This, in turn, permits further analysis of the cost function solely in terms of these composite prices.

An alternative way to interpret the structure of a weakly separable cost function is offered by an argument similar to that used to motivate weak separability of the production function, that is, a two-stage production process. In the context of the cost function, however, one might think of a two-stage cost minimization process. In the first stage, the cost of producing a single unit of an aggregate input (the magnitude of which depends on the level of output) composed of a subgroup of the inputs is minimized. In the second stage, these aggregate inputs are combined in a cost-minimizing fashion to produce the final product y. If c^i is thought of as the cost of producing a single unit of the aggregate input, it can also be interpreted as the marginal cost of that input and, assuming marginal cost pricing, as the price of the aggregate input. As previously stated, each c^i function retains its interpretation as an aggregate input price that depends on the output level and prices of the inputs in the subgroup used to produce the aggregate input, but here, the interpretation of c^i is modified to recognize that each aggregate input is constructed in a cost-minimizing fashion. Notice, moreover, that each c^i being linearly homogeneous in the input prices in the ith group is particularly fortuitous because it implies that the aggregate price index accurately reflects equiproportional changes in these input prices.

The ability to decompose the cost minimization problem into two stages could prove very convenient for either theoretical or empirical analysis. One can easily imagine cases where a limited number of observations on prices and output would not support reliable statistical analysis if all inputs were considered in, say, estimating a cost function but where sufficient observations exist to support statistical analysis based on a fewer number of aggregate inputs. However, the previous results indicate that each aggregate input price itself depends on output. Thus, a new price index is required for each aggregate input at different output levels. Simplicity suggests that it would be convenient to possess aggregate price indexes that only depend on the prices belonging to the separable subgroup and not on output. Cost functions possessing this property are said to be *weakly separable in the extended partition,* where the extended partition is defined by $_0\hat{\mathbf{I}}$. If the cost function is weakly separable in $_0\hat{\mathbf{I}}$, it assumes the general form

$$c(w, y) = C^*(y, c^1(w^1), \ldots, c^m(w^m)).$$

Here C^* and each c^i assume the same general properties already described when the cost function was weakly separable in $\hat{\mathbf{I}}$.

Weak separability in the extended partition is a special case of the more general functional restriction that w_i and w_j, $(i, j) \in \mathbf{I}^k$, are separable from y in the cost function. By the usual definition, w_i and w_j are separable from y if the slope of the factor price frontier in (i, j)-space is independent of output. Using Shephard's lemma, this, in turn, implies that the elasticities of the ith and the jth cost-minimizing demands with respect to output are equal. In particular, cost functions that are consistent with a homothetic technology satisfy a very strong form of this type of separability where all derived-demand elasticities with respect to output are equal. As noted earlier, such cost structures offer a natural interpretation in terms of aggregate inputs that coincides closely with the present discussion.

Strong separability of cost function: The cost function is *strongly separable* in the partition $\hat{\mathbf{I}}$ if

$$\frac{\partial}{\partial w_t}\left(\frac{\partial c(w,y)/\partial w_j}{\partial c(w,y)/\partial w_i}\right)=0, \quad i\in\mathbf{I}^v,\, j\in\mathbf{I}^k,\, t\notin\mathbf{I}^k\cup\mathbf{I}^v. \tag{3.14}$$

Strong separability, therefore, implies that the ratio of optimal derived demands from any two groups only depends on the prices in those two groups and output. As with the production function, strong separability of the cost function implies weak separability but not vice versa. To represent the cost function in terms of aggregator and macrofunctions, it proves especially useful to assume that each aggregator $c^i(y,w^i)$ is differentiable and $m>2$. The cost function can then be represented as either

$$c(w,y)=\Gamma(y)\left(\sum_i^m c^i(y,w^i)^{p(y)}\right)^{1/p(y)}, \quad 0\neq p(y)<1, \tag{3.15a}$$

or

$$c(w,y)=\Gamma(y)\prod_{i=1}^m c^i(y,w^i)^{p^i(y)}, \quad p^i(y)\geq 0, \tag{3.15b}$$

and $\sum_i p^i(y)=1$. Each c^i exhibits properties 2B.1–2B.5 and can again be interpreted as sectoral cost functions or composite prices. The representation in (3.15a) is particularly interesting since it is a generalization of the CES function introduced in Chapter 1. The second is a generalization of the well-known Cobb–Douglas function. The first implies that the Allen elasticity of substitution between two inputs from separate groups is simply $1-p(y)$, which for a given output level is constant. Performing the same calculation for (3.15b) implies that all cross-group Allen elasticities of substitution equal 1. Hence, strong separability implies that across groups, all inputs are Allen substitutes of the same degree. There is only room for complementary behavior among inputs that belong to the same group.

When each group contains only one price $(m=n)$ and the cost function is strongly separable, the cost function is *pricewise separable*. The Cobb–Douglas cost function and CES functions are pricewise separable.

If the cost function is strongly separable in $_o\hat{\mathbf{I}}$ with all aggregator functions differentiable, then, for $m>2$, it can be represented as either

$$c(w,y)=\Gamma(y)\left(\sum_{i=1}^m c^i(w^i)^p\right)^{1/p}, \quad 0\neq p\leq 1,$$

or

$$c(w,y)=\Gamma(y)\prod_{i=1}^m c^i(w^i)^{p^i}, \quad \sum_{i=1}^m p^i=1.$$

where each c^i is linearly homogeneous. Accordingly, a cost function is strongly separable $_o\hat{\mathbf{I}}$ only if the underlying technology is homothetic.

3.3b   Equivalence of separable production and costs

The existence of a duality between $c(w, y)$ and $f(x)$ as well as the similarity of the definitions of separability might cause one to suspect that separability of $f(x)$ in $\hat{\mathbf{I}}$ implies separability of $c(w, y)$ in $\hat{\mathbf{I}}$. This is not generally true. Separability in costs generally implies something different about the underlying technology than a separable production function.

There are instances, however, where separability of $c(w, y)$ in $\hat{\mathbf{I}}$ implies separability of $f(x)$ in $\hat{\mathbf{I}}$ and vice versa. Proceeding with a discussion of these cases requires some definitions and further assumptions. The main result of this section is that $c(w, y)$ is weakly separable in the extended partition $_o\hat{\mathbf{I}} = \{0, \mathbf{I}^1, \mathbf{I}^2, ..., \mathbf{I}^m\}$ if and only if $f(x)$ is weakly separable in the partition $\hat{\mathbf{I}}$ *and* each aggregator function f^i is homothetic. Production functions satisfying this latter property are called *weakly homothetically separable*. Notice, in particular, that *this does not imply that $f(x)$ itself is homothetic*.

To demonstrate this claim, note that the first-order conditions for an interior solution require that

$$\frac{w_j}{w_k} = \frac{\partial f(x)/\partial x_j}{\partial f(x)/\partial x_k}, \quad (k, j) \in \mathbf{I}^i \ \forall i. \tag{3.16}$$

If $f(x)$ is weakly separable, the right-hand side of (3.16) only depends on x^i so it can be rewritten more suggestively as

$$\frac{w_j}{w_k} = g_j^i(x^i). \tag{3.16'}$$

Homotheticity of each f^i function implies that $g_j^i(\cdot)$ is homogeneous of degree zero, which gives

$$\tilde{w}_j = g_j^i(\tilde{x}^i, 1) = h_j^i(\tilde{x}^i), \tag{3.16''}$$

where $\tilde{w}_j = w_j/w_k$ and $\tilde{x}^i$ is the vector with typical element x_v/x_k for $(j, k, v) \in \mathbf{I}^i$. Since this is true for each $\mathbf{I}^i$ under weak homothetic separability, (3.16'') can be solved to obtain the vector-valued function

$$\tilde{x}^i = h^i(\tilde{w}^i),$$

where $\tilde{w}^i$ is the vector with typical element given by the left-hand side of (3.16''). Cost-minimizing input ratios are here independent of the level of output. Further, each vector of normalized inputs only depends on the corresponding subvector $\tilde{w}^i$. By Shephard's lemma, each element of $\tilde{x}^i$ can be represented as

$$\tilde{x}^i_j = \frac{\partial c/\partial w_j}{\partial c/\partial w_k} = h^i_j(\tilde{w}^i), \quad (j,k) \in \mathbf{I}^i. \tag{3.17}$$

Expression (3.17) implies that

$$\frac{\partial}{\partial w_t} \frac{\partial c(w,y)/\partial w_j}{\partial c(w,y)/\partial w_k} = 0, \quad (j,k) \in \mathbf{I}^i, \ t \notin \mathbf{I}^i, \tag{3.18}$$

and

$$\frac{\partial}{\partial y} \frac{\partial c(w,y)/\partial w_j}{\partial c(w,y)/\partial w_k} = 0, \quad j,k \in \mathbf{I}^i.$$

Thus, weak homothetic separability implies that the cost function is *both* weakly separable in factor prices and separable in output. Furthermore, the duality theorems that established a one-to-one correspondence between $c(w,y)$ and $f(x)$ ensure that weak homothetic separability is a necessary and sufficient condition for the cost function to be represented as $C^*(y, c^1(w^1), ..., c^m(w^m))$. Postulating a cost function in this general form in applied or theoretical work restricts the underlying production function to be weakly homothetically separable.

Previously, we saw that one way of interpreting a cost function weakly separable in the extended partition $_0\hat{\mathbf{I}}$ was as the culmination of a two-stage cost minimization process. In the first stage, the cost of producing a single unit of an aggregate input was minimized, and in the second stage, these aggregate inputs were combined in a cost-minimizing fashion to produce the output. For the prices of these aggregate inputs to be independent of output required weak separability in the extended partition. This implies that the associated production function is weakly homothetically separable in the associated input partition $\hat{\mathbf{I}}$. From an empirical perspective, the existence of a two-stage cost minimization process suggests one way of attacking empirical estimation of a cost function that depends on too many input prices to be handled efficiently for a given data set. That is, in the first stage, separate cost functions are estimated for the aggregate inputs using the prices of the inputs in the respective subgroups. In the second stage, these sectoral cost functions are interpreted as aggregate input prices and are used as the basis of estimating a cost function dependent on y and the aggregate input prices.

Exercise 3.3. An obvious extension of these results is to the case where each input aggregator $f^i(x^i)$ is linearly homogeneous. In this instance, $f(x)$ is homothetic in each subvector x^i. Use this condition to derive a general representation for the corresponding cost function.

One might expect these results to generalize to the case of a production function that is strongly separable with homothetic aggregators. Such a function is called *strongly homothetically separable*. As with weak homothetic separability, strong homothetic separability does not imply overall homotheticity of the production function. Unfortunately, it also does not imply that the associated cost function is simultaneously strongly separable in the partition $_0\hat{\mathbf{I}}$. The reason is simple enough. The first-order conditions for cost minimization require that

$$\frac{w_j}{w_v} = \frac{\partial f(x)/\partial x_j}{\partial f(x)/\partial x_v}, \quad j \in \mathbf{I}^i, \, v \in \mathbf{I}^m. \tag{3.19}$$

The right-hand side of (3.19), however, is not generally homogeneous of degree zero since it does not represent the ratio of derivatives of a homothetic function. Hence, the normalization utilized in (3.16) is not generally available, and we cannot proceed as in the prior proof. However, if $i = m$, the right-hand side of (3.16) is homogeneous of degree zero, and we can proceed as before. Thus, strong homothetic separability of the production function does imply weak separability of the cost function in the partition $_0\hat{\mathbf{I}}$. The converse, however, is obviously not true. For strongly separable production to imply strongly separable costs, it is necessary to also assume that each of the aggregator functions is itself linearly homogeneous, which in turn implies that $f(x)$ is homothetic. The preceding arguments can then be modified to establish that the associated cost function can be written in the form of (3.12). The same general result applies to factor-wise separable production functions.

3.3c   *Using separability*

So far, relatively little has been said about why one may want to specify separable cost or production functions. Quite obviously, assuming separability significantly restricts the form of the cost or the production function. For example, if it is assumed that the production function is factor-wise separable and homothetic, we know the exact form the cost function must take. However, the importance of separability lies a little deeper than the imposition of structure. As noted earlier, the natural interpretation of a production aggregator is as an aggregate input. Similarly, cost aggregators can be interpreted as sectoral cost functions or composite prices in the case of weak separability. However, if the production function is weakly homothetically separable, these composite input prices can be specified independent of the level of output. This leads to the natural interpretation of these cost aggregators as exact price indices for the associated aggregate inputs.

One of the most distressing realities of applied econometric analysis is that there is often insufficient data or computational ability to deal with more than a relatively few number of variables. In the area of econometric production analysis, this often leads to the aggregation of certain groups of inputs or outputs into aggregate input or output indexes that are then used to fit either cost or production functions. Aggregation is required by the fact that there are simply too many separate inputs into the production process to allow meaningful statistical analysis. As an example, consider a typical grains farmer who uses a variety of fertilizers, herbicides, and pesticides. At the same time, he or she also uses many types of capital equipment that variously might include a planter, disk, plow, combine, tractors, and so on. The list is quite long. Rarely will the econometrician have access to an array of data sources, econometric techniques, or computational facilities that will allow inclusion of all of the equipment as separate inputs to the production process even though they clearly are separate inputs. He or she is then faced with the traditional problem that economists have always been faced with when dealing with even the simplest problems. The solution is either simplify the problem in some manner or give up since the data is insufficient to permit further analysis. If the first course is chosen, the economist will usually arrive at some answer that is certainly flawed in some aspects. If the second is chosen, no answer is found since the problem is too complex and, therefore, should not be attempted. The second course seems rather nihilistic and dooms the economist to either purely theoretical analysis or analysis of extremely simple problems. Usually one is better off with some information, no matter how imperfect, than with no information. The concepts underlying separable cost and production functions are a partial answer to these problems. They afford the applied researcher with a way to go about isolating input categories that can be treated as fairly distinct and are capable of being aggregated. For example, one of the $c^i(w^i)$ may be a price index for an aggregate capital variable that would include the price of tractors, disks, and so on. Clearly, this is quite restrictive in that it makes some very distinct assumptions about how tractors or combines interact with noncapital inputs. But at least it is a start in the direction of answering the question. Moreover, the results of this section imply that the specification of a cost function in terms of some aggregate price indexes and output presumes the existence of a weak homothetic separability. Thus, studies like the Ball–Chambers study mentioned earlier clearly limit themselves to the family of weakly homothetically separate technologies.

3.4 Concluding remarks

This chapter and the one preceding it attempt to give the reader a thorough introduction to the dual approach to the theory of cost. An effort has been made to derive results in a step-by-step manner to allow the reader to become familiar with the mechanics of the dual approach. The best way to come to grips with the more modern techniques, especially if one is used to thinking in terms of the more traditional approach, is by grappling with a single optimization problem using the dual approach in a quite detailed manner. Once some degree of proficiency in handling cost functions is achieved, it is relatively straightforward to extend the analysis to other producer optimization problems.

Such problems (profit maximization) are the subject of the next chapter. As the reader will undoubtedly note, therefore, much of the development that follows is considerably more terse than the preceding discussion. The reasons for this are two: to prevent boring the reader with needless mathematical detail and to encourage the interested reader to exercise the facility with dual methods developed here to extend the analysis presented.

CHAPTER 4

The profit function

4.1 Introduction

If most economists were asked what they thought motivates firm behavior under certainty, they would likely respond "profit maximization." This chapter uses developments in preceding chapters to analyze the economic behavior of profit maximizers. In an attempt to economize as much as possible, the presentation relies heavily on the properties of cost functions developed in Chapter 2.

In almost all instances in Chapters 2 and 3, detailed and at places quite lengthy derivations of results were given. But this chapter takes a somewhat different course. Namely, much of the mathematical detail presented in Chapters 2 and 3 has been eliminated. There were two reasons for doing this: The first is that it hopefully encourages readers to use developments in Chapters 2 and 3 to derive formally the results cited here. Second, many of the arguments associated with the profit function are virtually equivalent to arguments made in Chapters 2 and 3. Quite literally, the reader only has to change the names slightly for the arguments to apply. Therefore, little seemed to be served by taking the reader over the same mathematical ground as covered previously.

Thus, what follows relies heavily on graphic techniques to motivate results intuitively while leaving it to the reader to provide the formal justification for many results. In some places, all that is done is to give readers the result while asking them to provide a proof using methods parallel to those developed in Chapter 2 or 3. A somewhat more formal treatment of a multioutput generalization of the single-output profit function is provided in Chapter 7. Readers desiring a more formal treatment of the profit function may wish to refer to that chapter after finishing the present one.

The reader should not infer from this lack of rigor that the cost or the production function should be considered more important than the profit function. In fact, just the opposite is true. But what is true is that like any other tool, dual methods can only be learned with practice. Fleshing out the derivations in this chapter hopefully will give the reader this practice.

120

The genealogy of the profit function is a little more distinct than that of either the cost or the production function. Hotelling clearly had conceptualized such a function in the 1930s. However, it was not until McFadden's work [and that of his associates at Berkeley] that the dual relationship between profit and production functions was exhaustively investigated. McFadden (1978a) and Gorman (1968) were among the first individuals to establish the existence of a duality between the profit function and the direct technology. Moreover, the work of McFadden and his associates was perhaps the principal impetus behind the revolution in empirical production analysis that exploited the theoretical developments of duality theory in applied contexts.

In what follows, the properties of profit functions are first derived. These properties of profit functions are then used to discuss the comparative statics of a profit-maximizing firm. Section 4.4 discusses the dual relationship between cost and profit functions using the natural conjugate relationship between these functions. Discussions of short-run profit maximization and the structure of profit functions conclude the chapter.

4.2   Definition of the profit function

Like the cost function, the profit function is the mathematical representation of the solution to an economic agent's optimization problem, in this case, profit maximization. By definition, the profit function is

$$\Pi(p, w) = \max_{x \geq 0}\{pf(x) - w \cdot x\}$$
$$= \max_{y \geq 0}\{py - c(w, y)\}, \tag{4.1}$$

where p is the output price producers take as given. The equivalence of the two representations in (4.1) is derived from the following logic. Separate profit maximization into two stages. The first stage, which may be intuitively thought of as the short run, involves maximizing profit for a given output. The second stage (the long run) is then to choose output to maximize long-run profit. When output is fixed, revenue is also fixed, and profits are maximized by minimizing costs. Hence, fixed-output profit maximization yields the same input configuration as cost minimization. Having devoted an entire chapter to discussing the properties of the cost function, the second representation in (4.1) offers a natural procedure for investigating the profit function. It also allows us to draw freely on arguments in Chapter 2 and, thus, in some instances mitigates the need for complicated mathematical arguments. Finally, this representation makes it easier to look at the dual relationship between cost and profit functions

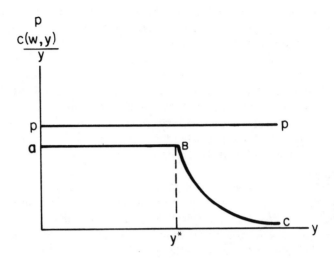

Figure 4.1 Possibility of infinite profit.

in a simple manner that relies on standard arguments in optimization theory.

The first order of business is to ascertain whether a solution to (4.1) exists. As it stands, the answer is, not necessarily! The reason is illustrated in Figure 4.1, which depicts an average cost function consistent with properties 2B.1–2B.6; average cost is given by the kinked curve ABC. The associated cost function is

$$c(w, y) = \begin{cases} ay, & 0 \le y \le y^*; \\ ay^*, & y^* \le y. \end{cases}$$

Although this cost function satisfies all of properties 2B in terms of y, it is obvious from Figure 4.1 that profit is not always bounded. For output levels approaching infinity, average cost approaches zero and profit goes to infinity. (Notice profit would be unbounded in Figure 4.1 even if average cost remained constant at a instead of declining as output grew above y^*.) Since a well-defined cost function is consistent with infinite profit, guaranteeing the existence of a solution to (4.1) requires further assumptions. The additional assumptions made are that $c(w, y)$ is continuous in y, and the set

$$\phi(p, w) = \{y : p \ge c(w, y)/y\}$$

is nonempty and compact (see Appendix).

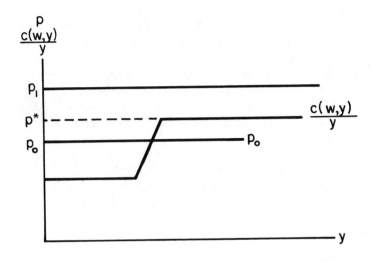

Figure 4.2 Maximum profit only locally defined.

The reader will recall from Chapter 2 that $c(w, y)$ was never shown to be continuous in y; to derive such a property, further assumptions on $f(x)$ would have been necessary [however, twice-continuous differentiability of $f(x)$ and strict quasi-concavity would have sufficed]. At present, however, we are trying to ensure that a maximum exists, and one method is to impose sufficient structure on the problem to satisfy the conditions of the Weierstrass theorem. The first step is to ensure that the objective function is continuous; this requires continuity of $c(w, y)$ in y. The second step, roughly put, is to rule out unboundedness and to guarantee that a maximum actually exists; this is the purpose of requiring $\phi(p, w)$ to be compact and nonempty. By imposing this condition, one limits the generality of the analysis. To see why, consider Figure 4.2, where two possible situations are illustrated. When the market price is less than p^*, say, p_0, profits are bounded, and a solution to (4.1) exists. However, when the market price is greater than p^*, say, p_1, profit is unbounded, and no solution exists. Consequently, the profit function is not well defined for all prices. Figure 4.2 graphically illustrates what our notation suggests, that is, $\phi(p, w)$ depends on both the price of output and input prices. In other words, being able to solve (4.1) for a particular (p, w) configuration does not ensure that one can solve (4.1) for all p and w. The ensuing analysis is, therefore, strictly local in nature and does not necessarily apply over all possible prices. Such an analysis is justified on two counts: In applied analysis, one rarely encounters data with an infinite range; moreover, one is usually hard-pressed to specify functions that simultaneously are empirically tractable and possess all requisite theoretical properties globally; and this assumption and the associated caveat, while important, are mainly mathematical in nature. In the real world, one does not observe either infinite profit or infinite output as is suggested by Figures 4.1 and 4.2. Therefore, reason suggests that something approximating this assumption applies. Having mentioned these caveats, it is important to note that $\phi(tp, tw) = \phi(p, w)$; that is, multiplying all prices by a positive scalar does not affect this set. Relative prices must change if the composition of $\phi(p, w)$ is to change. In what follows, always presume whenever necessary that this assumption does not preclude differentiation and related manipulations; moreover, the reader will not be constantly reminded that the arguments only strictly apply in a relatively small neighborhood.

Properties of the profit function: Armed with these assumptions, one can show that if $c(w, y)$ satisfies properties 2B.2–2B.6, then $\Pi(p, w)$ satisfies the following properties.

> *Properties of $\Pi(p, w)$ (4C):*
>
> 1. $\Pi(p, w) \geq 0$;
> 2. if $p^1 \geq p^2$, then $\Pi(p^1, w) \geq \Pi(p^2, w)$ (nondecreasing in p);
> 3. if $w^1 \geq w^2$, then $\Pi(p, w^1) \leq \Pi(p, w^2)$ (nonincreasing in w);
> 4. $\Pi(p, w)$ is convex and continuous in (p, w); and
> 5. $\Pi(tp, tw) = t\Pi(p, w)$, $t > 0$ (positive linear homogeneity).

Most of these properties are relatively self-evident and easily demonstrated. Furthermore, given the detailed derivation and discussion of closely related properties for $c(w, y)$ in Chapter 2 and the similarity of the arguments, it hardly seems productive to reproduce almost completely parallel arguments in a slightly different context. Hence, the following discussion of these properties is somewhat terse. Hopefully, this will encourage the reader to develop some of the arguments more completely; exercises are added for that purpose.

Property 4C.1 says that a producer never accepts negative profits if all inputs are perfectly variable. Intuitively, this should be obvious and is demonstrated by noting that the assumption of no fixed cost (property 2B.6) implies that producing at zero output yields

$$p \cdot 0 - c(w, 0) = 0.$$

An entrepreneur can always not produce and make zero profit. Therefore, if he or she chooses to do otherwise, profit cannot be negative.

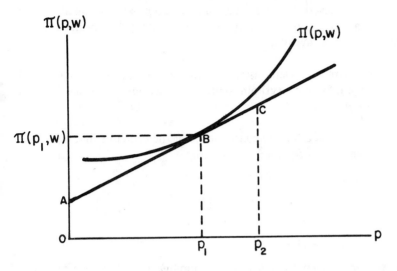

Figure 4.3 Hotelling's lemma and convexity of profit function.

Property 4C.2 is also easy to prove and should be intuitively clear. Suppose that at p^1 the individual chooses to produce an output equal to y^1. If price then rises to p^2, the individual always has the option of producing y^1 and making a profit of $p^2y^1 - c(w, y^1) \geq p^1y^1 - c(w, y^1) = \Pi(p^1, w)$. Therefore, the very worst that can be done is to increase profit by the amount $(p^2 - p^1)y^1$. Although perhaps not so transparent, property 4C.3 is also quite obvious and easy to show. Therefore, the reader is encouraged to do the next exercise.

Exercise 4.1. Show that the profit function is nonincreasing in w.

Property 4C.4 closely parallels the concavity of the cost function developed in Chapter 2. Thus, we only develop the convexity of $\Pi(p, w)$ in p graphically and leave it to the reader to develop a formal proof and parallel graphic arguments for w as an exercise. (Notice, however, that property 4C.4 is a special case of Lemma 15 developed in the Appendix; also see p. 270 for a formal proof.) Consider Figure 4.3, where the line segment emanating from A and going through B has a slope given by y_1, where y_1 is the profit-maximizing output for price p_1. At this price, profit is given by $\Pi(p_1, w)$. As demonstrated earlier, if price rises to, say, p_2, the producer can always keep output and thus cost constant but still increase profit by moving to C. However, since this represents the minimum that can be achieved, intuition suggests that $\Pi(p, w)$ as a function of p should lie above the line segment ABC, suggesting the upturned shape characteristic of convexity.

> **Exercise 4.2.** Demonstrate formally that $\Pi(p, w)$ is convex in (p, w). Develop a graphical argument that illustrates that $\Pi(p, w)$ is convex in w.

Property 4C.5 is a further consequence of the principle that only relative prices matter in economics. Formally,

$$\Pi(tp, tw) = \max\{(tp)y - c(tw, y)\}$$
$$= \max\{tpy - tc(w, y)\}$$
$$= t \max\{py - c(w, y)\}$$
$$= t\Pi(p, w),$$

where the second equality follows by the homogeneity of the cost function.

Until now, nothing has been said about the differentiability of the profit function. The result in property 4C.6 is analogous to Shephard's lemma:

6. If the profit function is differentiable in p and w, the unique profit-maximizing supply and derived-demand functions are

$$y(p, w) = \frac{\partial \Pi(p, w)}{\partial p} \quad \text{and} \quad x_i(p, w) = -\frac{\partial \Pi(p, w)}{\partial w_i} \quad \forall i,$$

where $y(p, w)$ and $x_i(p, w)$ are the respective profit-maximizing quantities. If unique profit-maximizing supply and derived demands exist, the profit function is differentiable (*Hotelling's lemma*).

As with the cost function, the partial derivatives of the profit function have important economic content. Moreover, there are important econometric implications associated with Hotelling's lemma; once a well-behaved profit function is specified, the lemma offers an easy way of recapturing well-behaved supply and derived-demand equations. Much more will be said about this in succeeding discussions, but for now let us construct a proof of the first part of the lemma. Suppose that y^1 is the profit-maximizing output for prices (p^1, w^1). The definition of the profit function then implies, for any other price configuration,

$$\Pi(p, w^1) \geq py^1 - c(w^1, y^1),$$

which in turn means that the function

$$L^*(p, w^1, y^1) = \Pi(p, w^1) - py^1 + c(w^1, y^1)$$

is minimized at p^1, w^1. The first-order condition for p and the envelope theorem (Appendix), respectively, require

$$\frac{\partial L^*(p^1, w^1, y^1)}{\partial p} = \frac{\partial \Pi(p^1, w^1)}{\partial p} - y^1 = 0,$$

$$\frac{\partial L^*(p^1, w^1, y^1)}{\partial w_i} = \frac{\partial \Pi(p^1, w^1)}{\partial w_i} + \frac{\partial c(w^1, y^1)}{\partial w_i} = 0.$$

When combined with Shephard's lemma, these equalities establish the result. This demonstration also establishes that the profit-maximizing derived demands equal the cost-minimizing derived demands evaluated at the profit-maximizing output. This result directly parallels the earlier result that long-run, cost-minimizing derived demand for variable inputs equals the short-run, cost-minimizing derived demand for variable inputs evaluated at the fixed-input vector that minimizes long-run cost. And, as before, this result offers a natural method of decomposing derived demands. In addition, second-order conditions for this problem imply that $\Pi(p, w)$ is convex in p. Also note that the matrix

$$\begin{bmatrix} \dfrac{\partial^2 \Pi(p, w)}{\partial p^2} & \dfrac{\partial^2 \Pi(p, w)}{\partial p\, \partial w'} \\[3mm] \dfrac{\partial^2 \Pi(p, w)}{\partial w\, \partial p} & \dfrac{\partial^2 \Pi(p, w)}{\partial w\, \partial w'} \end{bmatrix}$$

is symmetric and positive semidefinite. Hence, at least in the neighborhood of a solution to this minimization problem, $\Pi(p, w)$ must be convex in p and w since the Hessian matrix of a function is positive semidefinite if and only if the function is convex (see Appendix).

Rather than demonstrating the second part of Hotelling's lemma formally, I instead follow the example set by Chapter 2 and present an instance where profit-maximizing supply is not unique and then show that the associated profit function is not differentiable. Consider the cost function

$$c(w, y) = \begin{cases} ay, & 0 \le y \le y^*; \\ ay^* + b(y - y^*), & y^* \le y \le y^0, \ b > a; \\ ay^* + b(y^0 - y^*) + c(y - y^0), & y^0 \le y, \ c > b. \end{cases}$$

This cost function is illustrated graphically in Figure 4.4, from which it is apparent that $\phi(p, w)$ is nonempty and compact for $p < c$. For prices $p < a$, the profit-maximizing supply and, hence, profit are zero. When

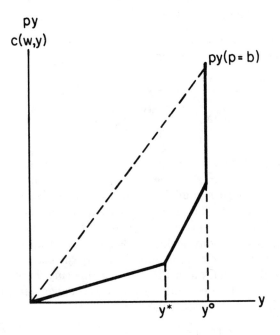

Figure 4.4 Maximizing profit.

$p = a$, profit is still zero, but the producer is indifferent as to whether 0, y^*, or any output between 0 and y^* is produced. When $b > p > a$, profits are maximized by producing at y^*, and profit is given by

$$\Pi(p, w) = (p - a)y^*.$$

When $b = p$, profit with output y^* is

$$(p - a)y^* = (b - a)y^*,$$

whereas if production occurs at y^0, profit is

$$py^0 - ay^* - b(y^0 - y^*) = (b - a)y^*.$$

Profit is the same whether y^* or y^0 is produced. Moreover, as is clear geometrically, profits are the same at any output level between y^0 and y^* when $p = b$. When $c > p > b$, profit is maximized at y^0 and is

$$\Pi(p, w) = (p - b)y^0 + (b - a)y^*.$$

This profit function is depicted graphically in Figure 4.5. Notice in particular that at prices (a) and (b), where a range of possible profit-maximizing

Π (p,w)

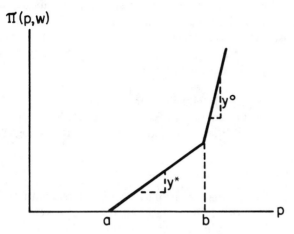

Figure 4.5 Profit for piecewise linear cost function.

outputs exists, the profit function is not differentiable. This point is pursued more thoroughly in the following example.

Example 4.1. Consider the family of technologies

$$c(w, y) = \begin{cases} \gamma y c(w), & 0 \le y \le y^*, \\ [\gamma y^* + \beta(y - y^*)]c(w), & y^* \le y \le y^0, \\ [(\gamma - \beta)y^* + (\beta - \delta)y^0 + \delta y]c(w), & y^0 \le y, \end{cases}$$

where $\gamma < \beta < \delta$ and $c(w)$ is any concave, linearly homogeneous, and nondecreasing function. For example, one might have

$$c(w) = \sum_{i=1}^{n} \frac{w_i}{\alpha_i} \quad \text{or} \quad c(w) = \min_{w}\{w_1/\beta_1, \ldots, w_n/\beta_n\},$$

that is, unit cost functions associated with a Leontief and a linear technology, respectively. By construction, the set $\phi(p, w)$ is compact so long as $p/c(w) < \delta$. And by arguments analogous to those just presented,

$$\Pi(p, w) = \begin{cases} 0, & 0 \le p/c(w) \le \gamma; \\ [p - \gamma c(w)]y^*, & \gamma < p/c(w) \le \beta; \\ [p - \beta c(w)]y^0 + [\beta - \gamma]y^* c(w), & \beta < p/c(w) < \delta. \end{cases}$$

The graph of this function parallels that presented in Figure 4.5, and this function satisfies properties 4C.1–4C.5. However, it does not satisfy Hotelling's lemma in all instances. Suppose that the linear technology applies; then there are instances (see Chapter 2) where no unique cost-minimizing demand exists and hence where no unique profit-maximizing derived demand exists. Moreover, when $p = \gamma c(w)$ or $p = \beta c(w)$, the profit function is not differentiable in p, and even though there may exist a profit-maximizing output level, it is not unique.

> **Exercise 4.3.** Verify Hotelling's lemma graphically (Figure 4.3) and that the profit function in Example 4.1 satisfies properties 4C.1–4C.5 for both the linear and the Leontief technologies.

4.3   Comparative statics and the profit function

When Hotelling's lemma applies, the profit function offers a natural and easy means of pursuing comparative static analysis. However, even if Hotelling's lemma does not apply, some very important inferences about derived-demand and supply behavior can be made by utilizing arguments that closely parallel the discussion in Chapter 2 of the fundamental inequality of cost minimization. Consider two separate price configurations (p, w) and (p^1, w^1). Corresponding to these $(n+1)$-tuples, define the profit-maximizing supply and derived demands by (y, x) and (y^1, x^1). By profit maximization, one obtains

$$py - wx \geq py^1 - wx^1 \quad \text{and} \quad p^1y^1 - w^1x^1 \geq p^1y - w^1x.$$

Adding these two inequalities yields the *fundamental inequality of profit maximization*

$$(p^1 - p)(y^1 - y) - (w^1 - w) \cdot (x^1 - x) \geq 0. \tag{4.2}$$

Even if the profit function is not differentiable and unique, profit-maximizing derived demands or supply does not exist, and expression (4.2) lets one infer the direction of change in supply caused by an increase in p. If only p changes,

$$(p^1 - p)(y^1 - y) \geq 0.$$

Supply cannot decrease if output price rises. Expression (4.2), therefore, is a very general affirmation of the basic laws of supply. Be they discontinuous, multivalued, or whatever, supply correspondences are not downward sloping in the price of output. The derivation of (4.2) only relies on the presumption that profits can be maximized and on no other specific restrictions on the cost or production functions. As such, it is likely one of the most general results that can be developed in economics. On the other hand, suppose that output price remains constant; then (4.2) implies

$$(w^1 - w) \cdot (x^1 - x) \le 0,$$

which is a restatement of the fundamental inequality of cost minimization from Chapter 2. Having demonstrated the ability to say something about comparative statics even in the absence of differentiability, let us now turn to an analysis of the properties of $x_i(p, w)$ and $y(p, w)$ that follow directly from the properties of the profit function.

Since $\Pi(p, w)$ is linearly homogeneous, Hotelling's lemma gives

$$y(tp, tw) = y(p, w), \tag{4.3}$$

$$x_i(tp, tw) = x_i(p, w), \quad i = 1, 2, \dots, n, \ t > 0.$$

That is, both output supply and derived demand are homogeneous of degree zero in p and w; only relative price changes affect supply or demand. Expression (4.3) is a direct consequence of $\phi(tp, tw) = \phi(p, w)$, which implies that the set of potentially, profit-maximizing outputs is invariant to proportional changes in prices.

Hotelling's lemma and differentiation give

$$\frac{\partial y(p, w)}{\partial p} \ge 0, \tag{4.4}$$

$$\frac{\partial x_i(p, w)}{\partial w_i} \le 0, \tag{4.5}$$

$$\frac{\partial x_i(p, w)}{\partial w_j} = \frac{\partial x_j(p, w)}{\partial w_i}, \tag{4.6}$$

$$\frac{\partial y(p, w)}{\partial w_i} = -\frac{\partial x_i(p, w)}{\partial p}. \tag{4.7}$$

Expressions (4.4) and (4.5) are restatements of the fundamental inequality of profit maximization for a twice-continuously differentiable profit function. They are direct consequences of the convexity of $\Pi(p, w)$ implying that the Hessian is positive semidefinite. Expressions (4.6) and (4.7) are *reciprocity* or *symmetry relationships* attributable to the twice-continuous differentiability of the profit function. As with cost minimization, expressions (4.3)–(4.7) are exhaustive in that they completely summarize the comparative statics properties of the derived demands and supply. Put another way, they represent a set of conditions on smoothly differentiable supply and derived-demand functions that ensure these functions can be "integrated" to recapture the technology, as represented by $c(w, y)$, that generated them. More will be said about this when the issue of duality is addressed. Although these conditions are exhaustive from a mathematical perspective, one can portray some of this information in an alternative fashion that may be illuminating intuitively. Specifically, as noted, one can decompose derived-demand responses to changes in p and w into two components, each of which has some interesting content.

Decomposing profit-maximizing derived demands: The proof of Hotelling's lemma showed that the partial derivative of the profit function with respect to w_i equals the partial derivative of the cost function with respect to w_i evaluated at the profit-maximizing supply. By Shephard's lemma, this partial derivative of the cost function equals the cost-minimizing demand for x_i. Hence, the profit-maximizing demand for x_i equals the cost-minimizing demand required to produce the profit-maximizing supply. This follows directly from our earlier discussion on partitioning profit maximization into two stages. In the first stage, the least cost way of producing output is found, and in the second, the profit-maximizing output is chosen. However, it is instructive to show directly that the profit-maximizing derived demands provide the least cost way to produce the profit-maximizing supply. Denote the vector of profit-maximizing demands by x^0, the profit-maximizing supply by y^0, and the least cost way to produce y^0 by x^*. By cost minimization, $wx^0 \geq wx^*$ since both x^0 and x^* belong to $V(y^0)$. But this implies that $py^0 - wx^* \geq py^0 - wx^0 = \Pi(p, w)$. Thus, if $x^* \neq x^0$, there are two possibilities. Either wx^* equals wx^0 and there is not a unique profit-maximizing derived demand vector (in this instance, Hotelling's lemma does not apply) or $wx^0 > wx^*$ and x^0 is not the profit-maximizing demand. Thus, if x^0 is the unique profit-maximizing demand, it must equal the cost-minimizing derived demand. Therefore, one can write

$$x_i(p, w) = x_i(w, y(p, w))$$

when Hotelling's lemma is applicable.

This last identity makes the following decompositions of the profit-maximizing derived-demand response to changes in p and w_j valid:

$$\frac{\partial x_i(p, w)}{\partial p} = \frac{\partial x_i(w, y^*)}{\partial y} \frac{\partial y(p, w)}{\partial p}, \tag{4.8}$$

$$\frac{\partial x_i(p, w)}{\partial w_j} = \frac{\partial x_i(w, y^*)}{\partial w_j} + \frac{\partial x_i(w, y^*)}{\partial y} \frac{\partial y(p, w)}{\partial w_j}, \tag{4.9}$$

where $y^* = y(p, w)$.

The intuition behind (4.8) is easily visualized with Figure 4.6. Let point B on isoquant y_0 be the original profit-maximizing point, and let p rise.

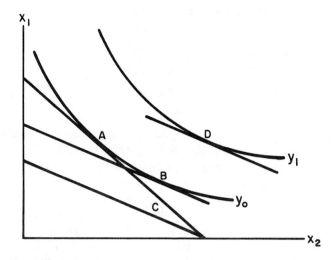

Figure 4.6 Decomposing comparative static effects.

The immediate response of output is to move out the expansion path to D; $\partial y(p, w)/\partial p$ in (4.8) represents this expansion. As output increases, however, the input mix adjusts; the extent to which the ith input adjusts is determined by how a cost-minimizing demand responds to changes in output.

One can also use expression (4.8) with expression (4.7) to establish an interesting relationship between output adjustment to changes in w_i and output adjustment to changes in p. Using the reciprocity relationship in (4.7) and some simple manipulation gives

$$\frac{\partial y(p, w)/\partial w_i}{\partial y(p, w)/\partial p} = \frac{-\partial x_i(w, y^*)}{\partial y}. \tag{4.10}$$

Since supply is nondecreasing in p, expression (4.10) implies that a change in w_i causes supply to adjust in the direction opposite to which the cost-minimizing demand for x_i adjusts when output rises. For example, whenever the ith input is normal, an increase in w_i will cause profit-maximizing output to decline. Conversely, if x_i is inferior, output rises if w_i rises. When the latter case prevails, we refer to output as being *regressive in w_i*.

Although expression (4.9) is more informative than earlier representations of $\partial x_i(p, w)/\partial w_j$, it can be written in several alternative forms by using results already developed. Namely,

$$\frac{\partial x_i(p,w)}{\partial w_j} = \frac{\partial x_i(w,y^*)}{\partial w_j} - \frac{\partial x_i(w,y^*)}{\partial y} \frac{\partial x_j(p,w)}{\partial p}$$

$$= \frac{\partial x_i(w,y^*)}{\partial w_j} + \frac{[\partial y(p,w)/\partial w_i][\partial x_j(p,w)/\partial p]}{\partial y(p,w)/\partial p}$$

$$= \frac{\partial x_i(w,y^*)}{\partial w_j} - \frac{[\partial x_i(p,w)/\partial p][\partial x_j(p,w)/\partial p]}{\partial y(p,w)/\partial p}. \tag{4.11}$$

The first of the three equations listed follows from applying the reciprocity relation (4.7); the next equality follows by applying (4.10); and the final equality follows by another application of the reciprocity relationship. Since each of the expressions in (4.11) is equivalent, which one is ultimately used is largely a matter of personal choice. The second two equalities are particularly attractive from an empirical perspective because they permit use of measures available from the profit function to recapture information about the properties of the cost-minimizing demands. These relationships demonstrate that a change in an input price evokes two analytically distinct adjustments; one is a pure substitution effect along a given isoquant (from A to B in Figure 4.6), and the other is a movement across isoquants associated with the output change induced by the factor price change. Of course, this decomposition is quite analogous (although not exactly) to the Slutsky decomposition familiar from consumer theory.

In the case of own-price effects, the last expression in (4.11) is interesting because it implies

$$\frac{\partial x_i(p,w)}{\partial w_i} \leq \frac{\partial x_i(w,y^*)}{\partial w_i}, \tag{4.12}$$

which is another manifestation of the Le Chatelier–Samuelson principle. Instead of comparing fixed- and variable-input adjustment, we now compare input adjustments associated with output-constrained profit maximization and unconstrained profit maximization. Expression (4.12) is a direct consequence of Hotelling's lemma. To derive that result, it was shown that

$$\Pi(p,w) \geq py^1 - c(w,y^1),$$

where y^1 is the profit-maximizing output for prices (p^1,w^1). Thus, one can visualize $py^1 - c(w,y^1)$ as a "short-run" profit function with the short run defined by output fixed at y^1. Given that this inequality holds and that the "long-" and "short-run" profit functions coincide at (p^1,w^1), that is,

$$\Pi(p^1, w^1) = p^1 y^1 - c(w^1, y^1),$$

$\Pi(p, w)$ is the upper envelope of the short-run (fixed-output) profit functions. Because $c(w, y)$ is concave in w, the short-run profit functions are convex in w. But the fact that $\Pi(p, w)$ is the upper envelope of these convex short-run functions means that its gradient in w must be more steeply sloped than the gradient of the short-run functions. Hotelling's lemma says that the gradient of each of these functions is the corresponding profit-maximizing derived-demand vector. Combining this with the envelope result means that the long-run derived-demand curves must be more steeply sloped than the short-run (cost-minimizing) derived demands, whence Equation (4.12).

Finally, upon converting (4.11) into elasticity form, one obtains

$$\epsilon_{ij}(p, w) = \epsilon_{ij} + \epsilon_{yj}(p, w)\epsilon_{ip}(p, w)/\epsilon_{yp}(p, w),$$

where

$$\epsilon_{ij}(p, w) \equiv \frac{\partial \ln x_i(p, w)}{\partial \ln w_j},$$

$$\epsilon_{yj}(p, w) = \frac{\partial \ln y(p, w)}{\partial \ln w_j},$$

$$\epsilon_{ip}(p, w) = \frac{\partial \ln x_i(p, w)}{\partial \ln w_j},$$

$$\epsilon_{yp}(p, w) = \frac{\partial \ln y(p, w)}{\partial \ln p}.$$

These results give calculating formulas for the various elasticities of substitution that are defined in Chapter 3.

Exercise 4.4. Calculate formulas for the cost-minimizing derived-demand elasticity, the Morishima elasticity, and the shadow elasticity in terms of the profit function.

Using results from previous chapters, it is easy to draw inferences about the properties of the decomposition in (4.9). For example, by the properties of the cost function, it follows that the matrix of substitution effects must be symmetric, singular, and negative semidefinite. Others are left to the reader as an exercise.

Exercise 4.5. Derive all of the properties of (4.9) using earlier results on $c(w, y)$.

Inputs x_i and x_j are *gross substitutes if*

$$\frac{\partial x_i(p, w)}{\partial w_j} = \frac{\partial x_j(p, w)}{\partial w_i} \geq 0.$$

That is, inputs are gross substitutes if, under profit maximization, usage of x_i varies positively with changes in w_j. We want to use this definition to consider gross substitutability closer. In particular, we examine instances where inputs are gross substitutes but Allen complements, or Allen substitutes but gross complements. Consider the latter instance first. By (4.9), x_i and x_j are Allen substitutes but gross complements only if the profit-maximizing effect is negative, that is,

$$\frac{\partial x_i(w, y^*)}{\partial y} \frac{\partial y(p, w)}{\partial w_j} \leq 0. \tag{4.13}$$

Thus, if these two inputs are to be gross complements, then either input i must be normal and y nonregressive or input i must be inferior and y regressive in w_j. From (4.10), however, y *is regressive* (nonregressive) in w_j *if and only if* x_j *is inferior (normal)*. Thus, a necessary condition for two goods to be gross complements when they are also Allen substitutes is that they both be normal or both be inferior.

Next consider the case where inputs are Allen complements but gross substitutes. This requires the left-hand side of (4.13) to be positive, and similar arguments establish that inputs change from Allen complements to gross substitutes only if one is normal and the other is inferior.

Given these results, one might ask what are the implications of gross substitutability or gross complementarity? By homogeneity,

$$\sum_j \frac{\partial x_i(w, p)}{\partial w_j} w_j = - \frac{\partial x_i(w, p)}{\partial p} p.$$

The right-hand side is negative if and only if x_i is a normal input. Thus, if x_i is normal,

$$\sum_j \frac{w_j}{x_i} \frac{\partial x_i(w, p)}{\partial w_j} \leq 0.$$

Suppose that in addition to x_i being normal all inputs are gross substitutes. This implies

$$\left| \frac{w_i}{x_i} \frac{\partial x_i(w, p)}{\partial w_i} \right| > \left| \frac{w_j}{x_i} \frac{\partial x_i(w, p)}{\partial w_j} \right|, \quad j \neq i,$$

that is, the absolute value of any single cross-price elasticity must be less than the absolute value of the own-price elasticity. On the other hand, if x_i is inferior,

$$\sum_j w_j \frac{\partial x_i(w, p)}{\partial w_j} \geq 0,$$

which implies that there must be at least one gross substitute for that input and further that the overall substitution effects must dominate the gross complementary effects.

4.4   Duality and the profit function

Chapter 2 argued that one can construct the input requirement set directly from the cost function and, moreover, that whenever a cost function satisfying properties 2B.1–2B.6 is specified, one can always derive an implicit input requirement set satisfying weak monotonicity, weak essentiality, nonemptiness, and convexity of the input requirement set. Accordingly, presuming the existence of a well-behaved cost function is equivalent to presuming the existence of a well-behaved input requirement set. The purpose of this section is to convince the reader that a similar relationship exists between the cost and the profit functions: Specification of a profit function implies the existence of a cost function. The approach taken, however, is slightly different from that used in Chapter 2. Here we rely on the mathematical theory of convex conjugates, which provides a method of inferring dual relationships between two convex functions. Although the analysis is grounded in this theory, it can be understood without prior knowledge of this theory. An attempt has been made to make the discussion as heuristic as possible while relying heavily on graphic illustration. The conjugacy between the cost and profit functions was the main reason for using the cost function to derive the profit function. However, a similar relationship also exists between the profit and the production functions. This latter relationship is explored in an exercise and an example that conclude this section. But the ultimate reason for using the conjugacy approach to examine the dual structure of cost and profit functions is to show the reader that more than one way of conceptualizing dual relationships exists. When the multioutput profit function is addressed in Chapter 7, we return to the approach used in Chapter 2 to analyze dual relationships.

Our starting point is the definition of the profit function at a given output price (p^1):

$$\Pi(p^1, w) = \max_{y \geq 0}\{p^1 y - c(w, y)\}$$

$$= p^1 y^1 - c(w, y^1).$$

Here y^1 is the profit-maximizing supply when the price configuration is (p^1, w). Even though y^1 is optimal for (p^1, w), there is no reason to expect it to be optimal in general. Indeed, if this were to be the case, supply would be perfectly inelastic. Hence, as a general rule,

$$\Pi(p, w) \geq py^1 - c(w, y^1),$$

which easily implies

$$c(w, y^1) \geq py^1 - \Pi(p, w). \tag{4.14}$$

Cost for any output level always provides an upper bound for the difference between revenue and maximum profit if profit is well defined and finite. In what follows, presume that the right-hand side of (4.14) is strictly bounded over p for a given (y^1, w) configuration. (Recall the earlier discussion of the related problem in defining maximum profit.)

On an intuitive level, therefore, it is reasonable that the implicit cost function

$$c^*(w, y) = \max_{p > 0} \{py - \Pi(p, w)\} \tag{4.15}$$

provides a good description of the technology that generated $\Pi(p, w)$. In what follows, it is shown that if $\Pi(p, w)$ satisfies properties 4C.1–4C.5, $c^*(w, y)$ locally satisfies properties 4B*.

Properties of $c^*(w, y)$ (4B):*

1. $c^*(w, y) \geq 0$, $w > 0$, $y > 0$;
2. if $w^1 \geq w$, then $c^*(w^1, y) \geq c^*(w, y)$;
3. $c^*(w, y)$ is concave and continuous in w;
4. $c^*(tw, y) = tc^*(w, y)$, $t > 0$;
5. if $y^1 \geq y$, then $c^*(w, y^1) \geq c^*(w, y)$;
6. $c^*(w, 0) = 0$; and
7. $c^*(w, y)$ is convex and continuous in y.

Before proceeding to a demonstration of the result, it is appropriate to comment briefly on the main differences between properties 4B* and properties 2B (those developed for the original cost function). These lie in 4B*.1 and 4B*.7. Property 2B.1 represented a strong inequality implying that the cost function is always strictly positive. However, this strong inequality was not utilized in the derivation of $\Pi(p, w)$. Hence, only the weaker inequality is manifested here. Second, $c(w, y)$ was assumed continuous and $\phi(p, w)$ was assumed compact to guarantee the existence of $\Pi(p, w)$. These assumptions are dually reflected in 4B*.7, which is somewhat stronger. More will be said about this later, for now we proceed to a quick demonstration of these results. Because of the similarity of related arguments for $\Pi(p, w)$, not much time will be spent trying to motivate these results intuitively.

To show 4B*.6, note that

$$c^*(w, 0) = \max_{p>0} \{p \cdot 0 - \Pi(p, w)\}$$

$$= \min_p \Pi(p, w) = 0$$

by the fact that profit is always nonnegative. To show 4B*.5, let p^1 solve (4.15) for y^1 and p for y. By definition, $c^*(w, y^1) = p^1 y^1 - \Pi(p^1, w)$, $c^*(w, y) = py - \Pi(p, w)$, and further $c^*(w, y^1) \geq py^1 - \Pi(p, w)$. But since $y^1 \geq y$, this last inequality implies that $c^*(w, y^1) \geq c^*(w, y)$, as required. And when this result is combined with 4B*.6, 4B*.1 follows directly. To show 4B*.2, let $c^*(w, y) = py - \Pi(p, w)$ and $c^*(w^1, y) = p^1 y - \Pi(p^1, w^1)$. Then, by (4.15), $c^*(w^1, y) \geq py - \Pi(p, w^1)$, which is greater than $py - \Pi(p, w)$ by the fact that $\Pi(\cdot)$ is nonincreasing in w. Concavity follows by the fact that the maximum value of function concave in a set of parameters is itself concave (see Lemma 14 in the Appendix). But $-\Pi(p, w)$ is concave in w by the properties of $\Pi(\cdot)$, and therefore, $c^*(w, y)$ has to be concave in w. Linear homogeneity follows by the following equalities ($t > 0$):

$$c^*(tw, y) = \max_{p>0} \{py - \Pi(p, tw)\}$$

$$= \max_{p>0} \{py - t\Pi(p/t, w)\}$$

$$= t \max_{p/t>0} \{(p/t)y - \Pi(p/t, w)\}$$

$$= tc^*(w, y).$$

Convexity of $c^*(w, y)$ for a twice-continuously differentiable cost function is equivalent to the traditional neoclassical assumption of rising marginal cost, which is usually taken to be a necessary condition for the existence of a stable equilibrium. Hence, 4B*.7 is well grounded in the neoclassical economic tradition and, therefore, should be quite intuitive. To demonstrate it formally, one needs to show that $c^*(w, y^0) \leq \theta c^*(w, y^1) + (1 - \theta)c^*(w, y)$ for $y^0 = \theta y^1 + (1 - \theta)y$. As before, define

$$c^*(w, y^1) = p^1 y^1 - \Pi(p^1, w),$$

$$c^*(w, y) = py - \Pi(p, w),$$

$$c^*(w, y^0) = p^0 y^0 - \Pi(p^0, w).$$

By (4.15),

$$c^*(w, y^1) \geq p^0 y^1 - \Pi(p^0, w) \quad \text{and} \quad c^*(w, y) \geq p^0 y - \Pi(p^0, w).$$

Evaluating $c^*(w, y^0)$ explicitly yields

$$c^*(w, y^0) = p^0[\theta y^1 + (1 - \theta) y] - \Pi(p^0, w)$$
$$= \theta(p^0 y^1 - \Pi(p^0, w)) + (1 - \theta)(p^0 y - \Pi(p^0, w)),$$

which when combined with the above inequalities yields the desired result.

Convexity of $c^*(w, y)$ means that profit maximization is never consistent with declining marginal costs. In a manner analogous to the discussion of nonconvexities of $V(y)$, a profit-maximizing firm simply "jumps" over nonconvex segments of the cost function. Whether or not $c(w, y)$ is convex, a well-behaved profit function always generates a convex cost function that is observationally equivalent to $c(w, y)$ in the sense that $c^*(w, y)$ generates the same profit function as $c(w, y)$. The easiest way to illustrate this is with Figure 4.7(a), where a nonconvex cost function that satisfies the compactness requirement on $\phi(p, w)$ is presented (as long as $p < \delta$, δ is the slope of the second line segment). The slope of the first line segment is given by, say, β, and as long as $p < \delta$, profits are bounded and are maximized by producing at y^*, where they equal $(p - \beta) y^*$. Now compare this with the convex cost function in panel (b), where up to y^* the slope of the cost function is β and beyond y^* the slope is δ. As long as $\delta > p > \beta$, profits are bounded and are maximized at y^*, where they equal $(p - \beta) y^*$. The profit functions generated by the convex cost function in (b) and the nonconvex cost function in (a) are both well defined over all $p \in (0, \delta)$ and are identical.

To reinforce the intuition, consider the smoothly differentiable nonconvex cost function in Figure 4.8 and profit associated with output price p^1 defining the ray $p^1 y$ that emanates from the origin. Since a nonconvex increasing function of y must "bend in" toward any such ray, profits at either y^* or y^0 are higher than at any output level in the nonconvex region of the cost function. A rational profit maximizer would never operate in the region $y^* < y < y^0$ if y^* and y^0 were available. Rather such an individual would simply "jump" over this nonconvex region. The observationally equivalent, convex cost function follows $c(w, y)$ up to y^*, proceeds along the broken line segment between y^* and y^0, and then follows $c(w, y)$ for $y^0 \le y$. Straightforward arguments verify that the associated profit function is kinked at $p = [c(w, y^0) - c(w, y^*)] / (y^0 - y^*)$.

Results developed in Chapter 2 imply that a sufficient condition for $c(w, y)$ to satisfy 4B*.7 is that $f(x)$ be concave. Under this assumption, $c^*(w, y)$ in fact equals $c(w, y)$. In other words, there exists a duality between $\Pi(p, w)$ and $c(w, y)$. On a somewhat more intuitive level, this result is pleasing since strict concavity rules out increasing returns for $f(x)$ satisfying property 1A.3a. The existence of increasing returns is one of the most frequently cited reasons for the nonexistence of maximum profits.

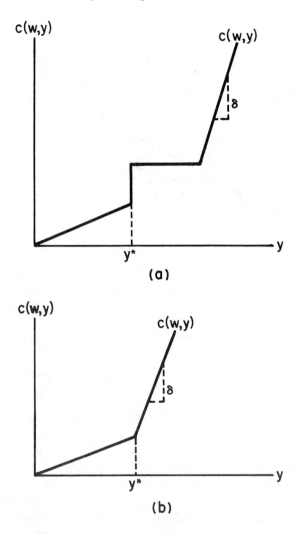

Figure 4.7 Observational equivalence of convex and nonconvex cost structures.

Preceding arguments suggest that if a flat segment in the cost function exists, the associated profit function is kinked at the price corresponding to the slope of the flat segment. By duality and analogy with arguments made in Chapter 2, therefore, flats in profit functions should be expected to map into kinks in cost functions. This and other points are pursued in the following example.

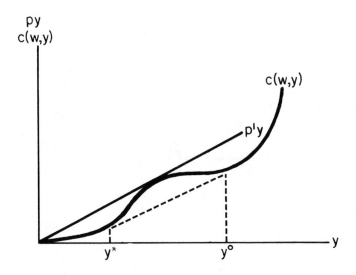

Figure 4.8 Profit maximization with nonconvex costs.

Example 4.2. Duality and the profit function. Consider the profit function defined over the limited price range

$$\Pi(p, w) = \begin{cases} 0, & 0 \le p \le \gamma c(w), \\ [p - \gamma c(w)]y^*, & \gamma < p/c(w) \le \beta, \\ [p - \beta c(w)]y^0 + [\beta - \gamma]y^* c(w), & \beta < p/c(w) < \delta. \end{cases}$$

This, of course, is the profit function derived in Example 4.1. It is represented graphically in Figure 4.9. Now consider problem (4.15). Before proceeding, note that the geometric depiction of (4.15) is quite similar to the geometric depiction of (4.1). Both involve maximizing the distance between a ray emanating from the origin and a function emanating from the origin. The only difference is that here we operate in output price space instead of output space. As long as $y \le y^*$, the maximum value of $py - \Pi(p, w)$ occurs at $p = \gamma c(w)$, whence

$$c^*(w, y) = \gamma c(w)y, \quad 0 \le y \le y^*.$$

However, when $y = y^*$, expression (4.15) is equally well maximized at $p = \gamma c(w)$, $p = \beta c(w)$, or any price in between. Using (4.15),

$$c^*(w, y^*) = \gamma c(w)y^*. \tag{4.16}$$

If $y^* < y \le y^0$, expression (4.15) is maximized at $p = \beta c(w)$; substitution implies

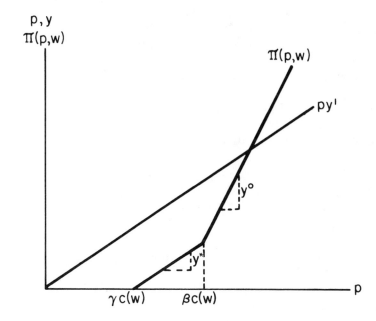

Figure 4.9 Deriving cost function from profit function.

$$c^*(w, y) = \beta c(w)y - [\beta - \gamma]y^*c(w)$$

$$= \gamma c(w)y^* + \beta c(w)(y - y^*). \tag{4.17}$$

When $y > y^0$, it is obvious from Figure 4.9 that the maximum in (4.15) is not well defined; one cannot recapture the cost function in this region. Combining (4.16) and (4.17) yields

$$c^*(w, y) = \begin{cases} \gamma c(w)y, & 0 \le y \le y^*, \\ \gamma c(w)y^* + \beta c(w)(y - y^*), & y^* < y \le y^0, \end{cases}$$

which is the cost function used to generate the profit function over the region $0 < p < \delta$. Inspection reveals that flat sections of this profit function map into kinked sections of the cost function, as expected.

To pursue the analysis further, it is convenient to specify the exact nature of $c(w)$. For illustration, suppose that $c(w) = \sum_{i=1}^{n} w_i/\alpha_i$. Arguments originally made in Chapter 2 then imply that

$$V^*(y) = \begin{cases} x_i \ge \dfrac{y\gamma}{\alpha_i}, & i = 1, \dots, n, \; 0 \le y \le y^*, \\ x_i \ge [\gamma y^* + \beta(y - y^*)]/\alpha_i, & i = 1, \dots, n, \; y^* < y, \end{cases}$$

is the technology dual to this profit function.

Example 4.3. Duality between production and profit functions. If a duality exists between the cost and profit functions, the structure of the cost function can be inferred directly from the profit function. Arguments developed in Chapter 2 then can be used to infer the structure of the input requirement set. This example starts by showing that the structure of the profit function implies something very specific about the structure of the Hessian matrix of the production function. Then, a conjugacy relationship between the production and the profit functions is developed. The profit-maximizing producer solves

$$\Pi(p, w) = \max\{pf(x) - wx\}.$$

If all inputs are strictly essential, we only need consider interior solutions, that is, $x(p, w) > 0$. For such a production function, the first-order conditions for profit maximization are

$$\frac{\partial f(x)}{\partial x_i} = \frac{w_i}{p}, \quad i = 1, 2, \dots, n.$$

The solution to these equations, if one exists, is the profit-maximizing input demand vector. Thus, applying the implicit function theorem to these equations gives the comparative statics properties of the derived demands. Differentiating the above at the optimum with respect to $w^* = w/p$ yields

$$\nabla_{xx} f(x(p, w)) \frac{\partial x(p, w)}{\partial w^*} = I_n$$

where I_n is an $n \times n$ identity matrix. Hence,

$$\frac{\partial x(p, w)}{\partial w^*} = \nabla_{xx}^{-1} f(x(p, w)).$$

That is, the matrix of partial derivatives of the derived-demand vector with respect to the input prices normalized by the output price is the inverse of the Hessian of the production function evaluated at the profit-maximizing solution. Notice that, by Hotelling's lemma,

$$\frac{\partial x(p, w)}{\partial w^*} = -\frac{\partial^2 \Pi(p, w)}{\partial w \, \partial w^*}$$

$$= -p \frac{\partial^2 \Pi(p, w)}{\partial w \, \partial w}.$$

Combining results demonstrates that at the profit-maximizing solution, the Hessian of the profit function in w is $-1/p$ times the inverted Hessian of the production function.

A conjugacy relationship also exists between $\Pi(p, w)$ and $f(x)$. By the definition of the profit function in (4.1),

$$\Pi(p^1, w^1) = p^1 f(x^1) - w^1 x^1,$$

where x^1 is the profit-maximizing derived-demand vector when prices (p^1, w^1) prevail. For any other price vector,

$$\Pi(p, w) \geq pf(x^1) - wx^1,$$

which suggests that a natural candidate for the production function dual to $\Pi(p, w)$ is

$$f^*(x) = \min_{w/p}\{\Pi(1, w/p) + (w/p)x\}.$$

The properties of $f^*(x)$ are pursued in the following exercise.

Exercise 4.6. Show that $f^*(x)$ defined in Example 4.3 is nondecreasing in x and concave in x and satisfies weak essentiality. Notice, in particular, that regardless of the shape of the original production function the conjugate function is always concave.

4.5 Short- versus long-run profits

A primary development in Chapter 3 was the Le Chatelier–Samuelson principle. As developments in this chapter illustrate, this principle is quite general – applying also to the relationship between cost-minimizing and profit-maximizing derived demands. This section takes up anew the case of fixed inputs. The main motivation is the observation that firms cannot always freely vary inputs. Short of explicitly introducing the time element into the consideration of producers' behavior, the traditional dichotomy between the long run and the short run seems the most efficient way to handle such problems. Because of the similarity of arguments and the attention devoted to the short-run problem in Chapter 3, in what follows, a largely graphic treatment that relies only peripherally on mathematical arguments is presented. Mathematical arguments (exactly identical to those employed in Chapter 3) are left to the reader as an exercise. Moreover, the successive relaxation of input constraints addressed in Chapter 3 is here left entirely as an exercise for the reader on which to hone his or her ability to manipulate economic concepts mathematically. Because of their importance, the reader is especially urged to pursue the exercises concluding this section.

As before, partition the input vector as (x^1, x^2), where x^2 represents the fixed inputs. By developments in Chapter 3, the short-run variable-cost function satisfies properties 2B.1–2B.6 under appropriate regularity conditions on $f(x)$. Define the *short-run variable-profit function* as

$$\Pi(p, w^1, x^2) = \max_{y \geq 0}\{py - c(w^1, y, x^2)\}.$$

Since $c(w^1, y, x^2)$ satisfies properties 2B.1–2B.6 in w^1 and y, earlier arguments imply that $\Pi(p, w^1, x^2)$ satisfies 4C.1–4C.5 in p and w^1. Moreover, if $c(w^1, y, x^2)$ is convex in y,

$$c(w^1, y, x^2) = \max_{p > 0}\{py - \Pi(p, w^1, x^2)\},$$

with the further conclusion that a duality exists between $c(w^1, y, x^2)$ and $\Pi(p, w^1, x^2)$. Since a derivation of these arguments only awaits the exact replication of earlier arguments, we leave them to the reader.

Short-run total profits are defined as

$$\Pi^s(p, w, x^2) = \Pi(p, w^1, x^2) - w^2 x^2.$$

By analogy with Chapter 3,

$$\Pi(p, w) = \max_{x^2} \Pi^s(p, w, x^2). \tag{4.18}$$

The proof of this relationship is quite intuitive and easily formalized. Expression (4.18) must hold because if it does not, a firm can increase profitability by proceeding in stages in solving its optimization problem. Since no costs or benefits have been attached to proceeding in stages (other than purely analytical), this cannot be the case, and (4.18) must apply. The importance of (4.18) is that it implies

$$\Pi(p, w) \geq \Pi^s(p, w, x^2) \quad \text{and} \quad \Pi(p, w) = \Pi^s(p, w, x^2(p, w)). \tag{4.19}$$

The long-run profit function is the upper envelope of the respective short-run profit functions. The functions coincide at the point where the fixed endowment vector is profit maximizing. This result applies in both output and input price space.

Let us first address the implications of (4.19) in terms of the output price. By (4.19), Figure 4.10 provides a reasonable depiction of the relationship between the long- and short-run profit functions. Geometrically, it is clear that $\Pi(p, w)$ must be "more" convex than $\Pi(p, w, x^2)$ in p if (4.19) is to hold. But assuming that both functions are twice-continuously differentiable, Hotelling's lemma implies

$$y(p, w) = y(p, w^1, x^2(p, w)),$$

where $y(p, w^1, x^2)$ is the short-run profit-maximizing supply. The fact that $\Pi(p, w)$ is more convex than $\Pi^s(p, w, x^2)$ when they coincide, however, yields the Le Chatelier–Samuelson relationship

$$\frac{\partial y(p, w)}{\partial p} \geq \frac{\partial y(p, w^1, x^2(p, w))}{\partial p}. \tag{4.20}$$

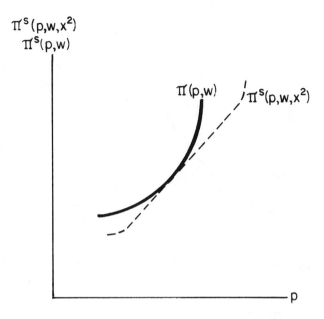

Figure 4.10 Le Chatelier–Samuelson principle for supply.

Expression (4.20) is easily reinforced by using the results of Exercise 3.2, where the reader was asked to verify that for a convex $c(w, y)$ short-run variable cost is "more" convex than $c(w, y)$, implying that the respective marginal-cost functions can be represented pictorially as in Figure 4.11. Suppose p is originally at P^*. Increasing or decreasing p calls forth less of an output response along the short-run curve; whence the result.

Parallel arguments can then be marshalled to demonstrate that

$$\frac{\partial x_i(p, w)}{\partial w_i} \leq \frac{\partial x_i(p, w^1, x^2(p, w))}{\partial w_i}, \quad i \in N^1. \tag{4.21}$$

Exercise 4.7. Develop a formal proof of expression (4.20) under the assumption that both $\Pi(p, w)$ and $\Pi^s(p, w, x^2)$ are twice-continuously differentiable. (*Hint:* use the methods developed in Chapter 3 to demonstrate the Le Chatelier–Samuelson principle.)

Exercise 4.8. Demonstrate the validity of expression (4.21) graphically and then derive it formally under the assumptions maintained in Exercise 4.7.

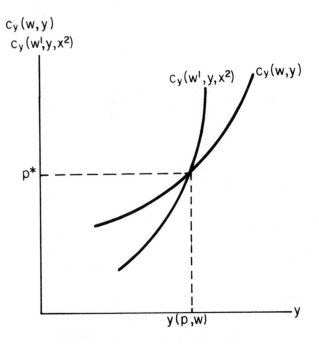

Figure 4.11 Le Chatelier-Samuelson principle.

Exercise 4.9. In Chapter 3, we demonstrated that if the input vector were partitioned, $x = (x^1, x^2, ..., x^k)$ (the higher the index, the more fixed the associated inputs),

$$\frac{\partial x_i(w, y)}{\partial w_i} \leq \frac{\partial x_i(w^1, ..., w^{k-1}, y, x^k)}{\partial w_i}$$

$$\leq \cdots \leq \frac{\partial x_i(w, y, x^2, ..., x^k)}{\partial w_i}, \quad i \in N^1.$$

Use parallel arguments to demonstrate that

$$\frac{\partial y(p, w)}{\partial p} \geq \frac{\partial y(p, w^1, ..., w^{k-1}, x^k)}{\partial p}$$

$$\geq \cdots \geq \frac{\partial y(p, w^1, x^2, ..., x^k)}{\partial p},$$

$$\frac{\partial x_i(p, w)}{\partial w_i} \leq \frac{\partial x_i(p, w^1, ..., w^{k-1}, x^k)}{\partial w_i}$$

$$\leq \cdots \leq \frac{\partial x_i(p, w^1, x^2, ..., x^k)}{\partial w_i}, \quad i \in N^1.$$

4.6   Structure of the profit function

Following the earlier discussions of the structure of production and cost functions, now turn to consideration of the implications of structural restrictions on $\Pi(p, w)$. The first issue is homotheticity. In what follows, all functions are presumed twice-continuously differentiable.

4.6a   *Homotheticity*

When $f(x)$ is homothetic, the profit function can be written in the equivalent forms

$$\Pi^*(p, c(w)) \quad \text{or} \quad c(w)\hat{\Pi}(p/c(w)), \tag{4.22}$$

where $\Pi^*(p, c(w))$ is linearly homogeneous in p and $c(w)$, and $c(w)$ is linearly homogeneous in w.

Thus, when the underlying technology is homothetic, the profit function can be expressed either as a linearly homogeneous function of the output price and a single aggregate input price [defined by the cost-minimizing way of producing $h(y)$] or as the product of an aggregate input price and a function homogeneous of degree zero in the output price and the aggregate input price.

Although these are equivalent forms, each is convenient for different purposes, and we shall use them interchangeably. Before proceeding with a derivation of (4.22), it is instructive to consider an intuitive argument that will hopefully convince the reader of the plausibility of this result. By Hotelling's lemma, writing the profit function in the form $\Pi^*(p, c(w))$ implies that profit-maximizing input ratios are independent of p. Arguments made in Chapter 2 indicate that cost-minimizing derived demands for homothetic $f(x)$ are independent of the output level. At a minimum, there seems to be a strong parallel between the consequences of homotheticity detailed in Chapter 2 and the first expression in (4.22). On an intuitive plane, independence of input ratios from output follows because as one proceeds out a ray from the origin in input space across different isoquants for a homothetic technology, one does not encounter differing marginal rates of technical substitution. If for a given input price configuration a particular ray gives the optimal input ratio, it continues to do so as long as input prices do not change. Our decomposition of profit-maximizing derived demands (4.8) demonstrates that the influence of p is manifested only through an output adjustment. Hence, if cost-minimizing input ratios are independent of output, the associated profit-maximizing ratios must also be independent of p.

Now to a formal demonstration. The results on derived-demand decomposition preceding (4.9) applied to a homothetic technology yield

$$x_i(p, w) = h(y(p, w)) \frac{\partial c(w)}{\partial w_i},$$

where $c(w)$ is linearly homogeneous in p. Obviously, $x_i(p, w)/x_k(p, w)$ is independent of p, and standard separability results give that $\Pi(p, w)$ can be written $\Pi^*(p, c(w))$. Since $c(w)$ is linearly homogeneous in w, the following equalities hold:

$$\Pi(tp, tw) = \Pi^*(tp, c(tw))$$
$$= \Pi^*(tp, tc(w))$$
$$= t\Pi^*(p, c(w)).$$

The third equality, a consequence of the linear homogeneity of profit functions, implies linear homogeneity of Π^* in p and $c(w)$. To establish the consequent equality between the first and second parts of (4.22), we could exploit directly the linear homogeneity of $\Pi^*(\cdot)$. A related, although slightly more cumbersome, method offers a useful means of obtaining an explicit representation of the profit function in certain circumstances.

By first-order conditions for profit maximization under homotheticity,

$$p = h'(y)c(w).$$

If $h(y)$ is strictly convex, this last expression can be solved by the implicit function theorem to get

$$y = H(p/c(w)).$$

By Hotelling's lemma, however,

$$\Pi(p, w) = \int \frac{\partial \Pi}{\partial p} \, dp = \int y \, dp = \int H\left(\frac{p}{c(w)}\right) dp.$$

Letting $H(p/c(w)) = \hat{\Pi}'(p/c(w))$ yields

$$\int H\left(\frac{p}{c(w)}\right) dp = c(w) \int \frac{\partial \hat{\Pi}(p/c(w))}{\partial p} \, dp$$

$$= c(w)\hat{\Pi}\left(\frac{p}{c(w)}\right),$$

as desired. The properties of the profit function in p require $\hat{\Pi}$ to be convex and nondecreasing. To reinforce the usefulness of the preceding approach, we encourage the reader to do Exercise 4.10.

Exercise 4.10. By results derived in Chapter 2, the cost function for a Cobb–Douglas technology assumes the form

$$c(w, y) = y^\alpha \prod_{i=1}^n w_i^{\beta_i}, \qquad \sum_{i=1}^n \beta_i = 1.$$

Use the method outlined in the preceding discussion to show that

$$\Pi(p, w) = \frac{A(\alpha - 1)}{\alpha} p^{\alpha/\alpha - 1} \left(\prod_{i=1}^{n} w_i^{\beta_i} \right)^{1/1 - \alpha},$$

where A is a constant integration.

So far, our analysis has succeeded in demonstrating that homotheticity implies that the profit function assumes one of the forms in (4.22). This does not necessarily mean, however, that the arguments can be reversed; that is, any time one can write a profit function in the form of (4.22), the associated cost function must be consistent with homotheticity. But by the dual nature of $\Pi(p, w)$ and $c(w, y)$, one would suspect this to be true. Fortunately, it is easy to use the conjugacy relationship in (4.15) to show that if $c(w, y)$ is not consistent with homotheticity, it is observationally equivalent to a cost function that is. In other words, one can always use (4.15) to generate a $c^*(w, y)$ that is factorizable as desired. If (4.22) applies,

$$c^*(w, y) = \max_{p>0} \{ py - c(w) \hat{\Pi}(p/c(w)) \}$$

$$= c(w) \max_{z>0} \{ zy - \hat{\Pi}(z) \}$$

$$= c(w) h^*(y), \tag{4.23}$$

where $z = p/c(w)$. By earlier results, $\hat{\Pi}$ is nondecreasing and convex in z, and therefore, it is legitimate to think in terms of a conjugate function for $\hat{\Pi}(z)$. Arguments directly paralleling the earlier discussion of the dual relationship show that $h^*(y)$ is convex and nondecreasing in y. Therefore, we have established that any time profit can be expressed in the form of (4.22), an implicit cost function assuming the general form of (4.23) can be constructed. By earlier results, (4.23) is consistent with the homothetic technology:

$$h^*(y) = f^*(x),$$

where $h^*(y)$ is convex and nondecreasing in y and $f^*(x)$ is linearly homogeneous. Under suitable differentiability assumptions, therefore, when $\Pi(p, w)$ satisfies (4.22), the underlying production function is

$$y = F(f^*(x)),$$

where F is a nondecreasing concave function.

Intuitively, profit maximization under homotheticity can be viewed as equivalent to choosing an aggregate input X to

$$\max\{ pF(X) - c(w)X \},$$

where, as before, $c(w)$ can be interpreted as the aggregate input price. To see why, recall that the first-order conditions for profit maximization under homotheticity require

$$h'(y) = p/c(w).$$

Also recall, however, that

$$h(y) - f^*(x) = 0 \quad \text{and} \quad y - F(f^*(x)) = 0$$

represent the same implicit function. Hence, differentiation reveals that

$$F'(f^*(x)) = 1/h'(y).$$

Then, letting X equal $f^*(x)$ and combining the above result with the first-order condition gives

$$pF'(X) = c(w)$$

as the first-order condition. This, of course, is the first-order condition for the problem defined in terms of the aggregate input.

4.6b   *Separability of the profit function*

We define the extended index set $_0\mathbf{I}$ for (p, w) by

$$_0\mathbf{I} = \{0, 1, 2, \ldots, n\}$$

where 0 is the index of the output price. The corresponding extended partition is

$$_0\hat{\mathbf{I}} = \{0, \mathbf{I}^1, \ldots, \mathbf{I}^m\},$$

where definitions of I^v are similar to those used in other chapters. Analogously, the associated partition of the input price vector is defined as

$$\hat{\mathbf{I}} = \{I^1, \ldots, I^m\}.$$

The first order of business is to discuss briefly the implications of weak and strong separability in the partition $\hat{\mathbf{I}}$. Weak separability of $\Pi(p, w)$ in $\hat{\mathbf{I}}$ implies that

$$\frac{\partial}{\partial w_v} \left\{ \frac{\partial \Pi(p, w)/\partial w_i}{\partial \Pi(p, w)/\partial w_j} \right\} = 0, \quad (i, j) \in \mathbf{I}^m, \ v \notin \mathbf{I}^m.$$

The associated profit function assumes the general form

$$\Pi(p, w) = \tilde{\Pi}(p, \Pi^1(p, w^1), \ldots, \Pi^m(p, w^m)).$$

As with the cost function, this type of separability implies that derived-demand ratios within groups are independent of input prices from other groups. Hence, an important consequence of weak separability in $\hat{\mathbf{I}}$ is that

$$\epsilon_{iv}(p,w)=\epsilon_{jv}(p,w), \quad (i,j)\in\mathbf{I}^m, \; v\notin\mathbf{I}^m.$$

To see why this result holds, recall that by Hotelling's lemma the definition of weak separability in the partition $\hat{\mathbf{I}}$ implies that

$$\frac{\partial}{\partial w_v}\frac{x_i(p,w)}{x_j(p,w)}=0, \quad (i,j)\in\mathbf{I}^m, \; v\notin\mathbf{I}^m.$$

Evaluating this derivative shows that the elasticities are equal. This result parallels, but is not equivalent to, the result that weak separability of $c(w,y)$ in $\hat{\mathbf{I}}$ requires

$$\epsilon_{iv}=\epsilon_{jv}, \quad (i,j)\in\mathbf{I}^m, \; v\notin\mathbf{I}^m.$$

Hence, weak separability of $\Pi(p,w)$ in $\hat{\mathbf{I}}$ does not necessarily imply weak separability of $c(w,y)$ in the same partition or vice versa. This nonequivalence is most apparent when one recognizes that converting (4.11) to elasticity form and applying the weak separability of $\Pi(p,w)$ in $\hat{\mathbf{I}}$ to the resulting compensated elasticity expression implies (see p. 135)

$$\epsilon_{iv}+\epsilon_{yv}\epsilon_{ip}/\epsilon_{yp}=\epsilon_{jv}+\epsilon_{yv}\epsilon_{jp}/\epsilon_{yp}, \quad (i,j)\in\mathbf{I}^m, \; v\notin\mathbf{I}^m,$$

or

$$\epsilon_{iv}-\epsilon_{jv}=\epsilon_{yv}(\epsilon_{jp}-\epsilon_{ip})/\epsilon_{yp}.$$

That is, weak separability of $\Pi(p,w)$ does not require the cost-minimizing derived-demand elasticities to be equal unless (assuming $\epsilon_{yv}\neq 0$) $\epsilon_{jp}(p,w)=\epsilon_{ip}(p,w)$, which implies that within-group input ratios are independent of the output price. More will be said about this presently, but for now, the main point is that separability of $\Pi(p,w)$ and $c(w,y)$ have different implications for the structure of technology.

Upon defining strong separability of $\Pi(p,w)$ in the partition $\hat{\mathbf{I}}$ as

$$\frac{\partial}{\partial w_v}\left\{\frac{\partial\Pi(p,w)/\partial w_i}{\partial\Pi(p,w)/\partial w_j}\right\}=0, \quad i\in\mathbf{I}^m, \; j\in\mathbf{I}^k, \; v\notin\mathbf{I}^m\cup\mathbf{I}^k,$$

it is immediate that

$$\Pi(p,w)=\tilde{\Pi}\left(p,\sum_{i=1}^{n}\Pi^i(p,w^i)\right),$$

$$\epsilon_{iv}(p,w)=\epsilon_{jv}(p,w), \quad i\in\mathbf{I}^m, \; j\in\mathbf{I}^k, \; v\notin\mathbf{I}^m\cup\mathbf{I}^k.$$

Rather than repeat a set of rather well-worn arguments, it is left to the reader to do Exercise 4.11.

Exercise 4.11. Demonstrate that strong separability of $\Pi(p,w)$ in $\hat{\mathbf{I}}$ and strong separability of $c(w,y)$ in $\hat{\mathbf{I}}$ are not equivalent. Derive sufficient conditions for them to be equivalent.

Let us turn to an investigation of separability in the extended partition $_0\hat{\mathbf{I}}$. To introduce this discussion, recall from above that a sufficient condition for weak separability of $\Pi(p, w)$ in $\hat{\mathbf{I}}$ to imply $c(w, y)$ weakly separable in $\hat{\mathbf{I}}$ is that $\epsilon_{ip}(p, w) = \epsilon_{jp}(p, w)$ for $(i, j) \in \mathbf{I}^m$. Another way of expressing this is that

$$\frac{\partial}{\partial p} \left\{ \frac{x_i(p, w)}{x_j(p, w)} \right\} = 0, \quad (i, j) \in \mathbf{I}^m.$$

This last result suggests that in addition to being independent of input prices from outside of the group, this input ratio is also independent of p. If this holds for all $\mathbf{I}^m$, Hotelling's lemma then suggests that the profit function is weakly separable in $_0\hat{\mathbf{I}}$ and expressible as

$$\Pi(p, w) = \breve{\Pi}(p, c^1(w^1), ..., c^m(w^m)). \tag{4.24}$$

Expression (4.24) is now apparently consistent with $c(w, y)$ weakly separable in $\hat{\mathbf{I}}$. Actually, however, much more than that can be shown. The principal result of this discussion is that weak separability of $\Pi(p, w)$ in $_0\hat{\mathbf{I}}$ implies weak separability of $c(w, y)$ in $_0\hat{\mathbf{I}}$ and vice versa. To demonstrate the first part of this result, note that when $\Pi(p, w)$ is weakly separable in $_0\hat{\mathbf{I}}$, one may take each c^i to be linearly homogeneous in each of its arguments and $\breve{\Pi}(\cdot)$ to be linearly homogeneous in p and the $c^i(w^i)$ functions by arguments directly parallel to ones utilized in the discussion in Chapter 3 of weak homothetic separability. Moreover, $\breve{\Pi}$ must be convex and nondecreasing in p if it is to be consistent with the properties of a profit function. An obvious interpretation of the right-hand side of (4.24) is that of a profit function expressed in terms of the output price and m aggregate input price indexes $c^i(w^i)$. Naturally, one expects it to be dual to a cost function expressible solely in terms of output and these same aggregate input indexes. This is now proven. Consider

$$c^*(w, y) = \max_{p > 0} \{ py - \breve{\Pi}(p, c^1(w^1), ..., c^m(w^m)) \}. \tag{4.25}$$

The envelope theorem applied to (4.25) gives

$$\frac{\partial c^*(w, y)/\partial w_i}{\partial c^*(w, y)/\partial w_j} = \frac{\partial c^v(w^v)/\partial w}{\partial c^v(w^v)/\partial w_j}, \quad (i, j) \in \mathbf{I}^v.$$

Since this equality holds for each index set, it follows that

$$\frac{\partial}{\partial w_k} \frac{\partial c^*(w, y)/\partial w_i}{\partial c^*(w, y)/\partial w_j} = 0, \quad (i, j) \in \mathbf{I}^v, \ k \notin \mathbf{I}^v,$$

and

$$\frac{\partial}{\partial y} \frac{\partial c^*(w, y)/\partial w_i}{\partial c^*(w, y)/\partial w_j} = 0, \quad (i, j) \in \mathbf{I}^v, \ \forall v.$$

Accordingly, the derived cost function $c^*(w, y)$ must be weakly separable in the extended partition $_0\hat{\mathbf{I}}$ and expressible as

$$c^*(w, y) = \hat{c}(y, c^1(w^1), \ldots, c^m(w^m)). \qquad (4.26)$$

Since each $c^i(w^i)$ is linearly homogeneous, so is c since overall linear homogeneity in w requires

$$c^*(tw, y) = \hat{c}(y, c^1(tw^1), \ldots, c^m(tw^m)),$$

$$= \hat{c}(y, tc^1(w^1), \ldots, tc^m(w^m)),$$

$$= t\hat{c}(y, c^1(w^1), \ldots, c^m(w^m)),$$

where the second equality is a consequence of the linear homogeneity of the c^i functions. Here, $\hat{c}$ is convex in y because the objective function in (4.25) is linear in y, and by now familiar results (see Appendix and the derivation of the properties of the profit function), the resulting maximal value function will be convex in y.

Suppose, on the other hand, that one starts out with a cost function satisfying (4.26). The associated profit function is

$$\Pi(p, w) = \max_{y \geq 0}\{py - \hat{c}(y, c^1(w^1), \ldots, c^m(w^m))\}. \qquad (4.27)$$

An application of the envelope theorem here and parallel arguments give

$$\frac{\partial \Pi(p, w)/\partial w_i}{\partial \Pi(p, w)/\partial w_j} = \frac{\partial c^v(w^v)/\partial w_i}{\partial c^v(w^v)/\partial w_j}, \quad (i, j) \in \mathbf{I}^v,$$

$$\frac{\partial}{\partial w_k}\left\{\frac{\partial \Pi(p, w)/\partial w_i}{\partial \Pi(p, w)/\partial w_j}\right\} = 0, \quad (i, j) \in \mathbf{I}^v, \; k \notin \mathbf{I}^v,$$

and

$$\frac{\partial}{\partial p}\frac{\partial \Pi(p, w)/\partial w_i}{\partial \Pi(p, w)/\partial w_j} = 0, \quad (i, j) \in \mathbf{I}^v.$$

Therefore, the profit function has to be weakly separable in the extended partition $_0\hat{\mathbf{I}}$, and given the linear homogeneity of the $c^i(w^i)$, $\hat{\Pi}$ must be nondecreasing and convex in p and linearly homogeneous in p and the $c^i(w^i)$.

In Chapter 3, $c(w, y)$ being weakly separable in the extended partition was shown to be equivalent to the production function being weakly homothetically separable in $\hat{\mathbf{I}}$. Coupled with the results in this section, this implies that weak homothetic separability of $f(x)$ enables one to conceptualize a profit maximization problem of the general form

$$\max_{\tilde{X}} pF(\tilde{X}^i, \ldots, \tilde{X}^m) - \sum_j c^j(w^j)\tilde{X}^j.$$

More to the point, however, the assumption of the existence of a profit function in terms of p and a vector of aggregate input price indexes implies that the associated technology must be weakly homothetically separable. The importance of this result largely lies in the great number of empirical studies that have been carried out at very high levels of aggregation using a single-output production function expressed in terms of several aggregate inputs.

Strong separability of $\Pi(p, w)$ in the extended partition $_{o}\hat{\mathbf{I}}$ implies

$$\Pi(p, w) = M\left(\phi(p) + \sum_{i=1}^{n} \phi^{i}(w^{i})\right).$$

By Hotelling's lemma,

$$\frac{\partial \Pi(p, w)/\partial w_i}{\partial \Pi(p, w)/\partial w_j} = \frac{\partial \phi^{m}(w^{m})/\partial w_i}{\partial \phi^{m}(w^{m})/\partial w_j}, \quad (i, j) \in \mathbf{I}^{m},$$

which by the property of derived demands must be homogeneous of degree zero in w^{m}. Hence, at a minimum, each $\phi^{i}(w^{i})$ should be homothetic by Lau's lemma, and we can write

$$\Pi(p, w) = M\left(p + \sum_{i=1}^{n} \tilde{\phi}^{i}[c^{i}(w^{i})]\right),$$

where each $c^{i}(w^{i})$ is linearly homogeneous in the respective w^{i}.

The conjugate relationship is then

$$c^{*}(w, y) = \max_{p}\left\{py - M\left[\phi(p) + \sum_{i} \phi^{i}(w^{i})\right]\right\},$$

from which it follows that

$$\frac{\partial c^{*}(w, y)/\partial w_i}{\partial c^{*}(w, y)/\partial w_j} = \frac{\partial \phi^{m}(w^{m})/\partial w_i}{\partial \phi^{v}(w^{v})/\partial w_j}, \quad i \in \mathbf{I}^{m}, j \in \mathbf{I}^{v}. \quad (4.28)$$

At a minimum, therefore, $c^{*}(w, y)$ must be strongly separable in the partition $\hat{\mathbf{I}}$ because from (4.28) the right-hand side of this expression is independent of any input prices not belonging to w^{m} or to w^{v}. Moreover, it is apparent that $c^{*}(w, y)$ is weakly separable in the extended partition $_{o}\hat{\mathbf{I}}$. This can be seen directly from (4.28) by noting that the right-hand side of that expression does not depend on the optimal value of p when $m = v$. Or, looking at it in another vein, strong separability of $\Pi(p, w)$ in the extended partition implies weak separability of $\Pi(p, w)$ in the extended partition. We already know from previous results that weak separability of $\Pi(p, w)$ in $_{o}\hat{\mathbf{I}}$ implies weak separability of $c^{*}(w, y)$ in $_{o}\hat{\mathbf{I}}$. The reader is encouraged to verify whether this result can be extended to strong separability of $c^{*}(w, y)$ in $_{o}\hat{\mathbf{I}}$.

Exercise 4.12. Determine whether or not $\Pi(p, w)$ being strongly separable in $_o\hat{\imath}$ implies that the conjugate cost function is strongly separable in $_o\hat{\imath}$.

The empirical relevance of this section lies largely in that weak separability of $\Pi(p, w)$ in $_o\hat{\imath}$ offers a theoretical justification for the estimation of a profit function in terms of a set of aggregate input price indexes. Studies doing that include Shumway (1983) and Antle (1984). Furthermore, it also shows that the associated technology must be consistent with weak homothetic separability in the original input bundle. On a logical level, there seems no reason to expect such a restriction to hold a priori. Moreover, most studies employing such an assumption typically do not have enough data to test its empirical relevance. Accordingly, it seems that such separability assumptions, whether explicit or implicit, provide a logical "greasing of the wheels" necessary for applied production analysis in its current state of the art. Although it may be necessary to permit such analysis, this does not mitigate either its importance or its restrictiveness. The best way to illustrate this problem is with the question every applied researcher must face when he or she utilizes such an assumption, Which inputs go into in each aggregate input? Although by no means trivial, the best answer one can hope for in most situations is one based on some hazy (and hopefully commonsense) partition of inputs that has at best shaky scientific foundations.

CHAPTER 5

Flexible forms and aggregation

Chapters 1–4 deal almost entirely with theoretical issues and only tangentially with applying these developments. There are basically two approaches to applied production analysis: econometric and mathematical programming. A relatively short book such as the present cannot hope to cover either in detail if it also provides a relatively complete treatment of theoretical issues. Thus, in writing this book, I have had to be somewhat selective in the topics covered. And in choosing materials for the more "applied" chapters, I have tried to focus on issues relevant to either the econometric or the mathematical programming approaches. The emphasis remains, however, on the econometric side in both this chapter and the next. This should not be interpreted as a judgment of the relative merits of either approach. Rather, it reflects the fact that most of my own work in applied production economics has been geared to the econometric approach.

This chapter deals with two issues that lie at the heart of applied production economics: functional form and aggregation. Apart from the obviously important contributions by Hanoch and Rothschild (1972), Varian (1983), Afriat (1972), and Färe, Grosskopf, and Lovell (1985), the first step in either the econometric or the programming approach is an assumption on the structure of technology. Traditionally, this meant specification of a production function involving very few parameters. However, recent advances in computer technology and multivariate statistical procedures have made it practical to handle much more complicated forms. With this increased ability has come an increased desire for generality in representing technology. This desire, largely spurred by the work of Diewert (1971), has led to much interest in what have come to be known as flexible functional forms. These are the subject of the first part of this chapter.

Most of the original empirical contributions utilizing a dual approach were at an aggregate level. The studies of Parks (1971), Binswanger (1974), and Berndt and Wood (1975) were all essentially industry-level studies. But as the reader will recollect from previous chapters, very little has been said about industry behavior. Rather, all theoretical developments have been cast at the firm level with individual entrepreneurs as the decision

158

makers. It is too much to hope that aggregation over firms places no restrictions on applied analysis. A consideration of some of these restrictions constitutes the second part of the chapter. The chapter closes with an example of an empirical study using a cost function.

Although much of what follows is geared to the econometric analysis of production relationships, apart from the example concluding the chapter, there is no formal discussion of econometric issues. In such a limited framework, one could only mention some of the econometric issues in passing. Suffice it to say that this chapter is not a cookbook on applying flexible forms to economic data. The discussion should acquaint the reader with the most important aspects of flexible forms and aggregation and bring the reader to the threshold of actual econometric work. The last example is used to give the reader a flavor of how flexible forms can be used in applied analysis. The details of the econometrics, however, are left to the reader; they should be thoroughly understood before any attempt is made to proceed with such analysis. A host of excellent texts on econometrics is available to help the reader.

Before proceeding with the business of the chapter, I want to pontificate a bit on my philosophy of choosing a functional form. First, one must keep the goal of the study firmly in mind when picking the form. Within the context of the problem, the form should be as general as possible and should restrict the ultimate outcome as little as possible. Second, choosing a functional form limits the range that the analysis can take. Once a general model is specified, classical statistical tests can only be conducted under the presumption that the general model is valid. Any conclusions drawn are only valid within the confines of that model. For example, suppose one wants to test whether the elasticity of substitution equals 2. A natural model might be the CES. If the null hypothesis of an elasticity of substitution of 2 is rejected, the appropriate conclusion is that if the technology indeed exhibits a constant elasticity of substitution, it is not 2. It is not valid to say, however, that the test demonstrates that the elasticity of substitution is never 2 because we have confined ourselves a priori to considering only constant elasticities of substitution. Making the latter assertion goes outside the confines of the model. Third, choosing a functional form is more a craft than a science. Classical statistical theory is silent about the choice of functional form. It presumes the researcher knows the most general model against which hypotheses of interest can be tested. Ideally, theory suggests form, but as will be clear, there are many numeric functions satisfying the requisite theory. Thus, choosing a flexible form requires judgment as well as knowledge. Finally, empirical analysis is an extension of theoretical analysis and is thus bound by the same logical strictures. Typically, theoretical analysis rules out logical absurdities, and it is left to empirical analysis to settle issues of magnitude, structure, and to some extent form. Everyone recognizes that theory is only as valuable as the assumptions are plausible; change an assumption and the results change. A major force militating for the increased use of mathematics in economics is the need to be explicit about one's assumptions. If one must assume a Cobb–Douglas form to get an answer, the answer is only strictly valid when the Cobb–Douglas assumption is. Although one might not realize this from any casual perusal of the literature, empirical analysis is as much, and perhaps even more, a prisoner of its assumptions as theoretical analysis. If we use a CES function to estimate the elasticity of substitution parametrically and the elasticity is in fact not a constant, the estimated elasticity is not strictly valid. This does not mean that this is not useful, but the situation is similar to that of trade policy makers who use results derived from the $2 \times 2 \times 2$ version of the Heckscher–Ohlin–Samuelson theory to make policy. There is a lot of room for error. Unfortunately, however, there is something unduly convincing about decimal points. Once seen in economic contexts, they tend to be believed. Therefore, one should always keep the maxim that analysis is only as good as its assumptions firmly in mind when doing empirical work. I think of empirical analysis as a rigorous form of theoretical investigation using real-world data.

5.1   Flexible functional forms defined

In specifying functional forms for applied production analysis, it is advantageous to have estimable relationships that place relatively few prior restrictions on the technology. To some extent, the last sentence is self-contradictory since specifying an estimable form that does not restrict the technology is usually difficult (if possible). Estimability typically implies a choice of form, and once the form is parameterized in accordance with received economic theory (homogeneity, convexity, etc.), duality guarantees the existence of a unique dual function. As a simple example, suppose that $f(x)$ is Cobb–Douglas. If an investigator utilizes a cost function linear in input prices, the applicability of the results is severely limited because such a cost structure presumes the existence of a Leontief and not a Cobb–Douglas technology. Thus, the search for functional relationships should expand considerably beyond those horizons suggested by the mathematically convenient forms utilized in previous chapters for expository purposes (Cobb–Douglas, Leontief, etc.). For, a priori, it seems unlikely that a real-world technology will assume any of these extremely simple forms.

A primary goal of this chapter is to investigate the properties of a family of relatively general functional forms. A good starting point for such a discussion is with a clear catalog of what might be accomplished by applied production analysis. Simply put, the primary goal of applied production analysis is empirical measurement of the economically relevant information that exhaustively characterizes the behavior of economic agents. For smooth technologies (i.e., those that are twice-continuously differentiable), this includes the value of the function (e.g., the level of cost), the gradient of the function (e.g., the derived demands), and the Hessian (e.g., the matrix of derived-demand elasticities). Therefore, in choosing a form, one rich enough in parameters to portray all of these effects independently without imposing prior constraints across effects should be the goal. For the sake of concreteness, suppose that one is investigating the primal technology (i.e., the production function). All of the economically relevant information is expressible in terms of the level of production, the vector of marginal productivities, and the matrix of elasticities of substitution. For an n-dimensional input vector, there are n marginal productivities, and the Hessian matrix contains n^2 elements. However, if the production function is twice-continuously differentiable, the Hessian is symmetric, and one need only consider the upper or lower triangular portion of the matrix. These triangular portions contain n diagonal elements and $\frac{1}{2}n(n-1)$ off-diagonal elements. Adding these separate effects [the dimension of the gradient, the number of elements in the upper or lower triangle of $\nabla_{xx} f(x)$] plus one term for the function value yields $\frac{1}{2}(n+1)(n+2)$ separate effects. Later, I shall show that this remains true for all versions of the technology. But for now, I want to emphasize that just as the choice of the functional form depends critically on its ultimate use, the number of parameters needed depends on the number of separate effects to be measured. As a gross example, one would never use a Cobb–Douglas function to investigate the magnitude of different elasticities of substitution since it forces all Allen elasticities to equal unity. The Cobb–Douglas, which has only $n+1$ parameters, cannot depict $\frac{1}{2}(n+1)(n+2)$ distinct effects without imposing restrictions across effects.

Besides measuring as many relevant effects as possible, research economy suggests choosing functional forms that are easy to estimate. The overwhelming attention that classical statistics has given to the linear model then suggests considering functional forms linear in parameters. One such form that remains quite general is the *general linear form*

$$h(z) = \sum_{i=1}^{k} \alpha_i b_i(z), \tag{5.1}$$

where each $b_i(z)$ is a known, twice-continuously differentiable, numeric function of z, and each α_i is a parameter (typically to be estimated).

The general linear form is attractive for several reasons: It can depict at least k distinct effects since it contains k parameters; and although it is linear in parameters, it is not linear in z. Finally, and most important, expression (5.1) can approximate (under relatively weak conditions) any arbitrary, twice-continuously differentiable function in the sense that the parameters of (5.1) can be chosen to ensure that, for any arbitrary $h^*(z)$,

$$h^*(z^0) = h(z^0),$$

$$\nabla_z h^*(z^0) = \nabla_z h(z^0), \tag{5.2}$$

$$\nabla_{zz} h^*(z^0) = \nabla_{zz} h(z^0).$$

That is, the parameters of (5.1) can be chosen such that its function value, gradient, and Hessian equal the corresponding magnitudes for any arbitrary $h^*(z)$ at z^0. Functions satisfying (5.2) are called *second-order differential approximations*.

The concept of a second-order differential approximation is important for applied production analysis because exhaustive information for smooth technologies is contained in the magnitudes represented in (5.2). For example, suppose $z = (p, w)$ and $h^*(z) = \Pi(p, w)$. Under some regularity conditions, an appropriately specified general linear form provides a second-order differential approximation to the true profit function regardless of whether the general linear form represents the true technology. Thus, a general linear form can approximate the level of profit, the derived demands and supply, and the behavior of derived demands and supply in response to changes in either p or w.

Demonstrating the validity of (5.2) is easy but notationally cumbersome. What is needed are appropriate regularity conditions in terms of the parameters that ensure that (5.2) holds. Put another way, we want to see if a unique vector $\alpha' = (\alpha_1, \ldots, \alpha_k)$ exists such that (5.2) holds. To start, note that for any twice-continuously differentiable function Young's theorem on the symmetry of partial derivatives implies that the Hessian only contains $\frac{1}{2}n(n+1)$ distinct elements, which, in turn, means that the left-hand side of (5.2) has only $\frac{1}{2}(n+1)(n+2)$ distinct expressions. Letting $k = \frac{1}{2}(n+1)(n+2)$ and using (5.1) gives

$$\frac{\partial h(z)}{\partial z_v} = \sum_{i=1}^{k} \alpha_i \frac{\partial b_i(z)}{\partial z_v},$$

$$\frac{\partial^2 h(z)}{\partial z_v \, \partial z_m} = \sum_{i=1}^{k} \alpha_i \frac{\partial^2 b_i(z)}{\partial z_v \, \partial z_m}.$$

Using these results, we then want to determine whether a parameter vector exists for which the general linear form approximates $h^*(z)$ in the sense of (5.2). To proceed, rewrite (5.2) in stacked vector form while remembering that the twice-continuous differentiability of $h^*(z)$ permits ignoring the lower triangle of $\nabla_{zz} h^*(z)$. This Hessian is stacked by taking each row of the upper triangle, transposing it, and placing it immediately below the elements of the previous row, which are all in turn placed below the elements of the gradient. Performing the indicated operation preceding yields

$$
\begin{bmatrix}
b_1(z), & b_2(z), & \ldots, & b_k(z) \\[2mm]
\dfrac{\partial b_1(z)}{\partial z_i}, & \dfrac{\partial b_2(z)}{\partial z_i}, & \ldots, & \dfrac{\partial b_k(z)}{\partial z_i} \\[2mm]
\vdots & & & \\[2mm]
\dfrac{\partial b_1(z)}{\partial z_n}, & \dfrac{\partial b_2(z)}{\partial z_m}, & \ldots, & \dfrac{\partial b_k(z)}{\partial z_n} \\[2mm]
\dfrac{\partial^2 b_1(z)}{\partial z_1^2}, & \dfrac{\partial^2 b_2(z)}{\partial z_1^2}, & \ldots, & \dfrac{\partial^2 b_k(z)}{\partial z_n^2} \\[2mm]
\dfrac{\partial^2 b_1(z)}{\partial z_1\,\partial z_2}, & \dfrac{\partial^2 b_2(z)}{\partial z_1\,\partial z_2}, & \ldots, & \dfrac{\partial^2 b_k(z)}{\partial z\,\partial z_2} \\[2mm]
\vdots & & & \\[2mm]
\dfrac{\partial^2 b_1(z)}{\partial z_n^2}, & \dfrac{\partial^2 b_2(z)}{\partial z_n^2}, & \ldots, & \dfrac{\partial^2 b_k(z)}{\partial z_n^2}
\end{bmatrix}
\begin{bmatrix}
\alpha_1 \\[2mm] \alpha_2 \\[2mm] \vdots \\[4mm] \\[4mm] \\[2mm] \alpha_k
\end{bmatrix}
=
\begin{bmatrix}
h^*(z) \\[2mm]
\dfrac{\partial h^*(z)}{\partial z_1} \\[2mm]
\vdots \\[2mm]
\dfrac{\partial h^*(z)}{\partial z_n} \\[2mm]
\dfrac{\partial^2 h^*(z)}{\partial z_1^2} \\[2mm]
\dfrac{\partial^2 h^*(z)}{\partial z_1\,\partial z_2} \\[2mm]
\vdots \\[2mm]
\dfrac{\partial^2 h^*(z)}{\partial z_n^2}
\end{bmatrix}
\tag{5.2'}
$$

The matrix on the left-hand side of (5.2′) is the Wronksian matrix and has as many columns as there are parameters of $h(z)$. If (5.2′) is to have a unique solution that is consistent with $h(z)$ approximating $h^*(z)$, there must be as many columns as there are rows; $h(z)$ must have $\frac{1}{2}(n+1)(n+2)$ parameters. Thus, $h(z)$ approximates $h^*(z)$ at z^0 if the Wronksian matrix is invertible at z^0, which requires that it have full rank equaling $\frac{1}{2}(n+1)(n+2)$. Put another way, if the determinant of the Wronksian of $h(z)$ does not vanish at z^0, then $h(z)$ can approximate any arbitrary twice-continuously differentiable function at z^0.

Besides approximating an arbitrary function in a second-order differential sense, expression (5.1) also can be formulated to represent a Taylor series approximation to an arbitrary function as follows. Let

$$
\alpha_1 = h^*(z^0)
$$

$$
\alpha_i = \frac{\partial h^*(z^0)}{\partial z_{i-1}}, \quad i = 2, \ldots, n+1,
\tag{5.3}
$$

$$
\alpha_j = \frac{\partial^2 h^*(z^0)}{\partial z_v\,\partial z_m}, \quad j = n+2, \ldots, \tfrac{1}{2}(n+1)(n+2),
$$

and

$$b_1(z^0) = 1,$$

$$b_i(z^0) = z_{i-1} - z_{i-1}^0, \quad i = 2, \ldots, n+1,$$

$$b_j(z^0) = \tfrac{1}{2}(z_v - z_v^0)(z_m - z_m^0), \quad j = n+2, \ldots, \tfrac{1}{2}(n+1)(n+2),$$

which, when combined with (5.1), yields the second-order Taylor series expansion. Forms that can be interpreted as a second-order Taylor series approximation to an arbitrary function are called *second-order numerical approximations.*

These developments indicate that the general linear form is attractive since it can approximate, in two general senses, any arbitrary twice-continuously differentiable function. Moreover, since it involves at least $\tfrac{1}{2}(n+1)(n+2)$ independent parameters, it should not impose many prior restrictions on the economic phenomena being measured. Forms that can be either second-order numerical or second-order differential approximations are usually referred to as *flexible functional forms.* The best way to underline what is meant by flexibility is by contrast with a form that is not flexible, the Cobb–Douglas. The parameters of a Cobb–Douglas cannot be chosen to satisfy either (5.2) or (5.3). In fact, the Cobb–Douglas is at best a first-order approximation. To see this more concretely, consider the Cobb–Douglas cost function introduced in Example 2.1. Results reported there indicate that all cross-price, derived-demand elasticities equal parameters of the cost function that by Shephard's lemma also equal the cost shares. Hence, first- and second-order effects are confounded in the Cobb–Douglas.

Example 5.1. The representation in (5.1) is more general (and therefore less manageable) than is necessary for many empirical applications. Often, tractability requires representing each $b^i(z)$ as a function of a subset of z. A relatively general, but tractable, version of (5.1) that contains as special cases the most commonly used flexible forms is the *generalized quadratic*

$$h(z) = \beta_0 + \sum_{i=1}^{n} \beta_i g_i(z_i) + \frac{1}{2} \sum_{i}^{n} \sum_{j}^{n} \beta_{ij} g_i(z_i) g_j(z_j), \tag{5.4}$$

where $\beta_{ij} = \beta_{ji}$ and each $g_i(z_i)$ is a known twice-continuously differentiable function of z_i. To verify (5.4) as a special case of (5.1), let

$$\beta_0 = \alpha_1, \quad \beta_i = \alpha_{i+1}, \quad \beta_{ij} = \alpha_v, \quad i = 1, 2, \ldots, n,$$

where v refers to the subscript of the element of α in (5.2) in the same row position as $\partial^2 h^*(z)/\partial z_i \, \partial z_j$, and

$$1 = b_1(z^0),$$

$$g_i(z_i) = b_{i+1}(z^0), \quad i = 1, 2, \ldots, n,$$

$$g_i(z_i) g_j(z_j) = b_v(z^0).$$

Completely analogous arguments demonstrate that the second-order Taylor series approximation is a special case of (5.4), so that the generalized quadratic is flexible in both senses.

Example 5.2. Consider the following problem: Approximate the Cobb–Douglas function

$$h^*(x) = 4x_1^2 x_2^2$$

at the point $x_1 = x_2 = 1$. At this point, the function value is 4, and the gradient is

$$\frac{\partial h^*}{\partial x_1} = 8x_1 x_2^2 = 8 \quad \text{and} \quad \frac{\partial h^*}{\partial x_2} = 8x_1^2 x_2 = 8.$$

Since the function is twice-continuously differentiable, the associated Hessian matrix is fully described by

$$\frac{\partial^2 h^*}{\partial x_1^2} = 8x_2^2 = 8, \qquad \frac{\partial^2 h^*}{\partial x_2^2} = 8x_1^2 = 8, \qquad \frac{\partial^2 h^*}{\partial x_1 \partial x_2} = 16x_1 x_2 = 16.$$

As a candidate to approximate this Cobb–Douglas function, consider

$$h(x) = a_0 + a_1 x_1 + a_2 x_2 + a_3 x_1^{1/2} + a_4 x_2^{1/2} + a_5 x_1 x_2.$$

Because the gradient plus the unique elements of the Hessian matrix for $h^*(x)$ and the function value consist of six terms, we have chosen to approximate $h^*(x)$ with a function linear in six parameters. The gradient for $h(x)$ is

$$\frac{\partial h}{\partial x_1} = a_1 + \frac{a_3}{2} x_1^{-1/2} + a_5 x_2 = a_1 + \frac{a_3}{2} + a_5,$$

$$\frac{\partial h}{\partial x_2} = a_2 + \frac{a_4}{2} x_2^{-1/2} + a_5 x_1 = a_2 + \frac{a_4}{2} + a_5,$$

and the appropriate elements of the Hessian are

$$\frac{\partial^2 h}{\partial x_1^2} = -\frac{a_3}{4} x_1^{-3/2} = -\frac{a_3}{4},$$

$$\frac{\partial^2 h}{\partial x_1 \partial x_2} = a_5,$$

$$\frac{\partial^2 h}{\partial x_2^2} = -\frac{a_4}{4} x_2^{-3/2} = -\frac{a_4}{4}.$$

Thus, the Wronksian version of expression (5.2) is

$$
\begin{bmatrix}
1 & 1 & 1 & 1 & 1 & 1 \\
0 & 1 & 0 & \frac{1}{2} & 0 & 1 \\
0 & 0 & 1 & 0 & \frac{1}{2} & 1 \\
0 & 0 & 0 & -\frac{1}{4} & 0 & 0 \\
0 & 0 & 0 & 0 & 0 & 1 \\
0 & 0 & 0 & 0 & -\frac{1}{4} & 0
\end{bmatrix}
\begin{bmatrix}
a_0 \\
a_1 \\
a_2 \\
a_3 \\
a_4 \\
a_5
\end{bmatrix}
=
\begin{bmatrix}
4 \\
8 \\
8 \\
8 \\
16 \\
8
\end{bmatrix}.
$$

The Wronksian matrix is nonsingular and can be inverted to obtain the following values for each a_i:

$$a_5 = 16, \qquad a_3 = a_4 = -32,$$

$$a_1 = a_2 = 8, \qquad a_0 = -32.$$

Example 5.3. Consider approximating the Cobb–Douglas function in Example 5.2 with the function

$$h(x) = a_0 + a_1 x_1 + a_2 x_2 + a_3 x_2 + a_4 x_1^2 + a_5 x_2.$$

At any point (but for convenience take the unit vector again), the reader should be convinced that the Wronksian associated with this function is singular. The reason is that the row of the Wronksian for the derivative $\partial^2 h / \partial x_1 \, \partial x_2$ is a null vector, as is that for $\partial^2 h / \partial x_2^2$.

A remaining issue to be addressed before moving on to more specific cases is exactly what is being modeled or approximated. The point is perhaps best illustrated by the observation that empirical studies in economics are commonly carried out in terms of the natural logarithms of variables. There are many arguments for proceeding in this manner, none of which need be repeated here. The fact remains, however, that it is not uncommon to transform economic variables before they are used in empirical analysis. If the transformation is invertible and single valued, no generality is lost in proceeding in this way when convenient. Similar reasoning applies here with only slight modifications. That is, often, it is convenient to use the generalized linear form when $h^*(z)$ is a known transformation of, say, the production or the profit function. If the transformation is known and twice-continuously differentiable, the general linear form remains flexible: Its parameters can be chosen to provide a second-order numerical or a second-order differential approximation.

To illustrate, suppose that one is ultimately interested in $\hat{h}(z)$, defined by

$$F^{-1}(h^*(z)) = \hat{h}(z),$$

where $F^{-1}(\ )$ is the inverse mapping of an appropriately defined transform (see Section 2.8a). Since $F^{-1}(\ )$ is known, it is easy to calculate

$$\nabla_z \hat{h}(z) = \frac{\partial F^{-1}(h^*)}{\partial h^*} \nabla_z h^*(z),$$

$$\nabla_{zz} \hat{h}(z) = \frac{\partial^2 F^{-1}(h^*)}{\partial h^{*2}} \nabla_z h^*(z) \nabla_z h^*(z)^T + \frac{\partial F^{-1}(h^*)}{\partial h^*} \nabla_{zz} h^*(z),$$

where the superscript T denotes transposition. If $h(z)$ is itself used to approximate $h^*(z)$, these results can be used to show that $F^{-1}(h)$ approximates $\hat{h}(z)$ in a second-order differential sense.

> **Exercise 5.1.** Show whether $F^{-1}(h(z))$ provides a second-order numerical approximation to $\hat{h}(z)$.

One of the most popular transformations of economic variables is the natural logarithm. This suggests considering the second-order numerical approximation of the logarithm of an arbitrary function $\hat{h}(z)$. Expanding in terms of the logarithm of the arguments and evaluating at $z^{0\prime} = (1, 1, \ldots, 1)$ obtains

$$\ln \hat{h}(z) \cong \ln \hat{h}(z^0) + \sum_{i=1}^{n} \frac{\partial \ln \hat{h}(z^0)}{\partial \ln z_i} \ln z_i$$

$$+ \frac{1}{2} \sum_i \sum_j \frac{\partial^2 \ln \hat{h}(z^0)}{\partial \ln z_i \, \partial \ln z_j} \ln z_i \ln z_j$$

since the natural logarithm of 1 equals zero. Letting

$$\ln \hat{h}(z^0) = \beta_0,$$

$$\frac{\partial \ln \hat{h}(z^0)}{\partial \ln z_i} = \beta_i,$$

and

$$\frac{\partial^2 \ln \hat{h}(z^0)}{\partial \ln z_i \, \partial \ln z_j} = \beta_{ij}$$

then gives

$$\ln \hat{h}(z) \cong \beta_o + \sum_{i=1}^{n} \beta_i \ln z_i + \frac{1}{2} \sum_i^n \sum_j^n \beta_{ij} \ln z_i \ln z_j. \tag{5.5}$$

The right-hand side of (5.5) is the *transcendental logarithmic* function (*translog* for short) and is interpretable as a second-order numerical approximation to an arbitrary $\hat{h}(z)$ in the neighborhood of $z^0 = 1$. The right-hand side of (5.5) is also a special case of the generalized quadratic form and, hence, a special case of the general linear form. Therefore, the translog, which has proven the most popular form in recent applied production economics, is flexible and can approximate arbitrary twice-continuously differentiable functions.

Example 5.4. The preceding discussion derived the translog as a special case of (5.1). Quite naturally, there are as many examples of similar approximations as there are unique monotonic transformations. Another that is quite well known is the function obtained by taking a second-order Taylor series expansion of the transformation of $\hat{h}(z)$, $\hat{h}(z)^p$, in terms of $z^{p/2}$ in the neighborhood of the null vector. The resulting approximation is

$$h(z)^p = \gamma_0 + \sum_{i=1}^n \gamma_i z_i^{p/2} + \frac{1}{2} \sum_{i=1}^n \sum_{j=1}^n \gamma_{ij} z_i^{p/2} z_j^{p/2},$$

which is called the *quadratic mean of order p*. Note in particular that if $\gamma_{ij} = 0$ for all i, j, the quadratic mean of order p degenerates to the CES function. A similar argument demonstrates that when $\beta_{ij} = 0$ for all i, j, the translog degenerates to the Cobb–Douglas.

Exercise 5.2. Decide whether the quadratic mean of order p is a second-order differential approximation to $\hat{h}(z)$ at $z^0 = 0$.

5.2 Approximation properties of flexible forms

The preceding section showed that a flexible form providing a second-order numerical or differential approximation to the transform of an arbitrary function also provides a second-order approximation to the function itself. Although important, this is to some extent tautological and, therefore, not very compelling. A deeper (and from an empirical perspective a more important) question is, Are these approximation properties preserved under the duality transformation? We have illustrated in several contexts that an indirect objective function (e.g., the cost function) can be used to reconstruct a primal function (e.g., the production function) that is observationally equivalent to the one that generated the indirect objective function. We now wish to determine whether this resurrection of the primal function destroys any of the approximation properties of the indirect objective function. The problem is perhaps best illustrated by an example. Suppose one has used an appropriate version of (5.1) to approximate a profit function. Will the cost function derived from applying the conjugacy relations to this approximation be an approximation to a cost function observationally equivalent to the cost function that generated the original profit function? If so, we have a strong result because the approximation to the profit function can be used to recapture all of the economically relevant information about the underlying cost function. And if this result holds between all primal and dual forms, the case for flexible forms is considerably strengthened.

The answer to the question posed in the previous paragraph is a modified yes. That is, the second-order differential approximation properties of a flexible form are preserved under the duality mapping. Although the answer is not an unqualified yes, the importance of the result is not diminished. To a large extent, it is the second-order differential approximation properties that appear the most important. It seems most important to have a firm grasp on the behavior of derived demands and related phenomena. In what follows, I only demonstrate this result for the dual mapping from profit to cost functions. There are two reasons for this: to emphasize the importance of profit functions in applied production analysis and to extend, however slightly, the existing literature. Blackorby and Diewert (1979) have already demonstrated this preservation property of flexible forms in the context of cost and production functions. By combining their results with ones to be derived here, it follows that such a relationship exists between profit and production functions.

The key to this demonstration is the recognition that the conjugacy relations developed in Chapter 4 allow one to express the gradient and the Hessian of the cost function solely in terms of the profit function. Recall from Chapter 4 that if a duality exists,

$$c(w, y) = \max_{p > 0} \{ py - \Pi(p, w) \}$$

$$= p^* y - \Pi(p^*, w), \tag{5.6}$$

where p^* solves the conjugate maximization problem. Applying the envelope theorem successively,

$$\frac{\partial c(w, y)}{\partial y} = p^*, \tag{5.7}$$

$$\frac{\partial c(w, y)}{\partial w_i} = -\frac{\partial \Pi(p^*, w)}{\partial w_i}, \quad i = 1, 2, ..., n.$$

The first-order condition for an interior solution gives

$$y - \frac{\partial \Pi(p^*, w)}{\partial p} = 0. \tag{5.8}$$

By (5.8) and the implicit function theorem,

$$\frac{\partial p^*}{\partial y} = [\partial^2 \Pi(p^*, w)/\partial p^2]^{-1}, \tag{5.9}$$

$$\frac{\partial p^*}{\partial w_i} = \frac{-\partial^2 \Pi(p^*, w)/\partial p\, \partial w_i}{\partial^2 \Pi(p^*, w)/\partial p^2}. \tag{5.10}$$

Differentiating expressions (5.7) using (5.9) and (5.10),

$$\frac{\partial^2 c(w, y)}{\partial y^2} = \left[\frac{\partial^2 \Pi(p^*, w)}{\partial p^2} \right]^{-1},$$

$$\frac{\partial^2 c(w, y)}{\partial y\, \partial w_j} = -\left[\frac{\partial^2 \Pi(p^*, w)/\partial p\, \partial w_i}{\partial^2 \Pi(p^*, w)/\partial p^2} \right], \tag{5.11}$$

$$\frac{\partial^2 c(w, y)}{\partial w_i\, \partial w_j} = \frac{(\partial^2 \Pi(p^*, w)/\partial p\, \partial w_j)(\partial^2 \Pi/\partial p\, \partial w_i)}{\partial^2 \Pi(p^*, w)/\partial p^2} - \frac{\partial^2 \Pi(p^*, w)}{\partial w_i\, \partial w_j}.$$

Using (5.6), (5.7), and (5.11) shows that elements of the gradient, the Hessian, and the value of the cost function can be expressed solely in terms of the profit function and p^*. Being able to specify a general linear form (call it $\hat{\Pi}$) satisfying (5.2) for $\Pi(p, w)$ means that (5.6), (5.7), and (5.11) can be used to verify that the conjugate cost function for (5.6) is a second-order differential approximation to the true cost function at (p^*, w).

5.3   Flexible forms for profit and cost functions

Preceding discussions maintained that there are $\frac{1}{2}(n+1)(n+2)$ economically relevant effects associated with a smooth production technology. Since the production function has n arguments while the associated profit and cost functions each have $n+1$ arguments, one might expect that designing a version of (5.1) for these latter functions involves a function with $\frac{1}{2}(n+3)(n+2)$ parameters to account for all the separate effects: the function value, a gradient with $n+1$ arguments, and a symmetric Hessian with $\frac{1}{2}(n+1)(n+2)$ independent terms. On the other hand, duality arguments suggest that both primal and dual functions offer equally good characterizations of all economically relevant information. This implies that some of the $\frac{1}{2}(n+3)(n+2)$ effects associated with, say, profit are not truly independent and can be expressed in terms of other effects. That this is so is easily demonstrated by using the relevant homogeneity properties to show that there exist $n+2$ separate restrictions not yet accounted for. The homogeneity of the profit function implies the following restrictions on the gradient and Hessian:

$$\Pi(p, w) = \sum_{j=1}^{n} \frac{\partial \Pi(p, w)}{\partial w_j} w_j + \frac{\partial \Pi(p, w)}{\partial p} p,$$

$$0 = \sum_{j=1}^{n} \frac{\partial^2 \Pi(p, w)}{\partial w_i\, \partial w_j} w_j + \frac{\partial^2 \Pi(p, w)}{\partial w_i\, \partial p} p, \quad i = 1, 2, \dots, n,$$

$$0 = \sum_{j=1}^{n} \frac{\partial^2 \Pi(p, w)}{\partial p \, \partial w_j} w_j + \frac{\partial^2 \Pi(p, w)}{\partial p^2} p.$$

When these $n+2$ restrictions are accounted for, only $\frac{1}{2}(n+1)(n+2)$ independent effects associated with the profit function remain. The following discussion concentrates on profit functions and leaves the extension of most results to the cost function to the reader.

Exercise 5.3. Show by the homogeneity properties of the cost function that there are only $\frac{1}{2}(n+1)(n+2)$ distinct effects associated with the gradient and the Hessian of a twice-continuously differentiable cost function.

In constructing a function to represent a profit function, one should include in the specification at least $\frac{1}{2}(n+1)(n+2) = k$ parameters. Hence, we start with the representation

$$\Pi(p, w) = \sum_{i=1}^{k} \alpha_i h_i(p, w), \tag{5.12}$$

where each $h_i(p, w)$ is twice-continuously differentiable. Expression (5.12), however, is not an adequate basis for the study of profit-maximizing firms; it ignores important information derived from the maximization hypothesis. Namely, (5.12) must satisfy properties 4C.1–4C.5 if it is to be a valid profit function. In particular, (5.12) must be both linearly homogeneous and convex. By definition, linear homogeneity implies

$$\Pi(tp, tw) = \sum_{i=1}^{n} \alpha_i h_i(tp, tw)$$

$$= t\Pi(p, w)$$

$$= t \sum_{i=1}^{n} \alpha_i h_i(p, w).$$

The second and third equalities suggest that for arbitrary α_i each $h_i(\cdot)$ function must be linearly homogeneous to ensure overall linear homogeneity.

Convexity is a somewhat more difficult problem. However, by standard results (see Appendix), sufficient conditions for (5.12) to be convex are for each α_i to be positive (negative) and each $h_i(p, w)$ function to be convex (concave). This suggests that one way to guarantee that functions like (5.12) are consistent with 4C.1–4C.5 is to pick each $h_i(p, w)$ so that it satisfies 4C.1–4C.5. For example, one might specify each $h_i(p, w)$ as an independent Cobb–Douglas of the form

$$h_i(p, w) = A_i \, p^{\gamma/(\gamma - 1)} \prod_{j=1}^{n} w_j^{\gamma_j/(1 - \gamma)},$$

where $\gamma > 1 = \sum_{i=1}^{n} \gamma_i$ and the parameters $(A_i > 0, \ \gamma_j > 0)$ are known and different for each $h_i(p, w)$. Therefore, arbitrary profit functions can be approximated by considering an appropriate linear combination of other profit functions.

Expression (5.12) is more general than is common in empirical analysis. Each $h_i(p, w)$ function usually depends on only a small subset of (p, w); frequently, it only depends on two prices. Of the functions depending on so few prices, perhaps the most general is a version introduced by McFadden (1978b):

$$\Pi(q) = \sum_{i=0}^{n} \sum_{j=0}^{n} \beta_{ij} q_i Q_{ij} \left(\frac{q_j}{q_i} \right), \tag{5.13}$$

with $\beta_{ij} = \beta_{ji}$ and where, for notational convenience, we denote $q = (p, w)$ with $q_0 = p$ and $q_i = w_i$. In (5.13), each $Q_{ij}(q_j/q_i)$ is automatically homogeneous of degree zero, implying that (5.13) is linearly homogeneous in (p, w). Assuming $\beta_{ij} \geq 0$ $(i \neq j)$ and each $Q_{ij}(q_j/q_i)$ is twice-continuously differentiable and convex ensures that (5.13) satisfies the curvature and smoothness properties associated with a well-behaved profit function. To satisfy the remaining properties, one needs $\partial \Pi(q)/\partial p$ to be nonnegative and $\partial \Pi(q)/\partial w_i$ to be nonpositive. Verification of these is left to the reader as an exercise.

Exercise 5.4. Derive restrictions on expression (5.13) to ensure its consistency with the monotonicity properties of profit functions.

Exercise 5.5. Expressions (5.12) and (5.13) can be valid representations of profit functions. In extending the results to cost functions, one must account for output effects as well as price effects. Specifically, consider the following candidate for a cost function:

$$c(w, y) = \sum_{i=1}^{n} \sum_{j=1}^{m} \gamma_{ij} w_i M^{ij}(w_j/w_i, y). \tag{5.14}$$

Determine whether (5.14) is a valid cost function. Is (5.14) a flexible form? If it is not, generalize it suitably.

Example 5.5. One of the earliest and most popular versions of (5.13) is the *generalized Leontief function*. The generalized Leontief profit function is defined by

$$Q_{ij} = -(q_j/q_i)^{1/2}. \tag{5.15}$$

The term on the right-hand side of (5.15) is convex, and as long as $\beta_{ij} > 0$ ($i \neq j$), the associated profit function

$$\Pi(p, w) = -\left[\beta_{00} p + 2p^{1/2} \sum_{j=1}^{n} \beta_{0j} w_j^{1/2} + \sum_{j=1}^{n} \sum_{i=1}^{n} \beta_{ij} (w_i w_j)^{1/2}\right]$$

is both convex and linearly homogeneous. By calculation and Hotelling's lemma,

$$y(p, w) = -\left[\beta_{00} + p^{-1/2} \sum_{j=1}^{n} \beta_{0j} w_j^{1/2}\right], \tag{5.16}$$

$$x_j(p, w) = p^{1/2} \beta_{0j} w_j^{-1/2} + \sum_{i=1}^{n} \beta_{ij} \left(\frac{w_i}{w_j}\right)^{1/2}. \tag{5.17}$$

Perhaps the most important thing to notice about (5.16) and (5.17) is that both are linear in parameters. If one has information on supply, derived demands, and prices, (5.16) and (5.17) provide a sound basis for estimation of the technology by multivariate regression techniques. (Also notice that the generalized Leontief is a special case of the quadratic mean of order p, where $p = 1$.)

5.4 Limitations of flexible functional forms

So far, very little has been said about the limitations of flexible forms. However, as any skeptic would suspect, they do not represent a panacea for applied production analysis. Although they are widely used in a variety of contexts and are approaching the status of such time-honored functions as the Cobb–Douglas and the CES in ubiquity, they do have limitations that are being increasingly recognized. The fact that they limit the range of technologies that can be characterized is, in itself, not surprising since fundamental duality results imply that any specification of a cost or a profit function places some restrictions on the technology. What has become distressingly apparent, however, is that these functions appear to be more limiting than many originally expected. The best way to introduce the substance of this analysis is with an example.

By Hotelling's lemma, the derived demand for the ith input (or supply if $i = 0$) associated with (5.13) is:

$$x_i(p, w) = -\sum_{j=0}^{n} \beta_{ij} \left[Q_{ij}\left(\frac{q_j}{q_i}\right) - \frac{q_j}{q_i} Q_{ij}'\left(\frac{q_j}{q_i}\right) + Q_{ji}'\left(\frac{q_i}{q_j}\right)\right].$$

Moreover,

$$\frac{\partial x_i(p, w)}{\partial q_v} = \beta_{iv}\left[\frac{q_v}{q_i^2} Q_{iv}''\left(\frac{q_v}{q_i}\right) + \frac{q_i}{q_v^2} Q_{vi}''\left(\frac{q_i}{q_v}\right)\right] \quad \text{when } i \neq v.$$

If each Q_{iv} is convex, the term in brackets is positive if all prices are positive. Since, to ensure convexity of $\Pi(p, w)$, we also assume that $\beta_{iv} \geq 0$ ($i \neq v$), expression (5.13) thus implies gross substitutability. That is, if each Q_{iv} is convex and each $\beta_{iv} \geq 0$, all inputs are gross substitutes and all inputs are also nonregressive.

Perhaps more serious than the above is the fact that generalized quadratic forms (e.g., the generalized Leontief, the translog, and the quadratic mean of order p) are very inflexible in representing separable technologies. This remains true regardless of whether one is trying to represent the function of interest or a monotonic transformation of it. (Recall that separability hinges on the ratio between various first partial derivatives; such ratios are invariant to monotonic transformations.)

For the generalized quadratic in (5.4),

$$\frac{\partial h(z)}{\partial z_i} = \beta_i g_i'(z_i) + \sum_{k=1}^{n} \beta_{ik} g_k(z_k) g_i'(z_i).$$

Hence,

$$\frac{\partial h(z)/\partial z_i}{\partial h(z)/\partial z_j} = \frac{g_i'(z_i)}{g_j'(z_j)} \frac{\sum_{k=1}^{n} \beta_{ik} g_k(z_k) + \beta_i}{\sum_{k=1}^{n} \beta_{jk} g_k(z_k) + \beta_j} \equiv \frac{g_i'(z_i)}{g_j'(z_j)} \frac{R_i}{R_j}.$$

If (5.4) is consistent with z_v separable from z_i and z_j, then

$$\frac{\partial}{\partial z_v} \frac{\partial h(z)/\partial z_i}{\partial h(z)/\partial z_j} = \frac{g_i(z_i)}{g_j(z_j)} \left(\frac{1}{R_j} \frac{\partial R_i}{\partial z_v} - \frac{R_i}{R_j^2} \frac{\partial R_j}{\partial z_v} \right).$$

$$= 0.$$

Or put another way,

$$R_j \frac{\partial R_i}{\partial z_v} = R_i \frac{\partial R_j}{\partial z_v}. \tag{5.18}$$

Substituting into (5.18),

$$\beta_j \beta_{iv} - \beta_i \beta_{jv} + \sum_{k=1}^{n} (\beta_{jk} \beta_{iv} - \beta_{ik} \beta_{jv}) g_k(z_k) = 0. \tag{5.19}$$

Since the $g_i(Z_i)$'s are arbitrary, numeric functions, expression (5.19) is only globally valid if

$$\beta_j \beta_{iv} = \beta_i \beta_{jv}, \quad \beta_{jk} \beta_{iv} = \beta_{ik} \beta_{jv}, \quad k = 1, 2, \dots, n. \tag{5.20}$$

Expression (5.20) represents $n+1$ restrictions on the parameters of (5.4). Notice, however, that these $n+1$ restrictions are imposed to ensure only that the following relationship holds:

$$\frac{\partial^2 h}{\partial z_i \partial z_v} = \left(\frac{\partial h/\partial z_i}{\partial h/\partial z_j} \right) \frac{\partial^2 h}{\partial z_j \partial z_v}.$$

This last equation represents only a single restriction on the $\frac{1}{2}(n+1)(n+2)$ economically distinct effects. Incorporation of (5.20), however, limits the number of free parameters to $\frac{1}{2}n(n+1)$. Imposing separability on the generalized quadratic involves parametric restrictions that result in more restrictions than originally desired. It is no longer valid to call the resulting form flexible since there are not enough free parameters left to depict the remaining distinct effects.

Having seen that imposing separability on (5.4) overparameterizes the restrictions, it is worthwhile to pursue this argument further. Rather than resorting to more tedious mathematical arguments emphasizing computation rather than inspiration, I shall state the basic results and leave it to the reader as an exercise to determine their ultimate validity. The result in expression (5.20) holds if and only if either $\beta_{iv} = \beta_{jv} = 0$ or i and j are separable from all other elements of z.

Exercise 5.6. Show that for the generalized quadratic form in (5.4) Z_i and Z_j are separable from Z_v if either $\beta_{iv} = \beta_{jv} = 0$ or z_j and z_i are separable from all other variables in the function. (This exercise only involves demonstrating sufficiency; necessity is much more complicated and perhaps is best left to only the most advanced readers.)

The ultimate conclusion to be drawn is that the generalized quadratic does not provide a very satisfactory method for testing separability restrictions. One needs to impose too much structure on the problem to accomplish the desired separability. The imposition of restrictions is not parsimonious, suggesting one should utilize more general relationships in considering separability.

Since the generalized quadratic cannot represent a separable technology flexibly, it is interesting to determine whether the general linear (or versions of it) places other easily recognized restrictions on the technology. For expression (5.13), the conjugacy relations imply that

$$c(w, y) = \max_p \left\{ py - \beta_{00} p - p \sum_{j=1}^n \beta_{0j} Q_{0j}\left(\frac{w_j}{p}\right) \right.$$

$$\left. - \sum_{j=1}^n \beta_{j0} Q_{j0}\left(\frac{p}{w_j}\right) w_j - \sum_{i=1}^n \sum_{j=1}^n \beta_{ij} w_i Q_{ij}\left(\frac{w_j}{w_i}\right) \right\}$$

is the cost function dual to (5.13). Here, $Q_{00}(1) = 1$ without loss of generality. Because the last term in braces is independent of p, the dual-cost function takes the form

$$c(w, y) = \Theta(w, y) + \phi(w), \tag{5.21}$$

where

$$\phi(w) = - \sum_{i=1}^{n} \sum_{j=1}^{n} \beta_{ij} w_i Q_{ij}\left(\frac{w_j}{w_i}\right),$$

$$\Theta(w, y) = \max_{p} \left\{ p\left(y - \beta_{00} - \sum_{j=1}^{n} \beta_{0j} Q_{0j}\left(\frac{w_j}{p}\right)\right) \right.$$

$$\left. - \sum_{j=1}^{n} \beta_{j0} Q_{j0}\left(\frac{p}{w_j}\right) w_j \right\}.$$

The cost function dual to (5.13) consists of two parts. The first part, $\phi(w)$, is linearly homogeneous and concave in w but independent of y; it may be thought of heuristically as a unit cost function for a constant-returns technology. The second part of the cost function is also linearly homogeneous and concave, but it is not independent of y. Hence, it too can be interpreted as a cost function.

Intuitively, therefore, the general linear profit function in (5.13) portrays a technology for a two-plant or two-tier operation. The first plant, corresponding to $\phi(w)$, represents that part of the productive process independent of output, that is, costs that are fixed. The second plant, corresponding to $\Theta(w, y)$, represents that part of the productive process dependent on output, that is, variable costs. Since $\Theta(w, y)$ can assume a number of different forms depending on the $Q_{ij}(\cdot)$ functions, (5.21) apparently is not unduly restrictive a priori. However, in the case of the generalized Leontief, expression (5.21) becomes much more restrictive. In that instance, applying the envelope theorem yields

$$\frac{\partial \Theta(w, y)}{\partial w_i} = p^{*1/2} \beta_{0i} w_i^{-1/2} \quad \forall i. \tag{5.22}$$

But (5.22) implies that all ratios $[\partial \Theta(w, y)/\partial w_i]/[\partial \Theta(w, y)/\partial w_j]$ are independent of y: In this instance, $\Theta(w, y)$ must be homothetic and expressible as $h(y)c(w)$. Thus, the technology dual to a generalized Leontief profit function is of the general form

$$c(w, y) = h(y)c(w) + \phi(w). \tag{5.23}$$

If the technology assumes the form of (5.23), it is called *quasi-homothetic* because it has straight-line expansion paths such as a homothetic technology. Unlike a homothetic technology, however, these expansion paths do not emanate from the origin. To see why, note that by Shephard's lemma for quasi-homothetic cost functions,

$$\frac{\partial x_i(w, y)/\partial y}{\partial x_j(w, y)/\partial y} = \frac{\partial c(w)/\partial w_i}{\partial c(w)/\partial w_j}.$$

As with a homothetic technology, the right-hand side is independent of output. Contrary to a homothetic technology, however, optimal input ratios do depend on the level of output.

As pointed out, a quasi-homothetic technology can be interpreted as associated with a production process carried out in two plants. In the first, cost is minimized in a fashion consistent with a homothetic technology. In the second, however, cost is independent of output; in short, $\phi(w)$ might be interpreted as a fixed cost of operation. Thus, a quasi-homothetic technology does not satisfy all of the properties of cost functions derived in Chapter 2 unless $\phi(w)$ equals zero, but in this case, the technology is consistent with homotheticity. Thus, the generalized Leontief profit function as represented here can only generate a cost function consistent with properties 2B if it is also consistent with homotheticity. Reversing the duality mapping yields

$$\Pi(p, w) = \max_{y}\{py - h(y)c(w) - \phi(w)\}$$

$$= \max_{y}\{py - h(y)c(w)\} - \phi(w)$$

$$= \hat{\Pi}(p, c(w)) - \phi(w),$$

which is the general structure of a profit function consistent with quasi-homotheticity. An alternative way to determine whether versions (5.13) imply quasi-homotheticity is to determine whether the subfunction

$$\beta_{00}p + \sum_{j=1}^{n} p\beta_{0j}Q_{0j} + \sum_{j=1}^{n} \beta_{j0}Q_{j0}w_j$$

is separable as required by homotheticity.

Exercise 5.7. Use the results in expression (5.21) to derive the exact cost function dual to the generalized Leontief profit function. This requires solving for $\Theta(w, y)$ in (5.21).

Before closing this section on the limitations of flexible forms, it is worthwhile to stress a point that is probably already apparent to many readers: Even if flexible forms are not restrictive, their ability to approximate arbitrary technologies is limited. The notions of approximation relied upon are local in nature: either a point approximation to the function, gradient, and Hessian or a second-order Taylor series expansion. Neither are truly global, and approximations based on them cannot be very exact for a wide range of observations.

To illustrate, consider a general linear form fitted by statistical means to a data set with, say, T observations. Suppose further that the observations consist of price and quantity data and that the fitted function is a profit function. If the fitted profit function is to provide a second-order differential approximation over the entire set of observations, expression (5.2) must apply at all T observations. For notational convenience, rewrite (5.2) as

$$A(t)\alpha = B(t), \tag{5.24}$$

where α is the $\frac{1}{2}(n+1)(n+2)$-dimensional vector of parameters, $A(t)$ is the Wronksian matrix on the left-hand side of (5.2′) when evaluated at observation t, and $B(t)$ is the vector on the right-hand side of (5.2′) defined similarly. Under usual circumstances, estimation yields a single estimate of the vector α; call it $\hat{\alpha}$. If the estimated technology is to be interpretable as a second-order differential approximation at all T observations, it must be true that

$$\hat{\alpha} = A^{-1}(1)B(1) = A^{-1}(2)B(2) = \cdots = A^{-1}(T)B(T).$$

Of course, the likelihood of this last expression actually holding, even approximately, is so small as to remove it from the reasonable range of consideration (see also White).

These arguments make it fairly clear just how limited the approximation properties of flexible forms are. However, many more arguments can be marshalled on this general topic. Rather than detailing a complete catalog, the argument is illustrated with one further example that is based on perhaps the most widely used flexible form, the translog. For the sake of concreteness, consider the translog cost function (a much more concrete example is detailed below)

$$\ln c(w, y) = \alpha_0 + \sum_{i=1}^{n} \alpha_i \ln w_i + \alpha_y \ln y + \frac{1}{2} \sum_{i=1}^{n} \sum_{j=1}^{n} \alpha_{ij} \ln w_i \ln w_j$$

$$+ \sum_{i=1}^{n} \alpha_{yi} \ln w_i \ln y + \alpha_{yy}(\ln y)^2, \tag{5.25}$$

where $\alpha_{ij} = \alpha_{ji}$. As shown, (5.25) can be interpreted as either a generalized quadratic or as a second-order Taylor series expansion around $w' = (1, 1, \ldots, 1)$, $y = 1$. Suppose the latter for the sake of argument. Then, to be consistent with the properties of a cost function, (5.25) must be consistent with both linear homogeneity and concavity in w. Linear homogeneity is simple enough for it requires

$$\sum_{i=1}^{n} \frac{\partial \ln c(w, y)}{\partial \ln w_i} = 1,$$

which upon manipulation gives the following parametric restrictions:

$$\sum_{i=1}^{n} \alpha_i = 1 \quad \text{and} \quad \sum_{i} \alpha_{yi} = \sum_{j=1}^{n} \alpha_{ij} = 0.$$

Now consider concavity: The right-hand side of (5.25) does not admit of parametric restrictions that make it globally concave in w. To demonstrate, consider the function $\alpha_{ii}(\ln w_i)^2$. Concavity requires that the second derivative of this function be nonpositive. But direct calculation reveals that this second derivative is

$$\frac{2\alpha_{ii}}{w_i^2}(1 - \ln w_i).$$

If $\alpha_{ii} \geq 0$, this expression takes the required sign only if $1 \leq \ln w_i$. Hence, no parametric restriction on α_{ii} ensures that the function is globally concave or concave even over the positive orthant.

5.5 Using flexible functional forms

The best way of interpreting these caveats and limitations is that the main attraction of flexible forms does not lie in their ability to closely approximate arbitrary technologies. They simply do not have this property. Therefore, it is probably counterproductive to think of a general linear form in terms of approximating the unknown, but true, structure. Rather, it seems more productive to recognize that estimation requires the specification of some functional form. In a classical statistical sense, specifying a functional form in empirical analysis is tantamount to an assumption that the underlying technologies are wholly consistent with that form. Therefore, the most likely contribution of the flexible forms lies not in their approximation properties but in the fact that they apparently place far fewer restrictions prior to estimation than the more traditional Leontief, Cobb–Douglas, and CES technologies. In most instances, they let measures like the elasticity of size and elasticities of substitution depend on the data. Hence, they can vary across the sample and need not be parametric as they are for most of the more traditional forms. If approximation is relegated to a second rank, how does one deal with failures like that of the translog's inability to be globally concave or global convexity of (5.13) implying gross substitutability? The best answer seems two-sided: First, functional forms should be developed that solve some of these problems and, second, in explicitly recognizing limitations of these forms, one should not expect more of them than they are capable of giving.

If the approximation properties of flexible forms are only local, they should only be interpreted locally. If imposing global concavity imposes unacceptable a priori restrictions, perhaps we should not strive for that. Maybe it is better to be content with convexity or concavity over the observed data points when using such forms. As an example of the points being emphasized here, return briefly to the discussion of separability for the generalized quadratic. Recall now that separability of z_i and z_j from z_v required

$$\beta_j \beta_{iv} - \beta_i \beta_{jv} + \sum_{k=1}^{n} (\beta_{jk}\beta_{iv} - \beta_{ik}\beta_{jv}) g_k(z_k) = 0.$$

Although this is a single nonlinear restriction, applying it globally translates into $n+1$ parametric restrictions. We overparameterize the restrictions by n degrees. Suppose, instead, that we are satisfied with a local restriction, namely, one that applies in the neighborhood of z defined by

$$g_k(z_k) = 0, \quad k = 1, 2, \ldots, n.$$

The separability restriction now becomes

$$\beta_j \beta_{iv} - \beta_i \beta_{jv} = 0.$$

If this last restriction is incorporated, the generalized quadratic places no further restrictions on separability among other pairs of its arguments. By limiting the scope of the analysis, we have, to some extent, generalized the ultimate applicability of our results and strengthened the plausible interpretations. Suppose we wish to test for global separability of z_i and z_j from z in the context of the generalized quadratic. If we impose (5.20) and test for its validity statistically, there are at least two reasons to expect rejection of the null hypothesis: The null hypothesis is false or the extreme version of separability involved is false. Since Occam's razor dictates choosing the latter, we have a test that is never truly capable of rejecting the null hypothesis. On the other hand, using the local approach allows us this flexibility at least over a limited range of the observations.

Before leaving the discussion of flexible functional forms, it is convenient to summarize in tabular form some of the more important results developed for various functional forms in the previous section. Table 5.1 details the properties of some of the most commonly encountered functional forms in economics: the Cobb–Douglas, the CES, the translog, the generalized Leontief, and the general linear form suggested in (5.21). The table lists the functional forms approximation properties, as well as the ability to restrict the parameters so as to ensure concavity and linear homogeneity, and finally the separability properties of each form.

Table 5.1. Some properties of common functional forms

Function	Approximation properties	Linear homogeneity	Concavity	Separability
Cobb–Douglas $h(z) = A \prod_{i=1}^{n} x_i^{\alpha_i} \quad (\alpha_i \geq 0)$	first-order Taylor series, first-order differential	$\sum_{i=1}^{n} \alpha_i = 1$	$\sum_{i=1}^{n} \alpha_i \leq 1$	z-wise separable
CES $h(z) = A \left(\sum_{i=1}^{n} \delta_i z_i^p \right)^{1/p}$	first-order Taylor series, first-order differential	linearly homogeneous		z-wise separable
Translog $h(z) = \alpha_0 + \sum_{j=1}^{n} \alpha_j \ln z_j$ $\quad + \frac{1}{2} \sum_i \sum_j \alpha_{ij} \ln z_i \ln z_j$ $(\alpha_{ij} = \alpha_{ji})$	second-order Taylor series, second-order differential	$\sum_j \alpha_j = 1; \quad \sum_i \alpha_{ij} = \sum_j \alpha_{ij} = 0$	not possible globally	not possible to restrict and maintain approximation properties
Generalized Leontief $h(z) = \sum_i \sum_j \gamma_{ij}(z_i z_j)^{1/2}$ $(\gamma_{ij} = \gamma_{ji})$	second-order Taylor series, second-order differential	linearly homogeneous	$\gamma_{ij} \geq 0 \quad (i \neq j)$	not possible to restrict and maintain approximation properties
General linear $h(z) = \sum_i \sum_j \beta_{ij} z_i z_j Q_{ij}\left(\frac{z_j}{z_i}\right)$ $(\beta_{ij} = \beta_{ji})$	second-order Taylor series, second-order differential	linearly homogeneous	$\beta_{ij} \geq 0$ and Q_{ij} concave $(i \neq j)$	

5.6   Aggregation over firms

Up to now, the only type of aggregation considered is that involving aggregation of inputs, input prices, or output. As a consequence, the aggregation discussion has revolved around various types of separability. There is another aggregation problem that is at least as important empirically as aggregation of inputs and input prices. That involves aggregation across firms. One of the most unattractive realities researchers face is that data generated and collected on a regular basis often do not conform to the data or variables conceptualized in theory. All previous developments have relied either explicitly or implicitly on a firm-level argument. However, researchers do not always have access to firm-level data that enable them to characterize satisfactorily the technology for a particular firm. Often, data are available only at a relatively high degree of aggregation, and one is reduced to estimating industry (or at best representative firm) functions on the basis of either cross-sectional or time-series data. In what follows, an attempt is made to address this issue by considering the aggregation of firm-level cost functions to the industry level. The aggregation of profit functions is left to the reader as an exercise. *All short-run cost or profit functions require aggregation over the fixed inputs* (Gorman, 1968).

The first order of business is to describe just what is expected from an aggregate or industry cost function. One property that seems especially attractive and almost indispensable is that industry costs equal the sum of costs for all firms in the industry. Thus, if $c(w, y)$ is the industry cost function and $c^i(w, y^i)$ is the ith firm's cost function (assume all firms face the same input prices), we want

$$c(w, y) = \sum_{i=1}^{m} c^i(w, y^i) \tag{5.26}$$

if there are m firms in the industry. The most important thing to note here is that, except for the most trivial cases, each firm will operate or want to operate at a different output level. Further, output generally enters individual cost functions in a nonlinear and at times quite complicated fashion. Matters are simple when each firm produces the same output (call it y^*) and each firm's production function is characterized by constant returns to scale. Then,

$$c(w, y) = \sum_{i=1}^{m} y^* c^i(w)$$

$$= y^* \sum_{i=1}^{m} c^i(w) = y \sum_{i=1}^{m} \frac{1}{m} c^i(w) = yc(w),$$

where $y = my^*$. Aggregation is easy because $c(w, y)$ is a multiple of a sum of concave functions and hence must be concave.

5.7 Linear aggregation of output

Matters change, however, when cost functions are nonlinear in output and all firms do not produce the same level of output. One might then wonder, what is the appropriate definition of industry output? The answer is that it depends on how one feels about the distribution of output across firms. If the distribution of output across firms does not matter, the most appropriate definition of aggregate output is the simple, unweighted sum of each firm's output:

$$y = \sum_i y^i. \qquad (5.27)$$

Any functional form capable of satisfying both (5.26) and (5.27) is now a candidate for an industry cost function. The question that we seek to answer is, do (5.26) and (5.27) limit the family of functional forms that are candidates for an industry cost function? If $c(w, y)$ is consistent with these conditions, the class of candidate functions is considerably restricted. Differentiation of $c(w, y)$ with respect to y^1 yields

$$\frac{\partial c(w, y)}{\partial y^i} = \frac{\partial c(w, y)}{\partial y} \frac{\partial y}{\partial y^i} = \frac{\partial c^i(w, y^i)}{\partial y^i}.$$

Thus,

$$\frac{\partial c(w, y)}{\partial y} = \frac{\partial c^i(w, y^i)}{\partial y^i} \quad \forall i$$

since $\partial y / \partial y^i = 1$. Aggregation consistency requires that each firm-level marginal cost equal aggregate marginal cost. Moreover, because this must apply regardless of the level of y^i, it follows that each firm-level marginal cost must be independent of y^i. Why do we obtain this result? The explanation lies in the fact that from the aggregate perspective, it is irrelevant which firm produces which units of output. To illustrate, consider redistributing some of firm i's output to firm j. What effect does this have on aggregate marginal cost? Because the level of y has not changed, aggregate marginal cost, and indeed total cost, should not change. The only way that this is possible is if the marginal costs for firms i and j are the same. This last result also implies that aggregate marginal cost is independent of aggregate output. This can be seen in a number of ways, but the easiest is to differentiate the preceding expression with respect to y^j ($i \neq j$) to obtain

$$\frac{\partial^2 c(w, y)}{\partial y^i \partial y^j} = \frac{\partial^2 c(w, y)}{\partial y^2} = 0.$$

Letting $\lambda(w)$ represent aggregate marginal cost,

$$\lambda(w) = \frac{\partial c(w, y)}{\partial y} \tag{5.28}$$

and integrating (5.28) over y gives

$$c(w, y) = \lambda(w)y + c^*(w), \tag{5.29}$$

where $c^*(w)$ is a constant of integration.

Expression (5.29) says that an aggregate cost function that is consistent with (5.27) must be consistent with a quasi-homothetic technology. More specifically, the aggregate cost function must be affine in output, that is, a translation of a linear function of aggregate output. This cost structure is subject to the same objections raised earlier about quasi-homothetic forms. It cannot satisfy the condition that $c(w, 0) = 0$ unless $c^*(w)$ itself equals zero, in which case the function would be consistent with the linear homogeneity of production. Thus, if we seek to define an aggregate cost function that depends on total industry output and satisfies all of the properties of $c(w, y)$ developed in Chapter 2, we are back at the linearly homogeneous technology used to introduce the aggregation problem at the beginning of this discussion.

Suppose that we dispense with the requirement that $c(w, 0) = 0$, and consider (5.29) as a valid short-run cost function where $c^*(w)$ represents fixed costs. [In a very real sense, the cost function depicted in (5.29) is short run because it treats the number of firms in the industry as exogenous. However, instances exist where the distribution of output affects industry structure.] Is there anything that can be said about the underlying technology? Because (5.29) implies quasi-homotheticity, the associated production function must have expansion paths that are straight lines but that do not ultimately emanate from the origin. Two possibilities for (5.29) are depicted in Figure 5.1(a) and (b). In panel (a), $c^*(w)$ is a positive number, whereas in panel (b), $c^*(w)$ is a negative number. In the second case, therefore, there exists a positive output

$$\hat{y} = -c^*(w)/\lambda(w)$$

for which costs are zero; output can be produced for free. And, in fact, for any $y \le \hat{y}$, costs of production are actually negative; the producer is being paid to produce output.

Consider the implications of (5.29) a bit further. First, monotonicity in y ensures that $\lambda(w)$ is positive. Furthermore, differentiating (5.29) establishes

$$\frac{\partial c(w, y)}{\partial w_i} = \frac{\partial \lambda(w)}{\partial w_i}y + \frac{\partial c^*(w)}{\partial w_i}.$$

So, by Shephard's lemma, each input demand is also affine in aggregate output. To satisfy homogeneity, it must be true that

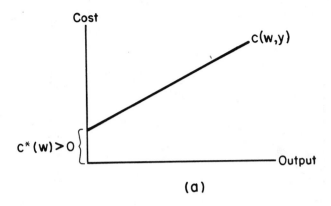

(a)

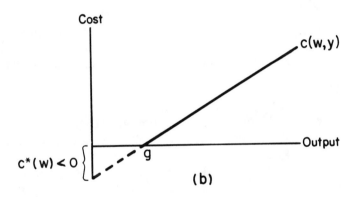

(b)

Figure 5.1 Quasi-homothetic cost structures.

$$\lambda(tw)y + c^*(tw) = t\lambda(w)y + tc^*(w),$$

which suggests that both $\lambda(w)$ and $c^*(w)$ are linearly homogeneous in w. Thus, one might think of both $\lambda(w)$ and $c^*(w)$ as unit cost functions for a constant-returns technology. This interpretation is further reinforced by noting that the aggregate cost function is concave in w if both $\lambda(w)$ and $c^*(w)$ are concave in w. For the cost function in (5.29) the elasticity of size is

$$\epsilon^*(w, y) = \frac{\lambda(w)y + c^*(w)}{y\lambda(w)}. \tag{5.30}$$

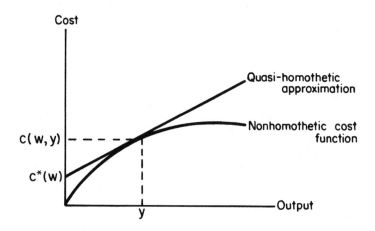

Figure 5.2   Quasi-homothetic cost as Taylor series approximation.

It is only possible for (5.29) to be consistent with constant returns to size if $c^*(w) = 0$. Thus, the ability of (5.29) to represent U-shaped average-cost curves appears severely limited. Now differentiate (5.30) with respect to y to obtain

$$\frac{\partial \epsilon^*}{\partial y} = -\frac{c^*(w)\lambda(w)}{[\lambda(w)y]^2}.$$

If $c^*(w)$ always equals zero, $\partial \epsilon^*/\partial y = 0$, and the average-cost curve is not U-shaped.

In general, (5.29) has limited ability to represent the type of cost curves usually encountered in economics. Furthermore, if $c^*(w)$ is positive, the aggregate cost function has an elasticity of size that is greater than 1 and exhibits increasing returns to size. The intuition here can be seen in several ways: First, consider (5.29) as a Taylor series approximation to a cost function that emanates from the origin. If the cost function being approximated by (5.29) does not switch from concave to convex or vice versa, then (5.29), with $c^*(w)$ greater than zero, approximates a concave cost function (see Figure 5.2). Second, recall the discussion of the elasticity of size in Chapter 2 (Section 2.3). There, we saw that the technology exhibits increasing returns to size if average cost decreases as output expands. For the technology described in (5.29), each small change in y changes average cost by $-c^*(w)/y^2$. Thus, as long as $c^*(w)$ is positive, average cost is declining. However, for large enough output levels, the cost function in (5.29) approximates constant returns to size because

$$\lim_{y \to \infty} \epsilon^*(w, y) = \lim_{y \to \infty} \frac{\lambda(w)y + c^*(w)}{\lambda(w)y} = 1.$$

On the other hand, if $c^*(w)$ is negative, the technology is always consistent with decreasing returns to size except for very large y where it is consistent with constant returns to size.

Another question is whether (5.29) can represent a homothetic technology. In general, the answer seems no. This follows because homotheticity requires that the cost function be written as $h(y)c(w)$. In the context of (5.29), this requires

$$c^*(w) = 0,$$

which, as we have already seen, implies the existence of constant returns to scale.

A positive aspect of (5.29) is that it offers a simple method of constructing a test for aggregation consistency. Suppose, for example, that one has available two flexible forms corresponding to the elements of (5.29) [call them $\tilde{\lambda}(w, y)$ and $\tilde{c}^*(w, y)$] that can be linearly homogeneous in w with at least one being a second-order approximation in y. Then, to test consistency with aggregation, it is sufficient to test consistency of the restrictions

$$\frac{\partial \tilde{c}^*(w, y)}{\partial y} = 0, \qquad \frac{\partial \ln \tilde{\lambda}(w, y)}{\partial \ln y} = 1.$$

The next issue to be addressed involves restrictions on firm-level cost functions needed to ensure they are consistent with aggregation. By the requirements for aggregation and previous aggregation results,

$$c(y, w) = \lambda(w)y + c^*(w)$$

$$= \lambda(w) \sum_i y^i + c^*(w)$$

$$= \sum_i c^i(y^i, w),$$

where the second equality follows by (5.27). If the $c^i(y^i, w)$'s are consistent with aggregation, each one must also be affine in y^i, that is,

$$c^i(y^i, w) = \lambda(w)y^i + c_i^*(w),$$

where $\sum c_i^*(w) = c^*(w)$.

An important implication of this result is that technical differences across firms are restricted to the $c_i^*(w)$ terms. Although one can aggregate cost functions derived from different technologies, the earlier discussion shows that this ability is limited. If each $c^i(w, y^i)$ is to satisfy the properties of a cost function derived in Chapter 2, fixed costs must not exist, implying that each $c^i(w, y^i)$ must be identically zero. So it is not possible to specify firm-level technologies satisfying properties 2B that allow for consistent aggregation across firms with nonidentical technologies in the long run. Only identical constant-returns technologies satisfy linear aggregation in the long run.

A natural conclusion is that any aggregate analysis of cost functions is very restrictive. For example, suppose each firm-level cost function takes the form

$$c(y^i, w) = \lambda(w) y^i + c^*(w) y^{i2},$$

where both $\lambda(w)$ and $c^*(w)$ exhibit all the requisite properties of unit cost functions. Such a function, although dual to a well-behaved production function, cannot support aggregate analysis. The family of firm-level functions capable of supporting aggregate analysis is usually quite small. However, this does not reflect a peculiarity of the cost function because the aggregation problems associated with well-behaved production and profit functions are at least as severe. As a simple example, consider the one-input case where the firm-level production function is

$$y_i = f_i(x_i).$$

As before, we impose linear aggregation conditions:

$$f(x) = \sum_i f_i(x_i) \quad \text{and} \quad x = \sum_i x_i,$$

where $f(x)$ is the industry production function and x is the aggregate industry input. Differentiating as above yields

$$\frac{\partial f(x)}{\partial x_i} = \frac{\partial f(x)}{\partial x} \frac{\partial x}{\partial x_i} = \frac{\partial f_i(x_i)}{\partial x_i}$$

so that, by similar arguments, the aggregate production function is affine in the aggregate input

$$f(x) = ax + c,$$

where c is a constant of integration.

As this indicates, it is not a peculiarity of the cost function that results in the stringent aggregation conditions derived. Rather, it is the linear aggregation rule that yields these results. Therefore, it may be worthwhile to relax these conditions. However, as the following example illustrates, relaxing the aggregation conditions must involve more than a trivial redefinition.

Example 5.6. Consider aggregation subject to (5.26) and the new output aggregation rule

$$y = \sum a_i y^i,$$

where each a_i is a positive constant. Here, the distribution of output across firms matters, and consequently, we expect to see that marginal cost across firms need no longer be the same. Differentiating (5.26) and the preceding and substituting yields

$$\sum_i \left(\frac{\partial c(w, y)}{\partial y} a_i - \frac{\partial c(w, y^i)}{\partial y^i} \right) dy^i = 0.$$

Because this equation must hold for arbitrary variations in each y^i, each firm-level marginal cost must be constant and equal to aggregate marginal cost times the appropriate weighting factor. Moreover, arguments exactly parallel to those presented show that aggregate marginal cost is constant and independent of output.

> **Exercise 5.8.** Linear aggregation of cost functions ensures that cost functions must be consistent with a very limiting type of quasi-homotheticity. This exercise is meant to reinforce the reader's understanding that these results are due to linear aggregation rules and not to anything peculiar to cost functions. Suppose that, instead, one is aggregating over firms operating in geographically distinct markets but producing the same commodity. All firms face different output prices (but for simplicity the same input prices), and the goal is to construct an aggregate profit function
>
> $$\Pi(p, w) = \sum_{i=1}^{m} \Pi^i(p^i, w),$$
>
> where the superscripts denote firm and p is the average price,
>
> $$p = \frac{1}{m} \sum_{i=1}^{m} p^i.$$
>
> Show that $\Pi(p, w)$ must be of the general form
>
> $$\Pi(p, w) = \Pi^0(w)p + \Pi^{00}(w).$$
>
> **Exercise 5.9.** As a consequence of Exercise 5.8, the corresponding aggregate profit function must be affine in the average price. This implies that aggregate supply is perfectly inelastic with respect to p. Derive sufficient conditions on $\Pi^0(w)$ and $\Pi^{00}(w)$ to

make $\Pi(p, w)$ consistent with the properties of a profit function. Show that the firm-level profit functions take the form

$$p_i \Pi^0(w)/m + \Pi_i^{00}(w),$$

where $\Pi^{00} = \sum \Pi_i^{00}$. What is implied about each firm's supply elasticity?

5.8   Nonlinear aggregation of output

The aggregate results developed, of course, depend on the rules by which aggregation must proceed, that is, expressions (5.26) and (5.27). Although it seems plausible that (5.26) should always hold, one might ask what is the consequence of relaxing (5.27)? Consider, then, rewriting (5.27) in the more general form

$$y = y(y^1, ..., y^m). \tag{5.27'}$$

Aggregate output need only be related to firm-level output by some stable function. One might now think of y as a representative output level rather than as aggregate output. Differentiating $c(w, y)$ with respect to y^i yields

$$\frac{\partial c(w, y)}{\partial y^i} = \frac{\partial c(w, y)}{\partial y} \frac{\partial y}{\partial y^i} = \frac{\partial c^i(w, y^i)}{\partial y^i}.$$

This expression implies

$$\frac{\partial y/\partial y^i}{\partial y/\partial y^j} = \frac{\partial c^i(w, y^i)/\partial y^i}{\partial c^j(w, y^j)/\partial y^j}.$$

Because the right-hand side of this last expression is independent of any y^k ($k \neq i$, $k \neq j$), the aggregation rule in (5.27') must be strongly separable:

$$y = y^*\left(\sum_{i=1}^m h^i(y^i)\right). \tag{5.27''}$$

Differentiation with respect to y^j ($j \neq i$) now establishes

$$\frac{\partial^2 c(w, y)}{\partial y^i \partial y^j} = \frac{\partial^2 c(w, y)}{\partial y^2} \frac{\partial y}{\partial y^i} \frac{\partial y}{\partial y^j} + \frac{\partial c(w, y)}{\partial y} \frac{\partial^2 y}{\partial y^i \partial y^j} = 0.$$

So, unlike the case of linear aggregation of output, aggregate marginal cost need not be independent of aggregate output. This last expression does establish that aggregate cost must be additively separable in the firm-level outputs and that

$$\frac{\partial^2 c(w, y)/\partial y^2}{\partial c(w, y)/\partial y} = \frac{\partial^2 y/\partial y^i \partial y^j}{(\partial y/\partial y^i)(\partial y/\partial y^j)}.$$

There are two possible cases here: Either $\partial^2 y/\partial y^i\,\partial y^j$ is zero (i.e., the aggregation rule is additively separable in y^i) or $\partial^2 y/\partial y^i\,\partial y^j$ is not zero. In the former, aggregate marginal cost is independent of y and the aggregate cost function degenerates to (5.29), with $y=\sum_{i=1}^n h^i(y^i)$. Using (5.26) yields

$$c(w, y) = \lambda(w)y + c^*(w)$$

$$= \lambda(w)\sum_{i=1}^m h^i(y^i) + c^*(w)$$

$$= \sum_{i=1}^m c^i(w, y^i).$$

The last equality implies

$$c^i(w, y^i) = h^i(y^i)\lambda(w) + c^{*i}(w).$$

Each firm-level cost function is quasi-homothetic as before but with an important difference: Marginal cost is not identical across all firms, and it is not independent of firm-level output.

In the second instance (i.e., when $\partial^2 y/\partial y^i\,\partial y^j$ is not zero), one can write

$$\frac{\partial^2 c(w, y)/\partial y^2}{\partial c(w, y)/\partial y} = k^*(y)$$

since, by hypothesis, $y^*(\ )$ is independent of w. The left-hand side of this expression is

$$\frac{\partial}{\partial y}\ln\frac{\partial c(w, y)}{\partial y},$$

and repeated integration over y yields

$$c(w, y) = h(y)c(w) + c^*(w).$$

That is, aggregation consistency requires that the aggregate cost function exhibit quasi-homotheticity. Using (5.26) and remembering that $c(w, y)$ must be additively separable in the y^i gives

$$c(w, y) = h(y)c(w) + c^*(w)$$

$$= c(w)\sum_{i=1}^m h^i(y^i) + c^*(w)$$

$$= \sum_{i=1}^m c^i(w, y^i).$$

So, again, we find

$$c^i(w, y^i) = h^i(y^i)c(w) + c^{*i}(w)$$

for aggregation consistency. In these equations, $h(y) = \sum_{i=1}^{m} h^i(y^i)$ is expression (5.27″) written in implicit form. For this instance, (a) marginal cost is not constant either for the aggregate function or for the individual firms and (b) homothetic production structures can be represented without forcing the imposition of a constant-returns technology. It is now possible to aggregate different technologies across firms because both $h^i(y^i)$ and $c^{*i}(w)$ can vary across firms. Thus, even if $c^{*i}(w)$ is forced to zero to ensure consistency with properties 2B, technology can vary across firms so long as the $h^i(y^i)$ terms are different. But then the degree of technical differences is somewhat limited. Suppose that each $c^{*i}(w)$ is set equal to zero. Then,

$$h^i(y^i)c(w) = \min\{wx : x \in V^i(y^i)\},$$

where $V^i(y^i)$ denotes the input requirement set for the ith technology. The fact that $c(w)$ is the same across all firms implies that

$$h^i(y^i)c(w) = h^i(y^i)\min\{wz : z \in V(1)\},$$

where $z = x/h^i$ and $V(1)$ is the input requirement set for a linearly homogeneous technology that does not differ across firms. In terms of our original definition of homotheticity, consistent nonlinear aggregation in the long run requires that each firm-level production function is a transform $(F)^i$ of the same linearly homogeneous function $f^*(x)$. Hence, input requirement sets are parallel across firms.

Exercise 5.10. Suppose that instead of expressing aggregate profit as a function of average price as in the two previous exercises it is a function of a representative price,

$$\Pi(p_0, w) = \sum_{i=1}^{m} \Pi^i(p^i, w),$$

where

$$p_0 = p^*(p^1, p^2, \ldots, p^n).$$

Develop the consequences of this respecification for aggregating profit functions.

*5.9   Some general aggregation results

So far, aggregate cost has been taken simply as the sum of each firm's costs. This implies that the distribution of costs across firms is irrelevant since redistributing cost from one firm to another does not affect total cost. A broader view of the aggregation problem permits the distribution of the functions to be aggregated as well as the distribution of the variable to be aggregated to matter. On an a priori basis, there is no reason to expect that both are unimportant. This section considers a more general aggregation problem that subsumes as special cases the two already considered. To focus attention on aggregation issues instead of the cost function, adopt new notation. A set of micro-level functions $g^i(k, z^i)$ is said to be aggregable if there exist functions $g(k, z)$ and z such that

$$g(k, z) = H(g^1, ..., g^m) \quad \text{and} \quad z = z(z^1, ..., z^m).$$

As before, the number of micro-level functions to be aggregated is exogenous, and all functions are at least twice-continuously differentiable.

Differentiate both equations with respect to z and the z^i to obtain

$$\frac{\partial g}{\partial z} dz = \sum_i H_i \frac{\partial g^i}{\partial z^i} dz^i \quad \text{and} \quad dz = \sum_i \frac{\partial z}{\partial z^i} dz^i,$$

where H_i is the partial derivative of H with respect to g^i. These two equations are the source of the general first-order restrictions on aggregable functions; substituting the second into the first yields

$$\sum_i \left\{ \frac{\partial g}{\partial z} \frac{\partial z}{\partial z^i} - H_i \frac{\partial g^i}{\partial z^i} \right\} dz^i = 0.$$

Because this equation must hold for arbitrary variations in the z^i, aggregation is only possible if

$$\frac{\partial g}{\partial z} \frac{\partial z}{\partial z^i} = H_i \frac{\partial g^i}{\partial z^i} \quad \forall i.$$

Since $\partial g/\partial z$ is independent of i, aggregation requires that the gradient of z be proportional to the gradient of H in z.

This proportionality condition allows us to deduce some very important structural characteristics relating z and H. Taking ratios yields

$$\frac{\partial z/\partial z^i}{\partial z/\partial z^j} = \frac{H_i(\partial g^i/\partial z^i)}{H_j(\partial g^j/\partial z^j)}.$$

This expression can be used to show that if z is separable in any partition of the z^i, H must be separable in the corresponding partition of the g^i. Define the partition $\hat{K}$ of the indexes of z and g by $(K^1, ..., K^v)$, where $v \le m$. Suppose that z is weakly separable in the partition $\hat{K}$; then,

$$\frac{\partial}{\partial z^k} \frac{\partial z/\partial z^i}{\partial z/\partial z^j} = 0, \quad (i, j) \in K^v, \ k \notin K^v.$$

By the proportionality result and the fact that both g^i and g^j are independent of z^k, this implies that

$$\frac{\partial}{\partial z^k} \frac{H_i}{H_j} = \frac{\partial}{\partial g^k} \frac{H_i}{H_j} \frac{\partial g^k}{\partial z^k} = 0, \quad (i,j) \in K^v, \, k \notin K^v,$$

provided that g^k is monotonic in z^k. This establishes the desired weak separability. A similar argument, left as an exercise to the reader, demonstrates that if z is strongly separable in the partition $\hat{K}$, then H is strongly separable in the corresponding partition for the g^i.

One might wonder why weak separability is an interesting structural restriction to impose upon the z function. It implies that there exist functions such that

$$z = \hat{z}(t^1(z_1), \ldots, t^v(z_v)),$$

where z_i is the subvector with elements whose indexes belong to the index set K^i. This is interpretable as implying that different subsets of the z^i are weighted differently in aggregation. For example, suppose that one is aggregating firm-level, short-run supply functions across firms with different levels of a fixed input. Here, z would be interpreted as the aggregate endowment of the fixed input, and weak separability means that certain groups of firms (e.g., on a regional basis) are treated differently in the creation of the aggregate input. The interesting fact is that this also implies that in creating the aggregate short-run supply function, these same firms' supply functions must be separately weighted.

Suppose now that the function aggregating the z terms is homothetic: This implies that the ratios of all its first partial derivatives are homogeneous of degree zero. By the proportionality result, the ratios of the first partial derivatives of H with respect to the z terms are also homogeneous of degree zero in the z^m because

$$\frac{\partial z(tz^1, \ldots, tz^m)/\partial z^i}{\partial z(tz^1, \ldots, tz^m)/\partial z^k} = \frac{\partial H(g^1(tz^1, k), \ldots, g^m(tz^m, k))/\partial z^i}{\partial H(g^1(tz^1, k), \ldots, g^m(tz^m, k))/\partial z^k} \quad \forall i, k.$$

The left-hand side of this expression equals the ratio of the partial derivatives of z evaluated at the unscaled ($t = 1$) z. Because the proportionality result holds over all z values, the value of the ratio on the right-hand side equals the ratio of these same partial derivatives for all i and k evaluated at $t = 1$. Hence, the ratio of the first partial derivatives of H with respect to the z must be homogeneous of degree zero, and by Lau's lemma on homothetic functions (see Appendix), H is homothetic in the z terms.

These results imply that a unique link exists between the H and the z functions. Obviously, not all H and z functions are consistent with aggregation. As an example, suppose that one tried to aggregate short-run

Table 5.2. *Aggregation results*

Problem Find $g(z, k)$ such that	
$$g(z, k) = H(g^1(z^1, k), ..., g^m(z^m, k))$$	
$$z = z(z^1, ..., z^m)$$	

H Linear $(H = \sum_{i=1}^{m} g^i)$

Linear z $(z = \sum_{i=1}^{m} z^i)$	Nonlinear z
$g(z, k) = v(k)z + m(k)$	$g(z, k) = v(k)h(z) + m(k)$
$g^i = v(k)z^i + m^i(k)$	$g^i = v(k)h^i(z^i) + m^i(k)$
$$m(k) = \sum_{i=1}^{m} m^i(k)$$	$$h(z) = \sum_{i=1}^{m} h^i(z^i)$$
	$$m(k) = \sum_{i=1}^{m} m^i(k)$$

H Nonlinear

weak separability of z ⟷ weak separability of H in g^i
strong separability of z ⟷ strong separability of H in g^i
homotheticity of z ⟷ homotheticity of H in z
H additively separable $(H_{ij} = 0)$;

$$h(z) = \sum_{i=1}^{m} h^i(z^i)$$

$$g(z, k) = v(k)h(z) + m(k)$$

$$\sum_{i=1}^{m} m^i = m(k)$$

industry supply using a weakly separable H for the supply functions but a linear z for the fixed factors specific to each firm. The proportionality result would be violated because this means combining a weakly separable H with a strongly separable and homothetic z. At a minimum, H must be specified as both strongly separable and homothetic before the issue of whether an aggregate industry supply function exists can even be legitimately posed. For without such consistency between H and z, aggregation is not possible. The results of this and the preceding sections on aggregation are summarized in tabular form in Table 5.2.

Example 5.7. Suppose that one wishes to aggregate according to the following rules:

$$g(k, z) = \sum_i g^i,$$

$$z = \sum_i a^i z^i + \frac{1}{2} \sum_i \sum_j b^{ij} z^i z^j,$$

where $b^{ij} = b^{ji}$. Differentiating and taking ratios yields

$$\frac{a^m + \sum_j b^{mj} z^j}{a^k + \sum_j b^{kj} z^j} = \frac{\partial g^m / \partial z^m}{\partial g^k / \partial z^k},$$

which in turn implies

$$\frac{\partial g^m}{\partial z^m} \left(a^k + \sum_j b^{kj} z^j \right) = \frac{\partial g^k}{\partial z^k} \left(a^m + \sum_j b^{mj} z^j \right).$$

This equality has to hold for all possible values of the z^v terms. Parametric expressions that are consistent with this are that

$$b^{ij} = 0 \quad (i \neq j).$$

These functional restrictions make z strongly separable. If each $g^i = z^i m^i(k)$, then H is both strongly separable and homothetic in the z^i terms. Does this imply any further functional restrictions on z? (*Hint: z* must be both strongly separable and homothetic.)

Exercise 5.11. Show that if H is additively separable in the z^i (i.e., $H_{ij} = 0$), then $g(z, k)$ must be additively separable in the z^i and $g^i = m(k) h^i(y^i) + g^i(k)$.

Example 5.8. In preceding sections, a great deal of time was spent discussing the various properties of flexible forms analytically. To put some meat on the bones of this analytical skeleton, this example presents a discussion of an empirical study using a specific functional form, the translog. This study was conducted by Ball and Chambers (1982) and has already been alluded to in previous chapters. It represents a cost function study of the meat products industry in the United States. As such, it was carried out at a very high level of aggregation and, therefore, represents at least an implicit incorporation of some of the input aggregation results discussed in earlier chapters.

The analysis assumes the existence of an aggregate cost function for the meat products industry,

$$c(w_k, w_L, w_E, w_M, w_S, y, t),$$

where w_k is the price of capital equipment, w_L is the price of labor, w_E is the price of energy, w_M is the price of intermediate materials, w_S is the price of capital structures, y is aggregate industry output, and t is an indicator of technical change (see next chapter). Since each input price obviously corresponds to an agglomeration of other input prices, the Ball–Chambers model assumes that the underlying technology is weakly homothetically separable. To estimate the model, a translog form was chosen to represent the cost function:

$$\ln c(w, y) = \beta_0 + \sum_{i=1}^{n} \beta_i \ln w_i + \frac{1}{2}\beta_{yy}(\ln y)^2 + \frac{1}{2}\sum_{i}^{n}\sum_{j}^{n}\beta_{ij}\ln w_i \ln w_j$$

$$\times \beta_y \ln y + \sum_{i=1}^{n}\beta_{yi}\ln y \ln w_i + \beta_T t + \frac{1}{2}\beta_{TT}t^2 + \sum_{i=1}^{n}\beta_{Ti}t \ln w_i,$$

where $\beta_{ij} = \beta_{ji}$. By Shephard's lemma, the cost shares associated with this technology are the logarithmic derivatives of the preceding:

$$S_i(w, y) = \beta_i + \sum_j \beta_{ij}\ln w_j + \beta_{yi}\ln y + \beta_{Ti}t.$$

If this translog function is to be consistent with linear homogeneity in the vector of input prices, the parameterized cost shares, which are the logarithmic derivatives of $\ln c(w, y)$, must sum to 1. Hence,

$$\sum_{i=1}^{n}\beta_i + \sum_i\sum_j\beta_{ij}\ln w_j + \ln y\sum_i\beta_{yi} + t\sum_i\beta_{ti} = 1.$$

For this restriction to apply globally,

$$\sum_{i=1}^{n}\beta_i = 1, \qquad \sum_i\beta_{ij} = 0, \qquad \sum_i\beta_{yi} = 0, \qquad \sum_i\beta_{Ti} = 0.$$

The reader can easily verify that incorporating these restrictions into the model reduces the size of the parameter space to exactly the number of distinct economic effects (remember the addition of t). As was demonstrated earlier, the translog cannot be made globally concave by imposing prior restrictions on the parameters.

If this cost function is to be consistent with a homothetic technology, it must factorize as

$$c(w, y) = h(y)c(w).$$

Applying this directly to the translog function requires some slight manipulation since we have expressed the cost function in transformed form. Taking antilogs yields

$$c(w, y) = \exp\left(\beta_0 + \sum_{i=1}^{n}\beta_i \ln w_i + \frac{1}{2}\beta_{yy}(\ln y)^2 + \frac{1}{2}\sum_i\sum_j\beta_{ij}\ln w_i \ln w_j\right.$$

$$\left. + \sum_{i=1}^{n}\beta_{yi}\ln y \ln w_i + \beta_T t + \frac{1}{2}\beta_{TT}t^2 + \sum_{i=1}^{n}\beta_{Ti}t \ln w_i\right)$$

$$= \exp\left(\beta_0 + \sum_{i=1}^{n} \beta_i \ln w_i + \frac{1}{2} \sum \sum \beta_{ij} \ln w_i \ln w_j + \beta_T t \right.$$

$$\left. + \frac{1}{2}\beta_{TT} t^2 + \sum_{i=1}^{n} \beta_{Ti} t \ln w_i \right)$$

$$\times \exp\left(\frac{1}{2}\beta_{yy}(\ln y)^2 + \sum_{i=1}^{n} \beta_{yi} \ln y \ln w_i + \beta_y \ln y + \beta_{Ty} \ln yt \right),$$

where the second equality is a consequence of the law of exponents. If this function is to be consistent globally with homotheticity, it must, therefore, be true that $\beta_{yi} = 0$ for all i. In this case, the cost flexibility is

$$\frac{\partial \ln c(w, y)}{\partial \ln y} = \beta_y + \beta_{yy} \ln y + \beta_{Ty} t.$$

By this last result, the associated technology is homogeneous only if $\beta_{yy} = 0$.

In this study, output was taken to be an index of various outputs and was measured only at the industry level. Therefore, the issue of consistency with aggregation is real and should not be ignored in the empirical analysis. By the preceding results, aggregation consistency, at a minimum, requires the cost function to be consistent with quasi-homotheticity. However, this cost function can always be written as

$$c(w, y) = \phi(w) m^*(w, y).$$

There are only two possible ways for this to be consistent with quasi-homotheticity: It may be consistent with homotheticity, and parametric restrictions for this are detailed above, or the function $m^*(w, y)$ itself is consistent with quasi-homotheticity. Notice, however, that

$$m^*(w, y) = \exp\left(\frac{1}{2}\beta_{yy}(\ln y)^2 + \ln y \sum_{i=1}^{n} \beta_{yi} \ln w_i + \beta_y \ln y + \ln y \beta_{Ty} t \right)$$

and there are no parametric restrictions that will make this consistent with quasi-homotheticity. Hence, consistency in aggregation always requires homotheticity for the model under consideration.

In the present framework, estimation of the share equations is not sufficient since the parameters determining the cost flexibility $(\beta_y, \beta_{yy}, \beta_{Ty})$ only appear in the cost function. Thus, additive disturbances are assumed for each share equation and the cost function. These disturbances are presumed intertemporally independent, multivariate normal with zero mean and with nonzero contemporaneous covariances. The contemporaneous covariance matrix for the disturbances of the cost and share equations is singular since the share equations must sum to unity for every sample point. That is, suppose the observed share equation is denoted $\hat{S}_i$, and the true share is S_i. They are related by $\hat{S}_i = S_i + e_i$, where e_i is the ith disturbance. Since observed shares always sum to 1, as do the true shares, we must then have

$$\sum_{i=1}^{n} e^i = 0.$$

At least one disturbance term is a linear combination of the others. This, in turn, implies that the variance and covariances for this disturbance term can be expressed in terms of the variance and covariances of other error terms, whence the singularity. Barten showed that singularity of this type can be handled by dropping a single equation in estimation. Estimation results are independent of the equation dropped under the maintained assumptions on the error structure. If there is significant autocorrelation, however, parameter estimates are not invariant to the equation dropped.

Maximum-likelihood estimation permits hypothesis testing with the log-likelihood ratio (λ), which is the natural logarithm of the ratio of the likelihood function computed under null and alternative hypotheses. The statistic $-2 \ln \lambda$ is asymptotically distributed as chi-square with degrees of freedom equal to the number of independent restrictions imposed.

Results for the alternative versions of the model are reported in Table 5.3. Based on the calculated log-likelihood ratio statistics, the null hypotheses of homotheticity, homogeneity, and constant returns to scale are rejected. Considering the homotheticity test first, notice that the calculated chi-square with 16 degrees of freedom at the 0.01 level is 16.81. Since both homogeneity and constant returns to scale imply homotheticity, it is not surprising that the data do not support the imposition of these restrictions. However, if the null hypothesis of homogeneity is tested against the alternative hypothesis of homotheticity, it is not possible to reject homogeneity. To assume homogeneity, therefore, is not much more restrictive than homotheticity for the meat products industry.

These hypothesis tests also rule out the possibility that the estimated cost function is consistent with aggregation. Therefore, results based on its analysis must presume the existence of an aggregate cost minimizer since within the translog form the data do not seem to be consistent with aggregation over firms.

Bibliographical notes

The discussion on flexible forms relies on a variety of sources, but the main inspiration comes from the excellent paper by Fuss, McFadden, and Mundlak (1978)

Table 5.3. *Parameter estimates for meat products cost function*

	Homotheticity	Homogeneity	Constant returns
β_{KK}	0.0106 (0.0008)	0.0109 (0.0008)	0.0105 (0.0008)	0.0077 (0.1271)
β_{KL}	0.0112 (0.022)	0.0140 (0.0026)	0.0136 (0.0025)	0.0102 (0.4813)
β_{KE}	−0.0011 (0.0003)	−0.0015 (0.0004)	−0.0015 (0.0003)	−0.0011 (0.2674)
β_{KM}	−0.0220 (0.0019)	−0.0247 (0.0023)	−0.0239 (0.0022)	−0.0168 (0.3252)
β_{KS}	0.0013 (0.0004)	0.0013 −	0.0013 −	−0.0001 −
β_{LL}	0.0268 (0.0096)	0.0433 (0.0097)	0.0384 (0.0088)	−0.0380 (0.3395)
β_{LE}	0.0052 (0.0007)	0.0053 (0.0012)	0.0043 (0.0011)	−0.0029 (0.3023)
β_{LM}	−0.0443 (0.0084)	−0.0652 (0.0087)	−0.0593 (0.0077)	0.0265 (0.5186)
β_{LS}	−0.0011 (0.0014)	0.0026 −	0.0030 −	0.0042 −
β_{EE}	0.0007 (0.0002)	0.0004 (0.0007)	0.0013 (0.0007)	0.0019 (0.0472)
β_{EM}	−0.0065 (0.0006)	−0.0059 (0.0010)	−0.0055 (0.0010)	0.0012 (0.2616)
β_{ES}	0.0017 (0.0003)	0.0017 −	0.0014 −	0.0009 −
β_{MM}	0.0788 (0.0080)	0.1028 (0.0095)	0.0959 (0.0082)	−0.0034 (0.1875)
β_{MS}	−0.0060 (0.0013)	0.0070 −	−0.0072 −	−0.0051 −
β_{SS}	0.0019 (0.0004)	0.0014 −	0.0015 −	0.0001 −
β_{K}	0.0069 (0.0175)	0.0067 (0.0046)	0.0064 (0.0044)	0.0040 (0.0082)
β_{L}	−0.0265 (0.0555)	0.0420 (0.0167)	0.0496 (0.0148)	0.1501 (0.0175)
β_{E}	0.0222 (0.0073)	-9.60×10^{-5} (0.0021)	0.0004 (0.0022)	0.0094 (0.0035)
β_{M}	1.0002 (0.0763)	0.9468 (0.0131)	0.9391 (0.0114)	0.8338 (0.0137)
β_{S}	−0.0028 (0.0083)	0.0045 −	0.0045 −	0.0027 −

Table 5.3 *(cont.)*

	Homotheticity	Homogeneity	Constant returns
β_Y	−22.8205 (0.2510)	−2.9459 (2.1095)	0.4510 (0.1586)	− −
β_0	56.2085 (0.2909)	3.0837 (4.5777)	8.2582 (0.6516)	−36.3416 (10.3709)
β_{YY}	5.6451 (0.1203)	−0.6005 (0.4875)	− −	− −
β_{YK}	0.0007 (0.0041)	− −	− −	− −
β_{YL}	0.0199 (0.0136)	− −	− −	− −
β_{YE}	−0.0052 (0.0016)	− −	− −	− −
β_{YM}	−0.0180 (0.0185)	− −	− −	− −
β_{YS}	0.0026 (0.0019)	− −	− −	− −
β_T	0.6051 (0.0323)	−0.0098 (0.0071)	−0.0115 (0.0080)	18.2012 (4.5561)
β_{TT}	0.0062 (0.0005)	0.0025 (0.0004)	0.0022 (0.0003)	−1.0829 (0.2563)
β_{YY}	−0.1497 (0.0087)	− −	− −	− −
β_{YK}	3.35×10^{-5} (9.24×10^{-5})	9.57×10^{-6} (4.80×10^{-5})	2.43×10^{-5} (4.78×10^{-5})	−5.1711 (1.7724)
β_{KL}	−0.0019 (0.0003)	−0.0017 (0.0001)	−0.0016 (0.0001)	0.0001 (0.0001)
β_{TE}	3.31×10^{-5} (3.82×10^{-5})	-7.80×10^{-5} (2.44×10^{-5})	-7.75×10^{-5} (2.52×10^{-5})	5.66×10^{-5} (4.18×10^{-5})
β_{TM}	0.0019 (0.0004)	0.0018 (0.0002)	0.0017 (0.0002)	−0.0004 (0.0002)
β_{TS}	-6.66×10^{-5} (3.87×10^{-5})	-3.10×10^{-5} −	5.70×10^{-5} −	5.1713 −
ln L	714.8009	689.1352	688.7614	536.1564

and McFadden's (1978b) paper on the general linear profit function. The discussion of the separability inflexibility is my interpretation of results presented in the monograph by Blackorby, Primont, and Russell (1978). Similarly, the discussion of quasi-homotheticity and its relation to the generalized Leontief profit function is my interpretation of an outstanding paper by Lopez (1984). The results on aggregation are all essentially due to Gorman (1968) and Muellbauer (1975). The last section, on the general aggregation problem, relies on the work of Richmond (1976) and some unpublished work that I have carried on jointly with Rulon Pope.

)

CHAPTER 6

Technical change and its measurement

In preceding developments, the implicit assumption was that the state of technology was constant and that production was basically timeless. Common observation demonstrates that neither of these assumptions bear close scrutiny. This chapter is a partial attempt to rectify these shortcomings by recognizing the effects of technological advancements on the production process. Unfortunately, it is not a panacea, and more than anything else, what follows represents a catalog of ways that certain types of technical change can be measured. It is not, and is not meant to be, a complete explication of all the intricacies of the phenomenon of technical change.

Because of the focus on measurement, some discussion of the broader issues involved is worthwhile, for it is always important (but often forgotten in economic analysis) to know just exactly what is being assumed. As usual, first is the question, Why is there interest in measuring technical change and its effects? And the best answer is that since the time of the Luddites, and certainly much earlier, people recognized and were concerned that technical advances generally displace other resources (especially labor). This recognition caused classical economists witnessing the Industrial Revolution to analyze the consequences of technical advancement. Ricardo's (1973) controversial chapter "On Machinery" represents an early attempt to deduce the consequences of mechanization for "the interests of the different classes of society...."

The evaluation of the consequences of technical change, originally addressed by the classical economists, has its neoclassical reincarnation in the acute interest that modern growth models give to the effects of technical change on intertemporal growth patterns, resource allocation, and sectoral returns. An obvious outgrowth is the attention that production economists give to measuring and identifying *biased technical change*. At the root of most definitions of "biasedness" is an interest in the consequences of technical change for different sectors of society.

The advent of neoclassical growth models was almost exactly contemporaneous with increased efforts to describe production technologies by quantitative means – be they econometric, programming, or engineering approaches. Production economists using econometric techniques on

203

time-series data rapidly realized that they had to account for the evolution of technology. Econometric necessity and the fact that perception of technical advances usually requires the passage of time led to the wide-spread identification of technical change with a "time" term in the production function. This approach is sometimes disparaged as being more a measure of our ignorance than anything else. Like most such savings, this old saw contains more than a grain of truth. But even if it is true, should one be upset at being able to measure one's ignorance? Given the current state of knowledge, including a time term in production functions may not be perfect, but it is a workable alternative with some definite advantages (e.g., analytical and econometric tractability) over some other approaches. The following discussion focuses almost exclusively on this approach.

Before proceeding, however, it is worthwhile to sketch some alternatives. An obvious criticism to the simple inclusion of time in the production function is that it is a passive approach. It seeks to measure technical change without clearly defining just what is meant by the concept and, more importantly, without explaining what motivates technical change. It is as if the cotton gin and McCormick's reaper were just lying around waiting to be "found." An alternative approach, Hicks's (1963) *induced-invention hypothesis,* has received much attention. The induced-invention hypothesis suggests that technical change is a response to market phenomena such as relative price changes. Closely paralleling this hypothesis is the notion that technical change, among other things, is a consequence of investment in the quality of human and other forms of capital. Indeed, an early criticism of the residual approach to technical change centered on the need to adjust for qualitative changes in inputs. To some extent, these arguments are the essence of the embodiment hypothesis discussed here. Other strands of thought are almost as numerous as the strands of hair on a person's head. Probably every economist has his own idea of what causes technical change. And the obvious corollary to this is that no discussion of the topic will satisfy everyone. Faced with this reality, I chose to devote most of my attention to the type of technical change most often encountered in empirical studies, that is, the easiest to deal with analytically. I make the choice cognizant that many readers will see it as a decision on my part as to which approach is best. This is not the case. Rather, it is an attempt to deal with an intractable problem in an economic fashion.

In what follows, we consider two distinct but related approaches to measuring technical change. The first envisages time as continuous and expresses most measures of technical progress or regress in terms of differentials of production, cost, or profit functions. The second approach, although not denying the continuity of time, recognizes that data on most economic phenomena are only gathered at discrete intervals. This latter approach identifies measures that match closely with discrete interval data gathering by constructing indexes of technical change.

6.1 Production function and technical change

Representing technical change analytically is by no means a simple task. There are many issues to be addressed, not the least of which is a reasonable definition of technical change. One definition, which is heavily exploited because of its analytical tractability, is that technical change represents a shift in the production function over time. Put another way, a stable relationship between output, inputs, and time (as identified by t) is presumed to exist:

$$y = f(x, t), \qquad (6.1)$$

and technical change is measured by how output changes as time elapses with the input bundle held constant. When (6.1) is differentiable, the *rate of technical change* is defined as

$$T(x, t) = \frac{\partial \ln f(x, t)}{\partial t}. \qquad (6.1')$$

Although representation (6.1) may seem relatively innocuous, it is in fact a very strong assumption and is not always realistic. Everyday observation reveals many innovations and developments that one would like to subsume under the rubric of technical change but are not consistent with either (6.1) or (6.1'). As a concrete example, consider the introduction of Eli Whitney's cotton gin: clearly a case of technical change. But, just as clearly, it is not consistent with (6.1) since ginning required such new methods and new inputs (the gin itself) that it represented a whole new technology, that is, a new production function. The fundamental nature of the capital input had changed drastically. The technical innovation was *embodied* in the cotton gin itself in the sense that the gin had to be acquired to have access to the new technology. Expression (6.1), however, assumes that technical change does not require new inputs and further that the production function maintains the same basic form as time elapses. An explicit example of expression (6.1) might be something like the modified Cobb–Douglas $f(x, t) = AX_i^\alpha X_2^\alpha t\gamma$. Since the technical change described by (6.1) is not embodied in any particular input or groups of input, it is usually referred to as *disembodied technical change*. Representing embodied technical change analytically requires differentiating the production function itself as well as the input bundle over time; that is,

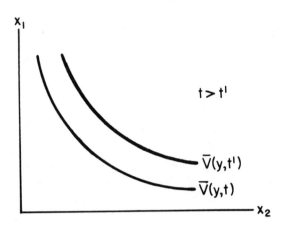

Figure 6.1 Progressive technical change.

$$y_t = f_t(X_t, t), \tag{6.2}$$

where $f_t(X_t, t)$ and $f_T(X_T, T)$ need not be the same functional forms and the components of the input X_T and X_t may be different. In the cotton gin example, X_T would include the gin whereas X_t would not. Unfortunately, embodied technical change consistent with (6.2) is very difficult analytically. Therefore, the remainder of this chapter confines itself to depictions of disembodied technical change.

Incorporating technical change into the analysis of input requirement sets requires some obvious changes in notation. Redefine the input requirement set

$$V(y, t) = \{x : f(x, t) \geq y\}.$$

If $t > t^1$, technical change is said to be *progressive* if $V(y, t^1) \subseteq V(y, t)$, that is, if it expands the input requirement set and allows input bundles formerly incapable of producing output y to produce y. Technical change is *regressive* for $t > t^1$ if $V(y, t) \supseteq V(y, t^1)$; that is, it shrinks the input requirement set by eliminating input bundles from the input requirement set. Figure 6.1 presents an illustration of progressive technical change. Notice, in particular, that this definition of progressive and regressive technical change does not categorize technical change consistent with the situation depicted in Figure 6.2, where the passage of time leads to a new isoquant that intersects the original isoquant. To accommodate such phenomena, define *locally progressive technical change* for a differentiable production function as that associated with $T(x, t) \geq 0$ and *locally regres-*

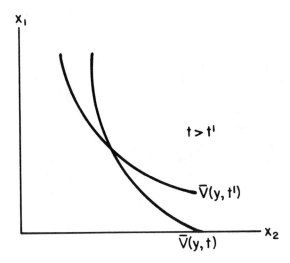

Figure 6.2 Locally progressive technical change.

sive technical change as $T(x, t) < 0$. Although regressive technical change may appear somewhat hard to swallow a priori, phenomena like those illustrated in Figure 6.2 are fairly commonplace. A possible example of locally regressive technical change could be a new technology (like high-yielding crop varieties) that requires very intensive committal of particular inputs (water and fertilizer) to be successful.

Because of situations similar to those in Figure 6.2 and because of concerns about technical change displacing inputs in production, a further taxonomy of technical change is often convenient. Since the time of Hicks (1963), it has been commonplace to classify technical change further according to its effect on relative input utilization. Hicks considered the case where x is a vector consisting of labor and capital. Technical change was defined as neutral if at points on the expansion path the marginal rate of technical substitution was independent of time. That is, the passage of time may shift isoquants, but in doing so, the marginal rate of technical substitution is not affected. Such an effect is depicted in Figure 6.3, where the expansion path is given by $0ABC$, and technical change moves the isoquant for output level y, as illustrated. As the reader has probably recognized, such changes closely resemble earlier definitions of separability. Letting K represent capital and L labor, it then follows that technical change is Hicks neutral if and only if

$$y = f(\phi(K, L), t); \tag{6.3}$$

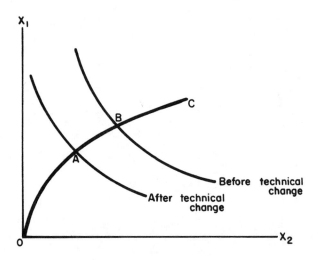

Figure 6.3 Hicks-neutral technical change.

that is, t is separable from K and L in production. Moreover, technical change can be Hicks neutral if and only if it is either progressive or regressive. This is easily seen by noting that the input requirement set for (6.3) can be written as

$$V(y, t) = \{K, L : f(\phi(K, L), t) \geq y\}$$
$$= \{K, L : \phi(K, L) \geq m(y, t)\},$$

where the second equality follows by the presumption that $\partial f / \partial \phi > 0$, and $m(y, t)$ is the function implied by solving the level set $\{\phi, t : f(\phi, t) = y\}$ for ϕ. To satisfy monotonicity in K and L, ϕ must be at least weakly increasing in K and L; progressive technical change can be perceived as effectively diminishing or increasing the level of $m(y, t)$ which the sub-production function $\phi(K, L)$ must exceed if K and L are to be elements of $V(y, t)$.

Hicks defined a concept of factor-using technical change in terms of the two-input production function. However, this definition has relatively little intuitive content in terms of an n-input model and consequently will not be presented here. In what follows, discussions of bias are restricted to those that can be expressed easily in terms of cost or profit functions.

An obvious way to generalize Hicks's concept of neutrality is to extend (6.3) to the many-input case. For what follows, the production function is defined as *Hicks neutral* if and only if it can be written as

$$y = f(\phi(x), t). \tag{6.4}$$

Although expression (6.4) is already quite restrictive, it is easy to show that a much more explicit a priori representation is obtained when production is both Hicks neutral and homothetic. If the technology is homothetic in x (Lau 1978a, 153), then

$$y = f(x, t) = H[f^*(x, t)],$$

where $f^*(x, t)$ is linearly homogeneous in x. For this technology to be consistent with Hicks neutrality, $f^*(x, t)$ must also be consistent with Hicks neutrality since the fact that

$$\frac{\partial f(x, t)}{\partial x_i} = \frac{\partial H}{\partial f^*} \frac{\partial f^*}{\partial x_i}$$

implies that

$$\frac{\partial}{\partial t} \frac{\partial f(x, t)/\partial x_i}{\partial f(x, t)/\partial x_j} = \frac{\partial}{\partial t} \frac{\partial f^*(x, t)/\partial x_i}{\partial f^*(x, t)/\partial x_j} = 0.$$

Performing the indicated differentiation yields

$$\frac{\partial^2 f^*(x, t)}{\partial x_i \partial t} \frac{1}{\partial f^*/\partial x_i} = \frac{\partial^2 f^*(x, t)}{\partial x_j \partial t} \frac{1}{\partial f^*/\partial x_j} \quad \forall i, j.$$

Assuming that $\partial f^*/\partial x_i > 0$ allows rewriting the preceding expression as

$$\frac{\partial \ln(\partial f^*/\partial x_i)}{\partial t} = \frac{\partial \ln(\partial f^*/\partial x_j)}{\partial t} \quad \forall i, j.$$

Because the derivative of the logarithm of each marginal productivity with respect to time is the same for all marginal productivities, this derivative is independent of x. These results imply that

$$\frac{\partial \ln(\partial f^*/\partial x_k)}{\partial t} = \phi^*(t) \quad \forall k.$$

Integrating and taking antilogs gives

$$\frac{\partial f^*(x, t)}{\partial x_k} = \exp[\phi(t)] \exp[m_k(x)],$$

where $\phi(t) = \int \phi^* \, dt$ and $m_k(x)$ is a constant of integration. Linear homogeneity of $f^*(x, t)$ then implies

$$f^*(x, t) = \sum_k \frac{\partial f^*}{\partial x_k} x_k$$

$$= \exp[\phi(t)] \sum_k \exp[m_k(x)] x_k$$

$$= A(t) m(x),$$

where $m(x)$ is linearly homogeneous since $f^*(x, t)$ must be. Letting a particular output level be denoted by y and applying the implicit function theorem assuming that $\partial H/\partial f^* \neq 0$ yields

$$h^*(y) = A(t)m(x),$$

where $h^*(y) = H^{-1}(y)$.

The input requirement set for this technology can be written as

$$
\begin{aligned}
V(y, t) &= \{x: A(t)m(x) \geq h^*(y)\} \\
&= \{x: m(A(t)x/h^*) \geq 1\} \\
&= h^*(y)/A(t)\{q: m(q) \geq 1\} \\
&= D(y, t)V(1),
\end{aligned}
\tag{6.4'}
$$

where the second equality follows by the linear homogeneity of $m(x)$, $V(1)$ is the input requirement set for a linearly homogeneous technology, and $q = A(t)x/h^* = x/D(y, t)$.

Augmenting technical change: Little has been said about how technical change actually affects production other than that it shifts the production function. One view of technical change is that it improves input efficiency. This concept is often referred to as *input-augmenting or factor-augmenting technical change* and can be represented as

$$f = f(\tilde{x}(x, t), t),
\tag{6.5}$$

where the notation denotes that production depends on an effective input vector $\tilde{x}(x, t)$ that in turn depends on the state of technology as well as the level of actual input usage (x). Moreover, it is often reasonable to expect that the effectiveness of the ith input only depends on how much of the ith input is committed to production. In the following, we only consider

$$\tilde{x}_i = \tilde{x}_i(x_i, t).$$

The case where x_j affects the effective input $\tilde{x}_i$ is left as a (difficult) exercise to the reader.

The idea behind factor-augmenting technical change is simple: Input quality varies with time so that, for example, hiring one unit of labor in year 1 does not necessarily yield the same effective labor units as in year 2. The passage of time makes a difference in how that input affects production. Notice, however, that this is not the same thing as what we have called embodied technical change because a stable relationship between output, input, and time still exists. Although the effectiveness of inputs varies over time, their essential character does not.

The rate of technical change associated with (6.5) now takes a slightly different form than in (6.1). But the reader should note that although the forms are different, they measure the exact same thing – the shift in the production function due solely to the passage of time. When the function is written as in (6.5), we presume more knowledge about how technical change actually affects production. Differentiating (6.5) with respect to t yields

$$\frac{\partial y}{\partial t} = \sum_i \frac{\partial f}{\partial \tilde{x}_i} \frac{\partial \tilde{x}_i}{\partial t} + \frac{\partial f}{\partial t}$$

or in percent terms,

$$\frac{\partial \ln y}{\partial t} = \sum \frac{\partial \ln f}{\partial \ln \tilde{x}_i} \frac{\partial \ln x_i}{\partial t} + \frac{\partial \ln f}{\partial t}.$$

Defining $\tilde{\epsilon}_i$ as the elasticity of output with respect to the effective input $\tilde{x}_i$ and $\tilde{\epsilon}$ as the scale coefficient with respect to the effective inputs, this expression becomes

$$\frac{\partial \ln y}{\partial t} = \tilde{\epsilon} \sum_{i=1} \theta_i \frac{\partial \ln \tilde{x}_i}{\partial t} + \frac{\partial \ln f}{\partial t},$$

where $\theta_i = \tilde{\epsilon}_i / \tilde{\epsilon}$. Thus, augmenting technical change has two components. The first is a scale expansion effect given by the elasticity of scale times a weighted average of the time rates of change of the various effective inputs. The second is a pure-shift effect that cannot be attributed to any particular input.

The unfortunate thing about expression (6.5) is that usually it is too general to be implemented empirically. Before (6.5) can serve as the basis for useful empirical analysis, one needs a more exact form. It is common to assume that an effective input can be written as

$$\tilde{x}_i = \lambda_i(t) x_i,$$

where $\lambda_i(t)$ is a numeric function of time. Substitution yields

$$y = f(\lambda_1 x_1, \ldots, \lambda_n x_n, t).$$

It is particularly interesting to consider the special case of technical change that is only factor augmenting:

$$y = f(\lambda_1 x_1, \ldots, \lambda_n x_n). \tag{6.6}$$

One reason for the interest in such input-augmenting technical change as (6.6) is that it generalizes the concept of Harrod neutrality that is central to many growth models. As originally introduced, Harrod neutrality applied to the two-input production function that we have already used in

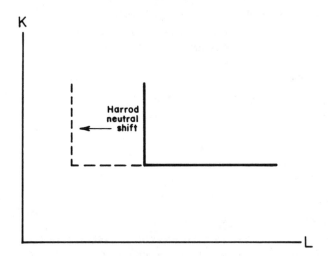

Figure 6.4   Harrod neutrality for Leontief technology.

conjunction with the discussion of Hicks neutrality. Instead of postulating independence of the marginal rate of technical substitution from t, Harrod neutrality postulated that only labor effectiveness changed over time, implying that all augmentation factors except labor equal 1. Harrod neutrality is depicted graphically in terms of the Leontief technology in Figure 6.4 as a horizontal displacement of the input requirement set.

For later analysis, it is convenient to define the *effective input requirement set for (6.6):*

$$\hat{V}(y) = \{\tilde{x} : f(\tilde{x}) \geq y\}. \tag{6.7}$$

Although it is not usually easy to relate $V(y, t)$ and $\hat{V}(y)$ for production functions of the general form of (6.6), there is one case that will prove of considerable interest. That is, consider the case where $\lambda_i(t) = \lambda(t)$ for all i; then we have

$$V(y, t) = \{x : f(\lambda(t)x) \geq y\}$$

$$= \lambda^{-1}(t)\{\lambda(t)x : f(\lambda(t)x) \geq y\}$$

$$= \lambda^{-1}(t)\hat{V}(y). \tag{6.8}$$

Production functions with input requirement sets of the general form of (6.8) will be called *equal-factor-augmenting production functions.* Notice, in particular, that if in addition to being equal factor augmenting, the production function is also homothetic in effective inputs, it can always be written in the Hicks-neutral form,

$$f(\tilde{x}) = H[\lambda(t)m(x)].$$

This last result is easily derived: Let the production function be homothetic in $\tilde{x}$; then, one must be able to write

$$f(\tilde{x}) = H[f^*(\tilde{x})],$$

where $f^*(\tilde{x})$ is linearly homogeneous. Combining this with the fact that all inputs have the same augmentation factor $\lambda(t)$ gives

$$f(\tilde{x}) = H[f^*(\lambda(t)x)]$$
$$= H[\lambda(t)f^*(x)],$$

as required when $m(x)$ is set equal to $f^*(x)$. The input requirement set for this technology can be written as

$$V(y, t) = [h^*(y)/\lambda(t)] V(1),$$

where $h^*(y)$ is the inverse mapping of the transform H and $V(1)$ is the unit-output input requirement set for $f^*(x)$. Thus, the input requirement set for an equal-factor-augmenting production function that is homothetic in effective inputs has the same general form as (6.4′).

6.2   Measurement of technical change from indirect objective functions

6.2a   *Technical change and the cost function*

This treatment of technical change closely parallels the earlier treatment of fixed inputs. In fact, one frequent interpretation of the technical change term t in the production function is as a fixed input. Accordingly, one should not be surprised that the incorporation of technical change in the form of (6.1) does not adversely affect most duality results. More to the point, if $V(y, t)$ satisfies the same restrictions placed on $V(y)$ to generate a cost function, the cost function

$$c(w, y, t) = \min_{x > 0}\{w \cdot x : x \in V(y, t)\}$$

will satisfy properties 2B.1–2B.6 (nonnegativity, nondecreasing, concave and continuous, and positively linearly homogeneous in w, nondecreasing in y, and no fixed costs). Related arguments also establish that the implicit input requirement set

$$V^*(y, t) = \{x : wx \geq c(w, y, t), \ w > 0\}$$

satisfies weak monotonicity, weak essentiality, quasi-concavity, and nonemptiness. Since the demonstration of this result is yet another replication of arguments developed in Chapter 2, it is left as an exercise for the reader.

Exercise 6.1. Suppose that $f(x, t)$ satisfies weak monotonicity, weak essentiality, quasi-concavity, and nonemptiness of $V(y, t)$. Derive the properties of $c(w, y, t)$ and show that the associated $V^*(y, t)$ satisfies the same properties as $V(y, t)$.

Furthermore, if $c(w, y, t)$ is differentiable in w, Shephard's lemma applies. The behavior of $c(w, y, t)$ in t is easy to categorize: If technical change is progressive, $c(w, y, t)$ is nonincreasing in t; if technical change is regressive, $c(w, y, t)$ is nondecreasing in t. The proof of these assertions rests in the recognition that progressive technical change, as defined above, expands the input requirement set. Hence, the minimum achieved on the expanded input requirement set can be no larger than the minimum achieved on the original input requirement set since the original cost-minimizing bundle remains feasible. Directly analogous arguments establish the relationship between regressive technical change and costs.

When the cost function and the production function are both differentiable, a unique relationship exists between the rate of technical change, the elasticity of size, and the derivative

$$\frac{\partial \ln c(w, y, t)}{\partial t} \equiv \theta(w, y, t),$$

which we now define as the *rate of cost diminution*. Our terminology anticipates that technical change diminishes cost. As already seen, this is not necessarily true, but the terminology is indicative of what one usually expects from technical change. Consider the Lagrangian

$$L = w \cdot x + q[y - f(x, t)], \tag{6.9}$$

where to avoid confusion with augmentation factors, q is a Lagrangian multiplier. Applying the envelope theorem and recalling from Chapter 3 that the optimal value of the Lagrangian multiplier for the cost minimization problem is marginal cost gives

$$\frac{\partial c(w, y, t)}{\partial t} = -\frac{q \, \partial f(x, t)}{\partial t}$$

$$= -\frac{\partial c}{\partial y} \frac{\partial f(x, t)}{\partial t}.$$

A little manipulation yields

$$\mathrm{T}(x(w, y, t), t) = -\epsilon^*(w, y, t)\theta(w, y, t) \tag{6.10}$$

where $x(w, y, t)$ is the bundle that minimizes (6.9) and $\epsilon^*(w, y, t)$ is the associated elasticity of size. An interesting implication of (6.10) is that if $\mathrm{T}(x, t)$ and $\theta(w, y, t)$ are both constants, the associated elasticity of size must also be constant. This in turn implies that the associated technology is always homogeneous of degree ϵ^*.

Exercise 6.2. If the production function exhibits a constant rate of technical change, say, T, then

$$\frac{\partial \ln f(x, t)}{\partial t} = T,$$

and integration yields

$$\ln f(x, t) = Tt + g(x).$$

Hence,

$$f(x, t) = \exp(Tt) \exp g(x) = \exp(Tt) h(x).$$

A similar argument establishes that if the rate of cost diminution is constant, say, θ,

$$c(w, y, t) = \exp(\theta t) c(w, y).$$

Use these two equations directly to argue that $g(x)$ must be homogeneous.

By (6.10), the rate of cost diminution overstates the rate of technical change if there exist decreasing returns to size, understates the rate of technical change if there are increasing returns to size, and exactly measures the rate of technical change only if there exist constant returns to size. Graphically, this is easily demonstrated by considering the average-cost function for the family of production functions characterized by constant rates of technical change, that is,

$$f(x, t) = \exp[g(x) + Tt], \tag{6.11}$$

where T is the constant rate of technical change (see Exercise 6.2). For any output,

$$\frac{\partial \ln[c(w, y, t)/y]}{\partial t} = \frac{\partial \ln c(w, y, t)}{\partial t} = -\frac{T(x(w, y, t), t)}{\epsilon^*(w, y, t)} = -\frac{T}{\epsilon^*(w, y, t)}.$$

Assuming (6.11) generates a U-shaped average-cost curve, the effect of technical change on average costs is depicted in Figure 6.5. There, $(AC)_0$ represents the average-cost curve before the advent of technical change, and $(AC)_t$ represents the average-cost curve after technical change. To the left of y^* the vertical distance between $(AC)_0$ and $(AC)_t$ is less than the rate of technical change, whereas to the right of y^* it is greater than the rate of technical change, and at y^* the distance exactly reflects T. Here, y^* represents the minimum average-cost point on $(AC)_0$.

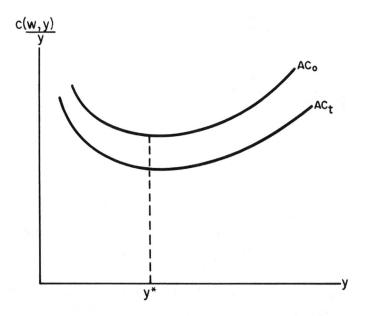

Figure 6.5   Rates of cost diminution and technical change.

The intuition behind the result depicted in Figure 6.5 is straightforward. As a general rule, technical progress raises the output obtainable for a given input bundle. Alternatively, it lowers the cost of obtaining a given output. If there exist size economies, expanding output decreases unit costs. Thus, the occurrence of technical progress in this region shifts the average-cost curve downward. At the same time, the implied percentage input saving, and at constant input prices the cost saving, must be less in percentage terms than the associated output expansion because of the size effect – hence the understatement of the effect of technical change. Alternatively, in the region of decreasing returns, the associated cost saving must be greater than the output expansion effect.

Cost-neutral technical change: It is convenient to categorize technical change in a similar manner to that developed for production functions. There, Hicks-neutral change was defined as equivalent to having an isoquant's slope independent of the state of technology. For the cost function, the analogous (but not equivalent) concept of *cost-neutral technical change* is

$$c(w, y, t) = c^*(\hat{c}(w, y), y, t),$$

where, without loss of generality, c^* is taken to be linearly homogeneous in $\hat{c}$ and $\hat{c}$ to be linearly homogeneous in w. Suppose that this did not hold. Then, taking the ratios of partial derivatives yields

$$\frac{\partial c(w, y, t)/\partial w_i}{\partial c(w, y, t)/\partial w_j} = \frac{\partial \hat{c}(w, y)/\partial w_i}{\partial \hat{c}(w, y)/\partial w_j} \quad \forall i, j.$$

Since $c(w, y, t)$ is linearly homogeneous in w, both sides of this equality must be homogeneous of degree zero in w by a property of homogeneous functions (see Appendix), and furthermore, Lau's lemma on homothetic functions then implies that $\hat{c}$ must be at least homothetic in w. Hence, $\hat{c}$ can be written in the general form $\hat{c}(w, y) = H[\check{c}(w, y)]$, where $\check{c}$ is now linearly homogeneous in w. Thus, $c(w, y, t) = c^*[(H(\check{c}(w, y)), y, t] \equiv c^{**}(\check{c}(w, y), y, t)$. For $c(w, y, t)$ to be linearly homogeneous in w requires

$$c(\Delta w, y, t) = c^{**}(\check{c}(\Delta w, y), y, t)$$
$$= c^{**}(\Delta \check{c}(w, y), y, t)$$
$$= \Delta c^{**}(\check{c}(w, y), y, t)$$
$$= \Delta c(w, y, t),$$

where the second equality follows by the linearly homogeneous nature of $\check{c}$, and the third and fourth equalities are consequences of the linearly homogeneous nature of $c(w, y, t)$. Thus, $c(w, y, t)$ can always be written in this fashion when it is characterized by cost-neutral technical change.

By the homogeneity properties,

$$c(w, y, t) = \hat{c}(w, y)c^*(1, y, t)$$
$$= A(y, t)\hat{c}(w, y)$$

if technical change is cost neutral. The implicit technology for a cost-neutral cost function is

$$V^*(y, t) = \{x: w \cdot x \geq A(y, t)\hat{c}(w, y), \ w > 0\}$$
$$= \{x: w \cdot x/A(y, t) \geq \hat{c}(w, y), \ w > 0\}$$
$$= A(y, t)\{Z: w \cdot z \geq \hat{c}(w, y), \ w > 0\}$$
$$= A(y, t)V^*(y), \quad (6.12)$$

where $Z = x/A(y, t)$ and $V^*(y)$ is an implicit input requirement set for a technology not undergoing technical change. Notice in particular the extreme similarity between (6.12) and the input requirement set for an equal-factor-augmenting technology. Specifically, (6.12) is an input requirement set for a technology experiencing equal-factor-augmenting technical change of a more general type than previously discussed. Here, augmentation factors depend not only on the state of technology but also on output. For any given output, a cost-neutral technology acts exactly as if it were an equal-augmenting technology. But across output levels it behaves differently.

Cost neutrality offers an intuitive feel for the concept of technical neutrality. By Shephard's lemma, cost neutrality means that cost-minimizing input ratios are independent of the state of technology. And if the technology is not neutral, a natural definition of biasedness is that technical change evinces a greater percentage adjustment in one input than in another; that is, it changes cost-minimizing input ratios. As such, there are at least $(n^2 - n)/2$ potential forms of relative bias. For example, technical change could enhance the utilization of capital relative to that of land while diminishing the utilization of capital relative to fertilizer in the production of an agricultural commodity. To further complicate the issue, many define the bias of technical change in terms of its effects on cost shares. Technical change is, therefore, often said to be unbiased (share neutral) if it leaves relative cost shares undisturbed; that is,

$$\frac{\partial}{\partial t} \frac{S_i(w, y, t)}{S_j(w, y, t)} = 0 \quad \forall i, j.$$

This last equation only holds for all i and j if

$$\frac{\partial}{\partial t} \ln \frac{S_i(w, y, t)}{S_j(w, y, t)} = 0$$

for arbitrary i and j; thus,

$$\frac{\partial}{\partial t} \ln S_i(w, y, t) = \frac{\partial}{\partial t} \ln S_j(w, y, t)$$

for arbitrary i and j. For this equality to apply for all w and regardless of the shares in question, the derivative of the logarithm of the share with respect to time must be the same for all shares:

$$\frac{\partial}{\partial t} \ln S_i(w, y, t) = m^*(y, t)$$

for all possible i. Remember that the linear homogeneity of the cost function implies that cost shares must add to 1 regardless of the level of t, w, or y. Using the preceding equality then yields

$$\frac{\partial}{\partial t} \left(\sum_i^n \ln S_i(w, y, t) \right) = nm^*(y, t)$$

$$= 0,$$

where the second equality follows by the fact that the derivative of the sum of the cost shares with respect to time must equal zero since this sum is always equal to 1. This implies that $m^*(y, t)$ itself equals zero so that the derivative of the logarithm of all cost shares with respect to time must also equal zero. Cost shares are, therefore, independent of the state of technology if technical change is share neutral. Bringing these results together gives the following expression for the ith cost share:

$$S_i(w, y, t) = n_i(w, y).$$

Integrating this last expression over w_i while recognizing that the ith cost share equals $\partial \ln c(w, y, t)/\partial \ln w_i$ gives

$$\ln c(w, y, t) = v(w, y) + u(y, t),$$

where $v(w, y) = \int n_i(w, y)\, dw_i$ and $u(y, t)$ is a constant of integration. Exponentiating both sides of this expression yields

$$c(w, y, t) = \exp[v(w, y)] \exp[u(y, t)]$$

$$= A(y, t)\hat{c}(w, y);$$

that is, share-neutral technical change is equivalent to cost-neutral technical change.

As far as creating a taxonomy of effects associated with technical change, the concepts of share or factor biases can be very convenient. Technical change is often said to be input-j using if

$$\frac{\partial \ln S_j(w, y, t)}{\partial t} > 0$$

and input-j saving if the opposite inequality holds. On the other hand, many individuals define biased technical change in terms of the partial derivative of $x_i(w, y, t)$ with respect to t. For clarity's sake, *share-using (saving) technical change* is that characterized by the first instance and *input-using (saving)* technical change is that characterized by the latter.

Example 6.1. Much of the original interest in the bias of technical change concerned how technical change affected various sectors of the economy. This concern is best reflected in the concept of share neutrality and the implications of the existence of share-biased technical change. Consider an economy whose aggregate production possibilities are characterized by a national product function exhibiting constant returns to scale (this assumption underlies, e.g., most general equilibrium analysis in international trade). From Chapter 2, this aggregate technology is equally well characterized by the associated dual-cost function:

$$yc(w, t),$$

where y is real national product and w is the vector of all factor prices in the economy. With constant returns to scale, all profits are exhausted in the payment of inputs so that

$$py = yc(w, t).$$

Here p is the price of the aggregate product, which for simplicity is treated as determined completely in international markets. In this context, cost shares represent the share of each group of factor owners in national income. Thus, technical change that is cost neutral and, consequently, share neutral does not affect the share of factors such as capital and labor in national income. Technical change of this sort does not enhance the relative economic position of one set of factor owners vis-á-vis that of any other set of factor owners. On the other hand, technical change that is not cost neutral will change the relative economic position of various sets of factor owners. For example, if technical change is labor using, the share of labor in national income goes up, and consequently, the share of at least one other factor of production in national income must go down.

Coincidence of cost neutrality and Hicks neutrality: Cost neutrality and Hicks neutrality are very similar, but not identical, concepts. This is best illustrated by first ascertaining what cost neutrality implies about the factor price frontier. Cost neutrality means that the curvature of the factor price frontier is independent of t. In terms of Figure 6.6, cost neutrality means the factor price frontier responds to technical change by shifting in a parallel manner, say, from c_0 to c_t. This implies that for any given w cost-neutral technical changes leave optimal input ratios unaltered. Translating these results in terms of the isoquant map using the results of Section 2.4b, cost neutrality means that technical change preserves the marginal rate of technical substitution along rays from the origin in input space (see Figure 6.7).

Recall from Figure 6.1 that Hicks neutrality requires that the marginal rate of substitution be independent of technology at points on the expansion path. Comparing these results with those in Figures 6.6 and 6.7 demonstrates that the two concepts only coincide when the expansion path is linear. This suggests that a necessary condition for the equivalence of the two concepts is the presence of homotheticity. To formalize these arguments, consider the implicit input requirement set associated with a cost-neutral technology. By expression (6.12),

$$V^*(y, t) = A(y, t) V^*(y)$$

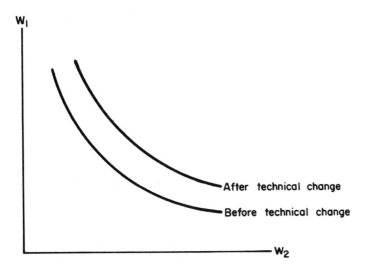

Figure 6.6 Cost-neutral technical change.

when the technology is cost neutral. The technology for a Hicks-neutral production function can be written as

$$V(y, t) = \{x : f(\phi(x), t) \geq y\}$$
$$= \{x : \phi(x) \geq \hat{h}(y, t)\}$$
$$= \hat{V}(\hat{h}(y, t)),$$

where $\hat{V}$ is the input requirement set associated with $\phi(x)$. Thus, the coincidence of cost and Hicks neutrality requires

$$A(y, t) V^*(y) = \hat{V}(\hat{h}(y, t)).$$

But, by duality, the cost function for the Hicks-neutral technology must be observationally equivalent to the one that generated the left-hand side of the preceding expression. The cost function for the Hicks-neutral technology is

$$c(w\ y, t) = \min\{wx : x \in \hat{V}(\hat{h})\}$$
$$= \tilde{c}(w, \hat{h}(y, t)).$$

Hicks neutrality, therefore, means that both output and the state of technology only affect cost via the pseudo-output variable $\hat{h}(y, t)$. If the technology is also to be cost neutral – implying that the slope of the factor price frontier is independent of time – the slope of the factor price frontier

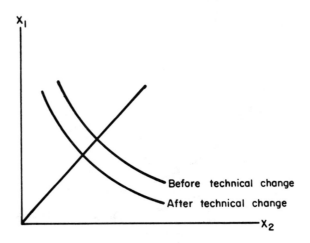

Figure 6.7   Cost-neutral technical change.

must also be independent of output because the factor price frontier is only independent of t if it is first independent of $\hat{h}(y, t)$. More formally, the i, j optimal input ratio equals

$$\frac{\partial \hat{c}(w, \hat{h}(y, t))/\partial w_i}{\partial \hat{c}(w, \hat{h}(y, t))/\partial w_j} = m_{ij}(w, \hat{h}(y, t)).$$

Cost neutrality then requires that

$$\frac{\partial}{\partial t} m_{ij}(w, \hat{h}(y, t)) = \frac{\partial m_{ij}}{\partial \hat{h}} \frac{\partial \hat{h}}{\partial t} = 0.$$

So unless $\hat{h}$ is independent of t (this means that costs do not depend on the state of technology), cost neutrality requires m_{ij} to be independent of $\hat{h}$. But it then follows that m_{ij} is independent of output, and by results reported in Section 2.3b [see Equation (2.30)], this cost function is then consistent with homotheticity.

Factor-augmenting technical change and the cost function: Cost-neutral technical change can always be interpreted as either diminishing (if technical change is progressive) all input prices or increasing all input prices (regressive technical change). Because cost neutrality and factor augmentation, therefore, appear closely related, a similar phenomenon might be expected there as well. This is easy to demonstrate. Consider the factor-augmenting technology $f(x, t) = f(\lambda_1 x_1, \ldots, \lambda_n x_n)$ described by (6.6). The

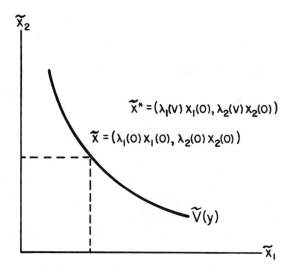

Figure 6.8 Cost minimization and input-augmenting technical change.

associated cost function can be expressed in terms of the effective input vector $\tilde{x} = (\lambda_1 x_1, \ldots, \lambda_n x_n)$ as

$$c(w, y, t) = \min\{w \cdot x : \tilde{x} \in \hat{V}(y)\}$$
$$= \min\{\tilde{w} \cdot \tilde{x} : \tilde{x} \in \hat{V}(y)\}$$
$$= c(\tilde{w}, y),$$

where $\tilde{w} = \{w_1/\lambda_1, w_2/\lambda_2, \ldots, w_n/\lambda_n\}$. Thus, the cost function associated with a factor-augmenting technology like (6.6) can always be interpreted in terms of input price diminishment or effective input prices with effective input prices given by the input prices divided by the augmentation coefficient.

A graphical representation is presented in Figure 6.8. Let the effective input combination denoted by $\tilde{x}$ belong to $V(y)$. Prior to the change in the augmentation factors $\tilde{x}$ is consistent with x at the level $\{x_1(0), x_2(0)\}$. If both λ_1 and λ_2 increase from, say, $\lambda_1(0)$ and $\lambda_2(0)$ to $\lambda_1(v)$ and $\lambda_2(v)$, the original x combination is consistent with an effective input combination $\tilde{x}^*$, say, that is greater than $\tilde{x}$. If the original input bundle were cost minimizing, a strictly cheaper way to produce y must now exist because under monotonicity $\tilde{x}^* \in V(y)$ but so is $\tilde{x} = (x_1^* \lambda_1(0)/\lambda_1(v), x_2^* \lambda_2(0)/\lambda_2(v))$. However, the cost associated with acquiring this last input bundle is strictly less than the cost associated with the original input bundle.

6.2b   *Technical change and the profit function*

The profit function accounting for technical change is

$$\Pi(p, w, t) = \max_{y \ge 0} \{ py - c(w, y, t) \}.$$

If $c(w, y, t)$ possesses properties 4B*.1–4B*.6, $\Pi(p, w, t)$ is a well-behaved profit function, and the conjugate cost function

$$c^*(w, y, t) = \max_{p > 0} \{ py - \Pi(p, w, t) \}$$

also possesses properties 4B*.1–4B*.6. To characterize the behavior of profit in terms of t, using the properties of $c(w, y, t)$ developed earlier proves convenient. If technical change is progressive, profit is nondecreasing in t. Progressive technical change implies $c(w, y, t) \le c(w, y, t^1)$ if $(t > t^1)$; let $y(p, w, t^1)$ be the profit-maximizing supply for (p, w, t^1). Under progressive technical change,

$$py(p, w, t^1) - c(w, y(p, w, t^1), t) \ge py(p, w, t^1) - c(w, y(p, w, t^1), t^1).$$

Even if supply does not adjust to the change in technology, profits cannot decrease. But, in general, supply adjusts, and by definition $\Pi(p, w, t)$ is at least as large as the left-hand side of this expression. A parallel argument establishes that regressive technical change tends to diminish profits.

Cost-neutral technical change means the cost function assumes the form $A(y, t)c(w, y)$. It will now be shown under what circumstances cost-neutral and profit-neutral technical change are equivalent. *Profit-neutral technical change* is technical change that leaves profit-maximizing input ratios undisturbed. For twice-continuously differentiable technologies, this gives profit functions of the general form

$$\Pi(p, w, t) = \Pi^*(\hat{\Pi}(p, w), p, t). \tag{6.13}$$

By Hotelling's lemma and the properties of profit functions,

$$\frac{\partial \Pi(p, w, t)/\partial w_i}{\partial \Pi(p, w, t)/\partial w_j} = \frac{\partial \hat{\Pi}(p, w)/\partial w_i}{\partial \hat{\Pi}(p, w)/\partial w_j}$$

is homogeneous of degree zero in p and w. Thus, by Lau's lemma, $\hat{\Pi}(p, w)$ is homothetic in p and w, and as earlier arguments established, no generality is lost by thinking of it as linearly homogeneous in p and w. Now,

$$\begin{aligned}
\Pi(\gamma p, \gamma w, t) &= \Pi^*(\hat{\Pi}(\gamma p, \gamma w), \gamma p, t) \\
&= \Pi^*(\gamma \hat{\Pi}(p, w), \gamma p, t) \\
&= \gamma \Pi(p, w, t) \\
&= \gamma \Pi^*(\hat{\Pi}(p, w), p, t), \quad \gamma > 0. \tag{6.14}
\end{aligned}$$

The second equality follows by the presumed linear homogeneity of $\hat{\Pi}$; the third equality is a consequence of the presumed overall homogeneity of $\Pi(p, w, t)$ and implies the fourth equality, which shows that Π^* must be linearly homogeneous in $\hat{\Pi}$. Using these results with the definition of profit-neutral technical change then gives

$$\Pi(p, w, t) = \hat{\Pi}(p, w)\Pi^*(1, p/\hat{\Pi}(p, w), t)$$

$$= \hat{\Pi}(p, w)\Pi^0(p/\hat{\Pi}(p, w), t). \tag{6.15}$$

Now it is time to determine if cost-neutral technical change implies that profits assume the same general form as (6.15). By definition, profits associated with cost neutrality are

$$\Pi(p, w, t) = \max_{y \geq 0}\{py - A(y, t)\hat{c}(w, y)\}. \tag{6.16}$$

Applying the envelope theorem to (6.16) yields

$$\frac{\partial \Pi(p, w, t)}{\partial w_i} = -A(y, t)\frac{\partial \hat{c}(w, y(p, w, t))}{\partial w_i};$$

thus,

$$\frac{\partial \Pi/\partial w_i}{\partial \Pi/\partial w_j} = \frac{\partial \hat{c}(w, y(p, w, t))/\partial w_i}{\partial \hat{c}(w, y(p, w, t))/\partial w_j}.$$

When technical change is cost neutral, t only affects profit-maximizing input ratios [remember, Hotelling's lemma implies that the left-hand side of this equality is the (i, j) optimal input ratio] through the profit-maximizing supply. For t to have no affect on profit-maximizing input ratios, these ratios must be independent of the level of output. But by preceding results and results in Chapter 2, this implies that the underlying technology is homothetic.

More formally, note that presuming that $\partial y(p, w, t)/\partial t \neq 0$ means that the derivative of the above ratios with respect to t can equal zero only if

$$\frac{1}{\partial \hat{c}/\partial w_i}\frac{\partial^2 \hat{c}(w, y, t)}{\partial w_i\, \partial y} = \frac{\partial^2 \hat{c}(w, y, t)}{\partial w_j\, \partial y}\frac{1}{\partial \hat{c}/\partial w_j} \quad \forall i, j.$$

Of course, earlier results tell us that this restriction is equivalent to homotheticity of $\hat{c}$.

Before pursuing more algebra on this topic, it is worthwhile to understand intuitively why cost neutrality and profit neutrality are not always equivalent. Cost neutrality means that optimal input ratios for either the cost minimizer or the profit maximizer are independent of the state of technology – *so long as output is held constant*. But one also expects the optimal output choice by a profit maximizer to depend on the state of technology. Certainly, we do not observe the same production pattern in

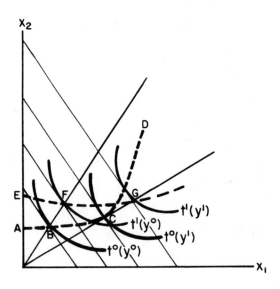

Figure 6.9 Profit-neutral and cost-neutral technical change.

all industries throughout time even when all prices grow at roughly the same rate. Thus, even if for a given output the profit-maximizing input ratios are independent of t, changes in t usually induce changes in profit-maximizing output. These output changes in turn induce changes in optimal input ratios unless the technology is homothetic.

Figure 6.9 illustrates these results pictorially. Let y^1 and y^0 represent the profit-maximizing outputs after and before technical change, respectively. The isoquants associated with these output levels before and after technical change are $\{t^0(y^0), t^0(y^1)\}$ and $\{t^1(y^0), t^1(y^1)\}$, respectively, in Figure 6.9. (The isoquants prior to technical change are distinguished by t^0; those after technical change are distinguished as t^1.) For given input and output prices, the expansion path for the old technology is BCD, whereas the expansion path for the new technology is EFG. Profit- and cost-neutral technical change requires that the optimal input ratio be invariant to the state of technology; that is, the expansion path for both the old and the new technology proceed through the same input combinations, and moreover, the optimal input ratio must be independent of the profit-maximizing level of output. Pictorially, this implies that B and G must lie on the same ray from the origin. This can only happen if both the old and the new expansion paths are linear, implying homotheticity as previously derived formally.

Returning to our earlier discussion of cost functions, we find that cost neutrality is consistent with homotheticity when $c(w, y, t)$ assumes the general form

$$A^*(y, t)\hat{c}(w). \tag{6.17}$$

Note, in particular, that Hicks neutrality and homotheticity jointly produce such a cost function. The associated profit function is of the form

$$\hat{\Pi}(w)\Pi^0(p/\hat{\Pi}(w), t). \tag{6.18}$$

To see that (6.18) is observationally equivalent to (6.17), note that the conjugacy relations imply

$$c^*(w, y, t) = \max_{p > 0}\{py - \hat{\Pi}(w)\Pi^0(p/\hat{\Pi}(w), t)\}$$

$$= \hat{\Pi}(w) \max_{p/\hat{\Pi}(w)} \{p/\hat{\Pi}(w)y - \Pi^0(p/\hat{\Pi}(w), t)\}$$

$$= \hat{\Pi}(w)A^*(y, t).$$

The converse proposition is left as an exercise for the reader:

Exercise 6.3. For a cost function consistent with cost neutrality and homotheticity, profit maximization requires

$$\frac{p}{\hat{c}(w)} = \frac{\partial A(y, t)}{\partial y},$$

which, if the implicit function theorem applies, yields the following expression for profit-maximizing supply:

$$y(p, w, t) = y^*(p/\hat{c}(w), t).$$

Use this equation to show that the associated profit function assumes the general form of (6.18).

Apparently, therefore, Hicks neutrality, cost neutrality, and profit neutrality are the same phenomenon only when the technology is also homothetic.

The effect of input-augmenting technical change on the structure of the profit function is easy to ascertain using previous results. When the technology is input augmenting, as in (6.6), one obtains

$$\Pi(p, w, t) = \max_{y > 0}\{py - c(w, y, t)\}$$

$$= \max_{y \geq 0}\{py - c(\tilde{w}, y)\}$$

$$= \Pi(p, \tilde{w}).$$

Table 6.1. *Technical change and production, cost, and profit functions*

	Hicks neutrality	Cost neutrality
$V(y, t)$	$\hat{V}[m(y, t)]$	$A(y, t)V(y)$
$c(w, y, t)$	$c(w, m(y, t))$	$A(y, t)\hat{c}(w, y)$
$\Pi(p, w, t)$	$\displaystyle\int \frac{\partial c(w, m[y(p, w, t), t])}{\partial w_i}\, dw_i$	$\displaystyle\int A[y(p, w, t), t]\,\frac{\partial\hat{c}(w, y(p, w, t))}{\partial w_i}\, dw_i$

Hence, input-augmenting technical change retains its interpretation as input-cost-diminishing technical change, meaning that it is profit enhancing since profits are nonincreasing in $\tilde{w}$. A particularly neat version of input-augmenting technical change involves an equal augmentation coefficient for all inputs – call this coefficient $\lambda(t)$. Then, since $w = \tilde{w}\lambda(t)$, one obtains by the linear homogeneity of the profit function that

$$\Pi(p, w, t) = \Pi(p, \tilde{w})$$

$$= \Pi(p, w/\lambda(t))$$

$$= \Pi(p\lambda(t), w)/\lambda(t).$$

Input-augmenting technical change of this form can be viewed as enhancing the effective per-unit return from producing a given output. As this rises, one expects supply to expand with the concomitant rise in revenues and income. However, the associated supply expansion only generates marginal returns equal to p and not $p\lambda(t)$ so that returns must be normalized back to original price units by dividing by the augmentation factor.

Exercise 6.4. Results of this chapter are summarized in Table 6.1, which delineates the various forms of neutrality in terms of its effect on $V(y, t)$, $c(w, y, t)$, and $\Pi(p, w, t)$. Several of these results were not derived in the text, and these are left as an exercise to the reader.

Example 6.2. To illustrate some of these concepts, consider the technical change component of the Ball–Chambers cost function discussed in Example 5.8. For the translog cost function presented there, the rate of cost diminution is

Profit neutrality	Joint Hicks–cost–profit neutrality	Input augmenting
$\{x: w \cdot x \geq \tilde{c}(w, y, t)\}$	$D(y, t) V(1)$	$\{\tilde{x}: f(\tilde{x}) \geq y\},$ $\tilde{x}_i = x_i \lambda_i(t)$
$\tilde{c}(w, y, t) = \max\limits_{p}\left[py - \hat{\Pi}(p, w)\Pi^0\left(\dfrac{p}{\hat{\Pi}(p, w)}, t\right)\right]$	$A(y, t) c(w)$	$c(\tilde{w}, y),$ $\tilde{w}_i = w_i / \lambda_i(t)$
$\hat{\Pi}(p, w)\Pi^0(p/\hat{\Pi}(p, w), t)$	$\hat{\Pi}(w)\Pi^0(p/\hat{\Pi}(w), t)$	$\Pi(p, \tilde{w}),$ $\tilde{w}_i = w_i / \lambda_i(t)$

$$\theta(w, y, t) = \beta_T + \sum_{i=1}^{n} \beta_{Ti} \ln w_{it} + \beta_{TY} \ln y_t + \beta_{TT} t.$$

The estimates of $\theta(w, y, t)$ for the last six years of the sample are reported in Table 6.2 along with the calculated elasticity of size. If these estimates are correct, the meat products industry underwent locally regressive technical change during this period (somewhat akin to the situation depicted in Figure 6.2). Although this may seem somewhat implausible at first glance, it fits well with the stylized facts of the industry that suggest overexpansion in plant size and capital utilization at precisely the same time that demand for meat products dropped off rapidly. Hence, it is often argued that the industry failed to "grow" into the technology it developed.

Because the cost function was estimated in translog form, it is particularly easy to investigate the biases of technical change in this instance. By simple differentiation,

$$\frac{\partial S_{it}}{\partial t} = \beta_{Ti} \quad \forall i.$$

To examine whether or not this cost function is potentially consistent with cost neutrality, notice that exponentiation yields

$$c(w, y, t) = \exp[\beta_0 + \beta_T t + \beta_\gamma \ln y + \tfrac{1}{2}\beta_{TT} t^2 + \tfrac{1}{2}\beta_{YY}(\ln y)^2 + \beta_{TY} t \ln y]$$

$$\times \exp\left(\sum_{i=1}^{n} \beta_i \ln w_i + \frac{1}{2} \sum_{i=1}^{n} \sum_{i=1}^{n} \beta_{ij} \ln w_i \ln w_j \right.$$

$$\left. + t \sum_{i=1}^{n} \beta_{Ti} \ln w_i + \sum_{i=1}^{n} \beta_{iy} \ln w_i \ln y \right).$$

Hence, cost neutrality here requires that $\beta_{Ti} = 0$ for all i. In other words, cost neutrality for the translog implies that cost shares are independent

Table 6.2. *Estimated elasticity of size, cost flexibility, and rate of cost diminution, U.S. meat products industry, 1970–76*

	ϵ^*	n	θ
1970	0.9654	1.0357 (0.2935)	−0.0088 (0.00686)
1971	0.8464	1.1814 (0.2964)	−0.0071 (0.00689)
1972	1.1379	0.8787 (0.2900)	−0.0173 (0.00676)
1973	2.4484	0.4084 (0.2814)	−0.0321 (0.00671)
1974	1.6057	0.6227 (0.2884)	−0.0288 (0.00686)
1975	13.0937	0.0763 (0.2764)	−0.0455 (0.00692)
1976	2.6164	0.3821 (0.2839)	−0.0396 (0.00703)

Note: Numbers in parentheses are standard errors.
Source: Ball, V. E., and R. G. Chambers. "An Economic Analysis of Technology in the Meat Products Industry." *AJAE* 64(1982): 699–708.

of time. A parametric test of these restrictions using the log-likelihood ratio statistic described earlier rejected cost neutrality. The estimated coefficients under the null hypothesis of cost neutrality and the resulting log-likelihood value are reported in Table 6.3.

Exercise 6.5. For the cost function discussed in Example 6.2, calculate the rate of technical change. Derive parametric restrictions for the translog that make it consistent with share neutrality. Discuss the implications of this last result in terms of the separability discussion of Chapter 5.

6.3   Divisia indexes and rate of technical change

Economists have long known that it is sometimes possible to observe the rate of technical change without estimating the production or any indirect objective function. Moreover, this way of measuring the rate of

Table 6.3. *Estimated coefficients for translog cost function for U.S. meat products industry under cost neutrality*

β_{KK}	0.0082
	(0.0007)
β_{KL}	0.0193
	(0.0027)
β_{KE}	−0.0011
	(0.0002)
β_{KM}	−0.0272
	(0.0025)
β_{KS}	0.0008
	—
β_{LL}	0.0344
	(0.0163)
β_{LE}	0.0039
	(0.0007)
β_{LM}	−0.0631
	(0.0159)
β_{LS}	0.0065
	—
β_{EE}	0.0014
	(0.0003)
β_{EM}	−0.0061
	(0.0009)
β_{ES}	0.0019
	—
β_{MM}	0.1078
	(0.0162)
β_{MS}	−0.0114
	—
β_{SS}	0.0022
	—
β_{K}	0.0008
	(0.0073)
β_{L}	0.3567
	(0.0411)
β_{E}	0.0094
	(0.0035)
β_{M}	0.6039
	(0.0477)
β_{S}	0.0202
	—

Table 6.3 *(cont.)*

β_Y	−30.0957
	(8.4300)
β_0	70.9975
	(17.7500)
β_{YY}	7.4298
	(2.0034)
β_{YK}	−0.0014
	(0.0021)
β_{YL}	−0.0679
	(0.0132)
β_{YE}	−0.0037
	(0.0008)
β_{YM}	0.0777
	(0.0143)
β_{YS}	−0.0047
	−
β_T	0.7420
	(0.1895)
β_{TT}	0.0068
	(0.0012)
β_{TY}	−0.1837
	(0.0455)
β_{TK}	−
	−
β_{TL}	−
	−
β_{TE}	−
	−
β_{TM}	−
	−
β_{TS}	−
	−
$\ln L$	691.1086

technical change closely resembles methods of measuring productivity. Because the measurement of technical change is often the focus of many empirical studies, considering alternatives that allow measurement without prior estimation is worthwhile. In this and later sections, the focus is on direct methods of measuring technical change. Perhaps the oldest of these approaches having some firm theoretical content is the Divisia index.

The key to measurement hinges on the recognition that actual input utilization depends on time. Total differentiation of

$$y = f(x, t)$$

with respect to time yields

$$\frac{dy}{dt} = \sum_j \frac{\partial f}{\partial x_j} \frac{dx_j}{dt} + \frac{\partial f}{\partial t}.$$

Dividing through by y gives

$$\frac{d \ln y}{dt} = \sum_j \epsilon_j \frac{d \ln x_j}{dt} + T(x, t).$$

This expression has $n+1$ observable terms ($d \ln y/dt$ and $d \ln x_i/dt$, $i = 1, 2, \ldots, n$) and $n+1$ unobservable terms [$T(x, t)$ and the n output elasticities ϵ_i]. To make $T(x, t)$ observable, one must find a way to make the ϵ_i observable. Fortunately, this can be easy: Under profit maximization, the output elasticities equal input shares in total revenue. Hence, when profits are maximized, one has

$$\frac{d \ln y}{dt} = \sum_j \frac{w_j x_j}{py} \frac{d \ln x_j}{dt} + T(x, t)$$

or

$$T(x, t) = \frac{d \ln y}{dt} - \sum_j \frac{w_j x_j}{py} \frac{d \ln x_j}{dt}. \qquad (6.19)$$

One can measure $T(x, t)$ by subtracting from the rate of output change a weighted sum of input utilization rates of change. If input and output prices, supply and input utilization, and rates of output and input change are observed, $T(x, t)$ can be calculated without estimation. However, this result only applies exactly to data generated continuously. And since most economic data come in discrete observations, (6.19) can only be approximated. A common approximation is

$$T(x, t) = \ln y_t - \ln y_{t-1} - \sum_{i=1}^{n} \frac{1}{2}[V_{it} + V_{i,t-1}][\ln x_{it} - \ln x_{i,t-1}], \qquad (6.20)$$

where y_t is output at time t, x_{it} is input i utilization at time t, and V_{it} is the ratio of the cost of input i at time t to revenue at time t. As the time interval goes to zero, (6.20) approaches (6.19).

The expression after the minus sign in (6.19) is the *Divisia input index,* whereas the third term on the right-hand side of (6.20) is the *Tornqvist approximation* to the Divisia index. Expression (6.20) only involves observable data, and in principle, market data can approximate the rate of technical change without estimation of the cost, production, or profit functions.

The ability to use observed data to calculate directly the rate of technical change depends critically on the assumption of profit maximization. Suppose that individuals are actually cost minimizers. The elasticity of output with respect to the jth input then equals $w_j x_j / y (\partial c / \partial y)$ [see Equation (2.22) and the accompanying discussion]. Marginal cost is not observable but equals the ratio of average cost to the size elasticity. So, under cost minimization, expression (6.19) becomes

$$T(x, t) = \frac{d \ln y}{dt} - \epsilon^*(w, y, t) \sum_j (w_j x_j / c) \frac{d \ln x_j}{dt}. \tag{6.21}$$

To obtain $T(x, t)$ from data generated by cost minimizers, one must know the scale elasticity. Put another way, for any observed changes in y and the x_i's and any postulated value of $T(x, t)$, a size elasticity exists that makes the observed changes in y and the x_i's consistent with (6.21). The problem here is similar to the identification problem in econometrics, where a single structure is consistent with multiple families of parameters. Expression (6.21) says that any $T(x, t)$ (or for that matter ϵ^*) can be made consistent with a body of observed data simply by choosing the correct ϵ^*. Hence, expression (6.21) does not provide enough information, in general, to identify the rate of technical change solely from observable economic data. Therefore, measuring $T(x, t)$ requires estimation of the cost function to obtain a reasonable measure of $\epsilon^*(w, y, t)$ before using (6.21) in the computation of $T(x, t)$. But estimation of a cost function with a reasonably flexible specification using time-series data should also generate an estimate of $T(x, t)$. If time-series data are unavailable and estimation is carried out with only cross-sectional data or with very limited time-series data, then direct estimation of the cost function and use of (6.21) can provide a reasonable means of approximating the rate of technical change.

Exercise 6.6. Expression (6.21) can be used to estimate both the rate of technical change and the scale elasticity if one is prepared to assume that both are constant. Rewriting that expression yields

$$\frac{d \ln y}{dt} = T(x, t) + \epsilon^*(w, y, t) \sum (w_j x_j / c) \frac{d \ln x_i}{dt}.$$

Let both the scale elasticity and the rate of technical change be treated as constants (ϵ^* and τ, respectively) and assume that the errors generated by this assumption are independently, identically distributed across time with mean zero. Denote the error at time t as ν_t and the logarithmic derivatives of y and x_i with respect to time at time t as $\dot{y}_t$ and $\dot{x}_{it}$; the stochastic version of the preceding equation then becomes

$$\dot{y}_t = \tau + \epsilon^* \dot{x}_{it} + \nu_t.$$

The parameters ϵ^* and τ can be estimated by applying ordinary least squares to this equation. As an exercise, use the data reported in Tables 6.4a and 6.4b to estimate these parameters for the Canadian agricultural sector (see also Fuss and McFadden, 1978, chap. IV.2).

6.4   Rate of technical change and total factor productivity

Long before economists specified and calculated rates of technical change, attempts were made to measure technical progress. Many of these attempts focused on comparing average productivity statistics. Often, this degenerated to comparing average labor products over time. Differences in the average product of labor were then attributed to technical progression or regression. Gradually, it was realized that it was wrong to identify technical progress entirely with the change in the average product of labor, or any other input for that matter. More and more, it became apparent that all input utilization could be affected by technical change and that any measure of technical change should take this into account.

A partial answer to the dilemma was the introduction of the notion of *total factor productivity*. Grossly put, total factor productivity is the average product of all inputs. More precisely, it is the ratio of the output to an index of inputs. Let the index of inputs be denoted as X. Then *total factor productivity* (TFP) is

$$\text{TFP} = y/X. \tag{6.22}$$

Differentiating both sides of (6.22) logarithmically with respect to time gives

$$\dot{\text{TFP}} = \dot{y} - \dot{X}, \tag{6.23}$$

where a dot over a variable denotes the logarithmic derivative with respect to time (e.g., $\dot{y} = d \ln y/dt$). To make (6.23) operational, one must specify a form for the time rate of change of the aggregate input (i.e., $\dot{X}$). Consider first the index derived by taking the cost-share weighted average of the time rates of change of the individual inputs,

$$\dot{X} = \sum_j (w_j x_j/c) \dot{x}_j.$$

Substituting this expression into (6.23) and comparing with (6.21) reveals that choosing this input index implies that the rate of change of total factor productivity (TFP) equals $T(x, t)$ when production is characterized by constant returns to size. This index for $\dot{X}$ is the Divisia input index that is based on cost shares. In general, choosing the aggregate input index so that

Table 6.4a. *Farm input quantity indexes by aggregate farm input categories and output index, Canada, 1961–80 (base year 1961)*

Year	(1) Real estate	(2) Labor inputs	(3) Farm machinery	(4) Livestock	(5) Crop inputs	(6) Energy inputs	(7) Miscellaneous inputs	(8) Output index
1961	100.00	100.00	100.00	100.00	100.00	100.00	100.00	100.00
1962	102.24	96.16	101.42	94.18	104.54	100.25	100.84	125.33
1963	103.06	93.66	104.02	103.72	113.76	102.96	107.18	137.93
1964	103.54	89.52	107.99	112.36	123.16	106.71	115.60	128.60
1965	105.31	82.39	113.73	114.06	129.33	112.01	125.24	136.53
1966	107.59	77.17	118.16	110.63	144.01	117.85	127.58	152.86
1967	110.62	77.37	121.06	113.57	156.13	123.20	131.75	131.75
1968	113.68	72.15	123.31	110.99	155.01	125.04	133.33	142.90
1969	114.35	72.87	122.96	113.61	157.47	126.17	127.11	148.81
1970	120.34	67.93	121.60	113.16	161.02	127.90	128.21	137.62
1971	121.93	67.26	122.10	110.31	172.14	149.13	127.18	155.50
1972	127.60	62.78	126.30	117.20	183.73	153.04	129.97	145.39
1973	132.88	62.67	136.45	120.92	186.75	157.05	145.37	152.23
1974	138.20	63.69	151.66	136.61	187.60	159.58	149.36	144.46
1975	143.95	63.28	166.24	117.89	186.08	152.34	138.49	160.63
1976	148.18	60.94	183.32	118.78	194.54	154.16	154.89	175.56
1977	146.32	57.88	184.46	116.08	200.54	159.21	139.39	175.09
1978	146.45	58.85	192.33	113.07	224.45	168.31	141.95	183.18
1979	147.85	59.96	192.49	126.17	239.83	181.61	120.63	173.38
1980	150.00	56.61	194.02	150.44	240.89	183.06	125.96	177.89

Source: Brinkman, G. L., and B. E. Prentice. *Multifactor Productivity in Canadian Agriculture: An Analysis of Methodology and Performance, 1960–1980.* School of Agricultural Economics and Extension Education, University of Guelph, Guelph, Ontario, Canada, May 1983.

Table 6.4b. Indexes of farm input wages and index of total expenses on all farm inputs, Canada, 1961–80 (base year 1961)

Year	(1) Real estate	(2) Labor inputs	(3) Farm machinery	(4) Livestock	(5) Crop inputs	(6) Energy inputs	(7) Miscellaneous inputs	(8) Total constant dollar aggregate inputs expense
1961	100.00	100.00	100.00	100.00	100.00	100.00	100.00	100.00
1962	99.83	100.01	100.03	99.81	99.87	100.17	100.14	98.42
1963	100.04	100.02	100.00	100.27	99.86	99.98	100.62	98.80
1964	99.82	100.03	100.04	100.27	99.87	100.01	100.07	98.46
1965	98.86	100.02	100.08	99.95	99.90	100.16	100.20	96.22
1966	99.91	100.01	100.01	100.03	99.99	100.18	100.67	95.57
1967	99.98	100.02	100.00	99.79	99.92	100.27	99.97	97.97
1968	100.01	100.01	100.00	100.31	99.99	100.14	100.00	95.31
1969	99.88	100.00	100.02	99.76	99.96	100.24	100.27	96.02
1970	99.85	99.98	100.09	100.15	99.99	100.20	100.17	93.83
1971	100.03	100.02	100.07	100.32	99.92	100.02	100.21	95.65
1972	100.04	100.02	100.05	100.11	99.82	99.93	100.32	94.82
1973	99.95	100.04	100.03	100.34	99.92	100.06	100.49	97.18
1974	100.03	100.04	100.07	100.04	99.89	100.05	100.43	100.93
1975	98.98	100.04	100.10	100.09	99.85	100.12	99.82	101.64
1976	98.70	94.97	100.68	97.66	99.82	100.03	100.01	103.11
1977	99.95	99.99	100.06	99.93	99.83	100.02	100.58	101.50
1978	100.04	100.03	100.06	100.23	99.89	99.86	100.15	105.12
1979	99.97	100.00	100.06	100.39	99.90	99.95	100.78	107.72
1980	100.09	100.00	100.10	100.15	99.88	100.07	100.41	106.86

Source: Brinkman, G. L., and B. E. Prentice. Multifactor Productivity in Canadian Agriculture: An Analysis of Methodology and Performance, 1960–1980. School of Agricultural Economics and Extension Education, University of Guelph, Guelph, Ontario, Canada, May 1983.

$$\dot{X} = \sum (w_j x_j / py) \dot{x}_j$$

implies that the rate of change of total factor productivity equals $T(x, t)$ for a profit-maximizing firm. [This follows by comparing (6.19) with (6.23) when the latter definition of $\dot{X}$ is used in (6.23).]

Thus, average product measures, such as total factor productivity, can be meaningfully related to other technical change concepts by an appropriate choice of indexes. To explore this issue further, integrate both sides of (6.19) over time to obtain

$$\ln \frac{f(x, t)}{f(x, 0)} = \ln \frac{y_t}{y_0} - \int_0^t \left(\sum \frac{w_j x_j}{py} \dot{x}_j \right) dv,$$

where v is the variable of integration and 0 is some base year relative to which t is compared. Exponentiation of both sides of this last expression gives

$$\frac{f(x, t)}{f(x, 0)} = \frac{y_t}{y_0} \exp\left(-\int_0^t \sum \frac{w_j x_j}{py} \dot{x}_j \, dv \right). \qquad (6.24)$$

Recalling that $T(x, t) = \dot{\text{TFP}}$ when a Divisia input index is used gives

$$\int_0^t T(x, v) \, dv = \int_0^t \dot{\text{TFP}} \, dv = \ln \frac{\text{TFP}(t)}{\text{TFP}(0)}$$

$$= \ln \frac{f(x, t)}{f(x, 0)}.$$

Total factor productivity has a natural index number interpretation: Namely, the ratio of TFP's from two different time periods equals the ratio of the production function evaluated at two different time periods (or for two different states of technology) holding the input bundle fixed. Thus, expression (6.24) measures the shift in the production function due solely to changes in t. A visual interpretation of expression (6.24) is provided in Figure 6.10. There, the input bundle is held constant at x, and t ranges over the positive orthant. The measure in (6.24) is the ratio $0B/0A$, which equals the ratio of TFP(t) to TFP(0).

Expression (6.24), in effect, defines an index of the relative effectiveness of a given input bundle x in producing output for different states of the technology. The production function itself is an aggregation of inputs so that, by (6.24), the ratio of total factor productivity from two different time periods can also be interpreted as a measure of the effectiveness of the aggregate input X in producing output. If technical change makes this aggregate input more effective in producing output, this index is greater than 1. If technical change makes this aggregate input less effective in producing output, the index is less than 1. And finally, if technical change does not change the aggregate input's effectiveness, the index equals 1.

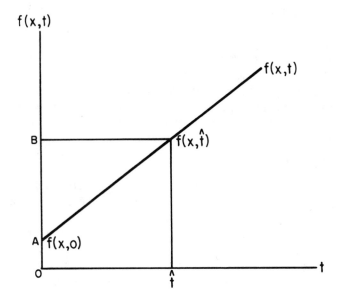

Figure 6.10 Indexes of technical change.

Total factor productivity has three closely related, but not exactly identical, interpretations: the average product of an aggregate input, a measure of the rate of technical change, and an index of input effectiveness in producing output before and after technical change. The main problem with implementing (6.24) is that it is based on continuous concepts whereas most data are gathered at discrete intervals. Thus, the time rates of change for the x_i (i.e., $\dot{x}_i$) must be approximated by their discrete counterparts. Of course, this leads to inexact calculation of the concepts involved. In the next section, ways to overcome this shortcoming are presented. Basically, the approach follows the course set by (6.24): Construct index numbers of technical change that can be exactly calculated from data gathered at discrete intervals.

6.5   Discrete measures of technical change

If one defines measures of technical change only in continuous terms, one can only approximate these concepts with discrete data. A partial solution is suggested by the left-hand side of (6.24). That is, measuring technical change in index number form is more appropriate. Because index numbers are defined over discrete intervals, this seems eminently reasonable. And as already seen, the production function provides a suitable way to aggregate inputs. There is a major drawback to this approach: Generally, it requires exact knowledge of the structure of the production function, and often it requires specific knowledge about the values of the parameters of the production function. Unfortunately, it is unusual to have such information in most practical instances. But there are specific cases where such an approach is appropriate and can yield fruitful results.

To grasp the method being proposed, consider a linearly homogeneous production function exhibiting Hicks-neutral technical change. Output at time t can then be written (see Table 6.1) as

$$y = A(t)m^*(x) = f(x, t),$$

where $m^*(x)$ is the linearly homogeneous production function associated with the input requirement set $V(1)$ in Table 6.1. Equation (6.24) suggests that a reasonable index of technical change is defined by evaluating the production function at an x with the technology or time variable changing. Such an index measures the shift in the production function solely due to the passage of time. For the preceding linearly homogeneous, Hicks-neutral production function, this index of technical change is

$$\frac{f(x, t)}{f(x, 0)} = \frac{A(t)}{A(0)}, \tag{6.25}$$

where again 0 is some base period against which the state of technology in time period t is to be compared. Here, the technical change index is the ratio of the multiplicative shift factors representing the Hicks-neutral effect.

The next question is whether it is possible to find an exact measure for (6.25) based on data observed at discrete intervals. The problem is simple if one observes market situations where the vector of inputs remains constant. In that case, (6.25) is simply the ratio of outputs at time t and time 0. Unfortunately, researchers rarely have this luxury in economics. Almost never do they have access to data from a controlled experiment that reduces the source of variation to one causal factor, the passage of time. Rather, economic data are usually observations from an active marketplace where the participants in the market follow some type of optimization behavior. Because the technology changes over time, an optimizing agent usually changes the input mix over time. Therefore, only comparing output levels over time using market-based data likely means the following comparison is being made:

$$\frac{y_t}{y_0} = \frac{f(x_t, t)}{f(x_0, 0)} = \frac{A(t)}{A(0)} \frac{m^*(x_t)}{m^*(x_0)} \neq \frac{A(t)}{A(0)}.$$

However, an exact index of technical change is

$$\frac{A(t)}{A(0)} = \frac{y_t}{m^*(x_t)} \frac{m^*(x_0)}{y_0}.$$

Thus, calculating the alternative input index $m^*(x_t)/m^*(x_0)$ yields, after appropriate manipulation, an index of technical change. Unfortunately, even in this restrictive case, this is not generally possible without knowing the exact form of $m^*(x)$. Suppose $m^*(x)$ can be written as

$$m^*(x) = \prod_{i=1}^{n} x_i^{\alpha_i}$$

so that the overall production function is Cobb–Douglas:

$$f(x, t) = A(t) \prod_{i=1}^{n} x_i^{\alpha_i},$$

where the constant term captures the effect of technical change and linear homogeneity requires $\sum_i \alpha_i = 1$. Even now calculation of the index is impossible without knowledge of the α_i's. In general, this leaves two possible courses. The first is to estimate directly the production function to get estimates of the α_i. A problem with this approach, aside from the actual problems of estimation, is that the resulting measure is only a statistical approximation. Comparing this approach with that outlined earlier, little has been gained, and the further problem of estimating the production function has been introduced. A second course suggested by (6.24) is less objectionable: Presume that data are generated by optimizing individuals. Specifically, assume that individuals are cost minimizers. Under this assumption, calculation yields

$$\epsilon_i = \alpha_i = \frac{\partial f}{\partial x_i} \frac{x_i}{y} = \frac{w_i x_i}{\sum w_i x_i} = S_i,$$

where the reader will recall from Chapter 1 that ϵ_i is the elasticity of output with respect to x_i [see Equation (1.6)]; the first equality follows by calculation; and the third equality follows because cost minimization implies that marginal productivities equal input prices divided by marginal cost (remember the optimal Lagrangian multiplier for the cost minimization problem equals marginal cost) and the further fact that linear homogeneity implies costs are linear in output.

So, if individuals are cost minimizers, the α_i parameters are cost shares that are observable from data on prices and quantities. The input index is then calculable as

$$\frac{m^*(x_t)}{m^*(x_0)} = \frac{\prod_{i=1}^{n} x_{it}^{S_{it}}}{\prod_{i=1}^{n} x_{i0}^{S_{i0}}},$$

and the technical change index becomes

$$\frac{A(t)}{A(0)} = \frac{y_t}{y_0} \frac{\prod_{i=1}^{n} x_{i0}^{S_{i0}}}{\prod_{i=1}^{n} x_{it}^{S_{it}}}, \tag{6.26}$$

which is exact and does not require estimation.

There are, of course, a number of problems with the measure in (6.26) that relate directly to the number of assumptions made to obtain it. Each assumption, linear homogeneity, Hicksian neutrality, Cobb–Douglas form, and cost-minimizing behavior, is critical to the derivation. Relax one and we will not obtain (6.25). Moreover, notice that the derivation assumes that the α_i parameters are constant. But cost minimization implies $\alpha_i = S_{i0} = S_{it}$. On an empirical basis, it will be extremely rare for cost shares to remain constant over time. Thus, this methodology is only applicable in limited circumstances. The real importance of (6.26) lies in the demonstration that an exact measure of technical change is derivable. It points the way for later developments. And a logical way to proceed is to relax assumptions sequentially to see if one can still find calculable measures of technical change.

Perhaps the most restrictive assumption is that $m^*(x)$ is a power equation. The Cobb–Douglas form is unattractive because of its separability properties and its limited ability to approximate other functions. One wonders whether it is possible to specify $m^*(x)$ to be flexible and still get observable measures of technical change. The answer is yes. To start, a result due to Diewert (1976) that simplifies further derivation is developed.

Consider the general quadratic function

$$h(Z) = \alpha_0 + \sum_i \alpha_i Z_i + \frac{1}{2} \sum_i \sum_j \alpha_{ij} Z_i Z_j$$
$$= \alpha_0 + \alpha^T Z + \tfrac{1}{2} Z^T A Z,$$

where $\alpha_{ij} = \alpha_{ji}$, $\alpha^T = (\alpha_i, ..., \alpha_n)$, $A = \{\alpha_{ij}\}$, and the superscript T denotes transposition. It follows that

$$h(Z^1) - h(Z^0) = \tfrac{1}{2} [\nabla_Z h(Z^1) + \nabla_Z h(Z^0)]^T [Z^1 - Z^0], \tag{6.27}$$

where $\nabla_Z h(Z^1)$ is the gradient of h at Z^1. To see this result, simply proceed by direct calculation:

$$h(Z^1) - h(Z^0) = \alpha^T Z^1 + \tfrac{1}{2} Z^{1T} A Z^1 - \alpha^T Z^0 - \tfrac{1}{2} Z^{0T} A Z^0$$
$$= \alpha^T (Z^1 - Z^0) + \tfrac{1}{2} Z^{1T} A (Z^1 - Z^0) + \tfrac{1}{2} Z^{0T} A (Z^1 - Z^0)$$
$$= \tfrac{1}{2} [\alpha + A Z^1 + \alpha + A Z^0]^T [Z^1 - Z^0]$$
$$= \tfrac{1}{2} [\nabla_Z h(Z^1) + \nabla_Z h(Z^0)]^T [Z^1 - Z^0],$$

where the second equality follows because for a symmetric matrix A, $Z^{1T} A Z^0 = Z^{0T} A Z^1$.

A reasonable extension of the Cobb–Douglas form is to assume $m^*(x)$ is the translog

$$\ln m^*(x) = \beta_0 + \sum_{i=1}^{n} \beta_i \ln x_i + \frac{1}{2} \sum_i \sum_j \beta_{ij} \ln x_i \ln x_j.$$

Using (6.27),

$$\ln m^*(x_t) - \ln m^*(x_0) = \frac{1}{2} \sum_i \left[\frac{\partial \ln m^*(x_t)}{\partial \ln x_i} + \frac{\partial \ln m^*(x_0)}{\partial \ln x_i} \right] (\ln x_{ti} - \ln x_{0i}),$$

which, taking antilogs, yields

$$\frac{m^*(x_t)}{m^*(x_0)} = \exp\left[\frac{1}{2} \sum_i \left(\frac{\partial \ln m^*(x_t)}{\partial \ln x_i} + \frac{\partial \ln m^*(x_0)}{\partial \ln x_i} \right) (\ln x_{ti} - \ln x_{0i}) \right].$$

$$(6.28)$$

If one can represent the right-hand side of (6.28) with observable data, (6.28) generates an observable technical change index consistent with the translog. But again this is easy since if

$$y = A(t)m^*(x),$$

it follows that

$$\epsilon_i = \frac{\partial \ln y}{\partial \ln x_i} = \frac{\partial \ln m^*(x)}{\partial \ln x_i} = S_i,$$

where again we use the fact that under constant returns and cost minimization the elasticity of output equals the cost share. Hence, one can write

$$\frac{A(t)}{A(0)} = \frac{y_t}{y_0} \exp\left[\frac{1}{2} \sum_{i=1}^{n} (S_{it} + S_{i0})(\ln x_{i0} - \ln x_{it}) \right]$$

$$= \frac{y_t}{y_0} \prod_{i=1}^{n} \left(\frac{x_{i0}}{x_{it}} \right)^{(1/2)(S_{it} + S_{i0})}.$$

$$(6.29)$$

Expression (6.29) corresponds exactly to the exponential of the right-hand side of (6.20). Thus, the Tornqvist index, derived earlier as an approximation, is an exact measure of technical change if the original production function exhibits Hicks-neutral technical change and can be closely approximated by a translog. Diewert has called (6.29) a *superlative index* of technical change because it is an exact measure of technical change for a functional form that is flexible.

These arguments can be applied to other flexible forms like the quadratic mean of order p and the generalized Leontief to derive other calculating formulas for superlative indexes of technical change. But this is left as an exercise to the reader.

Exercise 6.7. Suppose the production function is

$$f(x,t) = A(t) \left[\sum_{i=1}^{n} \sum_{i=1}^{n} \gamma_{ij} x_i^{p/2} x_j^{p/2} \right]^{1/p}.$$

Derive an index of technical change that is based only on observed data.

Indexes of technical change from cost and profit functions: A technical change index need not be specified solely in terms of the production function. The duality relationships imply that all economically relevant information can be recaptured from indirect objective functions, that is, the profit and cost functions. In what follows, these ideas are developed in a relatively complete fashion for the cost function; extension to the profit function is straightforward and is left as an exercise for the reader.

By the preceding discussion, it seems reasonable to examine indexes measuring how the passage of time changes the cost of producing a given output holding factor prices constant. Consider the following index of technical change:

$$\frac{c(w, y, t)}{c(w, y, 0)}. \tag{6.30}$$

Expression (6.30) gives the cost of producing y at time t relative to that of producing y at time 0 assuming that input prices are held constant at w. Expression (6.30) is virtually identical to cost-of-living indexes comparing how the cost of attaining a given level of well-being changes over time. To make the conversion complete, one would let y measure utility and the vector w be a vector of consumption prices instead of factor prices.

The measure in (6.30) does not always give the same measure of technical change as that defined for the production function. If the technology is both Hicks neutral and linearly homogeneous, the technical change index defined by (6.24) is

$$\frac{f(x,t)}{f(x,0)} = \frac{A(t)}{A(0)},$$

whereas the technical change index defined by (6.30) is

$$\frac{c(w, y, t)}{c(w, y, 0)} = \frac{[y/A(t)]c(w)}{[y/A(0)]c(w)}$$

$$= \frac{A(0)}{A(t)};$$

the two measures are reciprocals of one another in this instance. This result will not hold generally unless the cost function inherits the technical change properties of the production function. Before calculating formulas for the technical change index in (6.30), note that technical progress implies that (6.30) is less than 1, whereas technical regression implies that (6.30) exceeds 1.

Again, it is unlikely that data exist for which all the differences between costs can be attributed to technical change. Rather, calculation must be based on data where output, prices, and technology all vary. Therefore, we want to convert the ratio

$$\frac{c(w_t, y_t, t)}{c(w_0, y_0, 0)} \tag{6.31}$$

into an exact measure of (6.30). Under linear homogeneity and Hicks neutrality,

$$\frac{c(w_t, y_t, t)}{c(w_0, y_0, 0)} = \frac{y_t c(w_t)}{y_0 c(w_0)} \frac{A(0)}{A(t)},$$

which implies

$$\frac{A(0)}{A(t)} = \frac{C_t y_0 c(w_0)}{C_0 y_t c(w_t)},$$

where C_t is observed cost at time t. Deriving an accurate productivity index requires a functional form for c.

If $c(w)$ is the translog

$$\ln c(w) = \phi_0 + \sum_i \phi_i \ln w_i + \frac{1}{2} \sum_i \sum_j \phi_{ij} \ln w_i \ln w_j,$$

using (6.27) yields

$$\ln c(w_0) - \ln c(w_t) = \frac{1}{2} \sum_{L=1}^{n} \left[\frac{\partial \ln c(w_0)}{\partial \ln w_i} + \frac{\partial \ln c(w_t)}{\partial \ln w_i} \right] [\ln w_{i0} - \ln w_{it}]$$

and

$$\frac{c(w_0)}{c(w_t)} = \prod_{i=1}^{n} \left(\frac{w_{i0}}{w_{it}} \right)^{(1/2)(S_{i0} + S_{it})}.$$

The last equality follows because input cost shares equal the logarithmic derivatives of the cost function. Thus,

$$\frac{A(0)}{A(t)} = \frac{c_t y_0}{c_0 y_t} \prod_{i=1}^{n} \left(\frac{w_i^0}{w_i^t} \right)^{(1/2)(S_{i0} + S_{it})}. \tag{6.32}$$

Expression (6.32) is also a superlative technical change index since it is an exact index for a flexible technology.

Exercise 6.8. Let technology be consistent with a translog profit function. Develop an index of productivity based on

$$\frac{\Pi(p, w, t)}{\Pi(p, w, 0)}$$

that uses data for periods with different prices. The assumption of a linearly homogeneous production function implies that profit is either zero or infinity in both time periods. Thus, this assumption should not be employed in developing a technical change index. (*Hint:* Assume technology is Hicks neutral and homothetic and proceed from there or, alternatively, assume that the technology is profit neutral.)

Exercise 6.9. Suppose the cost function can be written as

$$c(w, y, t) = \frac{y}{A(t)} \sum \sum \beta_{ij} (w_i w_j)^{1/2}.$$

Derive an index of technical change corresponding to

$$\frac{c(w, y, t)}{c(w, y, 0)}$$

that is based only on observable data.

6.6   Measuring relative efficiency

So far, discrete measures of technical change have been addressed in a time context. As long as a single economic entity is being considered, this makes perfect sense, but once the issue of relative efficiency across firms is addressed, the passage of time is not required. For example, suppose one wants to determine whether a particular firm in an industry is more productive than another. One method is to assume that both firms have technologies that only differ by a multiplicative scalar,

$$y = A(\theta) f(x),$$

where $A(\theta)$ measures the relative technology for firms whose technical state of nature is characterized by the parameter θ. One discrete index of the relative efficiency of the two firms is $A(\theta_1)/A(\theta_0)$, where subscripts differentiate firms. If two firms use different input bundles, this index becomes

$$\frac{A(\theta_1)}{A(\theta_0)} = \frac{y_1}{y_0} \frac{f(x_0)}{f(x_1)}.$$

If $f(\ )$ is translog and linearly homogeneous, for cost-minimizing producers, the relative efficiency index is exactly (6.30) where time subscripts now refer to firms. Having defined discrete measures of technical differences allows one to use them for any discrete units – time or firms – with only minor notational changes.

> **Exercise 6.10.** Develop a discrete index of relative efficiency for two firms using any well-behaved cost function.

6.7 Technical change indexes without constant returns to scale

So far, all discrete measures of technical change or relative efficiency are based on the presumption of constant returns. However, it is important to derive measures of technical change or relative efficiency that do not require constant returns to scale, which excludes profit-maximizing firms from consideration unless one makes further assumptions about industry equilibrium. Therefore, in what follows, relax the constant-returns assumption and replace it with profit maximization. Consider the translog production function

$$\ln y_t = \alpha_0 + \sum_{i=1}^{n} \alpha_i \ln x_{it} + \frac{1}{2} \sum_i \sum_j \alpha_{ij} \ln x_{it} \ln x_{jt}$$

$$+ \beta_0 t + \beta_{00} t^2 + t \sum_{i=1}^{n} \beta_i \ln x_{it}.$$

By (6.27),

$$\ln y_t - \ln y_v = \frac{1}{2} \sum_i \left(\frac{\partial \ln y_t}{\partial \ln x_i} + \frac{\partial \ln y_v}{\partial \ln x_i} \right)(\ln x_{it} - \ln x_{iv})$$

$$+ \frac{1}{2} \left(\frac{\partial \ln y_t}{\partial t} + \frac{\partial \ln y_v}{\partial t} \right)(t - v).$$

First-order conditions for profit maximization require $\partial \ln y_t / \partial \ln x_i = V_{it}$ (as defined earlier), and this expression becomes

$$\ln y_t - \ln y_v = \tfrac{1}{2} \sum_i (V_{it} + V_{iv})(\ln x_{it} - \ln x_{iv}) + \tfrac{1}{2}(T_t + T_v)(t - v).$$

If units are arbitrarily chosen so that $t = 1$ and $v = 0$,

$$\exp\left[\frac{1}{2} (T_1 + T_0) \right] = \frac{y_1}{y_0} \prod_{i=1}^{n} \left(\frac{x_{i0}}{x_{i1}} \right)^{(1/2)[V_{it} + V_{i0}]}. \tag{6.33}$$

The right-hand side of (6.33) is similar to (6.29) [identical except that (6.29) is based on cost shares] and can be loosely interpreted in the same vein, that is, as a measure of the ratio of the average product of an aggregate input calculated at two different time periods. If the right-hand side of (6.33) is less than 1, it follows that

$$\tfrac{1}{2}(T_1 + T_0) < 0,$$

implying that technical regression exists in either period 0 or period 1 and, moreover, that if technical progression exists at all, it is dominated by technical regression. Thus, (6.33) measures the average rate of technical change for the two time periods.

Example 6.3. Two indexes of technical change. This example presents calculations based on an aggregate data set for Canadian agriculture during the period 1960–80 of two separate indexes of technical change. The indexes calculated are those presented in Equation (6.29) (the Tornqvist input index of technical change) and the index of technical change presented in Equation (6.32) (the Tornqvist index of technical change based on observed costs, output, and input prices). The indexes are both calculated with 1960 as the base year. Both indexes presume the existence of constant returns to scale and Hicks-neutral technical change. Therefore, the reader is cautioned against interpreting these indexes as anything more than an illustration of the procedures outlined previously. Actual measurement of technical change for this industry should involve a more thorough study of possible causes of technical change and alternative functional specifications. Both equations presume that the technology can be represented in translog form. The Tornqvist input index presumes that the technology is represented by a translog cost function.

It is interesting to examine the results of this analysis if only for illustrative purposes. Column 2 in Table 6.5 represents the level of output divided by the Tornqvist input index. Except for a few years in the sample, this index rises steadily. This suggests that output grew more rapidly than the input index, implying that Canadian agriculture underwent constant technical change. The third column of Table 6.5 represents the cost-based index of technical change. These numbers fall steadily throughout the sample with only few exceptions, suggesting that costs would fall throughout the sample period if input prices and output were held constant. Thus, they also suggest that Canadian agriculture is undergoing technical change. Furthermore, the numbers in column 3 of Table 6.5 are roughly the reciprocals of the numbers in column 2 of Table 6.5.

6.8   Summary

This chapter considers at least two distinct ways of viewing technical differences across firms or time. The first approach, defining technical change

Table 6.5. *Tornqvist input and
cost indexes using Canadian
agricultural data (base year 1960)*

Year	Input index	Cost index
1961	1.000	1.000
1962	1.268	0.785
1963	1.391	0.716
1964	1.299	0.765
1965	1.400	0.704
1966	1.570	0.625
1967	1.326	0.743
1968	1.464	0.667
1969	1.516	0.645
1970	1.422	0.682
1971	1.579	0.615
1972	1.468	0.657
1973	1.505	0.644
1974	1.388	0.705
1975	1.533	0.639
1976	1.627	0.597
1977	1.643	0.591
1978	1.660	0.589
1979	1.537	0.640
1980	1.578	0.621

in terms of derivatives of the production function, is the most traditional
and has a rich history to offer. The second approach, which defines technical differences in discrete terms, probably has just as long a history and
appeals directly to the intuition since we generally are faced with the necessity of using discrete data in applied production problems. Neither
approach is perfect since one approach only offers measurement by approximation whereas the other approach usually requires the choice of a
specific functional form.

Bibliographical notes

This chapter has drawn on a variety of sources. Important references that must
be mentioned are Solow (1957), Ohta (1974), Blackorby et al. (1976), and Diewert
(1976). Solow pioneered the Divisia index approach while Diewert was the first to
demonstrate the properties of the Tornqvist and other index numbers as exact for
flexible forms. Excellent examples of empirical studies using these methods can be
found in Ball (1985) and Capalbo and Denny (1986).

CHAPTER 7

Multioutput technologies

The chapter that closes this book serves several purposes. For readers who have endured the first four chapters, it represents a series of generalizations that should complete their introduction to applied production economics. For more advanced readers, bringing to the book an understanding of the more abstract concepts of a technology used in this chapter, it can and should serve basically as a replacement for Chapters 1–4. Readers of this ilk may find it convenient to use the first four chapters as an extended glossary. Finally, for individuals already well versed in production economics, this chapter provides a succinct summary in a common notation of results that are dispersed throughout the literature.

Writing this chapter has been fraught with pitfalls. Most apparent is that many of the arguments are necessarily at a higher level of abstraction and generality than earlier chapters. Some of the mathematical arguments that follow may seem elusive to some readers. On the other hand, this chapter is not a rigorous "formalization" of what has gone before. Although it is easiest to motivate intuition and understanding in the single-product case, there are matters of substance in the multioutput case that anyone interested in applied production analysis should comprehend; the multioutput case is not only of interest to mathematical economists. For these reasons, I have tried to keep the mathematical arguments closely in line with earlier chapters. As a consequence, not all results are proven formally. As elsewhere in the book, the mathematical arguments should be treated more as extended illustrations than as formal proofs. When it is expositionally convenient to do so, I have sacrificed mathematical formalities. But I do carry on the discussion in terms of a set-valued technology rather than a multioutput production or transformation function. There are several reasons for this. Most important of these is that it does not really complicate the mathematical argument. For example, the discussion of the multioutput cost function is exactly identical to that for the single-output case after $V(y)$ has been suitably redefined. Furthermore, there are issues relating to the aggregation of inputs and outputs where use of a multioutput production function unnecessarily limits the generality of the analysis to no good end in terms of either empirical or theoretical analysis. Finally, in my own way, I want to convince the reader

250

(as I did myself) that the multioutput case is really not as complex as we often think it to be. Arguments and intuition developed in the simplest of cases still basically apply, and the economics of a multioutput world, although somewhat more complicated, is for the most part not fundamentally changed.

Because this chapter covers both primal and dual representations of the technology, the discussion is at times somewhat terse. In some instances, little attempt is made to motivate arguments intuitively. Where very similar ground was covered before, just a sketch of the mathematical argument and a reference to the appropriate part of an earlier chapter is presented. This was done primarily because the intuition used here is practically identical to that for the single-output case. Readers interested in such heuristics can always refer to earlier chapters. Hopefully, this will reinforce in the reader's mind that here we address only a broader view of reality and not a fundamentally different topic area. Much less attention is paid to issues of functional structure here than in other chapters. The reason again is the same: With few exceptions, the details have already been covered in previous chapters, and extensions are fairly apparent and need little further intuitive or technical motivation. The generalizations we ignore but the reader may find important deal mainly with the functional structure of aggregate output functions (when they do exist). Finally, utilization of a set-valued technology ultimately removes some of the urgency of functional structure.

In what follows, I first discuss a primal representation of the technology. Then I turn to a brief discussion of several indirect objective functions and duality. The chapter closes with a treatment of various forms of input–output separability and nonjointness.

7.1   The primal technology

This section considers three closely related concepts of a technology: a production possibilities set, an input requirement set for a multioutput technology, and a producible-output set. The depictions of the technology used in this chapter are in reality simpler than concepts (e.g., the production function) used so far. The reason is that the current representation places fewer restrictions on the technology than earlier chapters. At the same time, however, the representation is so much more general than the production function that some may find this chapter more challenging than what has gone before. In what follows, differentiable technologies are only utilized in the discussion of functional structure. And even though the assumption of continuous differentiability greatly limits generality (e.g., it rules out Leontief technologies), the use of calculus techniques is so deeply entrenched within economics as to make some of these simpler arguments almost opaque to many. For that reason, an effort is made, through the use of examples and exercises, to relate these more general concepts to more familiar results.

Production possibilities sets: Our starting point is a specification of the technical possibilities that firms face. These are summarized by the production possibilities set T that gives all feasible input and output combinations. At its most general level, T may be defined in terms of an $(m+n)$-dimensional vector z that contains both outputs and inputs. Here, z is called the *net output,* or *netput,* vector; by convention, z_i is an output if it is positive (its production exceeds its use) and an input if it is negative (its use exceeds its production). Although there are intuitive advantages to dichotomizing firmly between inputs and outputs, doing so is limiting theoretically and empirically. Many real-world instances exist where entrepreneurs use a particular commodity as both an input and an output. A frequently cited example is the purchase and sale of manure by agricultural enterprises involved in both crop and livestock production. However, the intuitive advantages of maintaining a clear dichotomy between inputs and outputs is so great that I typically do so. Therefore, let y denote an m-dimensional vector of nonnegative, real-valued outputs and x denote an n-dimensional, real-valued vector of nonnegative inputs. Here, T is the set of all (x, y) combinations that are technically feasible given the existing state of technology.

In what follows, this menu of restrictions on T will prove convenient at different times:

Properties of T (7D):

1. T is nonempty;
2. T is a closed set;
3. T is a convex set;
4. if $(x, y) \in T$, $x^1 \geq x$, then $(x^1, y) \in T$ (free disposability of x);
5. if $(x, y) \in T$, $y^1 \leq y$, then $(x, y^1) \in T$ (free disposability of y);
6. for every finite x, T is bounded from above; and
7. $(x, 0_m) \in T$, but if $y \geq 0$, $(0_n, y) \notin T$ (weak essentiality).

Most of these properties closely parallel related properties for the production function. For the most part, they serve similar purposes. Property 7D.1 says that some feasible input–output combinations exist; that is, it assumes at its most basic level that a technology exists – outputs can be produced using inputs. Property 7D.2 is an essentially mathematical requirement that cannot, in fact, be contradicted by observable data. It guarantees that there are no holes in the boundary of T much in the same

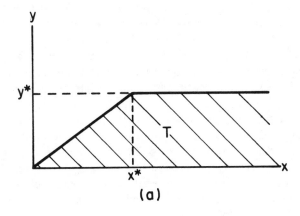

(a)

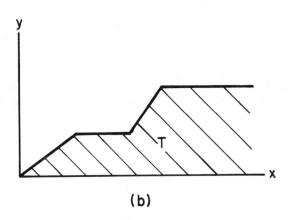

(b)

Figure 7.1 (a) Convex technology. (b) Nonconvex technology.

manner that we earlier assumed that the input requirement set for the production function had no "holes" (see Section 1.2). More formally, it requires that all of the accumulation or boundary points of T belong to T.

Property 7D.3 implies that any average of two technically feasible input-output configurations is also technically feasible. One might think of it as requiring the technology to be divisible in the following sense: Suppose $(x, y) \in T$ and $(x^1, y^1) \in T$ but that one wants to produce $\theta y + (1-\theta) y^1$ $(0 < \theta < 1)$; this should be feasible by utilizing a mixture of an operation sized θx and another operation sized $(1-\theta) x^1$. Figure 7.1(a) illustrates a

convex T; a nonconvex T is illustrated in 7.1(b). Property 7D.3 also generalizes the concept of a diminishing marginal rate of technical substitution.
Properties 7D.4 and 7D.5 are generalizations of the monotonicity properties of the production function. Simply put, they say that if x can produce a given output bundle, then a bigger input bundle can also produce
that output bundle. Extra units of the inputs do not hamper production.
On the other hand, 7D.5 implies that decreasing the output bundle does
not diminish the input requirement set. If x can produce y, it can also
produce all smaller output bundles. Again extra units of the inputs do
not get in the way of production. Property 7D.6 is a mathematical regularity condition that serves two purposes: to guarantee the existence of
a "production function" and to guarantee the existence of well-defined
extrema for the optimization problems that follow. Property 7D.7 simply
means that you cannot get something for nothing and that the origin belongs to T; that is, producing zero output is always feasible.

Input requirement sets: Several characterizations of T will prove convenient in what follows. The first generalizes the input requirement set to
the multioutput case. To preserve intuitive continuity and to emphasize
the basic similarity of definitions, retain the original notation and define

$$V(y) = \{x : (x, y) \in T\},$$

where it is understood that y is now a vector of outputs. As before, $V(y)$
represents the set of all input combinations capable of producing output
bundle y.

To reinforce intuition, consider the consequences of properties 7D for
$V(y)$. From 7D.1, $V(y)$ is nonempty for at least one finite output vector
since 7D.1 implies that at least one feasible input–output combination
exists. Notice, however, it does not imply that $V(y)$ is nonempty for all y.
Consider the technology portrayed pictorially by Figure 7.1(a) – output
levels greater than y^* are not achievable despite the fact that this technology obeys 7D.1–7D.7. Property 7D.3 implies that $V(y)$ is convex; to see
this, consider x and $x^1 \in V(y)$. By definition, $(x, y) \in T$ and $(x^1, y) \in T$,
which, together with the convexity of T, imply that $(\theta x + (1 - \theta)x^1, y) \in T$.
Thus, the boundary of $V(y)$ assumes the characteristic shape associated
with a diminishing marginal rate of technical substitution. Property 7D.4
implies that if $x \in V(y)$, then for $x^1 \geq x$, $x^1 \in V(y)$. Property 7D.5 means
that for $y^1 \leq y$, $V(y) \subseteq V(y^1)$. Finally, property 7D.7 can be recast in
terms of the input requirement set as $0_n \notin V(y)$ for $y > 0$.

Producible-output sets: Any technology satisfying 7D satisfies basically
the same properties (or obvious generalizations) for $V(y)$ as characterized

by the production function. Unlike the production function, however, T also characterizes interaction between different outputs. The easiest way to consider output interaction is the *producible-output set*

$$Y(x) = \{y: (x, y) \in T\}.$$

In words, the producible-output set represents all output bundles that can be produced using a *given* input bundle. In terms of Figure 7.1(a), the producible-output set $Y(x^*)$ is any output lying in the closed interval $[0, y^*]$. For smooth technologies (i.e., those that are twice-continuously differentiable), the outer boundary of this set is the *product transformation* curve familiar from general equilibrium analysis and the theory of international trade. As usually drawn, the product transformation curve is concave to the origin, implying an increasing rate of product transformation; the *rate of product transformation* is defined as the rate at which one output displaces another in a multiproduct technology with a fixed-input bundle. The boundary of $Y(x)$ exhibits an increasing rate of product transformation if T is convex. For a fixed x, increasing the production of a single output, say, y_1, at the expense of y_2 (holding all other outputs fixed) requires an increasing marginal opportunity cost in terms of units of y_2 foregone. To show that $Y(x)$ is consistent with an increasing rate of product transformation, one must show that $Y(x)$ itself, and hence its boundary, is convex. (In effect, this is equivalent to showing that the product transformation function is convex.) The demonstration is as follows: Suppose y and y^1 are both elements of $Y(x)$. An increasing rate of production transformation then implies that $\theta y + (1-\theta)y^1 \in Y(x)$, that is, that $\theta y + (1-\theta)y^1$ can be produced using only x. Notice, however, that since $(x, y) \in T$ and $(x, y^1) \in T$, by the convexity of T, $(\theta x + (1-\theta)x, \theta y + (1-\theta)y^1) = (x, \theta y + (1-\theta)y^1) \in T$, as required. Hence, it is legitimate to depict $Y(x)$ as in Figure 7.2.

The properties of $Y(x)$ can be inferred from properties 7D. By 7D.1, an x exists such that $Y(x)$ is nonempty. In some cases, the only element of $Y(x)$ may be the null vector because the existing input vector cannot produce a positive output. Such a situation is depicted pictorially in Figure 7.3. When $Y(x)$ is associated with input levels lower than x^*, no positive output level can be produced. Property 7D.4 says that if $x \geq x^1$, then $Y(x^1) \subseteq Y(x)$, whereas 7D.5 tells us that if $y \geq y^1$, then $y^1 \in Y(x)$ if $y \in Y(x)$. Property 7D.6 means that finite input bundles can only produce finite output combinations so that $Y(x)$ is bounded from above. Finally, property 7D.7 implies that although $0_m \in Y(0_n)$ any $y > 0_m$ cannot belong to this producible-output set. The only element of the producible-output set defined by the null input vector is the null output vector. In other words, you cannot get something for nothing: A technology that violates

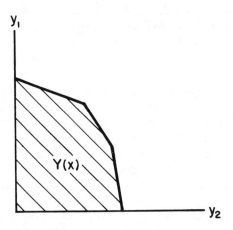

Figure 7.2   Producible-output set for convex T.

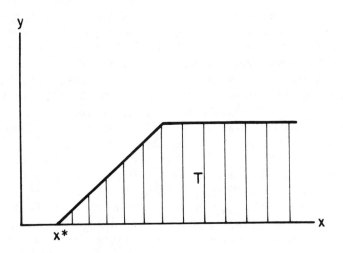

Figure 7.3 T possessing empty producible-output sets.

this property is depicted graphically in Figure 7.4. Even with a zero committal of inputs, output level y^* is feasible there.

Properties of producible-output sets (7E):

1. $Y(x)$ is nonempty and closed;
2.   if $y \in Y(x)$, $y^1 \leq y$, then $y^1 \in Y(x)$; if $x^1 \geq x$, then $Y(x^1) \supseteq Y(x)$;
3. $Y(x)$ is convex;

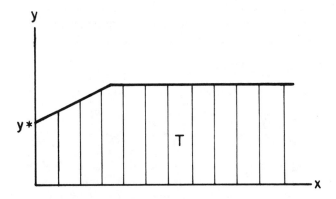

Figure 7.4 T with nonempty $Y(O_n)$.

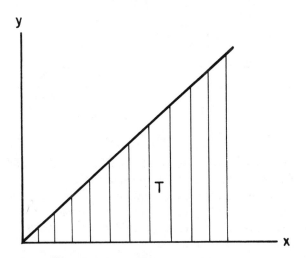

Figure 7.5 T exhibits constant returns to scale.

4. $Y(x)$ is bounded from above for finite x; and
5. if $y \geq 0$, $y \notin Y(0_n)$; $0_m \in Y(x)$.

Before discussing indirect objective functions, it is worthwhile to explore further the relationship between inputs and outputs. In the scalar output case, the notion of returns to scale is intuitive. In the multiproduct case, *T exhibits constant returns to scale if* $(x, y) \in T$ *implies that* $(\theta x, \theta y) \in T$ *for* $\theta > 0$. Graphically, this means that T is a cone emanating from the origin as depicted in Figure 7.5. In the single-input case, constant returns implies that all isoquants are evenly spaced and parallel. In the multioutput case, constant returns still implies that isoquants are evenly spaced. This is demonstrated by the following arguments:

$$V(ty) = \{x: (x, ty) \in T\}$$
$$= \{x: (x/t, y) \in T\}$$
$$= t\{x/t: (x/t, y) \in T\}$$
$$= tV(y),$$

where the second equality is a consequence of constant returns. Thus, the input requirement set for ty is just t times the input requirement set for y. It is then obvious that the frontiers of these two sets are parallel and the distance between these two frontiers in input space is just t. Turning to the producible-output set, one finds that under constant returns,

$$Y(tx) = \{y: (tx, y) \in T\}$$
$$= \{y: (x, y/t) \in T\}$$
$$= t\{y/t: (x, y/t) \in T\}$$
$$= t\{z: (x, z) \in T\}$$
$$= tY(x)$$

so that the producible-output set associated with tx is just a multiple of that associated with x. This means that constant returns to scale in the multioutput case implies evenly spaced and parallel product transformation curves as illustrated in Figure 7.6. The ratio $0D/0A$ in that figure gives the multiple (t) by which the entire input vector has been increased to shift the product transformation curve.

In the scalar output case, the notions of decreasing and increasing returns to scale are well defined and quite intuitive. Here, however, the situation is somewhat less clear because more than one output is involved. Although one can surely spell out relatively plausible definitions of increasing or decreasing returns to scale, the economic phenomena underlying much of the applied interest in scale economies seem best addressed in terms of cost and profit functions rather than T.

Example 7.1. Deriving $f(x)$ from T. T is a relatively obvious generalization of the production function. A production function satisfying properties 1A.1a, 1A.2a, 1A.3a, and 1A.4 [monotonicity, quasi-concavity,

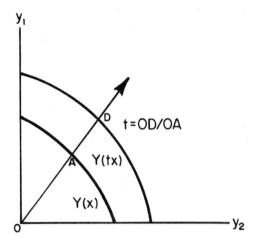

Figure 7.6 Producible-output sets for constant-returns technology.

weak essentiality, and nonemptiness of $V(y)$ for some x] can be derived
from a T satisfying 7D as the solution to

$$f(x) = \max\{y : (x, y) \in T\}$$
$$= \max\{y \in Y(x)\} \tag{7.1}$$

when y is a scalar. By 7D.2 and 7D.6, the maximum described in (7.1)
exists for all finite x since T is compact under these assumptions. Monotonicity requires that if $x^1 \geq x$, then $f(x^1) \geq f(x)$. Notice, however, that
7D.4 implies that for $x^1 \geq x$, $Y(x) \subseteq Y(x^1)$, which means that the feasible
set in (7.1) cannot shrink when x expands if it satisfies properties 7D.
Hence the maximum over $Y(x^1)$ can be no smaller than the maximum
over $Y(x)$. Quasi-concavity has already been demonstrated by showing
that $V(y)$ is convex in the multiproduct case. A direct proof applying to
(7.1) is: Define the solution to (7.1) when $x = x^i$ $(i = 0, 1, 2)$ as y^i; let $x^2 =
\theta x^0 + (1 - \theta)x^1$; suppose that both y^0 and $y^1 \geq y^*$; to demonstrate quasi-
concavity, we need to show that $y^2 \geq y^*$ as well. But by the convexity of
T, for x^2, output level $\theta y^0 + (1 - \theta)y^1 \geq y^*$ must always be available, implying by (7.1) that

$$f(\theta x^0 + (1 - \theta)x^1) \geq (\theta y^0) + (1 - \theta)y^1 \geq y^*,$$

which completes the proof. Weak essentiality follows from the fact that
we have already shown that $0_n \notin V(y)$ for $y > 0_m$ in the multiproduct case.
Properties 7D.1 and 7D.2 imply $V(y)$ is nonempty for some x.

The production function represents the boundary of T and not T itself. Here, $f(x)$ represents the set of technically efficient input–output combinations and not the set of technically feasible combinations. For example, it is portrayed in Figure 7.1(a) as the heavy line emanating from the origin and T.

Example 7.2. Transformation functions and T. A common representation of the multiproduct technology that does not dispense with differentiability is an implicit function of inputs and outputs:

$$Y(x, y) = 0.$$

An obvious special case is the scalar production function expressed in implicit form,

$$Y(x, y) = y - f(x) = 0.$$

This example discusses briefly the relationship between T and $Y(x, y)$. Although it is relatively straightforward (see, e.g., Diewert 1971, Shephard 1970) to derive $Y(x, y)$ directly from T, this example only covers a brief survey of the properties of $Y(x, y)$ that parallel those summarized in properties 7D.

Reexpress $V(y)$ and $Y(x)$ in terms of $Y(x, y)$:

$$V(y) = \{x : Y(x, y) \leq 0\} \quad \text{and} \quad Y(x) = \{y : Y(x, y) \leq 0\}.$$

Here it is obvious that $(x, y) \in T$ if $Y(x, y) \leq 0$. Assume that both of these sets are closed and nonempty to satisfy 7D.1 and 7D.2. Convexity of T can be manifested in several ways. The most obvious is the requirement that if $Y(y^0, x^0) \leq 0$ and $Y(y^1, x^1) \leq 0$, then $Y(\theta x^0 + (1-\theta)x^1; y^0 + (1-\theta)y^1) \leq 0$. This condition is satisfied if

$$Y(\theta x^0 + (1-\theta)x^1, \theta y^0 + (1-\theta)y^1) \leq \theta Y(y^0, x^0) + (1-\theta) Y(y^1, x^1)$$

or, in words, if $Y(y, x)$ is a convex function. For instance, a convex $Y(x, y)$ implies that $V(y)$ is also convex. By definition, let x and $x^1 \in V(y)$; then,

$$Y(x, y) \leq 0 \quad \text{and} \quad Y(x^1, y) \leq 0.$$

Using the convexity of $Y(x, y)$ yields

$$Y(\theta x + (1-\theta)x^1, \theta y + (1-\theta)y) = Y(\theta x + (1-\theta)x^1, y) \leq 0,$$

proving the convexity of $V(y)$, as desired.

Property 7D.4 requires that if $Y(x, y) \leq 0$, then $Y(x^1, y) \leq 0$ for $x^1 \geq x$. Suppose, in fact, that x belongs to the efficient input requirement set (i.e., the isoquant); then $Y(x, y) = 0$. Therefore, for the desired inequality to hold, $Y(x, y)$ cannot be increasing in x. Property 7D.7 implies that $Y(0_n, y) > 0$ for $y \geq 0_m$.

Exercise 7.1. One way to represent the product transformation function is

$$Y(y, x) = y_1 - m(y_2, \dots, y_m, x) = 0,$$

where

$$m(y_2, \dots, y_m, x) = \max\{y_1 : (x, y) \in T\}.$$

Derive the properties of this transformation function under the assumption that T satisfies properties 7D. Now show that the producible-output set defined by $Y(y, x)$ satisfies properties 7E.

7.2 Multioutput technologies and indirect objective functions

In the preceding section, it was seen that conceptualizing the technology as a set-valued relationship rather than in functional terms is more a matter of formalities than of economic substance. Using the properties of T, one can derive restrictions on $V(y)$, for example, that are almost identical to the restrictions used in the single-output case. Consequently, the arguments involved in the derivation of the multioutput counterparts of the cost and profit functions change only slightly, if at all. For that reason, we retain our original notation and denote the multioutput cost function as $c(w, y)$ and the multioutput profit function as $\Pi(p, w)$, where it is now understood that both y and p are m-dimensional vectors.

7.2a Multioutput cost function

Before proceeding with a derivation of the properties of $c(w, y)$, rewrite properties 7D in terms of $V(y)$ in a manner that makes them consistent intuitively with properties 1A of $f(x)$.

Properties of $V(y)$ (7A*):

1. If $x \in V(y)$ and $x^1 \geq x$, then $x^1 \in V(y)$; if $y^1 \geq y \geq 0$, then $V(y^1) \subseteq V(y)$;
2. $V(y)$ is a convex set;
3. $0_n \notin V(y)$ for $y \geq 0_m$ but $0_n \in V(0_m)$; and
4. $V(y)$ is nonempty and closed for finite y.

As the reader has undoubtedly noticed, properties 7A*.1–7A*.4 exactly parallel properties 1A.1a, 1A.2a, 1A.3a, and 1A.4 utilized in the derivation of the single-output cost function. Because none of those arguments were peculiar to the single-output case, demonstrating that $c(w, y)$ satisfies conditions 2B.1–2B.6 (actually this only requires the use of 7A*.1, 7A*.3, and 7A*.4) is easy. Hence, this task is left to the reader as an exercise:

Exercise 7.2. Suppose $V(y)$ satisfies 7A*.1, 7A*.3, 7A*.4. Show that $c(w, y) = \min\{w \cdot x : x \in V(y), w > 0\}$ is positive for $y > 0$ nondecreasing in w, concave and continuous in w, linearly homogeneous in w, equals zero when $y = 0_m$, and nondecreasing in y.

Also, notice that if $c(w, y)$ is differentiable in w, Shephard's lemma applies. A sufficient condition for $c(w, y)$ to be differentiable in w is that $V(y)$ be a strictly convex set (i.e., its boundary possesses no flat segments). Here again the intuition is basically the same as that developed in Chapter 2 and, therefore, is not repeated.

The comparative statics properties of derived demands for the multi-output case are essentially similar to those for the single-output case. When the cost function is not twice-continuously differentiable, the fundamental inequality of cost minimization still applies, and when the cost function is twice-continuously differentiable, the comparative static properties of derived demands is exhaustively characterized by the requirements that derived demands be homogeneous of degree zero in w; the sub-Hessian matrix $\nabla_{ww} c(w, y) = \nabla_w x(w, y)$ be negative semidefinite; the gradient of marginal costs $\nabla_y c(w, y)$ be homogeneous of degree 1 in w; and $\partial^2 c / \partial w_i \, \partial y_j = \partial^2 c / \partial y_j \, \partial w_i$.

7.2b   Revenue function

This section addresses a main point of departure between the single-output and multioutput cases. Here we are concerned with the maximum value that a given input endowment can produce. In the single-output case, maximizing the value derived from a given output bundle involves no economic choice since it implies operating at the point on the production function corresponding to the input endowment. Matters are different in the multioutput case because a given input bundle can produce the array of outputs summarized by the producible-output set. Revenue maximization then presents a true economic problem.

Before plowing through the mathematical arguments associated with revenue maximization, let me place it in a broader context. The most familiar utilization of revenue functions is in general equilibrium analysis and most especially in international trade. Most international trade models assume that a country maximizes the returns from its resource endowment and then uses these returns to trade in international markets. If the country is small relative to the rest of the world (i.e., it takes world prices as given), the first step in this process – maximization of revenue from a given resource endowment – is intuitively equivalent to an individual setting his or her budget constraint. As a result, the revenue function can be viewed as the purchasing power of a country's fixed-resource endowment. Second, standard, international trade assumptions theory assumes inputs do not move across borders just as individuals are assumed not to trade fixed inputs in the short run. For this and other reasons, the properties of revenue functions have implications that extend considerably beyond a simple characterization of the technology.

Define the *revenue function* as

$$R(p, x) = \max\{p \cdot y : y \in Y(x), \ p > 0\}. \tag{7.2}$$

Here p is an m-dimensional vector of strictly positive output prices. If $Y(x)$ satisfies properties 7E.1, 7E.2, 7E.4, and 7E.5, the revenue function defined in (7.2) satisfies:

Properties of $R(p, x)$ (7F):

1. $R(p, x) \geq 0$;
2. if $p \geq p^1$, then $R(p, x) \geq R(p^1, x)$;
3. $R(tp, x) = tR(p, x), \ t > 0$;
4. $R(p, x)$ is convex and continuous in p; and
5. if $x^1 \geq x$, then $R(p, x^1) \geq R(p, x)$.

The intuitive content of properties 7F parallels similar properties for other indirect objective functions. Therefore, I shall not spend a great deal of time motivating them heuristically. As an informal exercise, readers should try to motivate these properties on their own. (In pursuing this exercise, the reader is advised to consult Chapter 2, Section 2.2.) Property 7F.1 follows from the fact that 0_m is always producible by 7E.5; therefore, $R(p, x)$ can never be less than zero. To show property 7F.2, let y^1 be the solution to (7.2) when p^1 prevails. When prices rise to p from p^1, $Y(x)$ is unaffected. Hence, y^1 remains available and the worst that could be done is to produce at y^1 giving $R(p, x) = py^1 \geq p^1 y^1 = R(p^1, x)$ by supposition. Property 7F.3 is seen by

$$R(tp, x) = \max\{tpy : y \in Y(x), \ tp > 0\}$$

$$= t \max\{py : y \in Y(x), \ p > 0\}$$

$$= tR(p, x), \quad t > 0.$$

Convexity is slightly more difficult to show but is still easy. Let $p^2 = \theta p^0 + (1-\theta)p^1$ and y^i ($i = 0, 1, 2$) denote the solution to (7.2) when p^i ($i = 0, 1, 2$) prevails. By definition,

$$R(p^0, x) \geq p^0 y^2, \qquad R(p^1, x) \geq p^1 y^2.$$

But expansion reveals

$$R(p^2, x) = p^2 y^2 = [\theta p^0 + (1-\theta)p^1]y^2$$

$$= \theta p^0 y^2 + (1-\theta)p^1 y^2 \leq \theta R(p^0, x) + (1-\theta)R(p^1, x),$$

which completes the demonstration. Property 7F.5 follows from the fact that for $x \leq x^1$, property 7E.2 requires $Y(x^1) \supseteq Y(x)$. Since the producible-input set has not diminished in size, any output endowment remains feasible and the worst one can do is to produce at the old output bundle.

When $R(p, x)$ is differentiable in p, it satisfies a variant of the Shephard–Hotelling lemma derived earlier. That is, property 7F.6:

6.   If $R(p, x)$ is differentiable in p, a unique revenue-maximizing output vector exists with typical element

$$y_i(p, x) = \frac{\partial R(p, x)}{\partial p_i};$$

if a unique revenue-maximizing output vector exists, then $R(p, x)$ is differentiable in p (*Samuelson – McFadden lemma*).

Intuitively, property 7F.6 exactly parallels previous results on differentiability; therefore, there is no need to motivate it by using graphical examples. Moreover, the empirical importance of 7F.6 should be fairly obvious and needs little expansion. Therefore, only a demonstration of the first part of 7F.6 and a discussion of its implications for comparative static analyses follow. The second part of 7F.6 is not formally demonstrated but is addressed in an example.

As with the cost and profit functions when price p^0 prevails, one can write

$$R(p^0, x) = p^0 y^0,$$

where y^0 is the vector of outputs that maximizes (7.2) for price p^0. Notice, however, that $Y(x)$ is independent of p. Hence, y^0 must be feasible for any other output price vector. And the fact that it is not always chosen implies that

$$R(p, x) \geq p y^0,$$

which in turn implies that

$$L(y^0, p, x) = R(p, x) - py^0$$

attains a global minimum at $p = p^0$, where $L(y^0, p^0, x) = 0$. If $R(p, x)$ is differentiable, then first-order conditions for minimizing $L(y^0, p, x)$ yield

$$\frac{\partial R(p^0, x)}{\partial p_i} = y_i^0,$$

which establishes the first part of the Samuelson–McFadden lemma for differentiable $R(p, x)$. Notice that second-order conditions imply the convexity of $R(p, x)$ in p at p^0.

With properties 7F.1–7F.6 in hand, one has an easy method for carrying out comparative statics analysis for twice-continuously differentiable $R(p, x)$. Before proceeding with a brief analysis of that case, the reader should note that the solution to (7.2) satisfies the *fundamental inequality of revenue maximization:*

$$(p^1 - p^0)(y^1 - y^0) \geq 0.$$

Each revenue-maximizing output is nondecreasing in its own price regardless of any differentiability properties.

Exercise 7.3. Derive the fundamental inequality of revenue maximization. (*Hint:* Proceed in your arguments in a manner similar to those used to derive the fundamental inequality of profit maximization in Chapter 4.)

If $R(p, x)$ is twice-continuously differentiable, properties 7F imply

$$y(tp, x) = y(p, x), \quad t > 0;$$

$$\nabla_p y(p, x) = \nabla_{pp} R(p, x) \quad \text{is positive semidefinite;}$$

$$\nabla_x R(tp, x) = t\nabla_x R(p, x);$$

$$\frac{\partial^2 R(p, x)}{\partial x_i \, \partial p_j} = \frac{\partial^2 R(p, x)}{\partial p_j \, \partial x_i} = \frac{\partial y_j(p, x)}{\partial x_i}.$$

Given earlier results, the interpretation of these results is straightforward, and only the last two merit some additional comment. The gradient of $R(p, x)$ with respect to x is a vector of shadow prices because it gives the increase in revenue associated with an expansion in the input endowment. The results indicate that these shadow prices are linearly homogeneous in output prices. Thus, if all output prices increase proportionally, the shadow prices of all inputs increase by the same proportion. The last expression is similar to the earlier discovery that the change in marginal cost

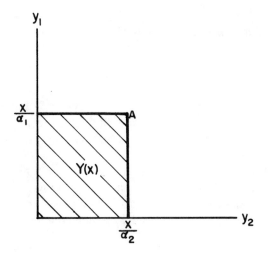

Figure 7.7 Fixed coefficient $Y(x)$.

associated with a change in an input price equals the change in that input's utilization eventuated by a change in y.

Example 7.3. Revenue functions for some special cases of producible-output sets. Consider the producible-output set illustrated in Figure 7.7. For convenience, assume that x is a scalar so that the technology associated with Figure 7.7 can be written as

$$Y(x) = \{y: y_1 \leq \alpha_1 x \text{ and } y_2 \leq \alpha_2 x; \alpha_1, \alpha_2 > 0\},$$

which is a natural counterpart of the Leontief, fixed-coefficient production function discussed earlier. It is easy to establish that this $Y(x)$ and its natural generalization

$$Y(x) = \{y: \alpha_i y_i \leq x, i = 1, \ldots, m; \alpha_i > 0\}$$

satisfy properties 7E.1–7E.5 (this is left as an exercise to the reader). Hence, the revenue function generated by applying (7.2) to this $Y(x)$ should satisfy 7F.1–7F.5. Moreover, it is clear geometrically from Figure 7.7 that regardless of the magnitude of $p > 0$, revenue is always maximized at vertex A, with $\alpha_i y_i(p, x) = x$. Hence, the associated revenue function is

$$R(p, x) = x \sum_{i=1}^{m} \frac{p_i}{\alpha_i},$$

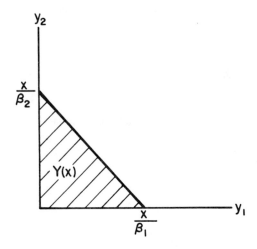

Figure 7.8 $Y(x)$ for linear (in outputs) technology.

which is linear in the output prices. Not surprisingly, therefore, a kinked $Y(x)$ maps into a linear revenue function. Notice in particular that $R(p, x)$ is always differentiable in p and that

$$y_i(p, x) = \frac{\partial R(p, x)}{\partial p_i},$$

as required by the Samuelson–McFadden lemma.

Now consider the technology

$$Y(x) = \left\{ y: \sum_{i=1}^{m} \beta_i y_i \le x; \ \beta_i > 0, \ i = 1, \ldots, m \right\},$$

which is illustrated in the two-output case in Figure 7.8, where the slope of the frontier of $Y(x)$ is given by $-\beta_2/\beta_1$. This technology is the counterpart for outputs of the linear production function. By the geometry of Figure 7.8 and by analogy with earlier arguments,

$$R(p, x) = \max\{p_1 x/\beta_1, p_2 x/\beta_2, \ldots, p_m x/\beta_m\}$$

$$= x \max\{p_1/\beta_1, p_2/\beta_2, \ldots, p_m/\beta_m\}.$$

This revenue function can be shown to satisfy properties 7F.1–7F.5, but $R(p, x)$ is not simultaneously differentiable in all output prices. Moreover, it is obvious from the geometry that at kinks in $R(p, x)$ (e.g., in the two-input case when $p_1/\beta_1 = p_2/\beta_2$) there is not a unique revenue-maximizing output. To see this clearly, suppose $p_i/\beta_i \le p_1/\beta_1 = p_2/\beta_2$. An equal revenue is achieved whether $y_i = 0$, $i \neq 2$, $y_2 = x/\beta_2$, or $y_i = 0$, $i \neq 1$, $y_1 = x/\beta_1$. Accordingly, we have an illustration of the second portion of the Samuelson–McFadden lemma.

Exercise 7.4. Verify that

$$Y(x) = \{y : y_i \alpha_i \leq x, \ i = 1, 2, \ldots, m, \ \alpha_i > 0\}$$

satisfies properties 7E. Verify directly that the associated revenue function

$$R(p, x) = x \sum_{i=1}^{m} \frac{p_i}{\alpha_i}$$

satisfies 7F.1–7F.5.

Exercise 7.5. Verify properties 7E for

$$Y(x) = \left\{ y : \sum_{i=1}^{m} \beta_i y_i \leq x, \beta_i > 0 \right\}.$$

Verify properties 7F for

$$R(p, x) = x \max(p_1/\beta_1, \ldots, p_m/\beta_m).$$

Exercise 7.6. Derive the comparative static properties of the technologies described in Exercises 7.4 and 7.5.

7.2c   *Multioutput profit function*

Three alternative, but equivalent, definitions of the multioutput profit function prove useful:

$$\Pi(p, w) = \max_{y,x} \{p \cdot y - w \cdot x : (x, y) \in T; \ w, p > 0\}$$

$$= \max_{y} \{p \cdot y - c(w, y) : w, p > 0\}$$

$$= \max_{x} \{R(p, x) - w \cdot x : w, p > 0\}. \tag{7.3}$$

The second equality is directly analogous to the profit decomposition discussed in Chapter 4. To demonstrate formally its validity, one must show that $x(p, w) = x(w, y(p, w))$, where $x(p, w)$ is the profit-maximizing derived-demand vector. But this is quite easy. Suppose in fact that

$$x(p, w) = x^1 \neq x(w, y(p, w)).$$

Then,

$$\Pi(p, w) = py(p, w) - wx^1$$

$$\geq py(p, w) - wx(w, y(p, w)).$$

But the inequality that follows from the definition of x^1 as profit maximizing then implies

$$wx^1 \leq wx(w, y(p, w)),$$

which violates the definition of $x(w, y(p, w))$ as cost minimizing unless

$$x^1 = x(w, y(p, w)).$$

So presuming that x^1 is profit maximizing but not cost minimizing implies a contradiction. Similar arguments reveal that the second decomposition is also valid. The formal demonstration is left to the reader as an exercise.

Exercise 7.7. Show that $y(p, x(p, w)) = y(p, w)$. The importance of these results lies mainly in the decompositions they offer for the comparative static properties of profit-maximizing outputs and derived demands. This point will be pursued shortly.

Even though the last two definitions of the profit function allow one to use the properties of $R(p, x)$ and $c(w, y)$ to infer the properties of $\Pi(p, w)$ (readers are encouraged to do this on their own), didactic goals seem best served at this point by developing the properties of $\Pi(p, w)$ directly from T. The motivation for proceeding in this manner should become apparent when we consider the restricted profit function and the duality between T and $\Pi(p, w)$ later. An advantage of this approach is that it demonstrates the generality of the profit function because, as it turns out, only properties 7D.1, 7D.2, 7D.6, and 7D.7 are utilized in the derivations. The resulting profit function, however, is observationally equivalent to one satisfying 7D.1–7D.7 (see the following discussion). The main result of this section is that if T satisfies 7D.1, 7D.2, 7D.6, and 7D.7, then $\Pi(p, w)$ defined by (7.3) satisfies:

Properties of multioutput profit function (7C*):

1. $\Pi(p, w) \geq 0$;
2. if $p \geq p^1$, $\Pi(p, w) \geq \Pi(p^1, w)$ (nondecreasing in p);
3. if $w \geq w^1$, $\Pi(p, w) \leq \Pi(p, w^1)$ (nondecreasing in w);
4. $\Pi(p, w)$ is convex and continuous in all its arguments;

5. $\Pi(tp, tw) = t\Pi(p, w)$, $t > 0$ (positive linear homogeneity); and
6. there exists fixed vectors $(\bar{y}, \bar{x})$ and $(\hat{y}, \hat{x})$ such that $\Pi(p, w) \geq p\bar{y} - w\bar{x}$ and $\Pi(p, w) \leq p\hat{y} - w\hat{x}$.

With the exception of 7C*.6, these properties and their intuitive explanations are virtually identical to properties 4C. [The importance of 7C*.6 will be apparent when we discuss the duality between $\Pi(p, w)$ and T.] The first step is to show that a maximum actually exists, but the conjunction of 7D.2 and 7D.6 implies that T is compact. And because $py - wx$ is continuous, a maximum exists on T by the Weierstrass theorem (see Appendix).

To show 7C*.1, note that 7D.7 implies that the origin is an element of T. The firm can always make zero profit by choosing the input–output combination $(0_n, 0_m)$. A rational individual always prefers this to any input–output combination yielding a negative profit, and rather than accept a negative output, the firm will not produce.

To show 7C*.2, let (x, y^1) be the profit-maximizing $(n+m)$-tuple associated with (p^1, w). Then $\Pi(p^1, w) = p^1 y^1 - w \cdot x$. Evaluate this same $(n+m)$-tuple at (p, w), remembering that T does not depend on any particular price configuration. This obtains $p^1 \cdot y^1 - w \cdot x \leq p \cdot y^1 - wx \leq \Pi(p, w)$ for $p \geq p^1$, where the last inequality follows by profit maximization and establishes the result. A parallel argument (left to the reader as an exercise) establishes 7C*.3. To show convexity, let (x^i, y^i) be the profit-maximizing $(m+n)$-tuple for price (p^i, w^i) $(i = 0, 1, 2)$, where $(p^2, w^2) = (\theta p^0 + (1-\theta)p^1, \theta w^0 + (1-\theta)w^1)$, $0 < \theta < 1$. By the definition of the profit function,

$$\Pi(p^0, w^0) \geq p^0 y^2 - w^0 x^2, \qquad \Pi(p^1, w^1) \geq p^1 y^2 - w^1 x^2,$$

whereas evaluating $\Pi(p^2, w^2)$ directly gives

$$\Pi(p^2, w^2) = \theta(p^0 y^2 - w^0 x^2) + (1-\theta)(p^1 y^2 - w^1 x^2).$$

Combining results yields the desired convexity. Linear homogeneity is by now obvious and is left to the reader as an informal exercise. To show 7C*.6, note that nonemptiness implies that at least one $(m+n)$-tuple must exist in T, say, $(\bar{x}, \bar{y})$. Then by profit maximization, one must have $\Pi(p, w) \geq p\bar{y} - w\bar{x}$, which establishes the first part of the result; the second part follows because T is bounded. In fact, one way to visualize $(\hat{x}, \hat{y})$ is to consider the solution to (7.3), which we denote as (x^*, y^*). Now consider a vector $\hat{y} > y^*$. By definition of the profit function, $(\hat{y}, x^*)$ cannot be feasible since $p\hat{y} - wx^* \geq \Pi(p, w)$. Here, however, the choice of $\hat{y}$ and x^* depends on (p, w) and is not fixed.

When differentiable, the multioutput profit function satisfies a version of *Hotelling's lemma,* that is, property 7C*.7:

7. the multioutput profit function is differentiable only if there exists a unique profit-maximizing supply or input, and if the function is differentiable, then

$$\frac{\partial \Pi(p, w)}{\partial p_i} = y_i(p, w) \quad \text{and} \quad \frac{\partial \Pi(p, w)}{w_i} = -x_i(p, w).$$

This version of Hotelling's lemma so closely parallels other versions that its proof is left to the reader:

Exercise 7.8. For the price configuration (p^0, w^0), denote the solution to (7.3) as (x^0, y^0). Use the fact that for arbitrary (p, w),

$$\Pi(p, w) \geq py^0 - wx^0$$

to establish the second part of 7C*.7. Show why this also implies that $\Pi(p, w)$ is convex.

The implications of the multioutput version of Hotelling's lemma are practically identical to those for the single-output case except that this version more forcefully underlines the importance of such results. In the multioutput case, the task of obtaining a closed-form solution to (7.3) after the specification of a relatively general technology, say, in the form of a smooth $Y(x, y)$ function, is, in many practical instances, insurmountable. Thus, practical methods of analyzing output and input relationships may not be available if the profit function is not used. If one wants to depict such interaction in an econometrically amenable form, specification of a differentiable profit function with the multioutput version of Hotelling's lemma is an attractive alternative.

Comparative statics and the multioutput profit function: Hotelling's lemma assumes even more importance when it is recalled that the properties of $\Pi(p, w)$ place exhaustive conditions on the behavior of profit-maximizing outputs and derived demands. By now in the discussion of other indirect objective functions, I would already have raised the specter of a fundamental inequality characterizing derived-demand and output behavior even in the absence of differentiability. The obvious analogue here is the generalization of the fundamental inequality of profit maximization to the multioutput case:

$$(p^1 - p)(y^1 - y) - (w^1 - w)(x^1 - x) \geq 0. \tag{7.4}$$

Expression (7.4) is derived in a manner analogous to the proof used in Chapter 4. Hence, its reproof here can be left for the willing reader. The main implication of (7.4) is a repetition of single-output intuition, but it remains worthwhile to point out. First, variation of any single-output (input) price causes the associated output (input) to vary in the same (opposite) direction. Consequently, any output supply correspondence is upward sloping in its own price whereas any derived-demand correspondence is downward sloping in its price. The second implication is more transparent if (7.4) is rewritten in discrete change notation:

$$\Delta p \, \Delta y \geq \Delta w \, \Delta x.$$

The inner product of output price change and output change always outweighs the inner product of input price change and input change regardless of how many prices vary. If, for example, only one output price and all input prices change, this yields (suppose $\Delta p_i > 0$)

$$\Delta y_i \geq \frac{\Delta w}{\Delta p_i} \, \Delta x.$$

The direct supply response effect on the ith output outweighs the weighted sum of all input adjustment. The importance of this last result is its ability to characterize supply response behavior for multiple price changes. Here, the own-price effect of supply expansion dominates all input adjustments. (Obviously, the inequality is reversed if $\Delta p_i < 0$.) A similar argument reveals that if only one input price adjusts ($\Delta w_i > 0$) and all output prices adjust,

$$\Delta x_i \leq \frac{\Delta p}{\Delta w_i} \, \Delta y.$$

Although this inequality does not necessarily imply that $\Delta x_i \leq 0$ in the face of multiple price changes, a definite upper bound is placed on the range of input variation.

For comparative statics analysis of a twice-continuously differentiable profit function, it is first convenient to recall the earlier notation $q = (p, w)$; that is, q is the $(m + n)$-dimensional vector of output and input prices. Then, using this notation, the comparative statics properties of the derived demands and output supplies are summarized by

$$z(tq) = z(q),$$

$$\nabla_q z(q) = \nabla_{qq} \Pi(q) \quad \text{(singular positive semidefinite matrix).}$$

The first equality is a consequence of the linear homogeneity of the profit function and Hotelling's lemma. The second expression also is a consequence of the linear homogeneity of the profit function since by Hotelling's lemma the Hessian of the profit function is the comparative statics matrix of the derived demands and supplies: Euler's theorem implies that every column of this matrix is a linear combination of the remaining columns. Hence, the comparative statics matrix is singular. Finally, the convexity of the profit function implies that its Hessian matrix is positive semidefinite.

These results, the first of which implies zero homogeneity in prices with the second implying the reciprocity relationship and downward-sloping derived demands and upward-sloping output supplies, exhaust the restrictions on input–output adjustment to price change.

By (7.3) on the decomposition of derived demands and output supplies,

$$y(p, x(p, w)) = y(p, w),\tag{7.5}$$

$$x(w, y(p, w)) = x(p, w).\tag{7.6}$$

Differentiating (7.5) with respect to p_j and w_k yields

$$\frac{\partial y_i(p, w)}{\partial p_j} = \frac{\partial y_i(p, x)}{\partial p_j} + \sum_{v=1}^{n} \frac{\partial y_i(p, x)}{\partial x_v} \frac{\partial x_v(p, w)}{\partial p_j};\tag{7.7}$$

$$\frac{\partial y_i(p, w)}{\partial w_k} = \sum_{v=1}^{n} \frac{\partial y_i(p, x)}{\partial x_v} \frac{\partial x_v(p, w)}{\partial x_k}.\tag{7.8}$$

Output adjustment to output price change is decomposable into two separate effects: a movement along the boundary of $Y(x)$ eventuated by the change in relative output prices and a shift of $Y(x)$ associated with the input adjustment caused by the change in relative prices.

Example 7.4. To illustrate, consider the technology

$$Y(x) = \{y : \alpha_1 y_1 + \alpha_2 y_2 \leq x^{1/2}; \ \alpha_1, \alpha_2 > 0\}.$$

The set $Y(x)$ is depicted graphically in Figure 7.9, which is essentially a replication of Figure 7.8 with the intersections on the axes changed. (Note that the multioutput profit function associated with the producible-output set depicted in Figure 7.8 is not well defined since that technology exhibits constant returns to scale.) Hence, the revenue maximization decision (the first stage of the profit-maximizing decision) is equivalent to maximizing the revenue from the linear technology

$$Y(\hat{x}) = \{y : \alpha_1 y_1 + \alpha_2 y_2 \leq \hat{x}\},$$

where $\hat{x} = x^{1/2}$. This technology (see Example 7.3) has a corner solution:

$$p_1 > \frac{\alpha_1}{\alpha_2} p_2 \Rightarrow y_1 = \frac{\hat{x}}{\alpha_1}, \quad y_2 = 0;$$

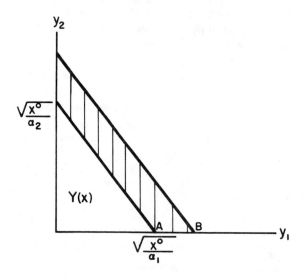

Figure 7.9 Decomposing multioutput supply response.

$$p_1 < \frac{\alpha_1}{\alpha_2} p_2 \Rightarrow y_1 = 0, \quad y_2 = \frac{\hat{x}}{\alpha_2}.$$

For $p_1 = (\alpha_1/\alpha_2)p_2$, the solution is ambiguous. Suppose that $p_1 > (\alpha_1/\alpha_2)$; the resulting profit maximization problem is

$$\max(p_1/a_1)x^{1/2} - wx$$

with the solution

$$x^{-1/2} = 2\alpha_1(w/p_1).$$

In Figure 7.9, this solution occurs at point A. Now suppose that p_1 rises. It still does not pay to produce y_2, but the profit-maximizing amount of $\hat{x}$ rises, as can be verified from the preceding. Hence, the original producible set $Y(x_0)$ expands by the shaded area and production of y_1 expands to point B. The most interesting aspect of this example is that it represents a case where the first term in (7.7) is zero but the second term forces satisfaction of the fundamental inequality of profit maximization.

> **Exercise 7.9.** The preceding discussion of Figure 7.9 assumed that the change in p_1 preserves the inequality of $p_1 > (\alpha_1/\alpha_2)p_2$. Suppose, rather, that p_1 decreases enough so that $p_1 < (\alpha_1/\alpha_2)p_2$. Convince yourself graphically that the fundamental inequality

of profit maximization is satisfied. Derive the associated effect
on the utilization of x and the production of y_2.

By expression (7.8) all profit-maximizing supply response to input price
change is in terms of an adjustment in $Y(x)$. Hence, for the situation depicted in Figure 7.9, a decrease in the price of x has the same qualitative
effect as an increase in p_1.

Turning to input adjustment to changes in (p, w), differentiation of
(7.6) yields

$$\frac{\partial x_i(p, w)}{\partial p_j} = \sum_{v=1}^{m} \frac{\partial x_i(w, y)}{\partial y_v} \frac{\partial y_v}{\partial p_j}, \tag{7.9}$$

$$\frac{\partial x_i(p, w)}{\partial w_k} = \frac{\partial x_i(w, y)}{\partial w_k} + \sum_{v=1}^{m} \frac{\partial x_i(w, y)}{\partial y_v} \frac{\partial y_v}{\partial w_k}. \tag{7.10}$$

Expressions (7.9) and (7.10) are the multioutput generalizations of the
input decompositions discussed in Chapter 4 [see especially Section 4.3,
Equations (4.8) and (4.9)]. As such, they require little further intuitive
motivation than to note that changes in derived demands associated with
an input price change have two components: The first is the usual substitution effect along the frontier of $V(y)$, and the second is associated with
an alteration of the output mix caused by the change in the relative profitability of the various outputs. All input responses to changes in output
prices feed through a change in the output mix.

So far we have not exploited the convexity properties of $\Pi(p, w)$ in the
discussion of multioutput decompositions. By symmetry of $\nabla_{qq}\Pi$ and
(7.9),

$$\frac{\partial y_v(p, w)}{\partial w_k} = -\frac{\partial x_k(p, w)}{\partial p_v} = -\sum_{r=1}^{m} \frac{\partial x_k}{\partial y_r} \frac{\partial y_r(p, w)}{\partial p_v}.$$

Substituting this expression into (7.10) gives

$$\frac{\partial x_i(p, w)}{\partial w_k} = \frac{\partial x_i(w, y)}{\partial w_k} - \sum_{v=1}^{m} \sum_{r=1}^{m} \frac{\partial x_i(w, y)}{\partial y_v} \frac{\partial y_r(p, w)}{\partial p_v} \frac{\partial x_k(w, y)}{\partial y_r}. \tag{7.11}$$

When $i = k$, one obtains yet another Le Chatelier–Samuelson result:

$$\frac{\partial x_i(p, w)}{\partial w_i} \leq \frac{\partial x_i(w, y(p, w))}{\partial w_i}.$$

This inequality follows because the second term on the right-hand side
of (7.11) is a quadratic form in the positive semidefinite, sub-Hessian
$\nabla_{pp}\Pi(p, w) = \nabla_p y(p, w)$ when $k = i$. The usual *short-run* versus *long-run*
interpretation of this result applies with the short-run again referring to

fixed-output profit maximization. Accordingly, the intuition associated with these results exactly parallels that developed in earlier chapters, to which the reader should refer for details. Put succinctly, the result is a consequence of the convexity and concavity properties of $\Pi(p, w)$ and $c(w, y)$ as well as their "envelope" relationships.

> **Exercise 7.10.** Use the decompositions (7.5) and (7.6) to show that the Le Chatelier–Samuelson principle applies to output behavior as well
>
> $$\frac{\partial y_i(p, w)}{\partial p_i} \geq \frac{\partial y_i(p, x(p, w))}{\partial p_i}.$$
>
> *Hint:* Make sure to use the properties of $R(p, x)$ in your derivation.

Example 7.5. Decomposing derived-demand and supply responses. Chapter 4 showed that one can express pure substitution effects solely in terms of the profit function. In the multioutput case, a similar result applies. First-order conditions for (7.3) yield

$$p = \nabla_y c(w, y(p, w)),$$

whereas the envelope theorem gives

$$-\nabla_w \Pi(p, w) = \nabla_w c(w, y(p, w)).$$

Assuming that both cost and profit functions are twice-continuously differentiable, implicit differentiation of the first equality yields

$$I = \nabla_{yy} c(w, y) \nabla_p y(p, w);$$
$$0 = \nabla_{yw} c(w, y) + \nabla_{yy} c(w, y) \nabla_w y(p, w).$$

Differentiating the envelope result yields

$$-\nabla_{ww} \Pi(p, w) = \nabla_{ww} c(w, y) + \nabla_{wy} c(w, y) \nabla_w y(p, w).$$

Combining the results with Hotelling's and Shephard's lemmas yields

$$\nabla_{ww} c(w, y) = -\nabla_{ww} \Pi(p, w) + \nabla_{pw}^T \Pi(p, w) \{\nabla_{pp} \Pi(p, w)\}^{-1} \nabla_{pw} \Pi(p, w).$$

As before, the matrix of substitution effects can be expressed entirely in terms of elements of the Hessian of $\Pi(p, w)$.

To give the reader a deeper understanding of this decomposition, some numerical examples may prove helpful. Recently, Lopez (1984) used cross-sectional data on Canadian agriculture to estimate a two-output, four-input profit function of the generalized Leontief form. The outputs were crops and animal products. The input categories were hired labor, operator and family labor, land and structures, and farm capital. In his model, Lopez also included dummy variables to account for regional differences and educational differences among operations. The resulting derived-demand and supply system is reported in Table 7.1, and the corresponding output supply and derived-demand elasticities are reported in Table 7.2.

Reexpressing the results obtained in elasticity form and using Table 7.2 gives Table 7.3, which summarizes the compensated output and input elasticities at the sample means. Table 7.3 reports compensated supply elasticities that correspond to the elements of $\nabla_{pp} R(p, x)$. As an informal exercise, the reader should verify that

$$\nabla_{pp} R(p, x) = \nabla_{pp} \Pi(p, w) - \nabla_{wp}^T \Pi(p, w) \{\nabla_{ww} \Pi(p, w)\}^{-1} \nabla_{wp} \Pi(p, w)$$

using the appropriate first-order condition and envelope result. The expression $\nabla_{pp} R(p, x)$ can be intuitively thought of as representing movement along the product transformation frontier that is associated with changes in relative output prices.

*7.2d Restricted profit function

Previous chapters devoted a lot of attention to short-run problems and other special cases. This section demonstrates that all such developments are special cases of a more general problem. In a sense, therefore, Chapters 2 and 4 and the rest of this chapter are superfluous because they all can be subsumed under the general rubric of the problem we are going to consider presently. Apparently, the first person to recognize this fact was McFadden (1978a) who exhaustively characterized the properties of the restricted profit function to be discussed here. However, the arguments utilized by McFadden go considerably beyond the mathematical confines of this book. Hence, what follows is intended more to give the reader a flavor of the generality of McFadden's work than as a rigorous exposition of his results.

In what follows, all discussion is in terms of a netput vector that we continue to denote as z. In the current notation, z need not be an $(m+n)$-dimensional vector, and to emphasize that fact, we presume only that $z \in \mathbb{R}^k$ (i.e., z is an element of the k-dimensional real space). We continue to describe the technology in terms of a production possibilities set. However, earlier presentations are modified by introducing a parameter vector θ; the interpretation of θ will become clear as the discussion progresses. Assume $\theta \in \mathbb{R}^l$. For notational conveniences, continue to use T to designate the production possibilities set and assume that the current T satisfies properties 7D.1 (nonemptiness), 7D.2 (closedness), 7D.6

Table 7.1. *Estimates of output supply and factor demand equations*

	Crop outputs	Animal outputs	Land and structure	Hired labor	Operator and family labor	Farm capital	Operator's education	Regional dummies
Crop outputs	−278.20 (706.20)	36.27 (73.88)	113.09 (80.45)	−3.201 (0.943)	−46.43 (70.97)	−83.55 (13.30)	−0.235 (0.389)	97.12 (160.30)
Animal outputs	36.27 (73.88)	1,495.80 (837.26)	−181.54 (84.95)	−547.06 (106.30)	−127.15 (83.27)	−752.63 (13.30)	1.143 (0.461)	−684.70 (188.30)
Land and structures	−113.09 (80.45)	181.54 (84.95)	−154.84 (25.98)	107.08 (17.99)	−11.62 (10.95)	52.97 (20.55)	0.274 (0.077)	200.26 (34.27)
Hired labor	3.201 (0.943)	547.06 (106.30)		32.67 (48.34)	−37.81 (12.65)	−23.27 (22.98)	−0.260 (0.067)	−54.72 (25.06)
Operator and family labor	46.43 (70.97)	127.15 (83.27)			405.50 (15.28)	8.522 (16.43)	0.011 (0.023)	16.26 (8.10)
Farm capital	83.55 (13.30)	752.63 (182.19)				1,213.10 (436.10)	0.499 (0.214)	21.43 (89.13)

Note: Numbers in parentheses are standard errors.
Source: Reprinted with permission from Lopez (1984).

Table 7.2. *Output supply and input demand elasticities*

| | Price of | | | | | |
	Crops	Animal products	Land and structure	Hired labor	Operator and family labor	Farm capital
Crop products	0.010	0.023	0.059	−0.002	−0.072	−0.022
	(0.006)	(0.048)	(0.042)	(0.008)	(0.109)	(0.003)
Animal products	0.012	0.472	−0.050	−0.240	−0.102	−0.091
	(0.025)	(0.089)	(0.023)	(0.046)	(0.067)	(0.022)
Land and structures	−0.212	0.335	−0.362	0.255	−0.051	0.035
	(0.151)	(0.157)	(0.085)	(0.043)	(0.048)	(0.013)
Hired labor	0.009	1.264	0.260	−1.240	−0.268	−0.025
	(0.003)	(0.317)	(0.261)	(0.654)	(0.089)	(0.024)
Operator and family labor	0.026	0.069	−0.005	−0.026	−0.065	0.002
	(0.039)	(0.045)	(0.004)	(0.008)	(0.057)	(0.003)
Farm capital	0.154	1.361	0.078	−0.054	0.037	−1.575
	(0.025)	(0.329)	(0.030)	(0.053)	(0.070)	(0.617)

Note: Numbers in parentheses are standard errors.
Source: Reprinted with permission from Lopez (1984).

(boundedness), and a modified version of 7D.7, that is, $(0_k, \theta) \in T$. This last assumption is made to ensure that the origin is an element of T. As usual, if $z_i > 0$, it is by convention an output, whereas if $z_i < 0$, it is an input. Also continue to use $q > 0$ as the notation for the netput price vector.

With these definitions, the *restricted profit function* is defined as

$$\Pi(q, \theta) = \max\{q \cdot z : (z, \theta) \in T\}. \tag{7.12}$$

A maximum exists since $q \cdot z$ is a continuous function while 7D.2 and 7D.6 ensure that the Weierstrass theorem applies. Assuming that 7D.1, 7D.2, 7D.6, and the modified form of 7D.7 apply, $\Pi(q, \theta)$ satisfies:

Properties of restricted profit function (7G):

1. $\Pi(q, \theta) \geq 0$;
2. $\Pi(tq, \theta) = t\Pi(q, \theta)$, $t > 0$;
3. $\Pi(q, \theta)$ is convex and continuous in q; and
4. there exist fixed vectors $\bar{z}$ and $\hat{z}$ that $\Pi(q, \theta) \geq q \cdot \bar{z}$ and $\Pi(q, \theta) \leq q \cdot \hat{z}$.

Table 7.3. *Compensated output supply and input demand elasticities*

Supply/Demand	Price of					
	Crops	Animal products	Land and structure	Hired labor	Operator and family labor	Farm capital
Crop products	0.007	−0.009				
Animal products	−0.095	0.098				
Land and structures			−0.482	0.434	−0.039	0.086
Hired labor			0.447	−0.377	−0.277	0.210
Operator and family labor			−0.001	−0.014	−0.036	0.051
Farm capital			0.193	0.525	0.740	−1.481

Source: Reprinted with permission from Lopez (1984).

Properties 7G are an abbreviated version of 7C*. The main difference is that there is no analogue to 7C*.2 and 7C*.3. The reason is that by not explicitly separating inputs from outputs, we lose the ability to ascertain monotonicity conditions. Rather than replicate a derivation of these results that is totally analogous to the derivation of 7C*, the reader should derive 7G.

Exercise 7.11. Show that if T satisfies 7D.1, 7D.2, 7D.6, and the modified form of 7D.7 already discussed, $\Pi(q, \theta)$ satisfies 7G.

This leads to the interpretation of the vector θ. Perhaps the most natural interpretation is that of a vector of fixed outputs and inputs not variable in the short run. Thus, $\Pi(q, \theta)$ is, in a sense, a short-run profit function; but in fact, it also generalizes $c(w, y)$, $R(p, x)$, and $\Pi(p, w)$. First, define θ as an m-dimensional vector of fixed outputs and z as an n-dimensional vector of inputs. In this instance, $z \leq 0$, and expression (7.12) is the negative of a cost function that will satisfy properties 7G with all signs reversed and convexity replaced by concavity. Notice that there are considerably fewer properties associated with 7G than 4B*. This is caused by not placing explicit restrictions on y. Moreover, now that z is a vector of inputs, it is easy to ascertain monotonicity properties in q.

Alternatively, suppose θ is an n-dimensional vector of fixed inputs and z is a vector of positive outputs. Then expression (7.11) is an obvious generalization of $R(p, x)$ after appropriate translations are made. Finally, let $z = (-x, y)$ and θ be a vector of parameters indexing the current state of the technology. Obviously, then, $\Pi(q, \theta)$ is the multioutput generalization of the single-output profit function admitting of technical change. This partial list of alternatives by no means exhausts the array of possible interpretations available for $\Pi(q, \theta)$. Virtually every theoretical development in this book is a special case of (7.12). The reader who has advanced this far should be very well equipped to provide intuitive motivation and possible empirical applications of (7.12).

This section closes by noting that $\Pi(q, \theta)$, if differentiable, satisfies a version of Hotelling's lemma, that is, property 7G.5:

5. If $\Pi(q, \theta)$ is differentiable in q, then the gradient $\nabla_q \Pi(q, \theta)$ equals the vector of profit-maximizing net outputs $z(q, \theta)$; $\Pi(q, \theta)$ is only differentiable if $z(q, \theta)$ is unique (Hotelling–McFadden lemma).

This first part of this lemma can be proven by a variety of means. Most of these demonstrations are available elsewhere. Therefore, we leave the demonstration to the reader.

*7.3   Duality and multioutput technologies

One of the main advantages of developing the scalar output cost function in terms of $V(y)$ rather than the production function is that results developed there are easily translated to the multioutput case. Such has to be the case because the arguments made to illustrate the dual relationship between the cost function and $V(y)$ in the single-input case can be repeated to convince the reader of a dual relationship in the multioutput case. Much the same is true for the relationship between multioutput $\Pi(p, w)$ and $c(w, y)$: These functions are conjugates, and the conjugacy arguments can be utilized to convince the reader of the dual relationship. So instead of walking the reader through arguments that closely parallel ones already developed, this section will illustrate the dual relationship between T and $\Pi(q, \theta)$. Since $\Pi(q, \theta)$ is the most general representation so far developed, demonstrating the plausibility of a dual relationship here should be sufficient to convince any remaining skeptics of the general nature of dual relationships.

The way to tackle this problem parallels previous developments of dual relationships and the various versions of the Shephard–Hotelling–Samuelson–McFadden lemmas. First show that various values of the restricted profit function can be used to segment netput space; then consider the intersection of all these segments. Since q does not affect T, by definition,

$$\Pi(q, \theta) \geq q \cdot z$$

for any $q > 0$ if $z \in T$. Geometrically, therefore, the hyperplane

$$\Pi(q, \theta) = q \cdot z$$

generated by a particular $\Pi(q, \theta)$ splits netput space into two half-spaces. The first represents all z such that $q \cdot z > \Pi(q, \theta)$ must be outside of T; otherwise, $\Pi(q, \theta)$ could not represent maximum profit over T. The second $\Pi(q, \theta) \geq q \cdot z$ should include all possible z's that are in T. As the discussion in Chapter 2 suggests, taking the intersection of all such half-spaces for all possible q gives a reasonable approximation to T. This suggests that

$$T^* = \{z : q \cdot z \leq \Pi(q, \theta) \text{ for all } q > 0\}$$

satisfies the same properties of T used to generate $\Pi(q, \theta)$.

The main result of this section is that if $\Pi(q, \theta)$ satisfies 7G, then T^* will satisfy 7D.1 (nonemptiness), 7D.2 (closedness), 7D.3 (convexity), 7D.6 (boundedness), and the modified version of 7D.7 that $(0_k, \theta) \in T$. As the reader will recall, it was not necessary to impose 7D.3 to get properties 7G for $\Pi(q, \theta)$. However, the fact that T^* satisfies convexity is a natural consequence of the presumed economic rationality of individuals, as illustrated in Chapters 2 and 4. And if T satisfies 7D.3, then $T = T^*$ (the proof of this goes beyond this text).

By definition, the half-space $qz \leq \Pi(q, \theta)$ is closed. And standard results imply that the intersection of an infinite number of closed sets is itself closed (see Appendix). Hence, T^* must be closed. To show nonemptiness, recall that by 7G.4 a fixed vector $\bar{z}$ exists such that

$$q\bar{z} \leq \Pi(q, \theta).$$

This in turn implies that $\bar{z} \in T^*$, yielding nonemptiness. Convexity is easily shown by arguments that by now should be standard to the reader. Suppose that z^0 and z^1 are both in T^*. This implies that

$$q \cdot z^0 \leq \Pi(q, \theta) \quad \text{and} \quad q \cdot z^1 \leq \Pi(q, \theta) \quad \text{for all } q > 0.$$

By the preceding, $q \cdot z^2 = q \cdot [\gamma z + (1 - \gamma)z^1]$ $(0 < \gamma < 1)$ satisfies these inequalities for all $q > 0$, and thus the result (see Appendix, lemma 4). Demonstrating boundedness requires the recognition that if, say, $z \in T^*$, then by 7G.4, $q \cdot z \leq \Pi(q, \theta) \leq q \cdot \hat{z}$; thus, $z \leq \hat{z}$ since $q > 0$.

Example 7.6. To illustrate how one would go from the profit function back to a production possibilities set, consider a technology that uses one input to produce a single output. As before, any input–output price pair defines a level set of the profit function

$$\{(x, y) : py - wx \leq \Pi(p, w)\}.$$

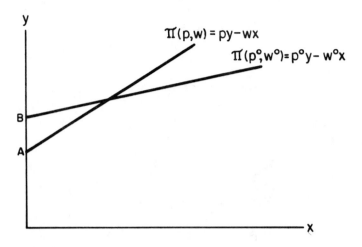

Figure 7.10 Duality between T and $\Pi(p,w)$.

This set is illustrated in Figure 7.10 by all points lying below the line segment emanating from A on the vertical axis. The distance $0A$ equals $\Pi(p,w)/p$. By the properties of the profit function, all technologically feasible input–output combinations must lie under this line segment; otherwise, there would exist input–output combinations consistent with a higher level of profit than $\Pi(p,w)$ when the price couple (p,w) prevails. Similar arguments reveal that all technologically feasible input–output combinations must lie below the line segment emanating from B on the vertical axis, which is consistent with a higher output–input price ratio than that emanating from A. Thus, the technology that defined $\Pi(p,w)$ must lie in the intersection of these two sets. Extending these arguments to all input–output price pairs eventually isolates an area consistent with the general properties of T.

Example 7.7. In the preceding, $R(p,x)$ was shown to be a special case of $\Pi(q,\theta)$, where $\theta = x$ and $q = p$. Thus, one can use arguments exactly paralleling those employed in Example 7.6 to retrieve $Y(x)$ from $R(p,x)$. Consider the half-space in output space defined by

$$H(p,x) = \{y : p \cdot y \le R(p,x)\}.$$

By the definition of $R(p,x)$, $Y(x) \subseteq H(p,x)$ since any $y \in Y(x)$ must automatically satisfy this inequality for any $p > 0$. The bounding hyperplane that defines this half-space is represented by the line segment AB in Figure 7.11. Anything below AB but above the origin is thus a candidate

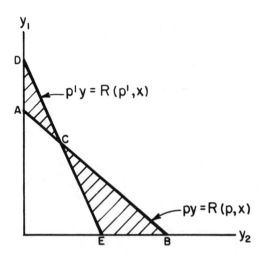

Figure 7.11   Constructing $Y^*(x)$ from $R(p, x)$.

for $Y(x)$. Now raise the relative price of y_2 slightly in Figure 7.11; let these prices be p^1. By the preceding, $Y(x) \subseteq H(p^1, x)$, but note now that the bounding hyperplane is DE. The shaded area labeled CEB, which belonged to $H(p, x)$, does not belong to $H(p^1, x)$. Conversely, the shaded area CDA belonging to $H(p^1, x)$ does not belong to $H(p, x)$. Just as clearly $H(p^1, x) \cap H(p, x)$ is the unshaded area ACE, which by observation is convex and satisfies the monotonicity requirements associated with $Y(x)$. Repeating these arguments for all p suggests that

$$Y^*(x) = \{y: p \cdot y \le R(p, x) \text{ for all } p > 0\}$$

is a good representation of the $Y(x)$ that actually generated $R(p, x)$.

Exercise 7.12. Develop a graphical representation of

$$T^* = \{q: q \cdot z \le \Pi(q, \theta) \text{ for all } q > 0\}$$

when $z = (-x, y)$.

Exercise 7.13. Derive an exhaustive set of properties for $Y^*(x)$ that follows from properties 7F for $R(p, x)$.

7.4   Structure of multioutput technology

Previous chapters discussed ways in which the technology can be restricted to make it more empirically and theoretically manageable. The generality

of T when contrasted with the limited generality of $f(x)$ should convince
the reader of the importance that functional structure assumes in the multioutput case. The same type of issues are involved here as earlier. All
too frequently there are simply too many outputs and inputs to be handled adequately by limited data sets. Even the most disaggregated empirical studies generally group several inputs or several outputs into indexes.
This section addresses, in some detail, those structural issues peculiar to
the multioutput case: input–output separability and nonjointness. I only
touch briefly on other structural issues peculiar to the multioutput case.
These, for the most part, are generalizations of results in other chapters.
In what follows, preserve the artificial split between inputs and outputs
to facilitate exposition. Moreover, all functions are presumed to be at
least twice-continuously differentiable when it is convenient to do so.

7.4a   *Restrictions on T*

In several instances, past chapters have used as an example an empirical
study by Ball and Chambers (1982) of the U.S. meat products industry.
In the discussion of those results, the reader may well have wondered just
what the output of this industry is. Actually, the output in that study was
an index of outputs that included different forms of meat products. Thus,
the Ball and Chambers study really investigated a multiproduct case utilizing some very restrictive assumptions on T. As shall be made clear from
consequent developments, the Ball–Chambers study maintained an assumption that for every $(x, y) \in T$ one could specify an output index $g(y)$
to be utilized as the output variable. When an index of output and a set
$\hat{T}$ exist such that $(x, g(y)) \in \hat{T}$ implies that $(x, y) \in T$, the technology is
separable in outputs. If T is separable in outputs, the input requirement
set generalizes the single-output case:

$$V(y) = \{x : (x, y) \in T\}$$
$$= \{x : (x, g(y)) \in \hat{T}\}$$
$$= \{x : (x, g) \in \hat{T}\}$$
$$= V(g).$$

Paralleling separability in outputs is the notion of separability in inputs. A technology is *separable in inputs* if an input index $m(x)$ and a set
$\tilde{T}$ exist such that if (x, y) is a producible set, then $(m(x), y) \in \tilde{T}$. As previously seen, output separability is particularly convenient for represent-
ing T in single-product terms. Input separability, on the other hand, is
particularly advantageous for representing T in terms of a single-input,
multioutput technology. A good illustration of such an instance is the

earlier discussion of Figure 7.8, which assumed the existence of a single input. Whereas output separability allowed Ball and Chambers to infer a single-output cost function, input separability, for example, allows one to think in terms of single-input revenue functions. When T is separable in inputs, the producible output set $Y(x)$ becomes

$$Y(x) = \{y : (x, y) \in T\}$$
$$= \{y : (m(x), y) \in \tilde{T}\}$$
$$= \{y : (m, y) \in \tilde{T}\}.$$

Example 7.8. Separability and product transformation function. Example 7.2 discussed the version of T that is given by the product transformation function $Y(x, y) = 0$. If $Y(x, y)$ is twice-continuously differentiable with no derivatives vanishing, output separability in the form $Y(x, g(y)) = 0$ implies by the implicit function theorem that one can also write

$$g(y) = m(x).$$

Similar arguments applied to the case of input separability will demonstrate that in this instance the two notions of input and output separability are equivalent.

The multioutput model has been used heavily in trade analysis. Most famous theorems associated with the Heckscher–Ohlin–Samuelson model were originally derived in the context of an economy using two inputs to produce two outputs. These models usually specify production as characterized by two separate production functions, $f^1(x^1)$ and $f^2(x^2)$. The only constraint across technologies is that total input utilization not exceed the aggregate input endowment. If input prices are predetermined, the technology is described completely by the expansion paths for these production functions. When both technologies exhibit constant returns to scale, the expansion paths are linear and emanate from the origin, as illustrated in Figure 7.12. Let the total input endowment be A in that figure. The constraint that $x^1 + x^2 = A$ then implies that production of y^1 is at B and production of y^2 is at C because these are the only points on the respective expansion paths that are consistent with cost minimization and complete utilization of the input endowment. (The vector sum of points B and C is A; Figure 7.12 is commonly referred to as the Lerner Pearce diagram.) Thus, how much of y^1 is produced depends on how much of y^2 is produced but only because each technology competes for a scarce input endowment. If the supply of all inputs were perfectly elastic, the level at which y^1 is produced is independent of the level at which y^2 is produced.

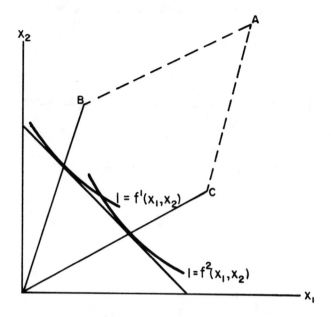

Figure 7.12 Equilibrium under nonjoint (in inputs) production.

When the technology exhibits interdependencies of this type only, production is nonjoint in inputs. More formally, T is *nonjoint in inputs* if, for every $(x, y) \in T$, there exist vectors $x^i \geq 0$ such that

$$y_i \leq f^i(x^i), \quad \sum_{i=1}^{m} x^i \leq x, \quad i = 1, 2, \ldots, m,$$

where $f^i(x^i)$ is a production function satisfying weak monotonicity, weak essentiality, nonemptiness, and closedness of the input requirement set.

To characterize the input requirement set associated with input non-jointness, notice that

$$V(y) = \left\{ x : x \geq \sum_{i=1}^{m} x^i; \ y_i \leq f^i(x^i), \ \forall i \right\}$$

$$= \{ \sum x^i : y_i \leq f^i(x^i) \}$$

$$= \sum_{i=1}^{m} \{ x^i : y_i \leq f^i(x^i) \}$$

$$= \sum_{i=1}^{m} V^i(y_i),$$

where $V^i(y_i)$ is the input requirement set associated with $f^i(x^i)$.

Another type of nonjointness is implied when one can write a separate input requirement function for each input. Here, T is *nonjoint in outputs* if, for every $(x, y) \in T$, there exists

$$x_i \geq g^i(y^i), \quad \sum_{i=1}^{n} y^i \geq y, \quad i = 1, 2, \ldots, n,$$

where $g^i(y^i)$ is nondecreasing, has a nonempty and closed producible-output set, and satisfies $g^i(0) = 0$.

The producible-output set for T is

$$Y(x) = \left\{ y : y \leq \sum_{i=1}^{n} y^i; x^i \geq g^i(y^i) \ \forall i \right\}$$

$$= \left\{ \sum_{i=1}^{n} y^i : x_i \geq g^i(y^i) \right\}$$

$$= \sum_{i=1}^{n} \{ y^i : x_i \geq g^i(y^i) \}$$

$$= \sum_{i=1}^{n} Y^i(x_i),$$

where $Y^i(x_i)$ is the producible-output set for $g^i(y^i)$. Intuitively, output nonjointness covers cases where one input is "separated" into a number of commodities. The best known examples are from agriculture and, in particular, the livestock industry, where, for example, a cow is separated into meat, leather, and offal. Geometrically, nonjointness in outputs means that for each input a separate product transformation surface exists, as illustrated in Figure 7.13. For a small, open economy with input endowment $x = (\bar{x}_1, \bar{x}_2)$, production occurs at y in Figure 7.13 if relative product prices are as illustrated.

Input and output nonjointness are often thought to exhaust the possible range of nonjointness. However, Kohli (1983) has recently introduced further definitions of nonjointness that are interesting. Kohli's first extension involves situations that arise under assembly line production techniques where all outputs proceed from one work station to another and at each work station a separate input enters the production process. This type of technology is here defined as Kohli output price *(KO)* nonjointness. Formally, T is *KO nonjoint* if, for any $(x, y) \in T$, nondecreasing input requirement functions satisfying weak essentiality and with nonempty and closed producible-output sets exist such that

$$x_i \geq g^i(y).$$

Notice, in particular, that $g^i(y)$ depends on the entire output vector produced and not just on a portion of it, as is the case with output nonjoint-

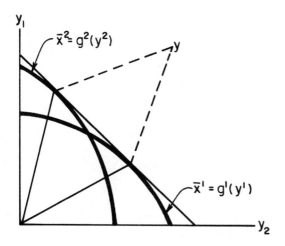

Figure 7.13 Nonjointness in outputs.

ness as already defined. KO nonjointness is a multioutput generalization of the single-input Leontief technology. Here, however, the input–output coefficients are replaced by the functional relationship $x_i/g^i(y)$. The associated input requirement sets are produced by right-angled isoquants:

$$V(y) = \{x : x_i \geq g^i(y), \ i = 1, 2, \ldots, n\}$$

$$= \bigcap_{i=1}^{n} \{x_i : x_i \geq g^i(y)\}$$

$$= \bigcap_{i=1}^{n} V^i(y),$$

where $\bigcap$ denotes the intersection operator and $V^i(y)$ is the input requirement set associated with $g^i(y)$.

The second type of nonjointness addressed by Kohli is perhaps best illustrated as generalizing the fixed-coefficient transformation function in Figure 7.7. As the reader may recall, that figure represents a single-input technology producing outputs in fixed proportions to input utilization. Thus, T is *Kohli input price (KI) nonjoint* if, for any $(x, y) \in T$, individual production functions satisfying weak monotonicity, weak essentiality, nonemptiness, and closedness exist such that

$$y_i \leq f^i(x), \quad i = 1, 2, \ldots, m.$$

The producible-output set for a KI nonjoint T is

$$Y(x) = \{y : y_i \le f^i(x), \; i = 1, \ldots, m\}$$

$$= \bigcap_{i=1}^{m} \{y_i : y_i \le f^i(x)\}$$

$$= \bigcap_{i=1}^{m} Y^i(x).$$

One might think of each $f^i(x)$ as a separate input index for each output. Note, in particular, that the entire input endowment is used in the production of all outputs.

7.4b   *Indirect objective functions and structural restrictions*

This section successively takes up separability and then nonjointness. When T is output separable, the cost function is

$$c(w, y) = \min\{w \cdot x : x \in V(y)\}$$

$$= \min\{w \cdot x : x \in V(g)\}$$

$$= \hat{c}(w, g(y)),$$

where $\hat{c}(w, g)$ is the cost function for the single-output technology $(x, g) \in \hat{T}$. If g is nondecreasing in y, $\hat{c}$ satisfies all of properties 2B with y replaced by g. In what follows, $\hat{c}$ is always assumed twice-continuously differentiable in all arguments.

The empirical significance of this last result has already been addressed in the discussion of the Ball–Chambers study. It permits estimation of a multioutput cost function using single-output techniques.

Example 7.9. In the single-output case, homotheticity implies that the production function can be transformed to a linearly homogeneous form: $h(y) = f^*(x)$. A natural generalization is to impose constant returns to scale on x and g in $\hat{T}$; then for any $t > 0$, $(x, g) \in T$ implies that $(tx, tg) \in \hat{T}$. When this holds, the cost function can be written as

$$c(w, y) = c(w)g(y),$$

where $c(w)$ is now the cost function associated with

$$c(w) = \min\{wx : (x, 1) \in \hat{T}\}.$$

To see why, consider the following arguments:

$$c(w, y) = \min\{wx : (x, g(y)) \in \hat{T}\}$$

$$= \min\{wx : (x/g(y), 1) \in \hat{T}\}$$

$$= g(y) \min\{wx/g(y): (x/g(y), 1) \in \hat{T}\}$$
$$= g(y)c(w).$$

To consider the implications of output separability for the profit function, start with the case where the marginal cost of producing the aggregate output $g(y)$ is a constant and equal to, say, λ. The profit function is then defined by

$$\Pi(p, w) = \max\{py - c(w, g(y))\}.$$

By the Kuhn–Tucker theorem (see Appendix), the first-order conditions for this problem are

$$p_i - \lambda \frac{\partial g}{\partial y_i} \leq 0, \quad y_i\left(p_i - \lambda \frac{\partial g}{\partial y_i}\right) = 0, \quad i = 1, 2, \ldots, m.$$

For an interior solution, one gets $y(p/\lambda)$, which is homogeneous of degree zero in p and λ. Generally, however, λ depends on both g and w so that although the preceding first-order conditions still apply,

$$y = y(p/\lambda(w, g))$$

is an implicit equation in the outputs (y) (Lau, 1978a). For arbitrary λ, profit associated with $y(p/\lambda)$ is

$$\Pi(p, w, \lambda) = py(p/\lambda) - c(w, g[y(p/\lambda)])$$
$$= H_1(p, \lambda) - H_2(p, w, \lambda).$$

Since $y(p/\lambda)$ is homogeneous of degree zero in p and λ, $H_1(tp, t\lambda) = tH_1(p, \lambda)$ and $H_2(tp, tw, t\lambda) = tH_2(p, w, \lambda)$ [the second equality exploits the properties of $\hat{c}(w, g)$]. But profit maximization implies

$$\Pi(p, w) = \max_\lambda \Pi(p, w, \lambda)$$
$$= \max_\lambda\{H_1(p, \lambda) - H_2(p, w, \lambda)\}$$

as the general form of the profit function under output separability.

Exercise 7.14. Show that if the technology is as described in Example 7.9,

$$\Pi(p, w) = c(w)\Pi^*(p/c(w)).$$

Notice the similarity between this representation and that for the single-product homothetic case. This technology is *output separable* and *input homothetic*.

The investigation of input separability in T starts with the revenue function. Under input separability,

$$R(p, x) = \max\{p \cdot y : y \in Y(x)\}$$
$$= \max\{p \cdot y : y \in Y(m)\}$$
$$= \hat{R}(p, m(x)),$$

where $\hat{R}(p, m)$ is the revenue function for a single-input technology. If m is nondecreasing in x, then $\hat{R}$ is nondecreasing in m.

Exercise 7.15. Suppose that T exhibits constant returns in y and $m(x)$; that is, if $(m(x), y) \in T$, then $(tm(x), ty) \in T$, $t > 0$. Show that, in this instance,

$$R(p, x) = \bar{R}(p) m(x),$$

where

$$\bar{R}(p) = \max_{v}\{p \cdot v : (1, v) \in T\}.$$

Such a technology is said to be *input separable* and *output homothetic*.

To examine the profit function for an input-separable T, parallel arguments to those made in the case of output separability are used. Under appropriate differentiability properties and the assumption of an interior solution, the solution to

$$\Pi(p, w) = \max_{x}\{R(p, m(x)) - w \cdot x\}$$

assumes the implicit form

$$x = x(w/\gamma),$$

where $\gamma = \partial R/\partial m$, the shadow price of the aggregate input. Since x is homogeneous of degree zero in w and γ, profit for arbitrary γ can be written as

$$\Pi(p, w, \gamma) = \hat{R}(p, m[x(w/\gamma)]) - w \cdot x(w/\gamma)$$
$$= H_3(p, w, \gamma) - H_4(w, \gamma),$$

where H_3 and H_4 are both linearly homogeneous [use the properties of $\hat{R}(p, m)$]. Thus, by profit maximization,

$$\Pi(p, w) = \max_{\gamma} \Pi(p, w, \gamma)$$
$$= \max_{\gamma}\{H_3(p, w, \gamma) - H_4(w, \gamma)\}$$

is the general form of the profit function for input separability.

Exercise 7.16. Show that if the technology is input separable and output homothetic,

$$\Pi(p, w) = \bar{R}(p)\Pi^{**}(w/\bar{R}(p)),$$

where Π^{**} is the normalized profit function

$$\Pi^{**}(u) = \max\{m(x) - u \cdot x\}.$$

This brings us to input nonjointness. By earlier results,

$$c(w, y) = \min\{w \cdot x : x \in V(y)\}$$

$$= \min\left\{w \cdot x : x \in \sum_{i=1}^{m} V^i(y_i)\right\}$$

$$= \sum_{i=1}^{m} \min\{w \cdot x^i : x^i \in V^i(y_i)\}$$

$$= \sum_{i=1}^{m} c^i(w, y_i),$$

where $c^i(w, y_i)$ satisfies properties 2B (Hall, 1973). Turning to the profit function,

$$\Pi(p, w) = \max\left\{p \cdot y - \sum_{i=1}^{m} c^i(w, y_i)\right\}$$

$$= \sum_{i=1}^{m} \max\{p_i \cdot y_i - c^i(w, y_i)\}$$

$$= \sum_{i=1}^{m} \Pi^i(p_i, w).$$

Here, properties 4C are satisfied for each Π^i. Input nonjointness implies that both the cost and profit functions are the sum of their single-product counterparts. Input nonjointness enhances econometric simplicity, for example, by implying that either $c(w, y)$ of $\Pi(p, w)$ can be modeled by their single-product counterparts with no loss of generality. By the preceding, input nonjointness requires

$$\frac{\partial^2 \Pi}{\partial p_i \partial p_j} = \frac{\partial^2 c}{\partial y_i \partial y_j} = 0 \quad \forall i, j.$$

Thus, for example, if a flexible form is used to model a multioutput technology, these last two equations yield parametric tests of nonjointness. After specifying a functional form, one can restrict it parametrically to accord with the above.

Example 7.10. Input nonjointness. To illustrate further the hypothesis-testing procedure being proposed, consider the results reported in Table

7.1. If this technology is consistent with input nonjointness, the cross-output-price terms in each supply equation should equal zero. From the magnitude of the coefficient and standard error reported in Table 7.1, this is not implausible since the confidence interval based on the asymptotic normality of these estimated coefficients blankets zero. That crops and livestock are input nonjoint is probably surprising if one recognizes that many livestock operations actually grow crops to feed to the livestock. For such operations, it is not immediately clear whether crops are inputs or outputs, and it is clear that there may be problems with always categorizing crops as an output. However, when one recalls the input categories Lopez (1984) used, the apparent anomaly is cleared up. Clearly, the data are highly aggregative in terms of number of inputs and number of outputs. And some precision and ability to discuss differences and characteristics of the technology were probably lost in aggregation.

One might wonder whether T can be simultaneously nonjoint in inputs and output separable. A necessary and sufficient condition for these two restrictions to apply simultaneously is that a $c^i(w, y_i)$ and $g(y)$ exist such that

$$\hat{c}(w, g(y)) = \sum_{i=1}^{m} c^i(w, y_i). \tag{7.13}$$

As the reader will recognize, expression (7.13) is mathematically equivalent to the nonlinear aggregation problem posed in Section 5.8. Hence, it is immediate from that discussion that a technology T is simultaneously input nonjoint and output separable if and only if it assumes a quasi-homothetic form. Intuitively, in Chapter 5, one was aggregating over different firms. Here, however, one can view the problem as one of deriving an aggregate output index that depends on each separate output. This will happen if and only if

$$c(w, y) = \sum_{i=1}^{m} g_i(y_i)\phi(w) + \theta(w)$$

with each $c^i(w, y_i)$ satisfying

$$c^i(w, y_i) = g_i(y_i)\phi(w) + \theta_i(w).$$

To demonstrate this result, use (7.13) to find that

$$\frac{\partial g/\partial y_i}{\partial g/\partial y_j} = \frac{\partial c^i(w, y_i)/\partial y_i}{\partial c^j(w, y_j)/\partial y_j},$$

which implies g must be strongly separable in y. Moreover, (7.13) implies

$$\frac{\partial^2 \hat{c}/\partial g^2}{\partial \hat{c}/\partial g} = \frac{-\partial^2 g/y_i y_j}{(\partial g/\partial y_i)(\partial g/\partial y_j)}.$$

As long as $\partial^2 \hat{c}/\partial g_g^2 \neq 0$, the left-hand side of this equation is independent of w since the right side is. Integration over g yields

$$\ln \frac{\partial \hat{c}}{\partial g} = a_0(g) + a_1(w).$$

Taking antilogs and integrating again yields

$$\hat{c}(w, g) = a_1(w) a_0^*(g) + a_2(w).$$

Using $c(w, g) = \sum_{i=1}^{m} \hat{c}^i(w, y_i)$ then implies $a_0^*(g) = \sum_{i=1}^{m} g_i(y_i)$, which satisfies strong separability.

Turning to $\Pi(p, w)$,

$$\Pi(p, w) = \max \left\{ p \cdot y - \sum_{i=1}^{m} g_i(y_i) \phi(w) - \theta(w) \right\}$$

$$= \max \left\{ p \cdot y - \sum_{i=1}^{m} g_i(y_i) \phi(w) \right\} - \theta(w)$$

$$= \sum_{i=1}^{m} \max \{ p_i \cdot y_i - g_i(y_i) \phi(w) \} - \theta(w)$$

$$= \phi(w) \sum_{i=1}^{m} \max \left\{ \frac{p_i}{\phi(w)} y_i - g_i(y_i) \right\} - \theta(w)$$

$$= \phi(w) \sum_{i=1}^{m} \Pi_i^* \left(\frac{p_i}{\phi(w)} \right) - \theta(w).$$

Thus, input nonjointness and output separability are only consistent if each particular output is produced according to a quasi-homothetic, single-output production function. If one rules out quasi-homotheticity as a working null hypothesis, the technology cannot be simultaneously separable and nonjoint.

Exercise 7.17. Consider the two-output, single-input technology $Y(y_1, y_2, x) \leq 0$. Show that imposing

$$\frac{\partial^2 x}{\partial y_1 \partial y_2} = 0$$

on this technology implies that it is simultaneously output separable and input nonjoint. Decide whether this result applies regardless of the number of outputs.

Output nonjointness has similar implications for $R(p, x)$ and $\Pi(p, w)$. Under output nonjointness,

$$R(p, x) = \max\{p \cdot y : y \in Y(x)\}$$

$$= \max\left\{p \cdot y : y \in \sum_{i=1}^{n} Y^i(x_i)\right\}$$

$$= \sum_{i=1}^{n} \{py^i : y^i \in Y^i(x_i)\}$$

$$= \sum_{i=1}^{n} R^i(p, x_i).$$

Here $R^i(p, x_i)$ is the revenue function for $Y^i(x_i)$. Using this result yields

$$\Pi(p, w) = \max_x \left\{\sum_{i=1}^{n} R^i(p, x_i) - w \cdot x\right\}$$

$$= \sum_{i=1}^{n} \max\{R^i(p, x_i) - w_i \cdot x_i\}$$

$$= \sum_{i=1}^{n} \Pi^i(p, w_i).$$

Here $R^i(p, x_i)$ and $\Pi^i(p, w_i)$ are single-input analogues of the general multioutput revenue and profit functions, respectively. As with input non-jointness, the general functions are sums of single-input analogues. An immediate implication is that each input's shadow price is independent of all other input levels,

$$\frac{\partial^2 R}{\partial x_i \, \partial x_j} = 0 \quad \text{for } i \neq j,$$

and that all profit-maximizing derived demands are independent of all other input prices; that is,

$$\frac{\partial x_i(w, p)}{\partial w_j} = -\frac{\partial^2 \Pi}{\partial w_i \, \partial w_j} = 0 \quad \text{for } i = j.$$

Therefore, one can always model each derived-demand function separately as a function of its own price and the output price vector.

Exercise 7.18. Analytically, it is interesting to know when T is simultaneously output nonjoint and input separable. As with input nonjointness and output separability, this is mathematically equivalent to an aggregation problem. Namely, find an $m(x)$ such that

$$\hat{R}(p, m(x)) = \sum_{i=1}^{n} R^i(p, x_i).$$

Show that this condition is satisfied if and only if

$$\hat{R}(p, m) = \phi^*(p) \sum_{i=1}^{n} g_i^*(x_i) + \theta^*(p)$$

with each

$$R^i(p, x_i) = \phi^*(p) g_i^*(x_i) + \theta_i^*(p).$$

Use this result to demonstrate that

$$\Pi(p, w) = \phi^*(p) \sum_{i=1}^{n} \Pi_i^{**} \left(\frac{w_i}{\phi(p)} \right) + \theta^*(p)$$

when T is simultaneously separable in inputs and nonjoint in outputs.

Analyzing the consequences of KO nonjointness for the cost function is neat because earlier discussion implies that the cost function is a generalization of the single-output Leontief cost function:

$$c(w, y) = \sum_{i=1}^{n} w_i g^i(y). \tag{7.14}$$

Each cost-minimizing derived demand is independent of factor prices. Thus, the associated factor price frontier is a flat surface in input price space as illustrated in Chapter 2 for the Leontief technology. Empirically, a null hypothesis of KO nonjointness requires a test of the null hypothesis that $\nabla_{ww} c(w, y)$ is the null matrix. Furthermore, as long as each $g^i(y)$ is nondecreasing in y, each input is normal. Rather than derive (7.14) directly, I show that such a cost function is observationally equivalent to a T that is KO nonjoint. Consider

$$V^*(y) = \left\{ x : w \cdot x \geq \sum_{i=1}^{n} w_i g^i(y) \text{ for all } w > 0 \right\}$$

$$= \left\{ x : \sum_{i=1}^{n} w_i(x_i - g^i(y)) \geq 0 \text{ for all } w_i > 0 \right\}$$

$$= \bigcap_{i=1}^{n} \{ x_i : x_i \geq g^i(y) \},$$

which establishes the result.

In light of the attention given to nonjointness and the obvious similarity of (7.14) with the input nonjoint case, one might be interested in cases where KO nonjointness coincides with other versions of nonjointness. Kohli output price nonjointness and input nonjointness exist simultaneously if and only if

$$c(w, y) = \sum_{i=1}^{m} c^i(w, y_i) = \sum_{i=1}^{n} w_i g^i(y).$$

Differentiation with respect to y_k yields

$$\frac{\partial c(w, y)}{\partial y_k} = \sum_{i=1}^{n} w_i \frac{\partial g^i(y)}{\partial y_k} = \frac{\partial c^k}{\partial y_k}.$$

If this is differentiated with respect to y_v $(v \neq k)$,

$$\frac{\partial^2 c(w, y)}{\partial y_k \, \partial y_v} = \sum_{i=1}^{n} w_i \frac{\partial^2 g^i(y)}{\partial y_k \, \partial y_v} = 0.$$

For this to hold for an arbitrary vector $w > 0$,

$$\frac{\partial^2 c(w, y)}{\partial y_k \, \partial y_v} = 0, \quad \text{and} \quad \frac{\partial^2 g^i(y)}{\partial y_k \, \partial y_v} = 0, \quad i = 1, 2, \dots, n,$$

for all k, v $(v \neq k)$. By standard results, therefore, $c(w, y)$ and each $g^i(y)$ are additively separable in y; that is,

$$g^i(y) = \sum_{j=1}^{m} g_j^i(y_j),$$

and the overall cost function is

$$c(w, y) = \sum_{i=1}^{n} w_i \sum_{j=1}^{m} g_j^i(y_j)$$

$$= \sum_{i=1}^{n} \sum_{j=1}^{m} w_i g_j^i(y_j)$$

$$= \sum_{j=1}^{m} \sum_{i=1}^{n} w_i g_j^i(y_j).$$

Each $c^i(w, y_i) = \sum_{j=1}^{n} w_j g_i^j(y_i)$, implying that every output production process is a generalization of the fixed-coefficient Leontief technology that has fixed proportions at each output level. However, the input–output coefficients are different for different output levels. The input requirement set is

$$V^*(y) = \left\{ x : w \cdot x \geq \sum_{j=1}^{n} w_j \sum_{i=1}^{m} g_i^j(y_i) \text{ for all } w > 0 \right\}$$

$$= \left\{ x : x_j \geq \sum_{i=1}^{m} g_i^j(y_i), \ j = 1, 2, \dots, n \right\}$$

$$= \bigcap_{j=1}^{n} \left\{ x_j : x_j \geq \sum_{i=1}^{m} g_i^j(y_i) \right\}.$$

The technology is both KO nonjoint and input separable if and only if it is observationally equivalent to a technology of the form: If $(x, y) \in T$, there exist functions $g_i^j(y_i)$ such that

$$x_j \geq \sum_{i=1}^{m} g_i^j(y_i).$$

That is, each input requirement function is independent of all other inputs and is additively separable in y.

Exercise 7.19. Show that if T is simultaneously input nonjoint and KO nonjoint,

$$\Pi(p, w) = \sum_{i=1}^{m} \tilde{\Pi}^i(p_i, w)$$

with

$$\tilde{\Pi}(p_i, w) = \max \left\{ p_i y_i - \sum_{j=1}^{n} w_j g_i^j(y_i) \right\}.$$

KO nonjointness and output separability are simultaneously consistent if and only if

$$c(w, y) = c(w, g(y)) = \sum_{i=1}^{n} w_i g^i(y).$$

The first equality requires all ratios of marginal costs to be independent of input prices. Using the second equality and differentiating gives

$$\frac{\partial g / \partial y_k}{\partial g / \partial y_v} = \frac{\sum_{i=1}^{n} w_i \, \partial g^i / \partial y_k}{\sum_{i=1}^{n} w_i \, \partial g^i / \partial y_v}.$$

By the separability of $c(w, g(y))$, the right-hand side must be independent of input prices. Differentiation with respect to arbitrary w_q yields

$$\frac{1}{\sum_{i=1}^{n} w_i \, \partial g_i / \partial y_v} \frac{\partial g^q}{\partial y_k} = \frac{\sum_{i=1}^{n} w_i \, \partial g_i / \partial y_k}{(\sum_{i=1}^{n} w_i \, \partial g_i / \partial y_v)^2} \frac{\partial g^q}{\partial y_v}$$

as a necessary condition for T to be simultaneously KO nonjoint and output separable. Hence, one must have

$$\sum_{i=1}^{n} w_i \left(\frac{\partial g^i}{\partial y_v} \frac{\partial g^q}{\partial y_k} - \frac{\partial g^i}{\partial y^k} \frac{\partial g^q}{\partial y_v} \right) = 0.$$

But for arbitrary $w > 0$, this implies that

$$\frac{\partial g^i / \partial y_v}{\partial g^i / \partial y_k} = \frac{\partial g^q / \partial y_v}{\partial g^q / \partial y_k} \quad \forall q.$$

This condition is satisfied if the $g^i(y)$ are isomorphic, that is,

$$g^i(y) = \hat{G}^i(\beta(y)), \quad i = 1, 2, ..., n.$$

The ratio of marginal cost is here given by the ratio $(\partial\beta/\partial y_i)/(\partial\beta/\partial y_j)$. Hence, our cost function becomes

$$c(w, y) = \sum_{i=1}^{n} w_i \hat{G}^i(\beta(y)),$$

and usual manipulations yield

$$V(y) = \bigcap_{i=1}^{n} \{x_i : x_i \geq \hat{G}^i(\beta(y))\}.$$

If the technology is simultaneously output separable and KO nonjoint, T can be characterized as a generalized version of the single-output Leontief production function. Here, however, the input requirement function for each input is a transformation of an aggregate output index, $\beta(y)$, so that it is a Leontief technology with nonconstant input–output coefficients.

The last topic discussed in this chapter is the effect of KI nonjointness on indirect objective functions. By an argument left to the reader,

$$R(p, x) = \sum_{i=1}^{m} p_i f_i(x).$$

Hence, revenue-maximizing supplies are perfectly price inelastic. The empirical implications of this result also should be quite obvious; they are left for the reader to ponder on his or her own. Here, we only consider the conjunction between KI nonjointness, output nonjointness, and input separability. The T is simultaneously KI nonjoint and output nonjoint if and only if

$$R(p, x) = \sum_{i=1}^{m} p_i f_i(x) = \sum_{i=1}^{n} R^i(p, x_i).$$

In a fashion completely parallel to KO nonjointness, this condition requires each $f^i(x)$ to be additively separable in x, that is,

$$f^i(x) = \sum_{j=1}^{n} f_j^i(x_j),$$

implying

$$R(p, x) = \sum_{i=1}^{n} \sum_{j=1}^{m} p_j f_i^j(x^i).$$

The dual producible-output set is

$$Y(x) = \left\{ y : p \cdot y \le \sum_{i=1}^{n} \sum_{j=1}^{m} p_j f_i^{j}(x_i); \; p > 0 \text{ for all } p \right\}$$

$$= \left\{ y : y_i \le \sum_{j=1}^{n} f_j^{i}(x_j) \right\}$$

$$= \bigcap_{i=1}^{m} \left\{ y_i : y_i \le \sum_{j=1}^{n} f_j^{i}(x_j) \right\}.$$

If the technology is both output nonjoint and KI nonjoint, the producible-output set is the intersection of the producible-output sets for m additively separable production functions each utilizing the same input bundle.

To close, consider instances where input separability and KI nonjointness coincide. By parallel arguments, the $f^{i}(x)$ functions must be isomorphic, so that

$$f^{i}(x) = F^{i}(\alpha(x)),$$

yielding the revenue function

$$R(p, x) = \sum_{i=1}^{m} p_i F^{i}(\alpha(x)).$$

Exercise 7.20. Show that if T is simultaneously input separable and KI nonjoint

$$Y(x) = \bigcap_{i=1}^{m} \{ y_i : y_i \le F^{i}(\alpha(x)) \},$$

that is, the producible-output set is the intersection of the producible-output sets for m single-output production functions that are isomorphic (i.e., can be interpreted as a transformation of a common production function depending on a common aggregate input).

Exercise 7.21. Show that if T is simultaneously KI nonjoint and output separable,

$$\Pi(p, w) = \sum_{i=1}^{n} \xi^{i}(p, w_i^{i}),$$

where

$$\xi^{i}(p, w_i^{i}) = \max \left\{ \sum_{j=1}^{m} p_j f_i^{j}(x_i^{i}) - w_i x_i \right\}.$$

Appendix: A brief mathematical review

Perhaps the only thing as inevitable as death and taxes in modern economics is that any book on technical economics will have a "self-contained" mathematical appendix. Rather than risk breaking such a firmly established tradition, I present a mathematical discussion that covers some pertinent facts that may be unfamiliar to some readers. By no means, however, is this appendix self-contained. Instead, it is probably best viewed as a mathematical glossary that should enable students possessing the usual doses of calculus and linear algebra to decipher some of the more technical points in the body of the text. The following discussion presumes, for example, that the reader understands the concepts of open and closed sets, continuity, and differentiability. The discussion is purposely somewhat informal, and only a few of the more obvious proofs are presented. Moreover, as in the body of the text, attention is restricted solely to $\mathbb{R}^n$, that is, n-dimensional real space.

Matrices and semi-definiteness: Any symmetric matrix $M \in \mathbb{R}^n \times \mathbb{R}^n$ is negative *semidefinite* if and only if

$$Q(M, Z) = Z'MZ \leq 0$$

for arbitrary $Z \in \mathbb{R}^n$. The $Q(M, Z)$ is often referred to as the quadratic form of the symmetric matrix M. If $Q(M, Z)$ is always strictly less than zero, M is called *negative definite*. The following lemma summarizes some important facts about negative semidefinite matrices.

> **Lemma 1.** $Q(M, Z)$ *is negative semidefinite only if*
> a. *its principal minors alternate in sign starting with a negative number;*
> b. *its principal submatrices are negative semidefinite; and*
> c. *the diagonal elements of $M(m_{ii})$ are nonpositive (i.e., $m_{ii} \leq$ 0).*

The principal minors of a matrix A are defined as the determinants of the matrices

302

$$\begin{bmatrix} a_{11} & a_{12} & \cdots & a_{1k} \\ a_{12} & a_{22} & \cdots & a_{2k} \\ \vdots & \vdots & & \vdots \\ a_{1k} & a_{2k} & \cdots & a_{kk} \end{bmatrix}, \quad k = 1, 2, \ldots, n,$$

where, for example, a_{ij} is the (i, j) element of A. To consider the notion of a principal submatrix, partition the set of integer indexes $u = 1, 2, \ldots, n$ for $\mathbb{R}^n$ into u_1 and u_2, which are mutually exclusive but exhaustive subsets, that is, $u = u_1 \cup u_2$ but $\phi = u_1 \cap u_2$, where ϕ denotes the empty set. The principal submatrix of A associated with the set of indices u_1 is the matrix obtained by deleting from A the rows and columns corresponding to the set of indices in u_2.

A symmetric matrix $M \in \mathbb{R}^n \times \mathbb{R}^n$ is *positive semidefinite* if and only if $-M$ is negative semidefinite. Alternatively, M is positive semidefinite if

$$Q(M, Z) \geq 0$$

for arbitrary $Z \in \mathbb{R}^n$. If $Q(M, Z) > 0$ for all Z, then M is called *positive definite*.

Lemma 2. $Q(M, Z)$ *is positive semidefinite only if*
a. *its principal minors are all positive;*
b. *its principal submatrices are positive semidefinite; and*
c. *the diagonal elements of M are nonnegative.*

The last lemma in this section considers the case of a negative (positive) definite matrix.

Lemma 3. *A negative (positive) semidefinite matrix is negative (positive) definite only if it is nonsingular. If A is negative (positive) definite, A^{-1} is negative (positive) definite.*

Some basic notions: Production economics relies heavily on the mathematical notion of a convex set. A set X is *convex* if for any x, y belonging to X, *the convex combination of x and y* defined by $\theta x + (1 - \theta) y$ also belongs to X for $0 \leq \theta \leq 1$. More intuitively, a set is convex if any weighted average of its elements also belongs to X. Examples of convex sets are the set of nonnegative real numbers, n-dimensional nonnegative real space, and the shaded area illustrated in Figure A.1. A nonconvex set is illustrated in Figure A.2, where it is clear that there exists a θ such that $\theta x + (1 - \theta) y = Z$ but Z does not belong to X as illustrated. Geometrically, the best description of a convex set is that a set is convex if any

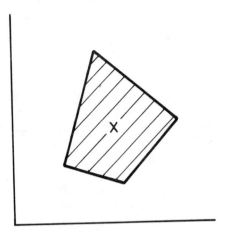

Figure A.1   Convex set.

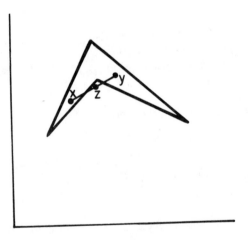

Figure A.2   Nonconvex set.

straight-line segment connecting any two elements of the set does not go outside the set.

The following basic lemma is central to the consideration of set-valued representations of the general technology:

Lemma 4. The intersection of a finite or infinite number of convex sets is convex.

Proof: We are interested in the set

$$V = \bigcap_{k \in K} X_k,$$

where K is the number of sets we are interested in (K can be either finite or infinite). By definition, any $x, y \in V$ also satisfy $x, y \in X_k$ for all $k \in K$. And since each X_k is convex, by supposition, $Z = \theta x + (1 - \theta) y \in X_k$, for all X_k and $0 \le \theta \le 1$. But since Z belongs to every X_k, $Z \in V$, and this completes the demonstration.

Lemma 4 is especially useful in the discussion of dual relationships since one of the easiest means of demonstrating a duality is by using an appropriately defined intersection of half-spaces. Before defining a half-space, however, let me demonstrate the earlier claim that n-dimensional, nonnegative real space (alternatively, the nonnegative orthant of real space) denoted $\mathbb{R}^n_+$ is convex. By definition,

$$\mathbb{R}^n_+ = \{x \in x \ge 0; x \in \mathbb{R}^n\}.$$

Here, x is an n-dimensional vector, $\mathbb{R}^n_+$ is n-dimensional real space, and the notation $x \ge 0$ means that no element of x is less than zero. Now if x and y belong to $\mathbb{R}^n_+$, their weighted average $z = \theta x + (1 - \theta) y$, $0 \le \theta \le 1$, must also belong to $\mathbb{R}^n_+$ since $z = \theta x + (1 - \theta) y \ge 0$.

A *half-space* is the set of all points lying on one side of a hyperplane in $\mathbb{R}^n$. More formally, the half-space $H(\alpha, q)$ is defined as

$$H(\alpha, q) = \{x : \alpha \cdot x \le q\}.$$

The half-space $H(\alpha, q)$ is illustrated graphically by the shaded area in Figure A.3. The n-dimensional vector α is termed the *normal* to the *bounding hyperplane* $K(\alpha, q) = \{x : \alpha \cdot x = q\}$. The reader should remember that the half-space $H(\alpha, q)$ depends both on the normal and the location parameter q; in general, if either α or q change, $H(\alpha, q)$ changes. Now suppose that $x, y \in H(\alpha, q)$. Then, it follows that $z = \theta x + (1 - \theta) y \in H(\alpha, q)$, for $0 \le \theta \le 1$. Thus, all half-spaces are convex, and Lemma 4 implies that the intersection of any number of half-spaces in $\mathbb{R}^n$ is itself convex. Readers can easily verify for themselves that the half-spaces defined by

$$H^*(\alpha, q) = \{x : \alpha \cdot x \ge q\}$$

are also convex. In passing, note that both $H^*(\alpha, q)$ define closed sets in $\mathbb{R}^n$.

A *half-space supports a set* X if X is a subset of the half-space, that is, is contained in the half-space, and if the bounding hyperplane of the half-space has a point in common with the boundary of X. Geometrically, a half-space supports a set if the set can be viewed as sitting on the bounding

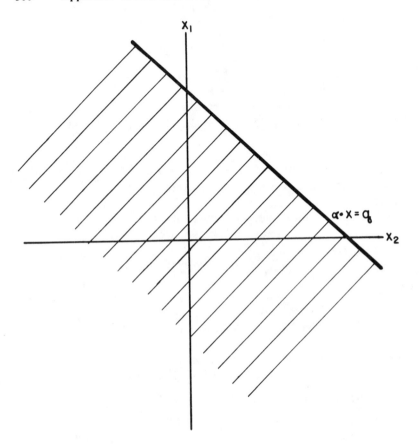

Figure A.3   Half-space $\{x_1, x_2 : \alpha_1 x_1 + \alpha_2 x_2 \le q\}$.

hyperplane of the half-space, as depicted in Figure A.4 for the half-space $H^*(\alpha, q) = \{x : \alpha \cdot x \ge q\}$.

The following result is basic to the modern theory of dual relationships:

> **Lemma 5 (Minkowski's theorem).** *A closed, convex set is the intersection of the half-spaces that support it.*

A proof of this result goes considerably beyond the mathematical confines of this book [interested readers might consult, e.g., Rockafellar (1970), 95–100]. But the intuition behind the result is easily demonstrated. As an example, consider the set X in Figure A.5. Since X is presumed closed, its boundary $CBDE$ belongs to X. Notice, however, that an equivalent way of defining X is

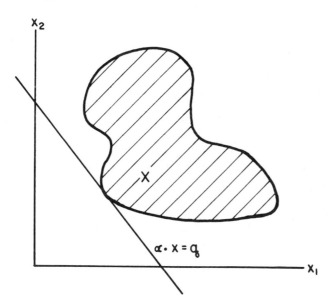

Figure A.4 Supporting half-space.

$$X = H^*_{GH} \cap H^*_{CF} \cap H^*_{AE},$$

where H^*_{GH} is the half-space generated by the bounding hyperplane of which GH is a segment; H^*_{CF} and H^*_{AE} are defined similarly. Since each of these half-spaces is closed and convex, the resulting X is itself convex and closed.

Now suppose, as is frequently the case in production economics, that we want to characterize a convex set with a smooth boundary as illustrated in Figure A.6. Unlike the situation illustrated in Figure A.5, infinitely many half-spaces support the closed convex set X. But by analogy with the discussion surrounding Figure A.5 and by Minkowski's theorem, that set X can now be reconstructed by considering the intersection of all of these supporting half-spaces, that is,

$$X = \bigcap_{\lambda \in \Lambda} H^*_\lambda,$$

where λ indexes the set of supporting half-spaces.

Up to this point, our discussion has proceeded entirely in terms of set concepts. At this point, it is convenient to turn to convexity and concavity of functions. A function $f\{f: \mathbb{R}^n \to \mathbb{R}\}$ is *convex* if, for any $x \in \mathbb{R}^n$, $y \in \mathbb{R}^n$,

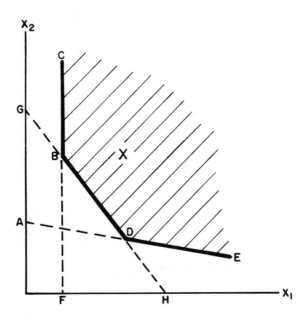

Figure A.5 Minkowski's theorem for convex sets.

$$f(\theta x + (1-\theta)y) \le \theta f(x) + (1-\theta)f(y),$$

where $0 \le \theta \le 1$. If the inequality is reversed, then f is *a concave function.* (In fact, all the results to be derived for convexity apply to concavity with the inequalities reversed; hence they are not repeated.) Intuitively, a function is convex if it assumes the shape of an up-turned bowl when it is graphed against any one of its n arguments holding all others fixed. Convexity also implies that a weighted average of x and y always yields a lower value of f than a weighted average of f evaluated at x and y. A geometric illustration of convexity is contained in Figure A.7 for the case when x is a scalar.

When f is twice differentiable, this intuitive description of convexity can be further strengthened, as the following lemma indicates:

Lemma 6. If $f: \mathbb{R}^n \to \mathbb{R}$ is convex and twice differentiable, then

$$\sum_{i=1}^{n} f_i(y)(x_i - y_i) \le f(x) - f(y)$$

for any $x, y \in \mathbb{R}^n$.

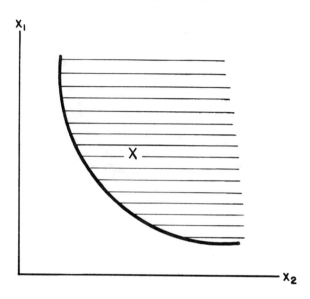

Figure A.6   Convex set.

In this lemma, f_i is the ith partial derivative of f. A sketch of a proof of this lemma is: Rewrite the definition of convexity as $f(y+\theta(x-y)) \le f(y)+\theta[f(x)-f(y)]$. The mean value theorem of calculus means we can rewrite the left-hand side as $f(y)+\sum_{i=1}^{n} f_i(y+\gamma\theta(x-y))\theta(x_i-y_i)$, $\gamma \ge 0$. Using this fact and rearranging yields the desired result upon letting γ go to zero.

The intuitive content of Lemma 6 is that any linear, Taylor series approximation of f at x always underestimates the function value. Thus, suppose that in Figure A.7, we take a first-order Taylor series approximation to f in the neighborhood of y. As labeled in that figure, the approximation to any other $f(x)$ will be somewhere along the line segment tangent to f at y; hence, the Taylor series first-order approximation always underestimates the function value, as the lemma suggests.

As should be clear from the illustration presented in Figure A.7, convexity implies that the value of the partial derivatives for f *rises* as the value of the argument rises. Notice, for example, that the tangent line segments in Figure A.7 become increasingly steeper. This, in turn, implies that when x is a scalar, the second derivative of f is positive when f is convex. For twice-continuously differentiable functions, $f'' \ge 0$ is, in fact, an alternate definition of convexity when x is a scalar. The following lemma extends this result to the n-dimensional case.

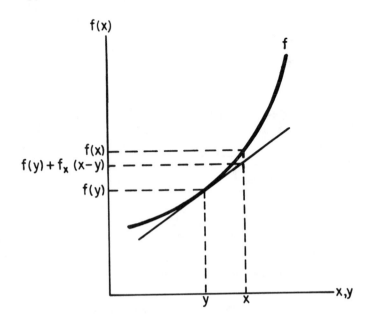

Figure A.7 Convex function.

Lemma 7. *If* $f: \mathbb{R}^n \to \mathbb{R}$ *is twice-continuously differentiable, it is convex (concave) if and only if its Hessian matrix is positive (negative) semidefinite.*

Rather than trying to prove this result directly, I shall only present an argument intended to make it intuitively plausible for the reader. Suppose, in fact, that f is convex. Now consider evaluating it at an arbitrary point $x + ty$, where t is a real scalar and x and y are n-dimensional vectors. Define the function

$$F(t) = f(x + ty).$$

Since f is convex in its arguments, $F(t)$ should be convex in t and $F''(t) \geq 0$. Evaluating $F''(t)$ at $t = 0$ obtains

$$F''(0) = \sum_{i=1}^{n} \sum_{j=1}^{n} f_{ij} y_i y_j \geq 0$$

for arbitrary y. This last expression, however, is a quadratic form in the Hessian of f and, thereby, implies that the Hessian is positive semidefinite.

Lemma 8. *If $f^i: \mathbb{R}^n \to \mathbb{R}$, $i = 1, 2, \ldots, k$, are convex functions, then $F: \mathbb{R}^n \to \mathbb{R}$, $F = \sum_{i=1}^{k} \alpha_i f^i$, is convex if $\alpha_i \geq 0$.*

Proof: By the convexity of each f^i,

$$f^i(\theta x + (1-\theta)y) \leq \theta f^i(x) + (1-\theta) f^i(y)$$

for $0 \leq \theta \leq 1$. But

$$F(\theta x + (1-\theta)y) = \sum_{i=1}^{k} \alpha_i f^i(\theta x + (1-\theta)y)$$

while

$$\theta F(x) + (1-\theta) F(y) = \theta \sum_{i=1}^{n} \alpha_i f^i(x) + (1-\theta) \sum_{i=1}^{n} \alpha_i f^i(y).$$

Using the inequality with these two equalities establishes the result.

Closely related to the concept of convexity of a function is the notion of quasi-convexity. A function $f: \mathbb{R}^n \to \mathbb{R}$ is *quasi-convex* if the set $\hat{V}(\alpha) = \{x: f(x) \leq \alpha\}$ is convex. Similarly, a function $f: \mathbb{R}^n \to \mathbb{R}$ is *quasi-concave* if the set $V(\alpha) = \{x: f(x) \geq \alpha\}$ is convex. Here, $\hat{V}(\alpha)$ and $V(\alpha)$ are called the *lower contour* and the *upper contour* sets, respectively, of f. The set $V(\alpha)$ is especially useful from an economic perspective because it can be closely identified with the concept of an isoquant or indifference curve. The following two lemmas further characterize quasi-convexity.

Lemma 9. *If $F: \mathbb{R}^n \to \mathbb{R}$ is convex (concave), then it is also quasi-convex (concave).*

Lemma 10. *A function $f: \mathbb{R}^n \to \mathbb{R}$ is quasi-concave if and only if $f(x) \geq f(y)$ implies that $f(\theta x + (1-\theta)y) \geq f(y)$ for $0 \leq \theta \leq 1$.*

Lemma 9 is easily demonstrated. Suppose x and y both belong to $\hat{V}(\alpha)$. By the supposed convexity of f, one has

$$f(\theta x + (1-\theta)y) \leq \theta f(x) + (1-\theta) f(y) \leq \alpha,$$

since $x, y \in \hat{V}(\alpha)$. Thus, $\theta x + (1-\theta)y \in \hat{V}(\alpha)$, as required. Lemma 10 is slightly more difficult to show, and here we only try to convince the reader of its validity by showing part of the proof. Suppose in fact that f is quasi-concave. This implies that if x and y belong to $V(\alpha)$, then $\theta x + (1-\theta)y$ also belongs to $V(\alpha)$ by definition. Now suppose further that by chance we have chosen y so that it is exactly on the frontier of $V(\alpha)$ [i.e., $f(y) = \alpha$]; the only way for $\theta x + (1-\theta)y$ to belong to $V(\alpha)$ is $f(\theta x + (1-\theta)y) \geq$

$f(y)$. But, by supposition, we already know that $f(x) \geq f(y)$ as required in the lemma. The basic idea here is simple. Whenever function values can be ordered as in Lemma 10, it is always possible to redefine $V(\alpha)$ in terms of the lower of the two function values. If f is quasi-concave, the function evaluated at the convex combination $\theta x + (1 - \theta)y$ must be no less than the function value used to define the upper contour sets. In passing, I remark that the boundaries of upper or lower contour sets (i.e., the sets $\bar{V}(\alpha) = \{x : f(x) = \alpha\}$) are often referred to as *level sets*. A good example of a level set is an indifference curve where α is now interpreted as a utility level and f as a utility function.

The following lemma, which is stated without proof, further characterizes quasi-concave functions that are also twice-continuously differentiable.

Lemma 11. *If $f \colon \mathbb{R}^n \to \mathbb{R}$ is a twice-continuously differentiable, quasi-concave function, the bordered Hessian matrix*

$$\begin{bmatrix} 0 & f_1 & \cdots & f_n \\ f_1 & f_{11} & \cdots & f_{1n} \\ f_2 & f_{12} & \cdots & f_{2n} \\ \vdots & \vdots & & \vdots \\ f_n & f_{1n} & \cdots & f_{nn} \end{bmatrix}$$

has successive principal minors that alternate in sign (beginning with a negative number) if f is evaluated at $x \geq 0$.

Essentially, this result says that a quasi-concave function has negative semidefinite, bordered Hessian matrices over the entire nonnegative orthant.

Maximization and its consequences: It is no exaggeration that most of neoclassical economics is based on the maximization postulate. Individuals are considered to be economically rational only if they arrive at their ultimate decisions as a result of some constrained maximization process. Practically all of the developments in this book hinge on the maximization postulate. This section presents a brief survey of some of the major results that are necessary to those discussions.

If maximization (or its natural counterpart, minimization) is to be the motivating force for analysis, the logical place to initiate the discussion is with conditions that guarantee the existence of a solution. As a trivial example, the affine function $\alpha + \beta x$, where $x \in \mathbb{R}$, has no finite maximum (minimum) value. To ensure the existence of a maximum, the device most frequently used in the book is the concept of compactness. A set $X \in \mathbb{R}^n$ is *compact* if it is closed and bounded. (This definition is a direct paraphrase of the Heine–Borel theorem.) Boundedness means exactly what it sounds like: One can always find a finite x or y both belonging to $\mathbb{R}^n$ such that for any $z \in X$, $y < z < x$. More technically, boundedness means that X must be contained within an open ball with a finite radius.

The importance of compactness is that it guarantees the existence of a minimum or maximum for any continuous function defined on the set. This should be intuitively clear from the above for if there exists $x, y \in \mathbb{R}^n$ such that for any $z \in X$, $y < z < x$, then for any continuous and increasing $f : \mathbb{R}^n \to \mathbb{R}$, one must have $f(x) > f(z) > f(y)$ for any $z \in X$. Closedness then implies that there exists an x_0, y_0 such that $f(x_0)$ for any $z \in X$ and $f(y_0) \leq f(z)$. This notion is formalized in the following lemma.

Lemma 12 (Weierstrass theorem). *Let X be a compact subset of $\mathbb{R}^n$ and $f : \mathbb{R}^n \to \mathbb{R}$ be continuous. Then, f achieves a maximum and a minimum on X.*

As a simple example of the applicability of this result, consider the affine function $\alpha + \beta x$ introduced earlier. If we restrict attention to the closed interval $0 \leq x \leq 1$, this function has a maximum at $\alpha + \beta$ and a minimum at α. Lemma 12 is perhaps the single most important result to many of the developments in the main part of the text.

In many economic applications, one is interested in problems of the general form

$$\max_{x \in \mathbb{R}^n_+} f(x, \alpha) \tag{A.1}$$

subject to

$$g(x, \alpha) \leq 0,$$

where α is a p-dimensional vector of parameters and $g(x, \alpha)$ is a vector-valued function [i.e., $g : \mathbb{R}^n \times \mathbb{R}^p \to \mathbb{R}^k$ $(k \leq n)$] that acts to define the range of feasible choices for the vector x as conditioned by the vector α. The most typical way to deal with such problems when both g and f are twice-continuously differentiable is to translate it into a Lagrangian function

$$L(x, \alpha, \lambda) = f(x, \alpha) - \lambda \cdot g(x, \alpha),$$

where $\lambda \in \mathbb{R}^k$ is a vector of multipliers and the dot notation implies an inner product. Necessary conditions for $x^* \geq 0$ to solve the original constrained maximization are given by the *Kuhn–Tucker* conditions

$$\nabla_x L(x^*, \lambda^*, \alpha) \leq 0,$$

$$x^* \cdot \nabla_x L(x^*, \lambda^*, \alpha) = 0,$$

$$\nabla_\lambda L(x^*, \lambda^*, \alpha) \ge 0,$$

$$\lambda^* \cdot \nabla_\lambda L(x^*, x^*, \alpha) = 0,$$

$$\lambda^* \ge 0.$$

Here, for example, $\nabla_x L(x, \lambda, \alpha)$ is the gradient of L with respect to x. The Kuhn–Tucker conditions will not be discussed in depth here. The reader can find accessible discussion in other texts.

The Kuhn–Tucker conditions imply an important result. Namely, if $x^* \ge 0$ solves the constrained maximization problem in (A.1), then

$$L(x^*, \lambda^*, \alpha) = f(x^*, \alpha)$$

since $\nabla_\lambda L(x, \lambda, \alpha) = g(x, \alpha)$. The value of the objective function evaluated at the solution to (A.1) is called the *indirect objective function* and is denoted by $\Phi(\alpha)$. Special cases of indirect objective functions are the cost, revenue, and profit functions discussed in the main body of the text. The next lemma is fundamental.

Lemma 13 (envelope theorem). *Suppose that $x^* > 0$ and that $g(x^*, \alpha) = 0$; then,*

$$\nabla_\alpha \Phi(\alpha) = \nabla_\alpha L(x^*, \lambda^*, \alpha) = \frac{\partial L}{\partial \alpha}(x^*, \lambda^*, \alpha).$$

To derive this result, notice that the first equality follows by our definition of the indirect objective function. To establish the second, one should first note that the solution to (A.1) depends explicitly on α, that is, $x^*(\alpha)$. Calculating the gradient yields

$$\nabla_\alpha L(x^*, \lambda^*, \alpha) = \nabla_x L(x^*, \lambda^*, \alpha) \frac{\partial x^*(\alpha)}{\partial \alpha} + \nabla_\lambda L(x^*, \lambda^*, \alpha) \frac{\partial \lambda(\alpha)}{\partial \alpha}$$

$$+ \frac{\partial L(x^*, \lambda^*, \alpha)}{\partial \alpha}.$$

For $x^* > 0$, $g(x^*, \alpha) = 0$, the Kuhn–Tucker conditions then imply that the second equality holds.

Lemma 13 is especially important in the derivation of cost-minimizing and profit-maximizing derived demands and supplies. That is, the change in the indirect objective function associated with adjusting x^* optimally for any change in α just equals the change in Lagrangian function holding x at x^*. This follows because the change in the indirect objective function for a change in x at the optimum is second-order small; otherwise, there would be room for adjusting x and improving the optimum. Therefore, any change in x induced by a change in α when evaluated at the

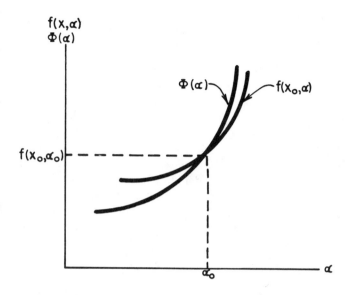

Figure A.8 Envelope theorem and convexity.

optimum has no first-order effect. Hence, the objective function only adjusts as it would if x were held constant at x^*.

More intuition on the envelope theorem can be grasped in the case where there are no constraints or where α does not affect the constraint set and α is a single parameter. Figure A.8 illustrates just such a case. Let α^0 be a particular value of the parameter and x^0 be the corresponding optimal choice of x given α^0. By definition, $\Phi(\alpha^0) = f(x^0, \alpha^0)$. Suppose, in fact, that we slightly change α holding x constant. Since x^0 does not generally remain the optimal choice as α varies from α^0, the graph of $\Phi(\alpha)$ over α must lie above that of $f(x^0, \alpha)$ over α. This, in turn, implies that $\Phi(\alpha)$ and $f(x^0, \alpha)$, although sharing at least one point in common, cannot intersect. Hence, they must be tangent to one another at α^0, implying, of course, the envelope result.

Besides the envelope result, however, the maximization hypothesis has further informational content. In what follows, we shall slightly redefine our problem (A.1) to the more general form

$$\max_{x \in X(\alpha)} f(x, \alpha). \tag{A.2}$$

To ensure that this maximum exists, we presume that $X(\alpha)$ is a compact set and that f is continuous in its arguments. The reader might note that for (A.1), $X(\alpha)$ is given by

$$X(\alpha) = \{x : g(x, \alpha) \leq 0\},$$

so that (A.2) is indeed a generalization of (A.1).

> **Lemma 14.** *Suppose $X(\alpha)$ is independent of α and f is concave in both x and α; then, $\Phi(\alpha)$ is concave in α.*

> **Lemma 15.** *Suppose the set $X(\alpha)$ is independent of α and f is convex in α. Then, $\Phi(\alpha)$ is convex in α.*

I only demonstrate Lemma 14 formally; Lemma 15 is illustrated graphically but is not formally derived. To demonstrate Lemma 14, consider the values α_i ($i = 0, 1, 2$) with x_i ($i = 0, 1, 2$) denoting the solution to (A.2) when α assumes the value α_i. Since, by hypothesis, $X(\alpha)$ is independent of α, x_0, x_1, x_2 are all feasible regardless of the value of α. If α_0 and α_1 are chosen such that $\alpha_2 = \theta\alpha_0 + (1 - \theta)\alpha_1$, $0 \leq \theta \leq 1$, demonstrating Lemma 14 requires demonstrating that $\Phi(\alpha_2) \geq \theta\Phi(\alpha_0) + (1 - \theta)\Phi(\alpha_1)$. Direct evaluation yields

$$\Phi(\alpha_2) = f(x_2, \theta\alpha_1 + (1 - \theta)\alpha_2) \geq f(\theta x_0 + (1 - \theta)x_1, \theta\alpha_0 + (1 - \theta)\alpha_1)$$

$$\geq \theta f(x_0, \alpha_0) + (1 - \theta)f(x_1, \alpha_1) = \theta\Phi(\alpha_0) + (1 - \theta)\Phi(\alpha_1).$$

The first inequality follows by the optimality of x_2 when α_2 prevails whereas the second equality is a consequence of the presumed concavity of f in both its arguments. The last equality establishes the desired result.

The best way to illustrate Lemma 15 is with Figure A.8, which was used to discuss the envelope theorem. Let x_0 be the optimal choice of x when $\alpha = \alpha_0$ (again we only present the scalar case). At α_0, $f(x_0, \alpha)$ and $\Phi(\alpha)$ coincide, but since $\Phi(\alpha) \geq f(x_0, \alpha)$ regardless of the value of α, the convexity of f in α implies that $\Phi(\alpha)$ should also be convex. In fact, it has to be more convex in α than $f(x_0, \alpha)$ to avoid having $\Phi(\alpha)$ and $f(x_0, \alpha)$ intersect. An important corollary follows by observing that if $f(x_0, \alpha)$ is linear in α, $\Phi(\alpha)$ must still be convex in α if it is to avoid intersection with $f(x_0, \alpha)$.

> **Corollary 1.** *If $f(x, \alpha)$ is linear in α and $X(\alpha)$ is independent of α, $\Phi(\alpha)$ is convex in α.*

Homotheticity: One of the most important concepts in modern production theory is the notion of homotheticity introduced by Shephard (1953) in his initial treatise on duality. The function $f(x)$ is *homothetic* in x if

$$f(x) = F[f^*(x)]$$

where $F(\cdot)$ is a strictly monotonic function of x and f^* is linearly homogeneous. Differentiating with respect to x_i and x_j yields, after taking ratios,

$$\frac{\partial f(x)/\partial x_i}{\partial f(x)/\partial x_j} = \frac{\partial f^*(x)/\partial x_i}{\partial f^*(x)/\partial x_j}.$$

Since $f^*(x)$ is linearly homogeneous, each of the derivatives on the right-hand side of this expression is homogeneous of degree zero. To see this, notice that, by the definition of linear homogeneity, $f(tx) = tf(x)$. Differentiating with respect to x_i yields

$$\frac{\partial f(tx)}{\partial x_i} t = t \frac{\partial f(x)}{\partial x_i},$$

which implies $\partial f(tx)/\partial x_i = \partial f(x)/\partial x_i$, whence homogeneity of degree zero. Thus, if a function is homothetic, the ratio of its first partial derivatives (if they exist) must be homogeneous of degree zero. This condition is clearly necessary for homotheticity of differentiable functions; the following lemma due to Lau (1978a) (and not proven here) establishes sufficiency;

> **Lemma 16 (Lau's lemma).** *If $f: \mathbb{R}^n \to \mathbb{R}$ is twice-continuously differentiable and has strictly nonzero first derivatives, it is homothetic if and only if the ratio of all possible pairs of these derivatives is homogeneous of degree zero.*

This lemma, which is used in almost every chapter, concludes our brief mathematical review.

Bibliography

Afriat, S. N., "Efficiency Estimation of Production Functions," *International Economic Review,* 13, 568–98 (1972).

Allen, R. C., and W. E. Diewert, "Direct Versus Implicit Superlative Index Number Formulae," *Review of Economics and Statistics,* 63, 430–5 (1981).

Allen, R. G. D., *Mathematical Analysis for Economists* (London: Macmillan, 1938).

Anderson, G. J., and R. W. Blundell, "Estimation and Hypothesis Testing in Dynamic Singular Equation Systems," *Econometrica,* 50, 1559–72 (1982).

Anderson, J. R., J. L. Dillon, and J. B. Hardaker, *Agricultural Decision Analysis* (Ames, Iowa: Iowa State University Press, 1977).

Anderson, R. W., "Some Theory of Inverse Demand for Applied Demand Analysis," *European Economic Review,* 14, 281–90 (1980).

Antle, J., "Structure of U.S. Agricultural Technology, 1910–78," *American Journal of Agricultural Economics,* 66, 414–21 (1984).

"Testing the Stochastic Structure of Production: A Flexible Moment-Based Approach," *Journal of Business and Economic Statistic,* 1, 192–201 (1983).

Appelbaum, E., "On the Choice of Functional Forms," *International Economic Review,* 20(2), 449–58 (1979).

Ball, V. E., "Output, Input, and Productivity Measurement," *American Journal of Agricultural Economics,* 67, 475–86 (1985).

Ball, V. E., and R. Chambers, "An Economic Analysis of Technology in the Meat Product Industry," *American Journal of Agricultural Economics,* 64, 699–709 (1982).

Barten, A. P., "Maximum Likelihood Estimation of a Complete System of Demand Equations," *European Economic Review,* 1, 7–73 (1969).

Barton, G. T., "Technological Change, Food Needs and Aggregate Resource Adjustment," *Journal of Farm Economics,* 40, 1429–37 (1958).

Berndt, E. R., and L. R. Christensen, "The Internal Structure of Functional Relationships: Separability, Substitution, and Aggregation," *Review of Economic Studies,* 40, 403–10 (1973).

Berndt, E. R., and M. A. Fuss, "Productivity Measurement Using Capital Asset Valuation to Adjust for Variations in Utilization," Working Paper 8125, Institute for Policy Analysis, University of Toronto, September 1981.

Berndt, E. R., and D. O. Wood, "Engineering and Econometric Interpretations of Energy-Capital Complementary," *American Economic Review,* 69, 342–55 (1979).

318

"Technology, Prices and the Derived Demand for Energy," *Review of Economics and Statistics,* 57(3), 259–68 (1975).

Binswanger, H., "A Cost Function Approach to the Measurement of Factor Demand and Elasticities of Substitution," *American Journal of Agricultural Economics,* 56, 377–86 (1974).

Blackorby, C., and W. E. Diewert, "Expenditure Functions, Local Duality and Second Order Approximations," *Econometrica* 47, 579–603 (1979).

Blackorby, C., and R. R. Russell, "The Morishima Elasticity of Substitution; Symmetry, Constancy, Separability and Its Relationship to the Hicks, and Allen Elasticities," *Review of Economic Studies,* 48, 147–58 (1981).

"Functional Structure and the Allen Partial Elasticities of Substitution: An Application of Duality Theory," *Review of Economic Studies,* 43, 285–93 (1976).

Blackorby, C., D. Primont, and R. R. Russell, *Duality, Separability and Functional Structure* (New York: North-Holland, 1978).

"On Testing Separability Restrictions with Flexible Functional Forms," *Journal of Econometrics,* 5, 195–209 (1977).

Blackorby, C., C. A. Knox Lovell, and M. C. Thursby, "Extended Hicks Neutral Technical Change," *Economic Journal,* 86, 845–52 (1976).

Brown, R. S., D. Caves, and L. Christensen, "Modelling the Structure of Cost and Production for Multiproduct Firms," *Southern Economic Journal,* 46, 256–73 (1979).

Brown, R. S., and L. Christensen, "Estimating Elasticities of Substitution in a Model of Partial Static Equilibrium: An Application to U.S. Agriculture, 1947–74," in *Modelling and Measuring Natural Resource Substitution,* E. R. Berndt and B. C. Field, eds. (Cambridge, MA: MIT Press, 1982).

Buse, R. C., "Total Elasticities – A Predictive Device," *Journal of Farm Economics,* 40, 881–90 (1958).

Byron, R. P., "A Note on the Estimation of Symmetric Systems," *Econometrica,* 50, 1573–6 (1982).

Capalbo, S. M., and M. G. S. Denny, "Testing Long-Run Productivity Models for the Canadian and U.S. Agricultural Sectors," *American Journal of Agricultural Economics,* 68, 615–25 (1986).

Carlson, S., *A Study in the Pure Theory of Production* (London: P. S. King & Son, 1939).

Cass, D., "Duality: A Symmetric Approach from the Economist's Vantage Point," *Journal of Economic Theory,* 7, 272–95 (1974).

Cassels, J. M., "On the Law of Variable Proportions." *Explorations in Economics* (New York: McGraw-Hill, 1936), pp. 223–36.

Caves, D. W., L. R. Christensen, and W. E. Diewert, "The Economic Theory of Index Numbers and the Measurement of Input, Output, and Productivity," *Econometrica,* 50, 1393–414 (1982a).

"Multilateral Comparisons of Output, Input, and Productivity Using Superlative Index Numbers," *Economic Journal,* 92, 73–86 (1982b).

"A New Approach to Index Numbers Theory and the Measurement of Input,

Output, and Productivity," Social Systems Research Institute Workshop Series No. 8112, University of Wisconsin, Madison, May 1981.

Caves, D. W., L. R. Christensen, and J. A. Swanson, "Economic Performance in Regulated and Unregulated Environments: A Comparison of U.S. and Canadian Railroads," *Quarterly Journal of Economics,* 96, 559–81 (1981a).

"Productivity Growth, Scale Economies, and Capacity Utilization," *American Economic Review,* 71, 994–1002 (1981b).

Caves, D. W., L. R. Christensen, and M. W. Tretheway, "U.S. Trunk Air Carriers, 1972–1977: A Multilateral Comparison of Total Factor Productivity," in *Productivity Measurement in Regulated Industries,* T. G. Cowing and R. E. Stevenson, eds. (New York: Academic, 1981), pp. 47–76.

Chan, M., W. Luke, and D. C. Mountain, "The Measurement of Total Factor Productivity in Canadian Agriculture," Working Paper No. 8113, Institute for Policy Analysis, University of Toronto, Toronto, February 1981.

Christensen, L. R., and W. H. Greene, "Economics of Scale in U.S. Electricity Power Generation," *Journal of Political Economy,* 84, 655–76 (1976).

Christensen, L. R., and D. W. Jorgensen, "The Measurement of U.S. Real Capital Input," *Review of Income and Wealth,* series 5, 293–320 (1969).

Cobb, C. W., and P. H. Douglas, "A Theory of Production," *American Economic Review,* 18, 139–65 (1928).

Deaton, A., "The Distance Function in Consumer Behavior with Applications to Index Numbers and Optimal Taxation," *Review of Economic Studies,* 47, 391–405 (1980).

de Janvry, A. C., "The Class of Generalized Power Production Functions," *American Journal of Agricultural Economics,* 54(2), 234–7 (1972).

Denny, M., and M. Fuss, "A General Approach to Intertemporal and Interspatial Productivity Measurement," Working Paper Series No. 8202, Institute for Policy Analysis, University of Toronto, Toronto, Canada, January 1982.

"Intertemporal Changes in the Levels of Regional Labor Productivity in Canadian Manufacturing," Working Paper 8131, Institute for Policy Analysis, University of Toronto, December 1981.

"Intertemporal and Interspatial Comparisons of Cost Efficiency and Productivity," Working Paper No. 8018, Institute for Policy Analysis, University of Toronto, December 1980.

"The Use of Approximation Analysis to Test for Separability and the Existence of Consistent Aggregates," *American Economic Review,* 67, 404–18 (1977).

Denny, M., M. Fuss, and L. Waverman, "The Measurement and Interpretation of Total Factor Productivity in Regulated Industries, with an Application to Canadian Telecommunications," in *Productivity Growth in Regulated Industries,* T. G. Cowing and R. E. Stevenson, eds. (New York: Academic, 1981), pp. 179–218.

Diewert, W. E., "Applications of Duality Theory," in *Frontiers of Quantitative Economics,* Vol. II, M. Intriligator and D. A. Kendrick, eds. (Amsterdam: North-Holland, 1974), pp. 106–206.

"The Theory of Total Factor Productivity Measurement in Regulated Industries," in *Productivity Measurement in Regulated Industries,* T. G. Cowing and R. E. Stevenson, eds. (New York: Academic, 1981), pp. 17–44.

"Aggregation Problems in the Measurement of Capital," in *The Measurement of Capital,* D. Usher, ed., *Studies in Income and Wealth,* Conference on Research in Income and Wealth NBER (Chicago, IL: University of Chicago Press, 1980).

"The Economic Theory of Index Numbers: A Survey," Discussion Paper No. 79-09, Department of Economics, University of British Columbia, March 1979.

"Superlative Index Numbers and Consistency in Aggregation," *Econometrica,* 46, 883–900, (1978a).

"Duality Approaches to Microeconomic Theory," Technical Report No. 281, The Economic Series, Institute for Mathematical Studies in the Social Sciences, Stanford University, October 1978b.

"Exact and Superlative Index Numbers," *Journal of Econometrics,* 4, 116–45 (1976).

"Functional Forms for Profit and Transformation Functions," *Journal of Economic Theory,* 6, 284–316 (1973).

"An Application of the Shepard Duality Theorem: A Generalized Leontief Production Function," *Journal of Political Economy,* 79, 481–507 (1971).

Epstein, L. G., "Generalized Duality and Integrability," *Econometrica,* 49, 655–78 (1983).

"Duality Theory and Functional Forms for Dynamic Factor Demands," *Review of Economic Studies,* 63, 81–96 (1981).

Färe, R., and R. W. Shephard, "Ray-Homothetic Production Functions," *Econometrica,* 45, 133–46 (1977).

Färe, R., S. Grosskopf, and C. A. Lovell, *Measurement of Efficiency of Production* (Boston: Klawer Nijhoff, 1985).

Farrell, M. J., "The Measurement of Productive Efficiency," *Journal of the Royal Statistical Society Series A,* 120, 253–90 (1957).

Ferguson, C. E., *The Neoclassical Theory of Production and Distribution* (Cambridge: Cambridge University Press, 1969).

"Substitution, Technical Progress, and Returns to Scale," *American Economic Review,* 55, 296–305 (1965).

Forsund, F. R., and L. Hjalmarsson, "Frontier Production Functions and Technical Progress: A Study of General Milk Processing in Swedish Dairy Plants," *Econometrica,* 47(4), 883–900 (1979).

Forsund, F. R., C. A. Knox Levell, and P. Schmidt, "A Survey of Frontier Production Functions and of Their Relationship to Efficiency Measurement," *Journal of Econometrics,* 13, 5–25 (1980).

Friedman, J. W., "Duality Principles in the Theory of Cost and Production Revisited," *International Economic Review,* 13(1), 167–70 (1972).

Frisch, R., "Annual Survey of General Economics Theory: The Problem of Index Numbers," *Econometrica,* 4, 1–38 (1936).

Fuller, W. A., "Estimating the Reliabilities of Quantities Derived from Empirical Production Functions," *Journal of Farm Economics,* 44, 82–99 (1962).

Fuss, M., "The Demand for Energy in Canadian Manufacturing," *Journal of Econometrics,* 5, 89–116 (1977a).

Fuss, M. A., "The Structure of Technology Over Time: A Model for Testing the 'Putty-Clay' Hypothesis," *Econometrica,* 45, 1797–822 (1977b).

Fuss, M., and D. McFadden (eds.), *Production Economics: A Dual Approach to Theory and Applications* (Amsterdam: North-Holland, 1978).

Fuss, M., D. McFadden, and Y. Mundlak, "A Survey of Functional Forms in the Economic Analyses of Production," in *Production Economics: A Dual Approach to Theory and Applications,* M. Fuss and D. McFadden, eds. (Amsterdam: North-Holland, 1978), pp. 219–68.

Gallant, R. A., "On the Bias in Flexible Functional Forms and an Essentially Unbiased Form," *Journal of Econometrics,* 15, 211–45 (1981).

George, H., *Progress and Poverty* (New York: Robert Schalkenbach Foundation, 1942).

Goldman, S. M., and H. Uzawa, "A Note on Separability in Demand Analysis," *Econometrica,* 32, 387–99 (1964).

Gorman, W. M., "Tricks with Utility Functions," in *Essays in Economic Analysis,* M. J. Artis and A. R. Nobay, eds. (New York: Cambridge University Press, 1976).

"Measuring the Quantities of Fixed Factors," *Value, Capital, and Growth,* J. N. Wolfe, ed. (Edinburgh: Edinburgh University Press, 1968), pp. 141–72.

Gould, J. R., "On the Interpretation of Inferior Goods and Factors," *Economica,* 48, 397–406 (1981).

Griliches, Z., "The Source of Measured Productivity Growth: United States Agriculture, 1940-60," *Journal of Political Economy,* 71, 331–46 (1963).

Hall, R. E., "The Specification of Technology with Several Kinds of Output," *Journal of Political Economy,* 81, 878–92 (1973).

Hanoch, G., "The Elasticity of Scale and the Shape of Average Costs," *American Economic Review,* 65, 492–7 (1975).

"Homotheticity in Joint Production," *Journal of Economic Theory,* 2, 423–6 (1970).

Hanoch, G., and M. Rothschild, "Testing the Assumptions of Production Theory: A Nonparametric Approach," *Journal of Political Economy,* 80, 265–75 (1972).

Haque, W., "Direct and Indirect Weak Separability," *Journal of Economic Theory,* 25, 237–54 (1981).

Hatta, T., and R. J. Willie, "Mosak's Equality and the Theory of Duality," *International Economic Review,* 23, 361–4.

Heady, E. O., "Marginal Rates of Substitutions between Technology, Land, and Labor," *Journal of Farm Economics,* 45, 137–45 (1963).

Heady, E. O., J. P. Madden, N. L. Jacobsen, and A. E. Freeman, "Milk Production Functions Incorporating Variables for Cow Characteristics and Environment," *Journal of Farm Economics,* 46, 1–19 (1964).

Hertel, T. W., "Applications of Duality and Flexible Functional Forms: The Case of the Multiproduct Firm," Research Bulletin 980, Department of Agriculture Economics, Purdue University, September 1984.

Hicks, J. R., *The Theory of Wages,* 2nd ed. (London: Macmillan, 1963).

Hotelling, H., "Edgeworth's Taxation Paradox and the Nature of Demand and Supply Functions," *Journal of Political Economy,* 40, 577–616 (1932).

Hulten, C. R., "Divisia Index Numbers," *Econometrica,* 41(6), 1017–26 (1973).

Johnson, W. E., "The Pure Theory of Utility Curves," *Economic Journal,* 23, 483–513 (1913).

Jorgenson, D. W., and L. J. Lau, "Duality and Differentiability in Production," *Journal of Economic Theory,* 9, 23–42 (1974).

Jorgenson, D. W., and M. Nishimizu, "U.S. and Japanese Economic Growth, 1952–1974: An International Comparison," *The Economic Journal,* 88, 707–27 (1978).

Just, R. E., and R. D. Pope, "Stochastic Specification of Production Functions and Economic Implications, *Journal of Econometrics,* 7, 67–86 (1978).

Kako, T., "An Application of the Decomposition Analysis of Derived Demand for Factor Inputs in U.S. Manufacturing," *Review of Economics and Statistics,* 62, 300–1 (1980).

Kohli, U., "Non Joint Technologies," *Review of Economic Studies,* 50, 209–19 (1983).

Kopp, R. J., "The Measurement of Productive Efficiency: A Reconsideration," *Quarterly Journal of Economics,* 96, 477–504 (1981).

Kuga, K., "On the Symmetry of Robinson Elasticities of Substitution: The General Case," *Review of Economic Studies,* 47, 527–31 (1980).

Lau, L. J., "Applications of Profit Functions," in *Production Economics: A Dual Approach to Theory and Applications,* M. Fuss and D. McFadden, eds. (Amsterdam: North-Holland, 1978a), pp. 134–216.

"Testing and Imposing Monotonicity, Convexity and Quasi-Convexity Constraints," *Production Economic: A Dual Approach to Theory and Application,* Vol. I, M. Fuss and D. McFadden, eds. (Amsterdam: Elsevier/North-Holland, 1978b), pp. 409–52.

"A Characterization of the Normalized Restricted Profit Function," *Journal of Economic Theory,* 12, 131–63 (1976).

"Profit Functions of Technologies with Multiple Input and Output," *Review of Economics and Statistics,* 54, 281–9 (1972).

"Duality and the Structure of Utility Functions," *Journal of Economic Theory,* 1, 374–96 (1970).

Lau, L. J., and P. A. Yotopolous, "Profit, Supply and Factor Demand Functions," *American Journal of Agricultural Economics,* 54(1), 11–18 (1972).

Lave, L. B., "Technological Change in U.S. Agriculture: The Aggregation Problem," *Journal of Farm Economics,* 46, 200–17 (1964).

Lave, L. B., "Empirical Estimates of Technological Change in United States Agriculture 1850–1958," *Journal of Farm Economics,* 44, 941–52 (1962).

Lopez, R. E., "Estimating Substitution and Expansion Effects Using a Profit Function Framework," *American Journal of Agricultural Economics,* 66, 358–67 (1984).

"Structural Implications of a Class of Flexible Functional Forms for Profit Functions," *International Economic Review,* 26, 593–601 (1983).

Marschak, J., and W. Andrews, "Random Simultaneous Equations and the Theory of Production," *Econometrica,* 12, 143–205 (1944).

Marsden, J., D. Pingry, and A. Whinston, "Engineering Foundations of Production Functions," *Journal of Economic Theory,* 9, 124–40 (1974).

Marshall, A., *Principles of Economics,* 9th ed. (New York: Macmillan, 1961).

McElroy, F. W., "Returns to Scale, Euler's Theorem and the Form of Production Functions," *Econometrica,* 37(2), 275–9 (1969).

McFadden, D., "Cost, Revenue and Profit Functions," in *Production Economics: A Dual Approach to Theory and Applications,* M. Fuss and D. McFadden, eds. (Amsterdam: North-Holland, 1978a), pp. 3–109.

"The General Linear Profit Function," in *Production Economics: A Dual Approach to Theory and Applications,* M. Fuss and D. McFadden, eds. (New York: North-Holland, 1978b).

Menger, K., "The Logic of Laws of Return: A Study in Meta-Economics," in *Economic Activity Analysis,* Oskar Morgenstern, ed. (Princeton, NJ: Princeton University Press, 1954), pp. 419–81.

Moore, H. L., *Synthetic Economics* (New York: Macmillan, 1929).

Morimoto, Y., "Neutral Technical Progress and the Separability of the Production Function," *Economic Studies Quarterly,* 25(3), 66–9 (1974).

Muellbauer, J., "Community Preferences and the Representative Consumer," *Econometrica,* 44, 979–99 (1976).

"Aggregation, Income Distribution and Consumer Demand," *Review of Economic Studies,* 42, 525–43 (1975).

Mundlak, Y., "Elasticities of Substitution and the Theory of Derived Demand," *Review of Economic Studies,* 35, 225–36 (1968).

"Specification and Estimation of Agricultural Production Functions," *Journal of Farm Economics,* 45, 433–42 (1963).

Nadiri, M. I., "Some Approaches to the Theory and Measurement of Total Factor Productivity: A Survey," *Journal of Economic Literature,* 8, 1137–78 (1970).

Nerlove, M., "Returns to Scale in Electricity Supply," in *Measurement in Economics: Essays in Memory of Yehuda Grunfeld,* C. F. Christ et al., eds. (Stanford, CT: Stanford University Press, 1963).

Newman, P., "Some Properties of Concave Functions," *Journal of Economic Theory,* 1, 291–314 (1969).

Ohta, M., "A Note on the Duality between Production and Cost Functions: Rate of Returns to Scale and Rate of Technical Progress," *Economic Studies Quarterly,* 25, 63–5 (1974).

Otani, Y., "A Simple Proof of the Le Chatelier–Samuelson Principle and the Theory of Cost and Production," *Journal of Economic Theory,* 27, 430–8 (1982).

Panzar, J. C., and R. D. Willig, "Economies of Scale in Multi-Output Production," *Quality Journal of Economics,* 91, 481–93 (1977).

Parks, R. W., "Price Responsiveness of Factor Utilization in Swedish Manufacturing," *Review of Economics and Statistics,* 53, 129–39 (1971).

Razin, A., "A Note on the Elasticity of Derived Demand under Decreasing Returns," *American Economic Review*, 64, 697–700 (1974).

Ricardo, D., *The Principles of Political Economy and Taxation* (London: J. M. Dent and Sons, 1973).

Richmond, J., "Aggregation and Identification," *International Economic Review*, 17, 47–56 (1976).

Ringstad, V., "Economics of Scale and the Forms of the Production Function: Some New Estimates," *Scandinavian Journal of Economics*, 80(2), 251–64 (1978).

Rockafellar, R. T., *Convex Analysis* (Princeton, NJ: Princeton University Press, 1970).

Russell, R. R., "Functional Separability and Partial Elasticities of Substitution," *Review of Economic Studies*, 42, 79–85 (1975).

Sakai, Y., "Substitution and Expansion Effects in Production Theory: The Case of Joint Production," *Journal of Economic Theory*, 9, 255–74 (1974).

"An Axiomatic Approach to Input Demand Theory," *International Economic Review*, 14, 735–52 (1973).

Samuelson, P. A., "Thunen at Two Hundred," *Journal of Economic Literature*, 21, 1468–88 (1983).

"The Fundamental Singularity Theorem for Non-Joint Production," *International Economic Review*, 7, 34–41 (1966).

Foundations of Economic Analysis (Cambridge, MA: Harvard University Press, 1948).

Sandler, T., and A. Swimmer, "The Properties and Generation of Homothetic Production Functions: A Synthesis," *Journal of Economic Theory*, 18, 349–61 (1978).

Schumpeter, J., *History of Economic Analysis* (Cambridge, MA: Harvard University Press, 1953).

Shephard, R. W., *Theory of Cost and Production Functions* (Princeton, NJ: Princeton University Press, 1970).

Cost and Production Functions (Princeton, NJ: Princeton University Press, 1953).

Shumway, C. R., "Supply, Demand and Technology in a Multiproduct Industry: Texas Field Crops," *American Journal of Agricultural Economics*, 64, 748–60 (1983).

Siebert, W. S., and J. T. Addison, "A Geometric Derivation of the Firm's Input Decision," *Australian Economic Papers*, 20, 142–9 (1981).

Solow, R. M., "Technical Change and the Aggregate Production Function," *Review of Economics and Statistics*, 39, 312–20 (1957).

Star, S., and R. E. Hall, "An Approximate Divisia Index of Total Factor Productivity," *Econometrica*, 44, 257–63 (1976).

Stevenson, R., "Measuring Technological Bias," *American Economic Review*, 70, 162–73 (1980).

Stigler, G., *Essays in the History of Economics* (Chicago, IL: University of Chicago Press, 1965).

Stigler, G. J., "Economic Problems in Measuring Change in Productivity," *Output, Input, and Productivity Measurement,* Studies in Income and Wealth: Vol. 25 Conference on Research in Income and Wealth, National Bureau of Economic Research (Princeton, NJ: Princeton University Press, 1961).

"The Cost of Subsistence," *Journal of Farm Economics,* 27, 303–14 (1945).

"Production and Distribution in the Short Run," *Journal of Political Economy,* 47, 505–27 (1939).

Tolley, H. R., J. D. Black, and M. J. B. Ezekiel, *Inputs as Related to Output,* U.S. Dept. of Agriculture Bulletin No. 1277 (1924).

Uzawa, H., "Production Functions with Constant Elasticities of Substitution," *Review of Economic Studies,* 29, 291–9 (1962).

Varian, H. R., "Non-Parametric Tests of Consumer Behavior," *Review of Economic Studies,* 50(1), 99–110 (1983).

Viner, J., "Cost Curves and Supply Curves," *Zeitschrift für Nationalokonomie,* 111, 23–46 (1931).

Wales, T. J., "On the Flexibility of Flexible Functional Forms: An Empirical Approach," *Journal of Econometrics,* 5, 183–93 (1977).

Walters, A. A., "Production and Cost Functions: An Econometric Survey," *Econometrica,* 31(1–2), 1–66 (1963).

White, H. J., "Using Least Squares to Approximate Unknown Regression Functions," *International Economic Review,* 21, 149–70 (1980).

Name index

327

Subject index